ORGANIZING URBAN AMERICA

Social Movements, Protest, and Contention

Series Editor: Bert Klandermans, Free University, Amsterdam

Associate Editors: Ron R. Aminzade, University of Minnesota
David S. Meyer, University of California, Irvine
Verta A. Taylor, University of California, Santa Barbara

Volume 28   Heidi J. Swarts, *Organizing Urban America: Secular and Faith-based Progressive Movements*

Volume 27   Ethel C. Brooks, *Unraveling the Garment Industry: Transnational Organizing and Women's Work*

Volume 26   Donatella della Porta, Massimiliano Andretta, Lorenzo Mosca, and Herbert Reiter, *Globalization from Below: Transnational Activists and Protest Networks*

Volume 25   Ruud Koopmans, Paul Statham, Marco Giugni, and Florence Passy, *Contested Citizenship: Immigration and Cultural Diversity in Europe*

Volume 24   David Croteau, William Hoynes, and Charlotte Ryan, editors, *Rhyming Hope and History: Activists, Academics, and Social Movement Scholarship*

Volume 23   David S. Meyer, Valerie Jenness, and Helen Ingram, editors, *Routing the Opposition: Social Movements, Public Policy, and Democracy*

Volume 22   Kurt Schock, *Unarmed Insurrections: People Power Movements in Nondemocracies*

Volume 21   Christian Davenport, Hank Johnston, and Carol Mueller, editors, *Repression and Mobilization*

Volume 20   Nicole C. Raeburn, *Changing Corporate America from Inside Out: Lesbian and Gay Workplace Rights*

Volume 19   Vincent J. Roscigno and William F. Danaher, *The Voice of Southern Labor: Radio, Music, and Textile Strikes, 1929–1934*

Volume 18   Maryjane Osa, *Solidarity and Contention: Networks of Polish Opposition*

Volume 17   Mary Margaret Fonow, *Union Women: Forging Feminism in the United Steelworkers of America*

For more books in the series, see page 300.

ORGANIZING URBAN AMERICA

Secular and Faith-based Progressive Movements

Heidi J. Swarts

Social Movements, Protest, and Contention
Volume 28

University of Minnesota Press
Minneapolis • London

Chapter 3 was previously published in
Transforming the City: Community Organizing and Political Change,
ed. Marion Orr (Lawrence: University of Kansas Press, 2006).

Published by the University of Minnesota Press
111 Third Avenue South, Suite 290
Minneapolis, MN 55401-2520
http://www.upress.umn.edu

Library of Congress Cataloging-in-Publication Data

Swarts, Heidi J.
 Organizing urban America : secular and faith-based progressive
movements / Heidi J. Swarts.
  p.   cm. — (Social movements, protest, and contention ; v. 28)
 Includes bibliographical references and index.
 ISBN-13: 978-0-8166-4838-2 (hc : alk. paper)
 ISBN-10: 0-8166-4838-7 (hc : alk. paper)
 ISBN-13: 978-0-8166-4839-9 (pb : alk. paper)
 ISBN-10: 0-8166-4839-5 (pb : alk. paper)
  1. Community organization—United States—Case studies.
 2. Community development, Urban—United States.   3. Urban
renewal—United States—Citizen participation.   4. ACORN
(Organization)   5. Religion and politics—United States.   I. Title.
 HM766.S88 2008
 307.3'4160973—dc22
                                                          2007046295

Printed in the United States of America on acid-free paper

The University of Minnesota is an equal-opportunity educator and employer.

15 14 13 12 11 10 09 08   10 9 8 7 6 5 4 3 2 1

Contents

Acknowledgments vii

Abbreviations xi

Introduction. Invisible Actors: Community Organizing, Agenda Setting, and American Social Movements xiii

1. Different Mobilizing Cultures: Congregation-based Organizing and ACORN 1

2. Religion and Progressive Politics: Congregation-based Community Organizing's Innovative Cultural Strategy 45

3. Experimenting with National Organizing Campaigns: ACORN's Innovative Political Strategy 71

4. Organizing Is a Numbers Game: St. Louis ACORN 91

5. A Seat at the Regional Table: Metropolitan Congregations United for St. Louis 110

6. *La Puebla Unida*: ACORN in the Sunbelt 127

7. The Power Is in the Relationship: San Jose PACT 142

8. The Results of Organizing 161

9. American Inequality and the Potential of Community Organizing 177

Appendix A Excerpts from "PICO Principles" 193

Appendix B Methodological Appendix 195

Appendix C Policy Outcomes for Selected National and Local Organizations since 1990 201

Appendix D   Agenda Setting: Selected Proposals Introduced
by Four Community Organizations since 1990   227

Notes   231

Bibliography   265

Index   287

Acknowledgments

There are many people to thank in the long process of preparing this book, and I apologize for anyone I may have inadvertently omitted. First, I want to thank all the organizers and members of St. Louis ACORN, Metropolitan Congregations United (MCU) for St. Louis, San Jose ACORN, and People Acting in Community Together (PACT) for their trust. They permitted me access to everything from individual staff supervision sessions, weekly staff meetings, and board meetings to negotiations with bank officers and massive demonstrations in the streets. I hope that this contribution to making their work visible will in a small way compensate them for their generosity and patience.

My first model of a passionate researcher (and wonderful boss) was Linda Flower of Carnegie-Mellon University. As her research assistant when I had just graduated from college, I will always remember her intellectual respect for me. My thanks to Linda and Tim Flower for providing models of grace and generosity.

I thank my mentors in organizing, first and foremost Mike Miller and Diana Miller, who have given me and continue to give me food for thought in too many conversations to remember. I first studied community organizing formally in a course at San Francisco State University with the late Tim Sampson. Thanks to everyone at the North of Market Planning Coalition in San Francisco's Tenderloin for stimulating my first reflections on the practice of community organizing. Conversations with other scholars and observers of community organizing, in person and over e-mail, were enlightening and fun. Thanks to Roger Karapin, John Krinsky, Doug

Hess, Peter Dreier, Steve Hart, Marshall Ganz, John McCarthy, and Art McDonald.

At Harvard Divinity School, I was lucky to be able to study social theory for three semesters with visiting professor Dunbar Moodie. He and Bill Gamson are inspiring models of intellectual rigor wedded to political commitment.

The communities of scholars of which I have been a part were wonderful incubators for thinking about movement dynamics and American politics. The dissertation from which this book grew was shepherded by what some have called the most supportive committee in history; thanks to Sidney Tarrow, Theodore Lowi, Mary Katzenstein, Elizabeth Sanders, and Penny Edgell. Cornell peers and friends provided intellectual stimulation and support; thanks to Matt Crozat, Wesley Edwards, Antonina Gentile, Peggy Kohn, Mingus Mapps, Matthew Rudolph, Anindya Saha, Lisa Sansoucy, John Schwartz, Aseema Sinha, Dan and Christina Sherman, and Kim Williams. While I was a graduate student, the Project on Contentious Politics sponsored by the Stanford Center for the Advanced Study in Behavioral Sciences and the Mellon Foundation was an embarrassment of riches, both intellectual and culinary, from 1996 through 1998. There I witnessed examples of collegiality that are unlikely to be exceeded, from Ron Aminzade, Jack Goldstone, Doug McAdam, Liz Perry, Bill Sewell, Sid Tarrow, and Chuck Tilly. It was a rare pleasure to be part of the working group on community organizing assembled by Marion Orr at Brown University during the 2004–5 year, including Rich Wood, Janice Fine, Clarence Stone, Mark Santow, Kathleen Staudt, Peter Burns, Bob Fisher, Rich Wood, and Dennis Shirley. A special thanks to Bill Gamson and the Boston College Department of Sociology for making possible a semester of leave during fall 2005 and to the members of MRAP, the Media and Movements Research and Action Project, for providing great company and a stimulating forum.

I am very fortunate to have colleagues at Rutgers University–Newark who embrace the study of grassroots politics in American cities. At the Maxwell School of Syracuse University, Suzanne Mettler and Grant Reeher encouraged me after reading an early manuscript draft. Warm appreciation to John Burdick and Robert Rubenstein, my colleagues and pals in PARC (the Program in the Analysis and Resolution of Conflict), along with Maxwell friends and colleagues Jim Bennett, Ásthildur Bernhardsdóttir, Keith Bybee, Audie Klotz, Sandy Lane, Don Mitchell, Grant Reeher, Radell Roberts, Mark Rupert, Hans Peter Schmitz, Katina Stapleton, Vitor Trindade, Hongying Wang, and many others for encouragement and support when it mattered most. The Dominick's restaurant gang was an oasis in the desert. Thanks also to political science department and PARC staff members Elizabeth Mignacca, Chris Praino, Jacquie Meyer, Candy Brooks, Tess Slater, and Stacy Bunce for their reliable help and support.

Many colleagues provided helpful feedback on the manuscript. Keith Bybee, Kristen Grace, Rob Kleidman, David Meyer, Kay Schlozman, Aseema Sinha, Bert Klandersman, Doug McAdam, Margaret Weir, and two anonymous reviewers read and commented on drafts or sections of my research. My excellent junior faculty writing group, including Elizabeth Cohen, Sarah Pralle, Hanspeter Schmitz, and Hongying Wang, provided invaluable feedback on manuscript chapters. Wise friend and expert editor Martha Nichols provided her usual perspicacious observations on the manuscript. Everita Silina, Ryan McKean, and Marie-Lou Fernandes provided valuable research assistance. Thanks to Jason Weidemann, Adam Brunner, and Nancy Sauro at the University of Minnesota Press for their patience and assistance.

I was able to conduct full-time fieldwork thanks to a National Science Foundation graduate fellowship as well as a Unitarian-Universalist Association dissertation scholarship. Additional support was provided by an Aspen Institute Nonprofit Sector Research Fund fellowship, a Philanthropic and Educational Organization (PEO) dissertation fellowship, and a Mellon graduate fellowship. Grants of hospitality as well as of funds made this research possible, from Clare Chance, Larry Berkowitz, and Sandy Tomita in St. Louis and Meg Durbin, Clinton Lewis, Eli, Gabriel, and Austin Lewis, and Michael Howard in San Jose.

I can't adequately thank my community of family and friends for their unflagging support. Elizabeth Cohen and Sarah Pralle were my steadfast compatriots and study companions in Syracuse. My love and thanks go to them and to Larry Berkowitz and Sandy Tomita, Ruth Buchman, Holly Christman, Rob and Carmel Crawford, Meg Durbin and Clinton Lewis, Diana Miller, the late Marilyn Spiro and the Spiro family, Kristen Grace, Rob Howe, Marcia Jarmel and Alana Jeydel, Eileen Kardos, Martha Nichols, Christina Rivers, Sandy Rose, Lisa Sansoucy, Aseema Sinha, Barbara Velarde Steines, Susan Tatje, Connie Van Rheenen, Brendan Wyly, and Kathryn Grace Wyly. The Unitarian-Universalist Fellowship of Big Flats, New York, and the First Unitarian Universalist Society of Syracuse exemplify community, and no one from my Euclid Terrace neighborhood bowls alone. Special thanks to Mary Ellen and Don for the most beautiful spot to read on Keuka Lake. I am lucky to have my brothers Andrew and Adam Swarts; my sisters-in-law Lorraine and Amy; my Blondes (Johnathan,

Jordan, and Hannah Swarts) and my Redheads (Michael and Emily Swarts); the Dolan-Faulkner clan; and the unconditional love of my late grandparents Charles Emerson and Cynthia Homet. My grandfather actually read my dissertation when he was ninety-three years old. I hope this astonishing act of devotion did not unduly shorten his life.

There are some to whom special thanks are due. I cannot adequately express my gratitude to Sid Tarrow. My parents, Lowell and Rachel Swarts, have supplied unwavering love and support. Harry Segal and Connie Van Rheenen, witnesses to the journey, know more than anyone else what it has required.

Abbreviations

ACORN	Association of Community Organizations for Reform Now
AME	African Methodist Episcopal, a historically black Methodist denomination
BOTY	Back of the Yards Neighborhood Council
CACI	Churches Allied for Community Improvement, part of MCU for St. Louis
CAP	Citizens' Action Program
CBCO	congregation-based or church-based community organizing
CBCOs	congregation-based or church-based community organizations
CCC	Center for Community Change
CCCC (C4)	Churches Committed to Community Concerns, part of MCU for St. Louis
CCHD	Catholic Campaign for Human Development
COPS	Communities Organized for Public Service
CRA	Community Reinvestment Act
CUCA	Churches United for Community Action, part of MCU for St. Louis
DART	Direct Action Research and Training
EITC	Earned Income Tax Credit
ESC	Ecumenical Sponsoring Committee, a predecessor of San Jose PACT
IAF	Industrial Areas Foundation
LIFT	Louisiana Interfaith Together

LOC	local organizing committee
MCU	Metropolitan Congregations United for St. Louis
NWRO	National Welfare Rights Organization
OCO	Oakland Community Organization
PACT	People Acting in Community Together
PICO	People Improving Communities through Organizing
RAL	refund anticipation loan
SJ ACORN	San Jose ACORN
SL ACORN	St. Louis ACORN
SMO	social movement organization
TEN	Transportation Equity Network
TWO	The Woodlawn Organization
WCTU	Women's Christian Temperance Union

Introduction

Invisible Actors: Community Organizing, Agenda Setting, and American Social Movements

In 2001, Santa Clara County, California, committed to providing health insurance to 100 percent of its children. From 2002 to 2004 the county recruited 25 percent more children into existing programs and enrolled another 15,000 children in a new program that brought $24.4 million in new funds into the county.

On November 2, 2004, George W. Bush won the presidential campaign in the state of Florida. Less well publicized was a ballot measure to raise the Florida minimum wage from $5.15 per hour to $6.15, with annual wage increases indexed to inflation. It passed by 72 percent, making Florida the first southern state to pass a minimum wage higher than the federal rate, immediately increasing 850,000 workers' annual full-time income by $2,000.

On August 10, 2005, President George W. Bush signed a $286 billion new transportation bill. Its pork barrel earmarks made headlines, but its redistributive features received little attention. These include a guarantee of more than $700 million in projects with provisions for low-wage job seekers. The bill also encouraged programs for low-income workers seeking new job skills on more than $200 billion of federal highway projects.[1]

These otherwise unconnected events share one feature: they were all instigated by mass-based community organizations of low- and moderate-income Americans—organizations that remain all but invisible behind the headlines. Health care for all Santa Clara County children was the brainchild of a labor-funded think tank and fifteen San Jose churches. The churches compose PACT (People Acting in Community Together), a community organization affiliated with the PICO (People Improving

Communities through Organizing) National Network. The Florida minimum wage campaign was led by ACORN (Association of Community Organizations for Reform Now), a thirty-eight-year-old national organization based in low-income neighborhoods. The Gamaliel Foundation, a network of church-based groups like PICO, led a coalition in lobbying successfully for redistributive programs in the 2005 transportation bill. Metropolitan Congregations United for St. Louis (MCU), a Gamaliel affiliate, helped lead this effort. Outside of the labor movement, ACORN and congregation-based community organizing are the most successful attempts to channel working-class organizing into policy influence.

Unlike national social movement organizations such as the Sierra Club or the Christian Coalition, these organizations are not well known. News coverage of the church-based groups may mention "priests" or "church leaders" but frequently does not name their organization. ACORN's protests are better publicized, but its policy innovations and national campaigns are less well known. In this sense, community organizations are invisible actors in American urban politics. Their invisibility is partly understandable; after all, community organizing by definition occurs in local communities. By the time they make national news, local organizing campaigns have usually gained allies and become subsumed in broader coalitions. Their proposals have been taken up by public figures or powerful government agencies. However, they play a critical role in agenda setting, representation, and policy making from below. Furthermore, while until recently their work has been largely local, they have increasingly become active in national campaigns. These grassroots organizations give voice to the voiceless and draw new constituencies into civic life. ACORN, the PICO Network, and the Gamaliel Foundation draw many thousands of poor and working-class citizens into meaningful civic engagement. Some groups are majority African American or Latino; others are among the most racially diverse social movement organizations in the nation.[2] They combine this voice-giving and empowerment function with political and policy gains that make a difference in their members' lives.

Voluntary associations' vital role in American public life is widely acknowledged, and federated mass-membership organizations have significantly influenced national social policies.[3] Even strictly local groups provided preexisting networks and resources for major national movements. For example, the Montgomery bus boycott, which ignited the most influential American movement of the twentieth century, drew heavily on such relatively invisible black Montgomery organizations as the Women's Political Council, the Interdenominational Ministerial Alliance, the Progressive

Democratic Association, the Citizens' Steering Committee, and of course, the churches.[4]

Community organizing as practiced by groups like ACORN, PICO, and the Gamaliel Foundation incorporates fewer Americans than the federated civic, fraternal, and service organizations that have received so much attention from scholars.[5] However, community organizing has steadily grown since Saul Alinsky practiced it in the 1940s, and its rate of growth has accelerated. A wide array of grassroots people's organizations use its methods, including hundreds of independent local organizations as well as those in this study, which are part of national associations. Some, such as ACORN, recruit neighborhood residents as both dues-paying members and activists. Others, like the groups in PICO and the Gamaliel Foundation, organizations of dues-paying institutions, primarily churches, emulate the model that the Industrial Areas Foundation (IAF) established in the 1970s.

At the center of this study are four local organizations and the three national associations to which they belong. However, the larger issue that motivates this book is the quality of American democracy. Economic inequality's dramatic increase since 1973 has produced a concentration of wealth among the top 1 percent of households in 2000 only slightly less than the top 1 percent in 1929, the most unequal period in the twentieth century.[6] Increasingly, economic inequality is linked through a number of mechanisms to political inequality. Throughout American history, collective action sustained in organized social movements from below has expanded rights and liberties and pressured the state to provide redistributive programs. Local organizations, when joined in federated national associations such as labor unions, women's civic associations, and fraternal organizations, provided the building blocks for effective coordinated political action.[7] Though often hidden from view, leaders have *intentionally* and *strategically* organized these movements that appear to well up and erupt from below.[8]

ACORN and congregation-based community organizations (CBCOs) are the leading contemporary models of community organizing for political power. Both styles of organizing have much to contribute to a broad, progressive movement for social change. They also raise important questions. In a time of declining public resources, a conservative resurgence, a fragmented and dispirited Left, and the dismantling of federal responsibility for social welfare, what can local grassroots organizing accomplish? Do ACORN and the church-based groups differ significantly in their methods and degrees of success? But the results they achieve are only part of the story. A fine-grained analysis of organizations can shed light on factors that constrain and enable other social movements in the United States. Their successes and failures are relevant not only for scholars of social movements, civic engagement, and policy innovation but for all those interested in redistributive movements in American politics.

The Argument of the Book

Different styles of organizing make different contributions to American urban politics and political participation. I argue that congregation-based community organizing (which I call CBCO for convenience)[9] has developed a unique and innovative *cultural strategy,* while ACORN is notable for its innovative *organizational and political strategy.* I do not mean that CBCO has not developed strategic and tactical innovations—indeed, it has. Nor do I suggest that ACORN lacks a strong mobilizing culture and collective identity. CBCO's unique contribution to the American organizing tradition is its combination of democratic deliberation, intensive leadership development, and a praxis that links the strategic pursuit of power to shared religious values. Several sociologists have investigated CBCO's organizational culture; this study explores its relation to American political culture. It also examines the PICO National Network and the Gamaliel Foundation, which are as large as the first CBCO network (the Industrial Areas Foundation) but not nearly as well known. There is no study that compares congregation-based organizing with ACORN or that considers the policy outcomes of three national organizations as well as four local groups.[10] There are no book-length scholarly treatments of the Gamaliel Foundation or ACORN.

Both *religion* and *class* account for CBCO's heightened attention to cultural elaboration. Its base in religion predisposes it to the use of shared symbols, language, and ritual. I argue that the need to unify its cross-class, multiracial membership leads it to perform more cultural work than ACORN does. In addition, it must develop a common language to bridge the different discourses of North American Christianity and power politics. In contrast, ACORN's membership is more homogeneous: lower income and predominantly African American and Hispanic. Its organizational culture is secular and populist, and ACORN usually does not need to work as hard to ideologically unify its more low-income membership. In chapters 1 through 3, I show how class, religion, and organizational logics help explain how the two approaches differ.

We need to know more about community organizing not just for its civic engagement impacts but for its policy innovations. These remain nearly invisible to scholars of public policy, who usually study the national level. When they do study local policy, scholars usually focus on public officials and bureaucracies even if a citizens' organization developed the concept and guided the legislation. This risks missing a critical aspect of policy innovation and diffusion.

This project is also motivated by an even more general issue in social science. Many studies of civic engagement and voluntary associations have approached their subjects at the macro level: analyses of changes in the ecology of organizations or large surveys of individual behaviors.[11] The macro level of analysis often obscures the role of individual and organizational innovations and strategic choices. The entrepreneurs who developed ACORN and congregation-based community organizations developed new strategies and tactics that, I argue, have been essential to achieving their results. Chapters 2 and 3 focus in depth on these contrasting cultural and political strategies. I mean for these accounts to help expand the theoretical space for agency in our understandings of grassroots movements and policy making.

Organizational Cultures and Processes

In this book I return to the central preoccupation of resource mobilization theory: the social movement organization. Piven and Cloward have famously argued that building stable, ongoing membership organizations hampers poor people's movements because it distracts from mobilizing mass disruption.[12] However, while building highly formal bureaucratic organizations may distract from collective action and certainly cannot substitute for it, effective collective action must be coordinated. Theirs and other structuralist accounts inevitably gloss over the leaders who, even if rich networks of potential activists exist, must develop ingenious appeals and tactics that will activate them—especially in a politically hostile national context. For example, from a distance, "bloc recruitment" of churches offers an obvious advantage in efficiency over ACORN's house-to-house recruitment. Indeed, this advantage is a major reason the method was adopted. However, even when appropriating existing networks, activists must constantly rebuild them and create new ones within institutions, which vary greatly in their degree of organization, network density, and member mobility and replacement.[13] It is fitting that research on social movement organizations is increasingly focused on such organizational factors as coalitions, leadership, strategy, and decision making.[14]

Organizations are excellent arenas for observing the cultural processes whereby people adopt new political ideas and identities, enter civic life, and learn new ways to exert influence. In her study of conflict styles in American religious congregations, Penny Edgell Becker writes that different organizational types mediate between "underlying variables" like size and polity [governance] and group processes, by institutionalizing patterns of authority and commitment that are related to, but not determined by, these structural features of the organization. They also mediate between larger cultural formations—traditions, ideologies, discourses—and social action at the local level.[15]

Local affiliates of larger organizations can reveal the continuities and the disjunctures between national and local organizational cultures. Studies can reveal the space leaders have in which to maneuver—or at least the possibilities they can see. The options leaders can envision are constrained by their own imaginations and the lenses their organizational cultures provide. These lenses color their perceptions of the political-economic context and what is politically feasible. More fundamentally, organizational cultures answer the questions "who are we?" and "how do we do things here?" They favor certain strategies and tactics and discourage others. Some tactics will be unthinkable, so some outcomes will be ruled out regardless of available resources or political opportunity. On the other hand, as they interact with their environment, organizations respond to external cues. If their goals are not well served by habitual ways of doing things, they can learn to do things differently.

While numerous factors outside an organization's control affect its impact, within their organizations activists exercise greater control over intervening variables such as the nature of its strategic deliberation, leadership training, issue framing, and member mobilization. Some of these organizational functions, such as democratic deliberation and leadership training, are valuable civic outcomes in their own right; others, such as framing issues and mobilizing members, are intermediate achievements that make some outcomes possible and foreclose others. Figure 1 primarily depicts internal features of community organizing.[16] I use the term *mobilizing culture* for two reasons. First, the process of mobilization is not just structural but cultural, that is, it involves shared meanings, norms, and practices. Second, as many have argued, this process includes more than does the "framing" approach to social movement cultures.[17] Mobilizing culture includes tacit norms and values that are nonstrategic and underlie more conscious strategic framing of group identity and issues. The congregation-based organizations may be more self-conscious in their use of ritual and symbol, but secular groups like ACORN have their own norms, values, lore, and assumptions about what constitutes community organizing.

Strategic capacity, Marshall Ganz's term, includes leaders' motivation, access to relevant knowledge, and deliberative and decision-making pro-

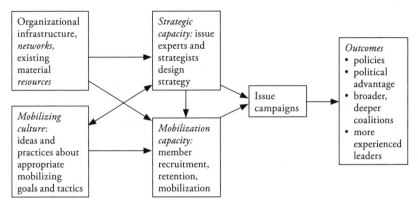

Figure 1. Relationship of organizational features to outcomes.

cesses ("Resources and Resourcefulness"). This concept helps rectify the invisibility of strategic choices in much of the social movement literature. It is specified separate from mobilizing culture to show that affiliates that share a general mobilizing culture can have different strategic capacities based on local differences.

Together, resources, mobilizing cultures, and strategic capacity produce *mobilization capacity,* the ability to mobilize constituents—a grassroots organization's fundamental source of power. Effective strategy and large numbers influence outcomes.

Why These Organizations?

This study compares two major styles of organizing: the organizing ACORN conducts in neighborhoods and the organizing that the PICO Network and Gamaliel Foundation conduct through religious congregations. I compare the processes and achievements of four community organizations over ten years, from 1997 to 2006, in two cities: St. Louis, Missouri, and San Jose, California. Each of the two cities has an ACORN chapter and a congregation-based organization.

All four organizations work primarily for political and policy changes, although three of them also provide some services to members. All are multi-issue organizations with modest budgets that seek power through mass mobilization. All are part of federated structures with local chapters, citywide or regional organizations, and statewide and national organizations. All have emerged from a common history of urban community organizing. However, the congregation-based organizations and ACORN have significantly different structures and mobilizing cultures.

ACORN is one of the few long-standing (thirty-eight years in 2008) national grassroots membership organizations that represents poor and working-class people's interests. It has chapters in eighty-five cities in thirty-seven states, national offices in six cities, and a new international division with offices in Canada, Peru, Mexico, and the Dominican Republic. It functions as a pressure group using protest, negotiation, and other tactics at the local, citywide, regional, and national levels. Because ACORN is not a 501(c)(3) nonprofit organization, it can also run and endorse candidates for office. ACORN's mainstay has been organizing neighborhood activist groups by signing up individuals through "door-knocking" house to house. Currently, ACORN is organizing living wage, antipredatory lending, community reinvestment, housing, state minimum wage increases, and other campaigns.[18]

Church-based organizations—federations of religious congregations—are the other fastest-growing type of community organization. Politically progressive and distinct from the religious right, they represent some of the most interesting efforts to forge diverse coalitions for social change. This study includes one member of each of two large national networks, federations of independent 501(c)(3) nonprofit organizations: the PICO organizing network (of which San Jose PACT is a member) and the Gamaliel Foundation (of which MCU is a member). Including both a PICO and a Gamaliel organization allows me to compare the norms of two different organizing networks that use the same general approach.

The data are drawn from a year of fieldwork (1997–98), interviews, and documents.[19] This included participant-observation of many meetings, campaigns, and events and numerous conversations with organization members and staff. Data include over two hundred interviews over ten years. These include semistructured interviews with seventy-five activists in the four local organizations and additional interviews with organizers and staff, city officials, members of other advocacy organizations, and others. Finally, I collected data on organizations' publicity, histories, budgets, funding, and campaigns from organizational files, other organizations, local newspapers, and city government departments.

Church-based Community Organizing's Innovative Cultural Strategy

Since the 1960s and 1970s, public interest groups have proliferated, along with movements for feminism, gay rights, environmentalism, Central American solidarity, antinuclear weapons, peace, and others.[20] Although these have been secular movements, churches and religious activists were heavily involved in many of them. However, liberal congregations' involve-

Table 1. Number of congregation-based organizing networks and ACORN chapters as of February 2006

National organization	Number of local groups	Number of states where active	Statewide federations or areas of concentration	Other countries where active, if any
IAF	56	21	Arizona Interfaith (5 projects), Texas Interfaith (10 projects), New York (6 projects)	UK, Canada, Germany
PICO National Network	50	17	California Project (17 projects), Louisiana LIFT (5 projects)	Rwanda
Gamaliel Foundation	55	20	Metropolitan regional organizations: Chicago MAC, Detroit MOSES, St. Louis MCU, Wisconsin (8 projects), Illinois (7 projects)	South Africa
DART (Direct Action Research and Training)	21	6	Florida Federation (10 projects)	
ACORN	85	37	Chicago, New York City, Boston, Ohio, Pennsylvania, Louisiana, Texas California (10 chapters), Florida (11 chapters)	Canada, Mexico, Dominican Republic, Peru

Note: Information compiled from interviews with Steve Kest, ACORN, August 4, 2004, Brooklyn, New York; Scott Reed, PICO, telephone interview, September 17, 2004; the Industrial Areas Foundation Web site, http://www.industrialareasfoundation.org/iafcontact/iafcontact .htm; the PICO Web site, http://www.piconetwork.org/; the Gamaliel Foundation Web site, http://www.gamaliel.org/; and the DART Center Web site, http://www.thedartcenter.org.

ment in left-of-center organizing has received far less attention than conservative religious activism. Rather than target a national political party, as the religious right has done, liberal churches have concentrated on local activism and limited national lobbying. CBCOs' tax-exempt status legally prevents them from partisan political activity such as endorsing candidates (although it permits unlimited educational efforts such as candidate forums, nonpartisan voter mobilization, and some lobbying). CBCOs have avoided endorsing candidates both due to these legal restrictions and because they want to retain access to politicians (they risk not having access to the person in an elected position if they supported the losing opponent).

The most provocative feature of church-based community organizing is not its political or policy outcomes but its innovative *cultural strategy*—ideas and practices that form a novel and effective amalgam of religion, political strategy, and American ideals. With these ideas and practices, CBCO is one of the few methods that successfully recruits and mobilizes a cross-race, cross-class membership. While churches are natural vehicles to recruit a cross-class membership, shared religious identity alone has not united Americans across class and race lines. It is a truism that the most segregated hour in America is eleven o'clock on Sunday morning. Organizers do conscious cultural work to forge a measure of unity from historic mistrust. In chapter 2 I analyze how the culture of church-based community organizing partially resolves tensions that have undermined American efforts at progressive reform. These are the class and racial divides, the liberal-conservative divide, altruism and self-interest, participatory democracy and efficiency, and privatism and public action. CBCO produces a distinctive "culture of commitment."[21]

CBCOs are far more attentive than ACORN to such organizational processes as training leaders and planning meetings with officials. However, it would be a mistake to assume that since CBCOs have produced noteworthy ideas and norms that borrow some language and rituals from religious culture that they are somehow less strategic. CBCOs articulate a religious basis for their political organizing, but their analysis of power and organizing techniques is portable to secular social movements. Organizing through churches was a conscious strategy of mobilizing both tangible and intangible resources, although it is *also* a sincere expression of religious values. The founders or top leaders of the three largest CBCO networks are either active Jesuits or Catholic seminary graduates, and many CBCO organizers are either members of the clergy or active religious laypersons.[22] Furthermore, CBCOs have produced numerous policy innovations: the living wage tactic was invented in 1994 by a powerful Baltimore CBCO, and San Jose PACT has developed innovations that have spread throughout California and the nation, such as comprehensive public safety programs and the use of tobacco settlement money to fund children's health care. However, CBCOs are unusual for their ideology of citizen action and the detailed organizing principles that they teach activists.

Religion and Progressive Change

Many Americans, including some scholars, see religion as an exclusively conservative force. They argue that because American religion is highly institutionalized it is interwoven and complicit with American power arrangements of race, sex, and class. Congregations' scope of action is restricted by members' class and racial loyalties and by church authorities, and they are greatly limited in tackling issues of sexuality and gender. Like other 501(c)(3) nonprofit organizations, their political activities are constrained by American tax law. Partisan politics can divide their members. In addition, American religious culture typically discourages conflict and contentious tactics.

However, American religion is neither an outmoded casualty of modernity nor a univocal conservative force. Religious texts and traditions are multifaceted and indeterminate and *always* interpreted by historically situated communities. When the social need and motivation arises, the politics of religious institutions can be virtually reversed. In the United States, religion has long been linked to politics of the left, right, and center. American Christianity played crucial roles in *simultaneously* maintaining and undermining (through abolitionism) the slave system. Religious institutions are sites of struggle and contestation like any others, and CBCOs are just one example of the closely braided relationship between religion and American social movements.[23]

Despite their limitations, churches may be the likeliest American institutions to serve as a base for widespread civic involvement.[24] Far more working-class people belong to churches than to unions. Because churches are the last institution remaining in many poor neighborhoods, those interested in improving urban conditions or protecting and expanding redistributive programs have had to confront religion's limitations but acknowledge its potential for mobilizing poor and working-class Americans. Chapters 1, 2, 6, and 8 analyze CBCO mobilizing culture and ideological achievements and present two cases of local organizations.

ACORN's Innovative Organizational and Political Strategy

ACORN mobilizes its scarce resources and membership using a wide array of tactics; known for boisterous confrontational protests, ACORN increasingly works in large coalitions, using a flexible and pragmatic array of insider and outsider strategies. Unlike some social movement organizations that seek exhaustive democratic deliberation, ACORN is instrumental and utilitarian, focused intently on raising funds, recruiting members, and implementing issue campaigns.[25] ACORN's constant experimentation with new tactics has made it a strategic innovator. Its structure as a single, centralized organization, its goal of building a national poor people's movement, and its infrastructure of national issue specialists helped enable ACORN to attempt ambitious national campaigns long before the CBCOs.

Also, ACORN's tremendous challenge as a poor people's organization to mobilize resources has motivated it to identify creative sources of funding, such as the private corporations it targets for reform. It began by using the Community Reinvestment Act (CRA) to pressure banks to offer new low-cost mortgages to low-income first-time homebuyers—and pay ACORN Housing Corporation to recruit and counsel them. ACORN then applied this corporate campaign strategy to numerous national banks and adapted it to other financial issues, such as home insurance and exploitative lending practices. Chapter 3 details ACORN's strategic innovations. These usually accomplish multiple goals simultaneously. For example, designing campaigns against banks extracted significant new funds for community reinvestment ($6 billion as of 2004).[26] It also funds ACORN to locate, screen, and train low-income borrowers. Some of these funds support organizing as well as service delivery, and recruiting homebuyers allows ACORN to reach potential new members.

ACORN staff organizers encourage members to lead, and neighborhood subgroups are free to tackle the issues that concern them, but major city and statewide campaigns are usually coordinated from the top. Central coordination by a cadre of seasoned, long-term national staff members provides efficiencies. Their continuity as staff helps mitigate the high turnover among necessarily low-paid local organizers. ACORN also has a dispersed national staff of issue experts who help craft campaigns and advise locals. This combines the expert knowledge of a public interest organization for poor people with the mass base of a federated membership organization active at local, state, and national levels.

Their relatively small numbers can make some local ACORN chapters seem like pesky gadflies. However, ACORN has forged increasingly broad alliances to achieve its goals. It has undertaken an enormous challenge—to organize and represent some of America's least powerful, poorest citizens on issues that would otherwise remain ignored. In the process it has empowered some unlikely leaders for political action. Chapters 1, 3, 5, and 7 explore ACORN's history and innovations in more detail.

St. Louis and San Jose: Urban Opposites

In recent decades, Americans began to observe a new phenomenon: cities in the warm southeast and southwest were growing rapidly, while the northeastern and midwestern industrial and manufacturing centers were losing population. These older manufacturing centers came to be called snowbelt or rustbelt cities, while the new, sprawling centers of immigration and high-technology growth are located in the sunbelt.

Organizational Type	St. Louis: *rustbelt; declining industrial city*	San Jose: *sunbelt; rapidly growing, high-technology city*
ACORN	St. Louis ACORN	San Jose ACORN
CBCO	MCU for St. Louis, a member of the Gamaliel Foundation, a national organizing network	PACT, a member of PICO, a national organizing network

Figure 2. Contrasting urban contexts of the organizations in the study.

St. Louis, Missouri, and San Jose, California, exemplify these two urban types. By 2003, St. Louis had lost 50 percent of its 1960 population. Its traditional manufacturing base continues to decline while the city struggles to shift to a high-technology economy. St. Louis has the typical black and white population of older industrial cities, with comparatively few Hispanics and Asians. In contrast, San Jose is in Silicon Valley, the model of explosive sunbelt growth and cutting-edge information economy. In Figure 2, a matrix of the four organizations illustrates the selection of cases. Because St. Louis and San Jose are stark examples of opposing types, their dynamics and influences on grassroots social movement organizations should be especially visible. Contrasting such different cities can reveal how organizations adapt to different external factors such as demographics, economy, and governing regimes. The data from four cases are only suggestive, of course, as numerous factors influence organizations.

Community Organizing and Public Policy

Local activism may be less salient in relatively centralized or closed polities, but it is especially important in the U.S. federal system, with its dispersed systems of authority that can be pitted against one another or abandoned in favor of more promising venues for policy reform. This allows mass-based voluntary associations to amalgamate local capacity vertically at the state and national levels or, alternatively, to adopt a horizontal strategy of "local gradualism."[27]

Grassroots community organizations make innovative public policy. Since they are unofficial actors, all too often they are invisible actors in public policy scholarship.[28] The policy literature tends to have a national focus and an elite-centered bias. In his study of federal policy making, Kingdon argued that "visible," or public, participants set agendas, while "hidden" participants, such as consultants and experts, propose specific alternatives. In his view, interest groups "affect the governmental agenda more by blocking potential items than by promoting them." Baumgartner and Jones's study of agendas and policy change acknowledges the role of citizen mobilization, especially how citizens' interest groups brought pressure *against* nuclear power, pesticides, and other potential threats.[29] In these narratives, the actors are public officials and other elites, and the role of grassroots movements is to protest policies initiated by others.

Yet social movements often generate demands that result in new policies and even propose the specific policies themselves.[30] Local grassroots organizations develop numerous policy innovations. Those in this study alone developed a multipronged public safety and anti-blight program, a model for the national program Weed and Seed; ACORN's Living Wage Resource Center, which assists and originates living wage campaigns in cities and states; pioneering antipredatory lending laws; the use of tobacco lawsuit settlements to fund new children's health-care programs; new low-cost private-sector mortgage programs; and a wide range of educational innovations, including charter schools, after-school centers, new urban "small schools," teacher home visits, and parent participation in schools. One local organization in this study, San Jose PACT, regularly researches, proposes, and wins numerous progressive policies. Examples include comprehensive programs for low-income immigrant families at a middle school, all coordinated by one person, and a package of forty anticrime programs that, at PACT's insistence, included prevention as well as suppression and enforcement.

Understanding the civic, political, and policy impacts of grassroots organizing also makes possible a fuller understanding of contemporary social movements.

Making Community Organizing Visible in Social Movement Theory

Community organizing unambiguously fits most scholars' definitions of "social movement," for example, Sidney Tarrow's "collective challenges by people with common purposes and solidarity in sustained interaction with elites, opponents and authorities."[31] However, most contemporary social movement theorizing is based on national or international movements. Except for work on the labor movement, European and North American scholarship is heavily influenced by middle-class movements. The relative invisibility of local movements and of class in North American social movement theory has partially obscured an important strain of American grassroots politics.

The primary focus on the national social movement has deemphasized the continuity of grassroots organizing in favor of the cyclical patterns of national movements and those rare historical moments when conditions encourage or demand mass national protest.[32] Also, an inclusive understanding of "social movement" makes it hard to analytically distinguish between the kind of national and international movements that occur, diffuse, and decline in cycles, and local organizing that proceeds relatively unaffected by national and international incentives to mobilize. Because the bulk of the literature concerns national social movements, or increasingly the fashionable topic of transnational mobilization, the fact is obscured that local activism has experienced rapid growth and involves far more American citizens than other forms.[33] This kind of local movement relies less on "moments of madness" and more on organizers and leaders with ongoing commitments to empowering the disempowered. These entrepreneurs explicitly seek to create an infrastructure that is relatively insulated from movement peaks and valleys—if not always in ability to win gains, at least in organizational continuity and mobilizing capacity. In the past thirty-five years, this capacity has steadily grown.

Different political opportunities help explain the different fates of St. Louis and San Jose church-based campaigns (see chapters 6 and 8), although many other variables contributed to their results, including resources and strategic capacity. However, a theoretical emphasis on political opportunity is not well equipped to explain why, nationally, community organizing has actually expanded in a hostile political climate. I argue that its growth focuses our attention on the strategic choices of movement entrepreneurs—how they have selected issues and designed campaigns to represent their constituencies' grievances in a process that is both culture-laden and strategic. The innovative mobilizing culture of CBCO and the resourcefulness and strategic innovation of ACORN place intention and agency in sharp relief.

Two Symbolic American Movement Traditions

One can discern a set of oppositions that characterize the way many participants and some scholars have thought about American social movements since the 1960s. As polarized distinctions, they do not describe real organizations so much as ideal types, in the Weberian sense; actual social movements combine elements of both types (see Figure 3). Yet these observable distinctions are some of the elements from which movements construct their identities. The features in the left-hand column characterize primarily middle-class moral reform movements such as abolition, temperance, and

Ideal Type A	Ideal Type B
Examples: moral reform movements; some "new" or "postmaterialist" movements	*Examples:* labor organizing and community organizing
protest	organizing
reactive	proactive
expressive	instrumental
moral	strategic
altruism	self-interest
purity	compromise
radical	moderate
virtue	power
like religion	like politics or economics
middle-class	working-class
predominantly white	racial associations not necessarily clear
tacitly feminine	tacitly masculine
countercultural	culturally mainstream
decision by consensus	decision by majority vote
emphasis on inclusive process	emphasis on political or policy outcomes
radical egalitarianism	hierarchical; traditional representative democracy
episodic	ongoing

Figure 3. Two ideal types of American social movements.

numerous others to the present day. Their moral fervor also animates campaigns that are justified by scientific or public health rationales, such as antismoking and antiobesity. It is not that they are never proactive and strategic, but that their identities and often tactics are historically more informed by the other traits. American religious or moral reform movements have a long tradition of distrusting politics because they are associated with godlessness, corruption, political machines, immigrants, and power for its own sake. For example, radical abolitionists found the world of power politics corrupt and morally repugnant, and only reluctantly turned to politics when "moral suasion" failed to convert slaveholders. The early Prohibition

Party, the Woman's Christian Temperance Union, and the Templars held any legal compromise of total prohibition to be immoral; likewise, segments of the Christian right abhorred compromise with the political system but were outflanked by the political realists among them.[34]

Twentieth-century American movements exhibit this cultural legacy, though often in secular guise. Activists fear that political compromise will damage the movement's purity of motive and vision. This secularized moralism influenced the radical wings of feminism, the antinuclear movement, twentieth-century peace movements, strands of the environmental movement, and others.[35] For example, Szymanski notes that radical pacifist Daniel Berrigan accused moderates of being "obsessed by the necessity of delivering results" and claimed that "the spiritual dismantling of the American empire is going to consume at least our lifetime." The Student Nonviolent Coordinating Committee (SNCC), a key civil rights movement organization, exemplified this spirit, although it certainly sought tangible results. Polletta shows how, in SNCC's early days, "a narrative of the sit-ins warranted SNCC as a kind of anti-organization . . . that was less interested in executing a well-planned agenda than in enacting in its own operation the society it envisaged, and that privileged direct and moral action over political maneuvering." SNCC members "also saw electoral politics as 'immoral' and antithetical to the moral protest that had animated SNCC's activism thus far."[36] This distinction structured the debate in 1963 between direct action and voter registration as a choice between whether

> the emphasis should be political or religious, spontaneous or rigidly political. . . . "Spontaneous" had come to refer to action not oriented to electoral politics, action motivated by religious commitment rather than strategic calculation, and action orchestrated by local groups rather than national committee. Its meaning went far beyond an absence of planning, but remained locked within a set of dualities: spontaneous versus political; political versus moral; moral versus instrumental.[37]

Consensus decision making in Quaker-rooted pacifist organizations influenced the culture of SNCC. After SNCC shifted to a black power identity, this cultural feature reversed its symbolic valence from black working-class to white middle-class.[38] Today the identity, ideology, and tactics of many contemporary anarchist, direct action, and youth-based movements draw heavily on the bundle of features in Ideal Type A.

While these bundles of oppositions are clearly ideal types, they help make sense of different movement organizations and, I argue, influence their mobilizing cultures and the tactics they choose. Maintaining an identity, whether drawn primarily from Ideal Type A or B, may influence strategic and tactical choices as well as (or instead of) rational means-ends analysis does. Ironically, a group or movement that sees itself as secular, rational, hard-nosed, and strategic may act in accord with this image even when it is less effective from an instrumental standpoint.[39]

Recent social movement scholarship has been disproportionately influenced by Ideal Type A. If an earlier generation of scholars themselves drew more on Type B—portraying movements as calculating rational actors busy mobilizing resources—the pendulum has long since swung in the other direction.[40] For example, James Jasper's *Art of Moral Protest* better describes movements that fit the left-hand than the right-hand column. He argues that "we often protest because our systems of meaning are at stake, because we have created villains, and villains must be attacked." This may be true for middle-class movements, but it is not for the community organizing in this book, which addresses stark unmet needs: class-based redistributive issues framed as place-based or religious-based. Jasper's expressive, moral, postindustrial movement members "regularly move from one cause to the next" and pursue alternative movement cultures partly for their own sake.[41] This does not characterize participants in community organizing, most of whom support families, do not identify with "activists," and are more likely to spend time in church, the PTO, or the Boy Scouts than protest the World Trade Organization.

Most scholars of American movements have not considered how contrasting class cultures may shape the forms, goals, and ideologies of non-class-based movements.[42] In addition, the *agency* of movement actors has been relatively invisible in social movement scholarship. North American social movement theory has had a strong structural bias. The influential political process approach to social movement scholarship highlighted the role of political opportunities (as well as mobilizing structures and issue framing) in stimulating the emergence of new movements. It was countered by a recent wave of scholarship focused on culture. However, both the political process and culturally oriented scholarship understate the role of individual creativity and strategic choice by movement entrepreneurs.[43]

Community organizations, like most other SMOs, occupy a terrain somewhere between the two ideal types described above. Community organizing has expanded and heightened its public challenges and national presence since the 1970s, even as national political opportunity has starkly declined. Since 2000, the national organizations in this study have responded to the Bush administration's onslaughts on national services and programs with unprecedented new organizing, national campaigns, and coalition building. This study considers both internal cultural processes and the urban political-economic contexts that constrain and enable their work.

Plan of the Book

I examine the cultures of community organizations at some length in chapters 1 and 2 because they help explain how movement organizations meet a number of challenges. Those less interested in organizational cultures and more in strategy and policy may wish to proceed directly to chapter 3, on ACORN's innovative political strategy, and the case studies that follow. Chapter 1 offers detailed portrayals of the contrasting mobilizing cultures of congregation-based community organizing and ACORN. The two cultures share basic assumptions about organizing drawn from Saul Alinsky, probably the single greatest influence on urban community organizing. However, distinct ideologies, collective identities, emotion norms, and assumptions about organizing pervade their organizational styles and guide action.

Chapter 2 focuses specifically on CBCO's innovative cultural strategy. One of the differences between CBCO and ACORN has to do with different class cultures: CBCO includes middle-class members, while ACORN generally does not. (Many organizers and staff members in *both* approaches have bachelor's or advanced degrees and are middle-class.) I contend that CBCO helps build a common identity among one of the most economically and racially diverse constituencies in the United States. I demonstrate how CBCO draws on religion and a practical theory of power to manage oppositions in American political culture and between the two ideal types of American social movements.

Chapter 3 argues that ACORN offers innovative organizational and political strategies different from and complementary to CBCO's strengths. Its structure as one centralized organization and its need for resources have spurred the development and dissemination of resourceful and varied tactics and targets. This has led it to become a leader in developing national campaigns.

Chapter 4 presents St. Louis ACORN, an organization with a long history of mobilization that was relatively depleted from recent ambitious but unsuccessful campaigns. The organization regained capacity with the staff resources and expertise that a national organization could provide. St. Louis ACORN offered the national office a setting to experiment with wage-increase campaigns, and ACORN diffused what it learned to subsequent campaigns.

Chapter 5 examines Metropolitan Congregations United for St. Louis, a congregation-based community organization. The chapter shows how this young organization trained its members in a sophisticated policy analysis of

St. Louis's urban problems. It confronted a local political system with few opportunities and went on to pursue more tractable issues in its campaigns for urban redevelopment. Its membership in the Gamaliel Foundation network of organizations gave it a vehicle in which to amplify its local work and influence state and national transportation policy.

Chapter 6 investigates San Jose ACORN, a young organization with a short history and few resources that nevertheless built capacity with disciplined organizers and unusually dedicated grassroots leaders.

Chapter 7 studies San Jose PACT, a congregation-based community organization affiliated with the PICO National Network. This organization combined a relatively long history and reputation, a pragmatic incremental strategy, and effective organizing and mobilizing practices to compile a record of impressive, agenda-setting outcomes.

Chapter 8 explores the results of community organizing based on the four local case studies as well as the three national organizations of which they are a part. The state and national campaigns of ACORN, the Gamaliel Foundation, and the PICO National Network show their strengths and weaknesses, but also significant accomplishments against great odds.

Chapter 9 looks ahead to the challenges facing community organizing. I argue that national coalition building has begun to transcend the balkanization that helps make the work of these organizations comparatively invisible. They will need far greater coordination and coalition building if this movement seeks meaningful gains for poor and working-class Americans.

1

Different Mobilizing Cultures: Congregation-based Organizing and ACORN

> *For people with much less experience with social policy than with socia-*
> *bility, the questions "What sort of people are we?" and "What do people*
> *like us want?" were as salient as "How do I coordinate with others who*
> *share my interests?"*
>
> —Elisabeth Clemens, *The People's Lobby*

In *Avoiding Politics: How Americans Produce Apathy in Everyday Life,* Nina Eliasoph suggests that "a crucial dimension of power is the power to create the contexts of public life itself. . . . Without this power to create the etiquette for political participation, citizens are powerless."[1] The organizations in this study all create distinct etiquettes and cultures of political participation. Organizations are not unified actors; even relatively small ones are complex, often with competing factions and conflicting interests. Nor can organizational culture be reduced merely to a set of tools that organizations self-consciously use strategically, although Ann Swidler's metaphor of a cultural toolbox captures the fact that organization leaders may consciously use some cultural features instrumentally.[2] An organizational culture is a set of interactive, institutionalized beliefs, norms, and practices and is therefore usually beyond the control of a particular actor or group of actors. Organizations are committed to broadly shared purposes, and elements of their cultures affect their success in realizing these purposes.

In this chapter, I compare something more specific, which I call *mobilizing culture:* CBCO and ACORN discourses, norms, and practices that influence the ability to mobilize members. Oberschall defines an organizational

culture as "a socially constructed, cognitive, normative and emotional meaning system which creates the central reality" of an organization.[3] It is a field
of relations among individuals made up of discourses (language, symbols)
and practices ranging from everyday routines to self-consciously expressive
rituals. The term "mobilizing culture" emphasizes that, for grassroots social
movement organizations, mobilizing people is fundamental, the source of
power that enables them to achieve their goals. It is valuable as civic engagement and essential for producing policy and political outcomes. For long-
term organizations, a mobilizing culture produces a collective identity—a
shared answer to the questions "What sort of people are we?" and "What
do people like us want?" These ways of thinking and acting support and
discourage certain behaviors and actions, thereby conditioning leaders' strategic choices.

This chapter presents key themes of participants' collective identities,
their activities in the process of organizing, and their perceptions of the
ultimate values that organizing serves. Data include organizational materials, fieldwork, and over two hundred interviews with observers, staff, and
seventy-five members of the four organizations (see appendices for more
on methods and data). For the CBCOs, this includes data from the national five-day trainings offered by the PICO Network and the Gamaliel
Foundation. In the CBCOs, national training is a crucial site of indoctrination in CBCO terminology and ideas.[4] I also observed an ACORN national convention (1998), a biannual event that is the largest gathering that
ACORN holds. The names of quoted individuals are pseudonyms in order
to protect individuals' identities.

This analysis of ACORN and CBCO cultures is organized according
to how their cultures help them perform essential tasks. Some tasks are
internal: organizations develop a collective identity meant to help recruit,
mobilize, and retain members. They impart an ideology and set of skills
that encourage members to act. They select and research issues and run
campaigns. They make numerous decisions, and these organizations seek
to do so not only effectively but democratically as well. Inevitably, conflicts
occur that they must resolve or at least manage. Organizations also perform critical tasks as they engage with outsiders. They need to challenge
and confront as well as to negotiate and collaborate with other political
actors. ACORN and the CBCOs must provide the conceptual and ideological resources to legitimate *both* contention and negotiation and decide
when to use each.

It is worth underscoring that the CBCOs and ACORN are far more
alike than different in their ultimate goals and ideology. Both seek popu-

list redistributive goals for low- to moderate-income Americans. Both seek some degree of democratic decision making among their grassroots base and value an empowered membership that "owns" the organization. Both also subscribe to a foundational belief that "leaders" (that is, the leading members—not the organizers or other paid staff) should and do run the organizations and that they are merely coached or trained by organizers.[5] This belief, a sacred principle of American community organizing, minimizes the vital role of the paid staff—organizers—in setting direction and leading the organization. In reality, authority is produced in a dynamic process in which the balance of power between members and organizing staff varies by organization. Though ACORN national staff direct the organization from the center more directly than CBCOs do or can, given their independent structure and boards, ACORN locals are often lively and participatory, and the national organization relies heavily on their experiences and problems to choose issue campaigns.

In separate sections for the CBCOs and ACORN, this chapter examines how they produce a collective identity; develop a political ideology, no matter how rudimentary; mobilize their members to act; sustain participation over time; train leaders; make decisions effectively and democratically; manage internal conflict; and confront and negotiate with authorities. Because norms of emotional expression influence mobilization, a discussion of the emotion culture of each organizational type is included in the section on mobilizing members.[6]

The Mobilizing Culture of Congregation-based Community Organizing

An Introduction to Congregation-based Community Organizing

CBCO is known variously as congregation-based, faith-based, broad-based, and institution-based organizing. There are perhaps two hundred congregation-based community organizations (CBCOs), each of which may include as few as ten or fifteen congregations or as many as eighty to one hundred. Some have broadened their base by adding labor unions, community development corporations, and other groups, but their staple is still religious congregations. CBCO traces its roots to the work of Saul Alinsky, who began organizing in Chicago in the 1930s. He founded the Industrial Areas Foundation (IAF) in 1940 to support his organizing. After he died in 1972 and senior staff member Ed Chambers took over as director, the IAF thoroughly redeveloped and systematized their organizing practices. In 1973 IAF organizer Ernesto Cortes first developed the current CBCO method in San Antonio, Texas. The organization as it was reorganized after 1972 is sometimes called the "new IAF." Communities Organized for Public Service (COPS) was founded in 1974 and is probably still the best-known CBCO.[7] COPS battled the city over regular flooding in the Hispanic barrio and won a major city bond issue and massive infrastructure improvements. These campaigns eventually brought together middle-class whites and poor Hispanics. COPS won over a billion dollars in improvements and played a decisive role in winning district elections that, combined with the city's 53 percent Hispanic population, helped shift the balance of power in San Antonio.[8] The success of COPS spawned the first CBCO statewide federation, the twelve-organization Texas Interfaith Network. Texas Interfaith covers almost all populated areas of Texas, has won numerous achievements, and has become a force in Texas state politics. The IAF has six regional clusters of a total of fifty-six U.S. CBCO groups as well as several international groups.

By the mid-1980s, thousands of community organizations had sprung up in response to the loss of urban resources from industrial abandonment, middle-class flight, and federal funding cuts. However, organizing neighborhoods house by house was labor-intensive and usually did not produce the mass base that organizing through institutions could. One of the few institutions remaining in the inner city was the church. Organizing entrepreneurs began to adopt the congregation-based structure and the IAF's distinctive ideology and practices. The four largest national CBCO organizations, known as networks because they consist of separate but allied organizations, are the IAF, PICO (People Improving Communities through Organizing) National Network, the Gamaliel Foundation, and DART (Direct Action Research and Training).[9] PICO operates a nineteen-federation California Project, similar to the IAF's Texas Interfaith Network, and another state consortium of locals, Louisiana Interfaith Together (LIFT). Gamaliel emphasizes metropolitan regionwide organizing, with the greatest concentration of locals in the Midwest and East. DART, concentrated in Florida, has twenty-three affiliates. All the CBCO networks recruit and train community organizers, assist clergy and other leaders in building new organizations, supervise organizing staff, and conduct national training sessions for members of their affiliates.

Saul Alinsky significantly influenced patterns of church and foundation support for community organizing. During the 1960s, the church's "labor priests" were replaced by priests active in community organizing and other areas.[10] After the riots following Martin Luther King Jr.'s assassination, churches allocated funds for racial justice programs. A group of priests helped organize the American Catholic bishops' response to urban unrest—a pledge of $50 million to come from an annual collection in American Catholic churches, by far the largest sum from an organized church.[11] Three of the priests who organized this effort had been trained by Alinsky in 1970, and they applied his view of community organizing to the fund's mission. The goal of the Catholic Campaign for Human Development (CCHD) is empowerment and self-determination for poor and working-class Americans rather than service provision or advocacy *for* them. The Campaign is informed by a North American version of liberation theology heavily influenced by Alinsky. The CCHD, still one of the largest funders of community organizing, issues grants to chapters of ACORN, CBCOs, single-issue coalitions, and other groups. Protestant and Unitarian-Universalist boards and foundations also fund organizing. Other sympathetic foundations include Ford and many smaller funders, some of which have formed consortia to support community organizing, such as the Neighborhood Funders Group and Interfaith Funders. However, funds are always scarce, so ACORN and the CBCOs rely on membership dues (family and congregation, respectively), grassroots fund-raising, and other sources of support (see chapters 5–8).

Elements of Congregation-based Community Organizing

With the development of COPS, IAF director Ed Chambers and organizer Ernesto Cortes began to focus on churches and families as "mediating institutions" between individuals and faceless corporations and bureaucracies. Chambers argued that movements, small civic associations, and local experts are all unable to generate continuous local power and citizen participation. Instead, he advocated (unsurprisingly) community-wide federations of churches because they had people, values, and money. The IAF continued to begin each new organization by forming a sponsoring committee of clergy and others that raised funds and lent credibility, and then held a founding convention. Raising funds before organizing and requiring congregational dues allow CBCOs to pay organizers as professionals. Salaries begin anywhere from $24,000 to $30,000, and seasoned organizers can make $60,000 or more.

Like other organizations influenced by Alinsky, CBCO groups address multiple issues to attract a broad membership, pick issues of widespread interest to maximize participation, and begin with small, easy-to-win issues that will empower participants. Good issues are "concrete, specific, and realizable." CBCOs identify issues through a labor-intensive process of individual interviews with church members, called "one-to-ones" or "relational meetings." This process aims to ensure that issues will be widely shared.

Each church has a team of leaders, the local organizing committee or the core team, that begins by conducting one hundred to four hundred (depending on congregation size) individual half-hour interviews to identify church members' values, interests, and concerns—what participants learn to call their "self-interest." From the interviews, each church's organizing team chooses issues with the help of organizers and national organizing network staff, who contribute their knowledge of context, strategy, and long-term goals.

CBCOs exert their power in "actions"—usually mass meetings that seek commitments from one or more public or corporate officials. Activists conduct these meetings with a formality more typical of a shareholders' meeting than grassroots protest. CBCO ideology relates organizing to religious ideas of justice and community, for example, by drawing on familiar biblical examples to illustrate organizing concepts. Jesus and the disciples are described as a local organizing committee; Jesus challenges his disciples just as an organizer challenges activists. The story of David and Goliath illustrates that, with a crafty strategy, sometimes those with less power can win.[12]

CBCO Mobilizing Culture: Building Solidarity through Common Identity

A CBCO forges unity and a collective identity among a highly diverse group by teaching a set of basic concepts and principles. The most concentrated opportunity for imparting these ideas is the national training sessions that each CBCO network offers several times a year, but they are reinforced in local training sessions and constant everyday use.[13] Participants in the PICO and Gamaliel Foundation trainings represented the full racial and socioeconomic diversity of the nation, from genteel white Southern Episcopalians to monolingual Mexican immigrant Catholics to mainline Protestant lesbian ministers to African American Pentecostals.[14] Participants in the summer 2000 national PICO training ranged from conservative Christians whose denominations refuse to ordain women to non-Christian Unitarian-Universalists whose churches ordain gays and lesbians. Political views may also vary widely; one staffer guessed that up to half the members in PICO churches were Republicans. Producing a common belief system, then, is paramount. Organizers draw from the language of Christianity as well as the history of community organizing.

One tool PICO Network trainers use to "convert" members to the CBCO model of organizing is a typology of social action designed to present congregation-based community organizing as the best type. It compares congregation-based community organizing with agencies and movements (see Figure 4). Agencies (social service providers) are presented as non-

	Congregation-based Organizing	Agency	Movement
Purpose	Develop leaders	Provide service	Change that will challenge status quo
Budget	$150,000–$400,000	Millions	Millions
Leadership	Multiple (20–25 trained leaders, self-interest driven, value-driven)	Director, a few others	Single (charismatic leader)
Action	Value-driven, multiple	Funding	Issues
Mobilization via	Networks, one-to-ones	Flyers, media	Media
Source of funds	Foundations, dues, individuals, businesses	Government	Donations
Ownership	Local	Government	Donors are implied

Figure 4. Types of social action, as presented at a PICO training session.

empowering, well-funded, and dependent on government (although in reality many agencies have small budgets from private sources). Movements are presented ambiguously but mostly negatively, with many of the traits of movement Ideal Type A (see Figure 3 in the Introduction). Of course, in reality, CBCO (and ACORN) organizers have dedicated their entire careers to organizing, not just in CBCOs but in movements for civil rights, labor, farmworkers, and others. Most organizers do, in fact, seek "change that will challenge the status quo." However, movements are presented as based on single issues, and thus they are vulnerable to decline when the issue disappears. CBCOs see multi-issue organizations based on shared values and social networks as a more stable basis for activism, a way around built-in obsolescence. Trainers also present movements as overwhelmingly ambitious, fast-moving, hard to control, and vulnerable to charismatic leaders—not far from media portrayals of social movements. (In reality, of course, movements include multiple organizations and leaders.) In contrast, a CBCO is presented as democratic (it develops many leaders), locally controlled, feasible because it has a small budget, and secure because of its diversified funding base.[15] Trainers hope participants will react as one activist did, who said firmly after the session, "Clearly, the CBCO is the best one."

The words "activist" and "rally" are pejorative to CBCOs because both are associated with movements. While ACORN unhesitatingly seeks to form a movement that will change the status quo, the CBCO view of movements as temporary, disorganized, and undisciplined stems from Ed

Chambers and the Industrial Areas Foundation and ultimately from Saul Alinsky.[16] As a veteran observer of Chicago politics, Alinsky saw his ideal as the *opposite* of a movement: an ongoing organization with seasoned leaders, a sort of democratic, populist political machine (the traits described for Ideal Type B, Figure 3 in the Introduction). "Activist" refers to individuals, sometimes called "lone rangers," who may be "very good people" but are "so obsessed with their ideas that they can't listen." Organizing is above all about *listening* for what motivates people. Thus, activists cannot build the all-important social networks necessary to a powerful organization. PICO leaders are exhorted to listen to others, not to impose their own goals; only by identifying other people's "pain"—which helps produce their self-interest—can they form the social networks that undergird power. A Gamaliel Foundation handbook instructs members conducting one-to-one interviews to "listen intently, especially for 'lead-ins' to stories: Getting them talking is important. Speak in order to draw them out. *A successful visit means the person visited is speaking at least 60% of the time.*"

In CBCO ideology, movements often have rallies—nonstrategic, expressive, symbolic demonstrations not designed to gain achievable results. In contrast, organizers see "actions" as strategic, instrumental, disciplined venues in which to make specific, negotiable demands and to win results. One organizer for a PICO-affiliated CBCO commented derisively, "They pay us too much for us to have rallies—we have to have actions." According to the typology in Figure 4, while movements supposedly have a single, charismatic leader, CBCOs have many leaders—in fact, according to this schema, their goal isn't to initiate change that will challenge the status quo but simply to develop leaders. Drawing these oppositions helps both organizers and leaders construct self-images as pragmatic, effective, democratically accountable, and long-lasting organizations. However, the emphasis on organizational process and local leadership development has sometimes discouraged members *and* organizers from envisioning a national movement with ambitious national goals.

Building Solidarity through Religious Identity

Within contemporary American Christianity there is a bewildering array of theologies and cultures, from fundamentalist to liberal, flamboyantly expressive to stiffly reserved, politically far-right to left. CBCOs draw on selected aspects of (primarily) Christian traditions and harness them to grassroots organizing. One way activists link their religion to organizing is by drawing on religious beliefs about social justice. Stephen Hart argues that faith-based community organizing builds on the Protestant realism of

Reinhold Niebuhr, the Catholic social justice tradition, and liberation the-ology.[17] Several Catholic priests and laypersons spoke of the "preferential option for the poor" as a litmus test by which to judge CBCO work and were uneasy when campaigns seemed "middle-class." Others cited Catholic social teachings. One Methodist laywoman compared PACT's work to Methodism as "a social church" and to the United Methodist Women's focus on women's and children's issues.

Perhaps to counter social mobility and rootlessness, an emphasis on family, community, and relationships is common to many churches. Par-ticipants articulated these themes in interviews, along with faith and love. Staff at one PACT Catholic church described their vision for the church in the coming year:

[to] continue the work of building a community of faith and love . . . to join together as a community against the problems in our neighborhood; to be a family; we need to get in touch with where people are—what are their dreams, concerns, their pain?

PACT and MCU churches easily wove these themes into their neighbor-hood organizing. Religious organizers and pastors believe that CBCOs, through building the relational infrastructure needed to mobilize hundreds and thousands of people into action, can help heal damaged communities emotionally and spiritually as well as materially. In contrast to Christian conservatives, these activists define problems socially, not individually, and seek solutions not in God's individual soul saving but through building the Kingdom of God in community.[18]

Along with a shared commitment to social justice, shared personal faith helps produce a collective identity. One activist explained that mem-bers' "commonality is their faith, not necessarily they all believe in the same thing, but at least there is a faith base." Clergy members see CBCO as furthering their own agendas, from "bringing about the Kingdom of God on earth" to "spreading the gospel," "evangelism," or just church growth. In particular, CBCO gives many pastors a tool to reshape churchgoers' commonsense "pew theology" of *individual* salvation to a "public theology" of *collective* Kingdom building here on Earth.

The religious base of activism is a double-edged sword; it gives clergy not only a political standard with which to judge their theology but also a theo-logical standard with which to judge CBCO activism. Pastors are sensitive to being used for their mobilizing capacity if the CBCO is merely "church based but not faith based." The power politics that CBCOs encourage have run up against priests' religious beliefs. For example, chapter 6 describes a major MCU action opposing federal legislation that would have fatally weakened the Community Reinvestment Act (CRA).[19] MCU invited a key member of the Senate Banking Committee, Missouri senator Christopher "Kit" Bond, to meet with 2,500 church members. Bond did not come and instead sent an aide who had not read the bill. The priest who chaired the meeting reported that the aide

> was getting mauled. The people started booing. Now, here's my mistake. When the people started booing, I needed to step back onto the stage and tell the people that's not the way to do it. . . . I just said, Senator Bond has got to change his mind. I just kind of threw it back at her, like, you deserved this. He deserved this, but she didn't. But then the real clincher for me was after the meeting. Without exception, every single organizer in the room thought that that was the highlight of the meeting. For me that was the absolute low point. Were we gathering here as church, or were we not?

However, the priest noted that "there were 2,500 people in the room, and 1,800 of them are probably close to poor," and his organizers were "seeing this as a great moment for them." The priest's understanding of Christian behavior influenced his etiquette of contention: he was reluctant to polarize the conflict and cast the aide as an opponent. But to his organizers, the moment of empowering the disempowered enacted a higher justice.

Within MCU, "Christian" had a wide range of meanings: some leaders and churches saw unstinting challenge to authorities as the best expression of their faith. At the other extreme, at least one church dropped out of the organization because, as one MCU board member reported sarcastically, "We were so mean to that lady, it was just *violent* confrontation." To combat this kind of perception, some organizers distinguish between *public* and *private* roles and relationships. The Gamaliel Foundation in particular emphasized that tough confrontation that would be unacceptable with one's intimates is appropriate and necessary in the public sphere.

Not just beliefs but also rituals drawn from religious practice help build shared identity. Many churches in Gamaliel-affiliated groups have held prayer walks in which participants tour an area and pray at sites of special concern. In St. Louis, one Catholic church held a prayer walk after Sunday mass. The 150 worshippers along with their alderman walked by sites of shootings, a drug house, the high school, and a housing complex the organization was helping to rebuild. The organizer had urged the priest-leader to make the action more "hard-hitting" by challenging their alderman to speed up the housing renovation, but the priest "toned it down." Thus the action was more symbolic than political, serving to build collective identity, frame neighborhood issues as moral and religious, and build consensus. The risk of such symbolic tactics is precisely that without a larger strategy, symbolic expression will substitute for effective political action. However, the advantage is that they build collective identity and the kind of "expansive culture" that motivates long-term commitment.[20]

Perhaps the most distinctive element that religion imparts to activism is religious faith itself: the strength it provides for risk taking and the capacity for endurance over the long term. Although other activists may have a strong faith in secular ideologies, these are not usually as pervasive and culturally legitimate as religion. One PACT trainer explained, "You never finish, because you're disciples. Because the work is never over, you have to pace yourself, withdraw, and reemerge again." A PACT member described a difficult campaign: "We knew it was uphill. You know that song, 'Be not afraid, I'll be before you always'—I think that helped me to help the [local organizing committee] members to say, you know, we can't do everything."

Building Solidarity through an Ideology of Organizing

CBCO members learn new concepts with which to understand and justify their work. At training sessions, PICO leaders learned that three major systems dominate social life: political, economic, and religious. Trainees were told that religion exerts moral claims over the other two systems but that religion's role has declined relative to politics and economics. By itself, this claim would be compatible with conservative religious views. However, organizers circumvented conservative implications by teaching that declining communities are caused not by individual moral decline or big government but a "criminal economic system" with inadequate oversight by government. One organizer asked, "What faith doesn't believe that health care is a basic human right? But the public debate is around money—what it will cost."

CBCOs emphasize members' firsthand experience for several reasons. First, they believe direct, personal experience is what motivates people. Second, appeals by members to officials, the media, and the public based on direct experience provide unassailable authority. However, this emphasis also rests on something deeper—an American distrust of intellectuals and experts and a faith in the concrete over the abstract.[21]

One exercise illustrates CBCO's typically nonideological, inductive method of building consensus on grievances and attempting to create "tension"—a felt contradiction—between participants' ideals and reality.[22] Participants decided a minimum monthly budget for a family of four should be over $2,000. Their organizer then asked them to calculate a month's earnings from the minimum wage: $1,000. The group listed resulting socio-economic pressures on families and neighborhoods (second jobs, drugs and prostitution, debt, overcrowding, divorce, etc.). Participants' own experiences built a case for the Social Gospel—the view that poverty and its associated conditions are rooted not in personal immorality but economic conditions.

Developing a Theory of Power

All the CBCO networks teach their members a political ideology in the form of easy-to-remember aphorisms. PICO's version is distributed as a set of "PICO Principles." PICO teaches its members that power is

> the ability to act
> neutral
> a necessary part of being: all of us are given power by
>   our creator
> a product of relationships and grows through relationships

One of CBCOs' biggest challenges is teaching Christians to embrace and domesticate political power. American Christianity has been associated with meekness and turning the other cheek, so organizers work hard to replace such associations with images of the angry, righteous Jesus overturning the moneylenders' tables in the temple. The following exchange from a training session illustrates how organizers try to complicate members' easy distinction between pure, good religious power and impure, corrupt political power:

> MEMBER 2: Isn't Jesus' power different than political power? Because it comes from God?
> ORGANIZER: You are raising the issue that power in the secular realm is different. Why?
> MEMBER 2: Christian power is releasing power.
> ORGANIZER: Power-with and power-over can both be legitimate. When conditioned, we sit in our chair when the bell rings [i.e., we consent to authority over us for agreed-upon social purposes].
> MEMBER 3: God in me, that's—
> ORGANIZER: Isn't God also in the mayor?

In his analysis of congregation-based organizing ideology, Stephen Hart has observed the ambiguity of the CBCO theory of power.[23] CBCOs present power as a noncoercive, neutral force that can be used for good or ill, depending on which values it serves. However, CBCOs see their organization as an actor in a field of contention; to realize their values, they must coerce other political actors because "power is taken, not given." Consistent with American social movement Ideal Type A, these church members share with feminists and other activists the fear of becoming, through politics, like those who use their power to dominate. They root power in religious values to try and prevent its abuse.

Self-Interest Moves People, But Self-Interest Changes

Self-interest is a core theme of organizing in the Alinsky tradition. It was never Alinsky's ultimate rationale for organizing, but was meant to recruit those uncommitted to activism and to challenge privileged liberals who denied they had any power-seeking interests when they sought to help the poor.[24] Alinsky and his followers argued that through struggle and reflection, activists would come to broadly identify with other Americans' concerns, across the barriers that keep them apart. However, an innovation of the IAF under Ed Chambers was to consistently link self-interest and fundamental values. PICO trainers do this by contrasting "self-interest" with "selfishness," arguing that "self-interest" became reduced and narrowed to mean "selfish" through the capitalist market system. To rehabilitate self-interest, one trainer told a parable of a farmer who selfishly sells a sick cow at a marketplace and loses his good reputation, which is ultimately against his long-term self-interest. Self-interest is redefined not only as collective and interpersonal, but as the concrete expression of values that transcend the individual. PICO sees values and self-interest as counterparts. Drawing on the Christian notion of incarnation, it sees self-interest as the embodied form of spiritual values, "the word made flesh."

Values

Although CBCOs invoke such abstract values as human dignity and justice, they are skeptical when members cite them as their only motivation for activism. When a trainer asked participants what got them into organizing, some gave answers such as "God tells us love your brother and sister," "because I can help," "my father did union and political organizing," and "God was getting me ready for something." The trainer assumed that their real motivations were both more visceral and less isolated and individual. After reading Exodus 2:23–25 aloud,[25] the trainer asked, "What are your own internal groanings or cries? Also, what goes on in your *communities*?" The assumption that political commitment is rooted in the direct experience of oppression was ill-equipped to accommodate more subtle or altruistic motives; however, another common PICO catchword is "passion"—one's deepest motivation. Adding the motivation of passion accommodated a wider range of motivations than immediate self-interest based on personal oppression.

Mobilizing through Networks: "Power Is in the Relationship"

PICO has developed an ideology in which, probably more than in any other CBCO network, power, politics, and self-interest are grafted onto relationships, values, and religion. This is reflected in the slogan "power is in the relationship." Participants learn that twenty- to thirty-minute interviews with church members are the most basic tool of mobilization. These interviews, or one-to-ones, are not casual conversations but are carefully focused to identify an interviewee's self-interest or passion—what they would "stand up for"—as well as to establish a relationship. The first step is to "surface the stories" and concerns. Only then do they "agitate"—through challenging questions, get people "pissed off about what's going on; mad enough to do something about it."

ACORN teaches paid organizers a similar series of steps for door knocking, the door-to-door home visits they make to recruit dues-paying members and participants. They learn how to make the pitch and close just like a salesperson. In contrast, a PICO trainer warned leaders that a one-to-one was

> not a commercial call. You're not trying to market an organization. For one thing, we may be associated with an issue they didn't like. Don't taint the conversation. Just find out what would make the neighborhood better.

While ACORN's metaphor for recruitment is sales, one PICO organizer joked that forming relationships is more like courtship: "One-to-ones are not simply to bring bodies. You know what it's like to have someone want you just for your body?" This illustrated the distinction CBCO makes between "organizing" and "mobilizing": mobilizing treats people like objects to be herded to rallies, but organizing gives people the ongoing skills to advocate for themselves.

One PICO organizer commented to leaders about revisiting the members they brought to a public meeting with officials (an action), "Aside from that first one-to-one, this is the most powerful thing you will ever do." This is a remarkable thing to say about such a noninstrumental activity. It illustrates the emphasis CBCOs place on building members' commitment, strengthening their social networks, and reflecting on their experiences of solidarity and empowerment. ACORN members have similar experiences. Although ACORN organizers typically debrief the results of an action with leaders and many pay attention to their leaders' development, ACORN does not emphasize individuals' personal development the way PICO does through reflection on their experiences and emotions.

Tension and Agitation

Co-optation of members by authorities is always a danger in community organizing. While ACORN elicits members' anger toward officials, CBCOs' identity as congregation based, as well as members' and perhaps some organizers' sense of Christian behavior, prevents outward displays of unruly aggression. Middle-class members may find even polite and formal styles of confrontation unpleasant or offensive. Instead, CBCOs' courtesy toward their objects of claims making helps prevent church members from perceiving politicians as vulnerable victims of rude activists, which might tempt them to defend the politician. CBCOs let activists know that officials are briefed ahead of time on what will be asked at public meetings. If a politician refuses activists' demands, then the tension that results is the politician's responsibility:

> If he chooses to stand up there and say, "No, it's more important to build a new stadium than fix crumbling neighborhoods," they [the politicians] make that choice. We believe in tension, in our private lives and in our public lives. Tension exposes the contradictions.

Tension with politicians is positive—a form of pressure that can expose contradictions between CBCO values and politicians' values or between what an official says and what she does. For example, PACT held a public meeting with Mayor Ron Gonzalez in 2000 to pressure the mayor to use city tobacco settlement monies for children's health care. The organizer reported, "Gonzalez was icy cold after forty minutes of lots of tension. They were raising the tension, but he didn't even throw us a bone, just read a prepared statement."

Organizers produce tension by "agitating" members, that is, aggressively challenging them by pointing out the contradiction between how things should be and how they are, or between members' own feelings or values and their actions. One trainer said, "Tension is the energy behind change. It's uncomfortable."

For PICO and PACT, agitation is overshadowed by values and relationships. In contrast, the Gamaliel Foundation emphasizes aggressively challenging participants (Gamaliel Foundation director Greg Galluzzo said, "Everything we say is designed to agitate people").[26] In weeklong training, Gamaliel trainers asked each participant whether he or she was

a "powerful person" in the "public arena." Some trainers aggressively challenged participants who claimed they were powerful, arguing that without
an organization they were actually powerless. Each was also asked to name
a hero. When someone could not do so, the trainer said, "If you can't name a
hero, it shows me you aren't really serious about being a hero yourself."
When one participant said she had a fearful voice in her head, one organizer
said, "This week we'll kick the stuffing out of it." With regard to a prospective leader with a difficult personality, he said, "You should send him to
training, we'll kick his ass." The nominal purpose of all this confrontation
is to evoke a reaction that agitates participants out of passivity and into active involvement.

Discipline and Control

CBCOs see many social movements as fitting social movement Ideal Type
A: loose, spontaneous, and expressive, while they see themselves more like
Ideal Type B, disciplined and instrumental. They pursue specific policy
outcomes and value organizational discipline and control. CBCOs see organizing through networks as more effective and more *predictable* than mobilizing outsiders through flyers, inducements, and the like. One mayoral
administrator-turned-organizer said he became a PICO organizer because he
was impressed with a method that allowed him to accurately predict a turnout of three thousand based on the networks that leaders could mobilize.

One San Jose PACT organizer's detailed plan for mobilizing a Catholic
church illustrates both the structural advantage of mobilizing through organized institutions and the disciplined practices that exploited that structural
potential. Her detailed plan for mobilizing the large, multiethnic church
listed the largest previous "Turnout from Church at a Federated [citywide]
Action" as 250; her goal, or "estimate for this action turnout," was 350. The
plan listed six allies of the church including neighborhood schools, community centers, and the local homework center (won by a PACT campaign);
what actions had been taken to recruit school students; and the mobilization plan for church members. This included six meetings with church subgroups; mobilization plans for Bible classes and the English, Spanish, and
Filipino choirs; a list of twenty leaders working on mobilization, including
two priests; plans to stuff church bulletins with announcements of the action; and estimates for how many buses would need to be reserved.

Trainers exhorted members often about the importance of one-to-one
interviews for building social networks ("relationships"), the basis of large
and predictable mobilization. One trainer asked, "Who here passes flyers?
Shame, shame, if you can't produce through your one-to-ones. Mobilization

is *business*. You take care of it personally, with a visit or a telephone call." Mobilization through flyers brings outsiders with no organizational history or accountability, who can undermine the scripted agendas and firm control of all interactions with authorities that are so important to CBCOs and that exemplify CBCOs' perceived difference from the spontaneity of movements.

Another example of the CBCO emphasis on discipline, predictability, and control is carefully planned meetings and public actions. This sacrifices spontaneous excitement but also prevents nasty surprises. In case one leader becomes overawed by authority, a second person is designated to take over the role of pinner, the person who pins down the official with challenging questions. If an official fails to attend, the group has a fallback plan. Activists learn this discipline by planning everyday meetings to the minute, with standard agenda items such as the reflection (a thought-provoking reading, religious or secular, relating the work to shared values).

CBCOs value discipline and efficiency, but they also value a democratic decision-making process.[27] Local church organizing committees often make decisions by mutual agreement, but formal board meetings usually take votes.

Organizers Train Leaders; Leaders Organize

There is a longstanding distinction in community organizing between organizers and leaders, with roots at least as far back as the civil rights movement, in SNCC (Student Nonviolent Coordinating Committee) and the SDS (Students for a Democratic Society). Polletta refers to "the tension between deferring and leading at the heart of organizing," and in particular the dread of well-educated outsiders "manipulating" the poor that they hope to empower.[28] For this reason SNCC organizers often played the role of Socratic questioner and were uneasy about leading directly. Community organizing often resolves this tension with a distinction between staff organizers and leaders (participants): "Organizers train leaders; leaders organize." CBCO leaders learn interpersonal and political skills, which include mobilizing people.

"New" social movements often emphasize radical egalitarianism and are uneasy with hierarchies of authority (consistent with Ideal Type A). In contrast, CBCOs believe differences in leadership potential are natural, but leaders can be developed and often are not defined so much by education or speaking ability as by commitment, courage, anger at injustice, and relational skills. The unapologetic assertion that "leaders are people who have followers"—i.e., people who respect them and will come to a meeting if asked—is part of CBCO's self-conception as political and psychological realists. There is wide access to leadership training, and organizers constantly seek new potential leaders.

Leaders mobilize others, serve on their local congregational organizing teams, and plan campaigns with organizers. CBCO places an unusual emphasis on training activists to research issues, policies, and political actors. In all four community organizations, local staff researched neighborhood and citywide issues. However, *members* of PACT and MCU mentioned research from five to ten times more frequently than members of either ACORN local did. Because ACORN nationally coordinates major campaigns, it has a national staff whose sole responsibility is to research issue campaigns. However, local ACORN leaders may conduct substantial research: in San Jose, strong ACORN leaders researched and compared different local school policies.

To some extent, CBCO networks emphasize developing leadership capacity as an end in itself.[29] PICO founder John Baumann stated, "We believe organizing is about people and people are about issues. Empowerment is spiritual as well as social."[30] Defining persons as both social and spiritual, and seeking to develop both, applies a holistic and Christian understanding of the person to CBCO leadership development. One Gamaliel Foundation affiliate reported its leadership training of underrepresented groups as an accomplishment in itself:

> Over 350 residents, mainly people of color and Hispanic residents from the lowest income neighborhoods in the city, have gained leadership skills as part of the Waterbury ordinance initiative. . . . Over 80 mostly low-income residents build experience with the legislative process. . . . Nine leaders were sent for 3–4 day leadership training in the Boston area. . . . Six Waterbury leaders developed extensive negotiating skills as community representatives on the ordinance development committee. . . . Board members received training in . . . major donor fundraising. . . . Six high school seniors who were involved in the Youth in Action program learned extensive community outreach skills.[31]

Forging Solidarity through Emotion Norms of Authenticity and Expression

Arlie Hochschild's *The Managed Heart* inspired much study of emotions at work. While business organizations may train employees to produce certain emotional responses and expressions, grassroots organizations may try to inspire feelings of connectedness that strengthen bonds among members, anger that motivates action, inspiration that bolsters commitment, or any number of other emotions. In addition to mobilizing emotions instrumentally, an emotional climate and norms operate tacitly in any organization. Organization emotion norms are often inflected by gender associations.

Some cultural regularities in PACT and MCU have widespread feminine associations (see the "Gender in Congregation-based Community Organizing" section).[32] Congregation-based organizing more than ACORN tends to name and discuss emotions as an integral part of organizing. Naming the emotional dimension of participants' experiences functions in several ways. Emotional dynamics are a constant of any human interaction; by encouraging staff and leaders to name them, conflictual emotions can become normalized and expressed so they dissipate and do not undermine the organizing. A norm of naming, discussing, and therefore accepting members' negative emotions helps members feel they belong and are fully accepted; feelings of belonging build solidarity and trust, strengthening members' bonds to one another or to their organizer. Also, emotions provide valuable information about how participants experience the work. The initial question MCU organizers asked in evaluations of meetings and actions was "How do you feel?"

In PACT, which had a woman director and three or four other women staff members, naming emotions was part of a larger pattern of attention to interactive processes. Staff had two one-and-a-half or two-hour staff meetings per week. These began with a check-in from each staff member that could include personal, emotional, and work-related concerns. Staff shared information, got advice, made commitments, and planned together. Thursday meetings featured a reflection prepared by a staff member, using a scriptural or secular text to link organizing to values.

Like any subculture, CBCOs have specific norms, and participants are freer to name some emotions than others. PICO organizers' emotion language is more about *fear* and *pain* than anger. Fear is an obstacle to be uncovered and named, and pain is a clue to people's self-interest. One PACT organizer coached an activist writing a presentation for a mass meeting with the mayor to focus on "what's painful in our community." In a staff report, a PACT organizer noted her difficulty organizing a church because she was "not able to tap into pain."

The CBCOs, especially those affiliated with PICO, consistently use emotion language in their public presentations. A PACT flyer for one campaign read:

> If budgets neglect our children, the neglect is felt as deep pain by our families—in children lost to drugs and gang violence. In these three years, PACT has reached out to over 8,000 families. We've heard optimism and

determination. But we've also heard frustration, pain, anger, and fear. At one elementary school, the students have arrived at school twice to find a dead child. . . . We are afraid. We are tired, but we are also determined.

Similarly, an MCU meeting program stated, "Fear of crime, our children lost to drugs and gangs . . . hospitals closing, abandoned buildings, middle-class flight . . . have weighed heavily on our hearts."

PICO organizers promote the tension that comes from challenging and agitation as productive because it leads to action:

> TRAINER: You have a lot of work to do! Now you'll see if you are fighters or wilters! It's anxiety-producing, but it's exciting, isn't it!
> MEMBER: Yeah!

New CBCO organizers internalize these norms and apply them to themselves as well as members. One young PACT organizer-in-training noted that at the annual all-PICO staff retreat, "The tension throughout the [staff] trainings was good."

Anger can be used to agitate members, as a PICO trainer did when he pounded a table and exclaimed, "The conditions of our community are unacceptable, and they're not going to change unless *you* make them change!" This was even more frequent among Gamaliel Foundation organizers, who agitated members aggressively to evoke their anger and mobilize them to action (see below, the section "Gender in Congregation-based Organizing").

Managing Internal Conflict

Since CBCO participants tended more often than the ACORN members to self-consciously name both hostile and positive emotions as an integral part of organizing, criticism and conflict became partially normalized. The norms of challenging and accountability accomplished this to some extent. Building relationships of trust as safe "containers" for challenges may also make criticism more palatable. As an MCU organizer exclaimed to an organizer he supervised, "You've got to get her [a leader] to license you to agitate her!" In the words of two PICO slogans, the organizer meant "Challenge is relational; a challenge outside of a relationship is an irritation" and "You don't have a relationship until it's been tested by a challenge."

One conflict illustrates how CBCO emotion norms provide tools for naming and resolving conflicts. PICO member organizations undergoing internal conflict can request an assessment by a team of top PICO staffers outside the organization. In one remarkable case, a PICO member organization's staff had a serious conflict with their director over the group's direction. A group of young, relatively new organizers felt the director was not providing a clear organizing vision or adequate supervision. The norms of directness, challenging, and accountability, seen as essential to organizational health, dictated that these staff members communicate directly with their boss rather than bury the conflict until it exploded or go over the director's head. The staff and director all agreed to conduct an outside assessment. A team of three senior PICO staff members visited the organization and together, in one week, conducted eighty-one one-to-one interviews with the organization's leaders and others familiar with it. In a difficult and emotional meeting, the PICO assessors presented their findings to the director—their colleague and friend—and they came to a consensus that the director should resign. Norms of emotional expression and open conflict resolution allowed the organization to resolve a fundamental conflict openly and aboveboard. It was not without pain and anger, but the organization's steering committee remained intact even though many of its members were friendly with the outgoing director.

Confronting and Negotiating with Authorities: "Who Do You Love?"

Organizing that tries to build powerful, mass-based organizations must somehow make claims on authorities. To motivate members to challenge authority and draw the boundary between "us" and "them," organizations must polarize their opponent. As Alinsky wrote, "Pick the target, freeze it, personalize it, and polarize it."[33] However, congregation-based organizing has developed a method of polite-but-firm polarization that is palatable for church members, many of whom would be unwilling to use protest tactics such as ones that ACORN typically uses. An organization's tactics must be in keeping with its collective identity.[34] CBCOs demonstrate power in large, formal, ritualistic mass meetings that make claims to authorities. These meetings with authorities are not spontaneous deliberation but carefully scripted political theater that enacts dramatized challenges to authorities in front of hundreds or thousands of church members. Mass meetings, or actions, are a CBCO's public face "frontstage," the site of claims making. They should not be confused with the scores of "backstage" meetings where authentic deliberation and debate, not political theater, take place.

Meetings or actions with authorities demonstrate power by mobilizing large numbers and by overturning deferential norms of interaction, insisting that authorities meet them on their turf, and by strictly controlling the agenda and how many minutes an official is allowed to speak. The opponent is polarized by the pinner, the member designated to pin down the official to yes-or-no answers. Activists are trained to push for yes-or-no commitments, knowing that politicians will avoid them if at all possible. Organizations hold rehearsals, and pinners practice their job. Getting a "no" answer is seen as preferable to "mush" because it will expose the authority as an opponent in the eyes of hundreds or thousands of people. Tight control of the proceedings helps avoid being manipulated by officials, although it can impart an artificial, staged quality to the proceedings.

One Catholic priest in St. Louis reported that his education in tactics from Gamaliel Foundation national training was "There are no rules. Make up your own rules." When a local politician went back on a commitment, the priest said,

> It just made me laugh when his response to why they weren't going to [uphold their commitment] was that "things change." So I said, "Well, things will change here too." I was . . . prepared to conduct a meeting in a way that would advantage us, and he would be isolated. Someone would meet him at the door and escort him in and he would not sit with any of us and not have a chance to talk with anyone to try to sway someone or schmooze them. We also had timed the meeting so that he came a half hour after it started so the crowd would be prepped on their part.

At a PICO California Project public meeting in Sacramento with state legislators, one PICO speaker deplored the San Francisco schools and then invited legislators to respond to the two thousand activists present. She warned sternly, "If we hear finger-pointing from our legislators, I will stop you. I will interrupt you. Assemblyman, you have five minutes." Activists unfamiliar with these norms may sympathize with politicians who are cut off or pressured by pinners (especially if they don't know the official has been thoroughly briefed by letter in advance). The PICO principle "Who do you love?" reminds activists that their allegiance should be to their congregations and families. To underscore that point, one PICO organizer mocked, "Who do we *love*? People with titles?"

"Who do you love?" also reminds leaders to keep their families' and congregations' interests in mind during fast-moving interactions with authorities, when leaders make snap decisions far removed from their congregations. When New York police shot unarmed Haitian immigrant Patrick Dorismond, priests from the PICO affiliate in Brooklyn, New York, refused to negotiate for police reforms until Mayor Rudolph Giuliani apologized to Dorismond's family.[35] Though insisting on this symbolic concession may seem counterproductive, the priests knew that if they accepted anything less they would lose face with their constituency.[36] The phrase "Who do you love?" is meant to help prevent activists from being seduced and co-opted in the midst of contentious interaction.

In their early histories, CBCOs more frequently engaged in the disruptive tactics typical of ACORN. One middle-class African American member in MCU reported that a bank manager in his neighborhood refused to meet with his church organizing committee, and about fifteen MCU members "sat in" at the bank until it would send an authoritative decision maker to meet at the church. In the resulting meeting, their church won security guards at all NationsBank locations in St. Louis. Other MCU constituents engaged in similar tactics. However, many church members, especially the middle class, disapprove of aggressive tactics, even the polite polarization of meetings. One MCU member reported that her fellow Catholics felt "'I came here to pray. Don't talk to me about politics or the community.' We were pushy and Christian people aren't supposed to be pushy; this caused many church people to be angry at our campaigns and blame us for bad outcomes." This is one reason CBCOs are less able to engage in disruption than ACORN. Another MCU leader reported in disgust that her chapter, trying to keep a local department store from closing, had to cancel an alternative Christmas carol–sing at the CEO's house due to members' reluctance. This activist had to call a reporter and tell him the protest was canceled. However, timidity is not the only reason that CBCOs engage in "contained contention" when they become mature and develop a track record; their electoral threat rather than protest is more likely to motivate politicians to negotiate with them.[37]

Gender in Congregation-based Organizing

Organizing, whether in the workplace or the community, along with other social movements, has a history of male dominance. This male dominance ranges from overt bias in hiring organizers to unconscious gender-related cultural norms. One senior network organizer told a woman organizer, "No Hispanic men will work for you!" However, more subtle gendered patterns are more common. Women CBCO organizers have confronted the same kinds of challenges as women in other professions.

CBCOs prevent gender from becoming a fault line in several ways. The fact that CBCO empowers working-class women at least as often as men goes a long way toward removing gender as a source of division. Also, organizations seldom frame issues in gendered terms or pick "feminist" issues such as domestic violence, pay equity for women, and the like. (Neither do labor unions: sexism in working conditions or pay can easily be framed in terms of general rights, fairness, or justice.) The issues men *and* women participants cite as most pressing affect entire families and communities: housing, social services, lack of jobs, education, public safety, transportation. One retired cannery worker, a Methodist active in San Jose PACT, did not describe herself as a feminist. However, she said, "I belong to United Methodist Women and our emphasis is on women, youth, and children and all issues that PACT is having right now. There [are] a lot of single moms . . . you don't make [as] much money historically as men. I know this because I worked forty years."

Perhaps the most subtle but widespread influence of gender in organizing is on gendered cultural norms. The culturally gendered aspects of MCU, PACT, and their associated networks all contrast with ACORN, but not in identical ways. The CBCOs share the relational philosophy of organizing, greater comfort with emotional expression, and an emphasis on personal growth that explicitly addresses emotions such as fear and the courage needed for risk taking. However, they combine this with an emphasis on building power. The Gamaliel Foundation places more emphasis than does PICO on stripping away members' fear of power through aggressive challenging. This alienated some Gamaliel activists, especially women. One woman pastor pulled her church from the organization after the weeklong training session. At one Gamaliel training, a racially diverse group of fifteen to twenty women gathered to discuss what they perceived as male notions of aggression and power. They found a sympathetic ear in national organizer and trainer Mary Gonzalez, the wife of Gamaliel director Greg Galluzzo. When women asked why their organizations didn't work on issues such as domestic violence or child care, Gonzalez applied the same analysis to her own organization as CBCOs would to any political structure. Gonzalez suggested that women needed to organize *within* the Gamaliel organizations to target its male establishment and put forward their own issues.

Compared to the Gamaliel Foundation, PICO seems like the kinder, gentler network. Nevertheless, women organizers claim the PICO Network shares in the masculine culture of organizing, especially in its early days. But compared to ACORN, *both* CBCOs exhibit traits associated in American culture with religion and the feminine. These include emotional expressiveness, including expressions of vulnerability; attentiveness to psychological experience and local group processes; a concern with community well-being; and attention to aesthetic and ceremonial meaning making—in this case, meanings conducive to organizing. To the extent that these characterize congregation-based organizing, they endow it with more culturally feminine qualities than ACORN. On the masculine-gendered side of the cultural divide lie the most instrumental aspects of organizing: tasks, numbers, and strategy rather than organizational processes, and, of course, power and aggression. These were more common in ACORN. A female labor organizer organizing women workers expresses a view of organizing strikingly similar to CBCO—one that the organizer describes as based on the experiences of "working women":[38]

> ORGANIZER: The key is organizing one-to-one, or one person at a time. It's a type of organizing based on building deep personal relationships by connecting workers to each other in important ways. It's not the kind of organizing that relies on market techniques or advertising. It's not about selling somebody something. You build a strong organization by connecting people to each other . . . the most important is listening. . . . They should not talk about the union; find other ways to get to know the person, to listen to their story. . . . Unions are cultural organizations and want the union to be connected to people's lives in a full way. The family is part of this. If you want to build a strong union you have to have room for the family.
> INTERVIEWER: The word "relationship" is a strong word. It suggests some duration of time to develop. Is that right?
> ORGANIZER: It certainly does take time. . . . I know this is a woman's way of looking at the world. Sometimes we talk about how men focus more on tasks or events and women more on relationships, but you can see it all the time in the organizing we do.[39]

The following section examines a very different mobilizing culture that cannot be understood apart from ACORN's history, authority structure, and institutional rules.

The Mobilizing Culture of ACORN

The ACORN Organizing Model

ACORN, the other type of organization included in this study, traces its roots to Alinsky, among other sources, but has developed its own distinct structure and set of practices. In 1970, just before Ernie Cortes began experimenting with organizing Mexican American churches, former organizers for the National Welfare Rights Organization (NWRO) tried a new experiment in Arkansas. This became the Arkansas Community Organization for Reform Now (ACORN).[40] Wiley and other NWRO organizers rejected Piven and Cloward's notion of loose mass mobilization in favor of ongoing mass organization.[41] They developed a model, unlike Alinsky's, that ignored existing groups and created a brand-new organization after a six-week campaign.[42] During the six weeks, the organizer identified needs and organized welfare recipients to confront the local welfare office. This six-week plan became the essence of the ACORN organizing model.

Wade Rathke and other organizers refined the six-week organizing drive, which was easily replicated by ACORN's raw, young, mostly white organizers. The organizer researched and analyzed the neighborhood, knocked on doors, made initial contacts, established an organizing committee, picked an issue, prepared for a neighborhood meeting, held the meeting, staged a collective action, and evaluated it. The organizer made twenty to forty contacts per day by knocking on doors. Following Cesar Chavez, who believed membership dues made an organization self-sufficient and helped members own the organization, ACORN organizers collected dues.

Although pay rates have significantly increased over the years, ACORN is known for low pay and long hours for organizers. The organization justified this by calling for movement-like dedication.[43] For this reason, ACORN has traditionally drawn highly committed, idealistic young people, often white, middle-class college graduates. However, in recent years it set a goal to dramatically increase the organizers of color; by 2003, 64 percent of ACORN's organizers were people of color.[44] The salary of organizers who stay with ACORN increases quickly. However, ACORN still faces a challenge in recruiting staff, as well as in raising its budget. ACORN funds have consistently come from three internal sources: dues from members, other internal fund-raising campaigns, and door-to-door canvassing in affluent neighborhoods (once a major national program, now defunct except at some locals). ACORN supplements these funds with foundation grants, just as CBCOs do, but ACORN is notable for its high percentage of internal fund-raising. In Delgado's account, internally raised funds increased from 27 percent in 1975 to 62.4 percent in 1981. In St. Louis ACORN, they were 80 percent of the budget.

ACORN's training booklet for members includes "Principles of ACORN": some of these are similar to Alinsky-style precepts, and a few suggest ACORN's special features. For example, the doctrine of the multi-issue organization is familiar: "Some organizations are devoted to a single issue, and whether they win or lose . . . the organization usually fades away. The advantage of being a multi-issue organization is the appeal to a broader number." When organizers help members develop a list of local concerns it must "be prioritized according to the criteria of what's winnable, what brings people into the organization." Also familiar is the imperative to develop grassroots leaders:

It is our responsibility, as leaders and organizers, to develop every member's leadership potential. . . . Develop new people by giving them opportunities to try new roles. Think of some small thing for that quiet member who seems so shy. Perhaps that person could hold the posterboard check-list at an action.

Other principles sound equally familiar, but hint at ACORN's particular distinctions, such as "SELF-SUFFICIENCY AND INTERNAL FINANCING": "Nobody will ensure our survival except ourselves . . . make fundraising planning a constant part of every plan."

The principle of "coordinating autonomy" understatedly suggests the organization's centralized direction on major issues, traditionally taboo in the "up from the grassroots" culture of community organizing: while "autonomy refers to the local independence of each group, city, and state to decide which issues to work on," "coordination . . . refers to the ability of the members of a group to work together and for the group to work with other ACORN groups in its city, state, and across the nation." ACORN's emphasis on action over planning or efficiency, at least for local groups, is evident:

Actions are the very heart that keeps that blood pumping. . . . A local group that sees a month go by without a single action [is] . . . a person undergoing cardiac arrest.

There is no such thing as a perfect action. . . . What's important is that the group acts. . . . Actions should be . . . imaginative, fun, and effective. . . . If the issue is getting a stop sign, don't send a letter to the street commissioner when your members can go in person to his office. . . . Other organizing objectives are accomplished by going in person—developing new leaders, giving members the experience of success through action.

ACORN's Collective Identity

Perhaps the most fundamental task confronting any organization is constructing a convincing and powerful meaning system that defines members' collective identity and mission. ACORN spends little time self-consciously constructing a collective identity, as the CBCOs do, and much time pursuing instrumental tasks—which is a key aspect of its collective identity. One ACORN organizer described a particularly successful city ACORN organization as having a "hard-core organizing culture," by which he meant a disciplined, organized, and productive organization.

Task-Oriented Radicals

Among staff perhaps more than members, ACORN's disheveled offices suggest that a professional-looking office is not a priority, as ACORN is doing more important things. Ironically, this image ran up against ACORN members' more working-class value of respectability. Both ACORN locals had cluttered, messy offices, but at San Jose ACORN, Hispanic women leaders volunteered to clean it. The St. Louis office was dirty and in bad repair; while members tolerated it, the office disturbed some because they felt it was bad public relations for an organization whose aim was to improve conditions for the poor: "The office is not clean and not because we haven't tried. . . . It's just never, ever clean. . . . You can see the holes in the ceiling . . . and that second-floor room is so dusty . . . people with allergies come in there and they actually get ill," one member complained.

Organizer dress is jeans and T-shirts, which distinguishes ACORN staff and many members from the "suits" in the power structure. One staff member laughed incredulously as he described seeing a former ACORN organizer who was "working for some legislator, wearing this *suit.*"

Oppositional Outlaws

ACORN derives much of its esprit de corps from its members' identity as militants unafraid to confront the powers that be. This identity as a uniquely militant organization is reinforced by contentious action. A story of how former Missouri senator Tom Eagleton "ran over" a member when trying to drive past rowdy ACORN demonstrators was part of St. Louis ACORN lore, as these two organizers' joking conversation illustrates:

> BILL: We've had some powerful moments.
> JACKSON: The ACORN way is the only way!
> BILL: We had one when we were trying to get arrested and the police had been told "Do not arrest them." They refused to arrest us!
> JACKSON: The best one was when we stopped traffic.
> BILL: The best one was when Eagleton *ran over* a couple of our members!
> JACKSON: He was so nervous! . . . Bill raised a bunch of hell! . . .
> BILL: I was so mad at that man. I cussed a senator. I wanted to get everyone else pissed off. . . . I went to block his car and he kept right on driving!

Observers sometimes criticize ACORN for seeking confrontation for its own sake. One former New Party organizer worked in the ACORN office and was hired, supervised, and ultimately fired by ACORN. He organized an independent ward organization for the New Party. He claimed that when members identified local problems and wrote to the chief of police and other officials, "every city official responded positively" and addressed the problems.[45] Obviously, not all city officials are this responsive. From ACORN's perspective, these could have been attempts at co-optation or a distraction from more significant campaigns.

Long-term ACORN organizers—not necessarily members—tend to see the organization as a solitary vanguard of principled leftists. Its Web site states, "ACORN stands alone in its commitment to organizing and winning power for low and moderate-income people."[46] For example, St. Louis ACORN sought an increase in the commission that one bank paid ACORN Housing for each successful loan candidate ACORN referred. Such commissions are a vital source of funding for the program and allow ACORN not to charge its low-income clients. An organizer said about the effort, "As usual, we're out on a limb fighting for these other organizations [that offer low-cost housing loans], and they're backstabbing us left and right." Similarly, a former ACORN director commented on the right-wing St. Louis Catholic hierarchy and congregation-based organizing that "no one with any self-respect or political commitment would work for a group like that. The word on the street is you've got to be a chump or a fascist to work with an IAF-like outfit." He also described a different group as "politically unprincipled" because it made a deal with the city in a campaign that competed with an ACORN campaign.

This self-image as the hardest-working, only truly radical community organization has sometimes helped ACORN justify moving into other organizations' geographic arenas.[47] However, after Reagan was elected in 1980, an ACORN memo by founding organizer Wade Rathke read, "ACORN has been the Lone Ranger of the Left too long. . . . Unions, political allies and church support are all essential. . . . We need some friends out there."[48] ACORN subsequently made more efforts to collaborate with allies. Since the 1990s, but particularly since 2000, ACORN has demonstrated far greater openness to building alliances, not only with labor unions and the CBCOs but with a wide range of advocacy groups (see chapter 3).

Volunteers into Activists

Activists from all four community organizations spoke frequently about the "community" in a general way. However, this way of speaking does not distinguish ACORN's political activism from run-of-the-mill community service and volunteer work. ACORN and the CBCOs had to acculturate members into activist, *political* organizations when many of their members had little political experience. This can be challenging in the American context, where apolitical volunteerism is the most acceptable and pervasive style of civic involvement.[49] ACORN responded by identifying itself as a confrontational direct action organization. However, local chapters could still be diverted from politics by more conventional community activities, such as mutual aid. San Jose ACORN organizer Sarah Rosen "cringed to admit" that the popular neighborhood cleanups its local chapters sponsored seemed "sort of service-y to me." They did not challenge the powers that be, train or politicize leaders, or gain power for the organization. She explained, "We've got sort of a grant [available from all city council members]. That's why I don't like it; the leaders just apply for it."

One middle-class St. Louis ACORN member's ward chapter had a similar idea:

> ARLENE: We thought we could attract seniors [with] a small service for these people over the holidays. We were willing to do it on our own. We had planned to Christmas carol in the neighborhood, actually. . . . We were going to take some little treats and interview these people and find out what they wanted us to do, because if they're joining as members, then we work for them here. Well, [her organizer] . . . couldn't relate to that at all. He said, "I'm not into all of this, but the only thing that I can tell you is that you need to do A, B, and C." Like stick to what we've got going on here, this is a political thing—he didn't say that, but that was how it came off.
>
> HS: What did you do about that?
>
> ARLENE: Well, it made me back down a little bit. You cannot expect them to pay their little dues every month and not see anything. So there are some speed limit signs up and down McGreery. These people don't walk up and down McGreery, what do they care? They still need to be able to see something for the membership dues that they are paying.

Arlene saw her chapter partly as providing services to the elderly, a small patronage system delivering services to woo a constituency. ACORN chapters have numerous picnics, barbecues, and dinner dances, but the primary goal is always fund-raising. Though Arlene's plan included identifying residents' needs (a possible basis for future campaigns), it also included nonpolitical services—community volunteering and socializing without an immediate instrumental goal—which did not fit ACORN's identity as a no-nonsense activist organization. Providing services also risked distracting the chapter from political organizing. What the CBCOs might see as relationship building that would develop a constituency, Arlene's organizer saw as a distraction from important political work.

Ironically, in its search for creative solutions to scarcity of resources, ACORN established the service-providing ACORN Housing Corporation, which recruits, screens, and educates first-time home buyers for below-market mortgage programs that ACORN wins from banks through the Community Reinvestment Act (see chapter 3). However, this program ingeniously combines *several* instrumental functions: it redistributes resources from banks to inner-city neighborhoods, recruits new potential members, mobilizes resources for ACORN to support Housing Corporation staff (and also organizing), and provides a valuable service to members, enabling many families to build equity for the first time.

ACORN also combined grassroots advocacy with service provision after Hurricane Katrina struck in late August 2005. ACORN's founder and chief organizer Wade Rathke, a New Orleans native, runs one of ACORN's national offices in New Orleans. The hurricane devastated the ACORN office, its members' homes (many in the Ninth Ward), and families torn apart by relocation. ACORN members advocated for their right to return to their homes, but like PICO, they engaged in enormous efforts simply to locate and identify their members, reunite families, and give their members a voice in the reconstruction planning.

Cultural Identities of ACORN Members

For both ACORN locals, the geographical community they represented was ethnically homogeneous. This raises the possibility that ethnic or racial identity could be used to assist the organizing process. A Christian identity was also widely shared among many St. Louis ACORN members.

Race and Religion in St. Louis ACORN

St. Louis ACORN closely fit the description of HAT, a black antitoxics community group in another study. Paul Lichterman writes that one of HAT's leaders did not often articulate a religious basis for her activism, and she did not always define her work as service to a specifically black community; she did not need to. She could take for granted a local moral universe of Christian charity and African American communal service in which public-spirited good deeds made sense and were worthwhile.[50]

As for HAT, in St. Louis ACORN the black church was assumed "background knowledge" for activists (see chapter 5). Norms such as deference to preachers, protest forms such as prayer vigils, and use of an opening prayer in meetings all expressed this cultural knowledge.[51] In meetings, religious members occasionally made comments like "Remember the hereafter, but don't forget your portion in this world!" and "I'm hoping and praying by the dear Lord that we can do better than we are now and get some good people so we can go up the mountain." Such religious expressions provided the black St. Louis flavor in ACORN's generic populism.

However, they were unofficial: ACORN saw them as part of members' private lives, not the organization's public life. At one ACORN national convention, some members (including the new St. Louis ACORN chairman, a minister) noticed that organizers had scheduled no religious services for Sunday morning, so members scheduled one and put it on the weekend's agenda.

As with religious identity, in St. Louis, black organizers' and members' informal invocations of racial identity were unofficial. In meetings and protests, members were free to express religious and racial aspects of their local identity, even as activists understood that ACORN represents more than one ethnic identity. Instead, interviewees saw ACORN's mission as standing for "the community": a populist organization that stood for "the small person," "your everyday citizen," or even more specifically, "for the downtrod [sic] of people who have no jobs or have jobs that don't pay them anything," or for "poor people who's not able to go into the mayor's office and say, hey, I have no health care whatsoever."[52]

Several members were disturbed at the St. Louis staff's choice to limit organizing to black north St. Louis: "I started looking around and there's hardly any white people and then I started telling them, hey look, this ain't no black organization. This is a poor folks organization and you can't tell me there ain't no poor white people out there." This member wanted St. Louis ACORN to cross local racial boundaries so it could enlarge its constituency and become stronger. However, ACORN is dramatically racially diverse at the national level, at least *among nonwhites*—a mix of African Americans, Puerto Ricans, Mexican Americans, and a few whites is evident to activists who attend the biannual national convention. The organization's ability to bring together an ethnically diverse group and to balance local self-expression with an overarching populist identity, is a significant achievement. ACORN organizers sometimes claim that the dire conditions for poor people make the need for unity self-evident. However, this glosses over the real cultural and strategic work ACORN does in choosing issues that can forge unity against its opponents and framing them inclusively.

Religion and Ethnicity in Hispanic San Jose

In contrast to St. Louis, the largely Hispanic San Jose ACORN did not incorporate any religious expression. The members came from a very different shared Catholic heritage in which vigorous religious expression by members is probably less typical. Like the St. Louis group, San Jose ACORN also understands itself as low and moderate income but sees itself even more strongly as a local neighborhood improvement association representing the community. As immigrants or the children of immigrants in an economically booming city, members may have a greater sense of upward mobility than African Americans in St. Louis do. San Jose ACORN also draws from a much smaller, more compact area than St. Louis ACORN. Members see themselves as working "to make the neighborhood better," to "help" and to "come together for" the community, and to "do things for our neighborhood."

In sum, ACORN tries to build a populist collective identity as low- to moderate-income people who are militant and oppositional. This allows it to bridge racial boundaries in the service of poor and working-class unity. Its task is made easier when local geographic areas are ethnically and culturally uniform. Then it tacitly draws on these ethnic identities to forge its solidarity.

ACORN's Political Ideology

ACORN does not impart a detailed political ideology to its members; it sees itself as an "action organization."

Populist

ACORN's ideology is a down-to-earth, nonsectarian populism. If there is one slogan that is ubiquitous in ACORN across the country, it is "The people—united—will never be defeated" or "El pueblo—unido—hamas sera vencido!" A rare, elaborated public statement of ACORN's ideology is its People's Platform. The platform was developed in 1978–79 to help forge a national identity from scattered local groups and to help cement a progressive political ideology that would flush out the more conservative members.[53] The platform, revised and approved by the national membership in 1980, is a veritable laundry list of progressive positions challenging corporate power and championing "the people" in energy policy, health care, housing, work, rural issues, community development, banking, taxes, and more. In what may be the most lyrical passage ever put to paper in ACORN's name, the platform's preamble brings to mind the populism of Frank Capra, Woody Guthrie, and John Steinbeck:

> We stand for a People's Platform, as old as our country, and as young as
> our dreams. We come before our nation, not to petition with hat in hand,
> but to rise as one people and demand . . . Enough is enough. We will

wait no longer for the crumbs at America's door. We will not be meek, but mighty. We will not starve on past promises, but feast on future dreams.[54]

Such visionary and lofty rhetoric is not typical of ACORN in practice, whose organizers focus relentlessly on raising dues, making telephone calls, raising funds, and reaching turnout goals. Organizers' ideals are less often articulated and more often inferred from their commitment to daunting work at low pay. However, members do share and express a populist sentiment; they see ACORN as an organization dedicated to "putting power in the hands of the small person or your everyday citizen," organizing for "the middle Americans and the poor Americans . . . so they can do things for themselves," or simply "people coming together for the community, trying to make their community better."

ACORN Members' Ideals

Activists interviewed from all four organizations discussed their motivations for participation. Figures 5a and 5b display the themes most commonly articulated by members of each of the four organizations.[55] These data suggest that the members' concerns have more in common than not. Activists in all four organizations frequently see their work as service to the community and conceive of issues in terms of their effect on families and children. The fact that black St. Louis ACORN members mention "rights" more often than the other groups may be a legacy of the civil rights movement.

"Family" was a concern common to all activists. Interestingly, "children," "kids," and "youth" were particularly topical for San Jose activists, whether PACT or ACORN members. This is probably because youth issues—education, safety, neighborhood services—were pressing concerns in San Jose. (They were even more dire in St. Louis, but there were many other issues, notably poverty, unemployment, and abandoned buildings, with which they competed.) Interestingly, none of the activists spoke most frequently about abstract "rights" or "justice." This suggests that community organizing may lend itself especially to the concrete issues of home, family, and children.

Mobilizing ACORN Members

Unlike CBCOs, ACORN organizers were usually directly responsible for mobilizing individual members. Organizers assumed that to mobilize a certain number they needed to get two or three times that many commitments to attend. This is labor-intensive work. Besides mobilizing regular

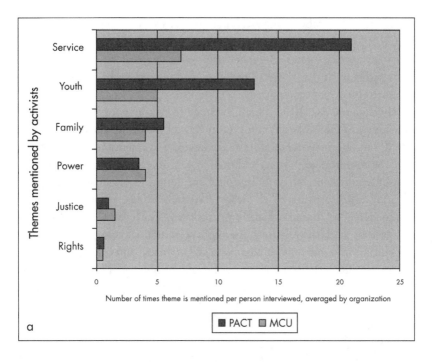

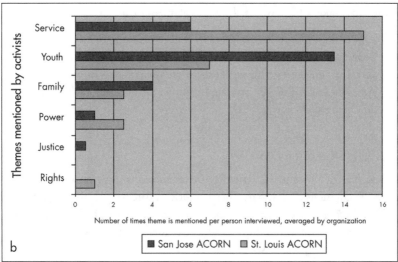

Figures 5a and 5b. Motivations to organize expressed by CBCO and ACORN activists.

neighborhood members, ACORN organizations with special functions, like ACORN Housing or the Community Jobs Hiring Hall, appeal to selective incentives (see chapter 5). In general, ACORN approaches mobilizing like sales, with a pitch that they call the "rap," complete with the close. This fast-paced, results-oriented approach is suited to organizing as a high-volume numbers game. ACORN, which lives day to day by constantly soliciting individuals to join, takes a shorter-term view of recruiting activists than the CBCOs do. Both approaches are goal oriented and intentional, but CBCOs have the resources to permit, and the ideology to encourage, a longer-term view of recruitment and mobilization. Some longtime organizers argue that when ACORN organizes well locally, like the CBCOs, its success is partly due to strong relational organizing practices.[56] However, for ACORN, an emphasis on building relationships might seem noninstrumental and "soft" in a culture whose identity is based on combativeness and confrontation.

In ACORN, the creation of social capital is not a goal in itself. Perhaps because organizers believe that having leaders mobilize through networks does not work, *building* social networks where they are weak is also not a priority. St. Louis staff wished to build latter-day ward "machines." However, social networks are built partly through noninstrumental interaction—that is, interaction whose goal is not primarily to accomplish tasks but to interact for its own sake. One San Jose leader explained it this way:

> CARLOS: I like socializing. Socializing is an ingredient that keeps people together, because when you do issues you work and when you socialize you get together with the people you enjoy working with.
> HS: Does ACORN give you opportunities to socialize or do you create them unofficially?
> CARLOS: I create them unofficially.

ACORN's Emotion Work

When ACORN organizers tried to incite emotions, they generally tried to evoke excitement and anger. These emotions directly inspire members to action. Excitement is energizing and empowering and can be used not just to stimulate action, but to build a collective identity as a powerful organization. The opening exercises at one ACORN national convention were an expressive ritual designed to produce collective excitement that would build shared identity and commitment. Each state's delegation marched into the plenary hall at the convention's opening, wearing its own special state T-shirt, shouting and chanting distinct chants. The California delegation, led by Latino members, chanted "Si se puente / California esta presente!"

Black members led the Californians in chanting some lines from a black pop song, "'Cause we're hot, we're hot, we can really shake 'em up, we're dynamite now—oh, yes we are!" When all 1,200 members had entered the room, they continued chanting, competing for dominance in a frenzied cacophony that raised participants' energy and excitement. When President Maude Hurd called the roll, each state presented its chant again as loudly as possible. This intense energy, combined with large, diverse groups of people, thrilled members who had never seen more than seventy-five or one hundred ACORN members together before. However, such symbolic exercises are usually directed against an external target. In St. Louis, anger was the most common emotion expressed in actions and was used to motivate activists to take disruptive direct action. In July 1997 ACORN's Jobs Committee invited seventy-five companies to come to a forum for job seekers, and only one company came. The organizer said staff knew they wouldn't come but planned the event to incite members' anger and motivate them to demand concessions such as hiring agreements. During actions, loud expressions of anger also help inflate the power of relatively small numbers, as one organizer demonstrated in an action at the mayor's office (see chapter 5).

Sustaining Participation over Time

ACORN and the CBCOs seek sustained participation because they strive for power through longevity and growth. The ability to switch from issue to issue gives them, in theory, a range of constituencies to replenish the organization and ensures that if one goal is met the organizations' reason to exist does not evaporate.[57] During the observation period, the St. Louis and San Jose chapters differed significantly in the level of ongoing, sustained participation by members. While ACORN's ideal was lasting participation from its active members, in practice the St. Louis chapter assumed that it would have to recruit an ever-shifting base of new participants. There were several reasons for this. The organization was at a low point in 1997–98, having lost several major campaigns, and participation was low. Their constituents were poorer on average than San Jose's members, and their lives may have been more precarious and unstable. Another was the view of organizing as a "numbers game," that particular individuals are not so important as long as a numerical total is achieved. San Jose ACORN had a stronger base of core leaders at this time.

Sustaining commitment from staff over time is also important for organizational development. Because of its low salaries and heavy workload, ACORN was prepared to lose organizers frequently. According to member Arlene, the organizer for her fledgling St. Louis ward group "was going to organize us and go. He wasn't going to be around long so we better catch on and learn the resources that we needed to use. . . . He started us out thinking that he was going to be gone at any minute, and sure enough that is how the end came for him—he was gone, just vanished." The organizer's abrupt departure after three months without notice or warning damaged the chapter's confidence and solidarity: "Because [the organizer] had not officially broken off this love affair that he created here . . . we had to regroup and figure out a way to tell our other members that he was gone." The organizer could leave without letting his chapter know because ACORN focuses on results—dues and members—more than interactive processes. To what extent this is driven by immediate resource needs or by organizational ideology remains to be investigated.

Training ACORN Leaders

ACORN seeks to train grassroots members, but this goal is less important than getting wins. Since ACORN relies heavily on its national staff for research, strategic planning, and a unified national direction, trained local leaders are less important to its mission than they are to the CBCOs. ACORN organizers did not talk about relationship building or social networks but focused on the nuts-and-bolts tasks of chairing meetings, dealing with politicians, and the like. Although it emphasizes leadership training much less than the CBCOs, ACORN offers local organizing training and sends promising leaders to national training sessions where they meet ACORN members from all over the country. In one instance, the exposure they got to leaders from other organizations allowed St. Louis leaders to challenge an organizational norm back home. The bylaws dictated that elected board members oversee the finances. However, the St. Louis director was accustomed to controlling the budget and expenditures himself. After a key St. Louis leader learned about this provision of the bylaws, back home he led a coup. He organized local board members to support his challenge to the director to institute a finance committee and require monthly budgets.

Often leaders get training through direct experience chairing a meeting, speaking to the media, or occupying a city office. One St. Louis leader said she "really wasn't comfortable speaking in front of a group. . . . The first time it happened was when we went to Senator [Christopher] Bond's office and they schooled me a little bit on the issue and then pushed me out front. I didn't appreciate being put up front like that, and I felt like I was not real prepared. And they said that's how it is, we baptized you." However, this leader learned to chair meetings the same way, and said, "The more you do it, the more comfortable it becomes."

ACORN leaders' most important role is to help plan and attend actions. Therefore, organizers typically do much of the research and planning and strongly guide leaders in strategy and tactics. But most ACORN members feel they learn a tremendous amount from the experience of organizing, both new skills and new knowledge about politics:

> It's a whole new thing that's opened up. . . . I could tell you every legislator, who they are, their address and telephone number . . . and sometimes the issues that they champion and stuff. But before, I couldn't tell you anything. I learned how to get things done, like talking to the alderman, speaking with the housing authorities, like that; telephone numbers, peoples [sic] to call.

The degree of local training and quality of local leadership varied greatly between St. Louis and San Jose. San Jose leaders conducted research themselves on local schools so they could propose reforms to their school district. As one explained, "We do the research first, we investigate, we come to a conclusion, and we have a target. That's our motto."

One neighborhood chapter in San Jose ACORN staged a surprise occupation of the office of its city council member, who had refused to meet with ACORN. The members were well briefed by their organizer in a meeting that explained the background on the grievance, plan of action, song and chant practice, and different plans of action to fit different circumstances and possible responses by the council member.

Making Decisions Effectively and Democratically

Unlike a business corporation, grassroots community organizations such as ACORN and the CBCOs explicitly strive for some degree of democratic decision making. This involves balancing the authority of paid organizers and staff with the authority of the members the organization seeks to empower. The case studies in chapters 5 and 7 present a detailed picture of ACORN members' awareness and active participation in their organization. This section notes several features that appear to be common to both the city chapters and to ACORN as a whole.

Like the CBCOs, ACORN has maintained the organizer-leader dichotomy in which decision-making power is supposed to rest with indigenous low-income leaders. At regular board meetings, ACORN leaders (elected from the membership), make decisions by vote or general agreement. Because ACORN is one nationally coordinated organization rather than a network of separate groups, ideas for issues, tactics, and strategy often come from staff, especially in major campaigns. The degree to which local leaders' concerns and ideas direct local organizing varied in the two chapters in this study.

ACORN has a split personality with regard to democratic decision making. According to the national bylaws, power formally rests with the membership through their elected representatives at the local, state, and national levels. However, power is shared with the national "Chief Organizer" (ACORN founder Wade Rathke) in personnel matters. Similarly, all local dues are sent to ACORN's New Orleans office, and checks are issued from there. Generally, local organizations' boards (of members) cannot hire and fire the staff who, in theory, work for them. In *all* community organizations, since staff are paid for their special knowledge and expertise, their knowledge endows them with great informal power. In ACORN, in practice, most power emanates from the center, from the leading national staff members with whom top city organizers work closely.[58] Leaders pick neighborhood-level issues that they care about, but organizers exert more influence on city and national campaigns. This may exact some cost in local empowerment and democracy; however, it produces a unity of national purpose that is harder for CBCOs to achieve.

Managing Internal Conflict

In the St. Louis organization, conflicts occurred among staff, among members, and between members and staff.[59] Members were not shy about expressing conflicts openly. However, among staff, these conflicts were handled privately rather than openly in public settings. The director tended to ignore conflicts among members when they broke out publicly, preferring to leave them to the members themselves to resolve. For example, in one training session two members belligerently challenged the authority of the board president (a long-running dispute); they finally left the training session to continue the dispute privately.

Race was a consistent dimension of conflicts between black members and staff and St. Louis's white director. Whether among staff members or between staff and members, conflicts were not addressed or resolved publicly but ignored or expressed privately. This may be because acknowledging the issue of racism within the organization would contradict its mission and was therefore taboo, especially in an organization that does not view emotional expression and open conflict resolution as an integral part of the organizing process (in contrast to a CBCO). Or special care may have been taken to shield intra-staff conflict from an outside observer. In any case, ACORN's identity and ideology are quite distinct from feminist-influenced new social movements, Ideal Type A, which focus on group process and interaction itself as a legitimate site of political struggle. Instead, internal conflicts were ignored in public settings, while attention was focused on the central unifying conflict—between ACORN and the authorities.

Negotiating with Authorities

ACORN confronts authorities dramatically, although chapters have become familiar with negotiation. However, ACORN's self-image deemphasizes negotiation and compromise in favor of contentious direct action.

We Raised Some Hell

Mounting direct action—demonstrations, pickets, office sit-ins, squatting, etc.—is important to ACORN's collective identity. The "ACORN Members' Handbook" reads:

> ACORN's experience is that direct action not only is the best way of winning, but also the best way to increase members' involvement. . . . To tackle a problem like getting a stop sign at a dangerous intersection, an ACORN neighborhood group might get 30 people together and come out to an "action" at the intersection, speak to the press, and hang up their own stop sign. . . . When they win the stop sign, all 30 of those ACORN members know that they are responsible for that victory. Those same people are then more likely to believe that by working together in a group, they can make changes happen.

Confrontational tactics are supposed to be fun for members. While activists are sometimes nervous about chairing meetings or speaking in public with little preparation, ACORN's atmosphere as a no-nonsense, confrontational action organization is exciting to members and organizers. ACORN is one of very few organizations that offer disenfranchised poor people "a chance to speak up and raise some hell." They don't make proposals, they make "demands." For example, Arlene, a middle-class black ACORN member, had to be coached to be confrontational. At her chapter's first action, she "gave [my alderwoman] a list of requests. James [her organizer] said they were *demands.*"

Figures 6a and 6b illustrate the activities that leaders from all four organizations most associated with their work. St. Louis ACORN leaders especially were more likely to speak of their organizing confrontationally, using words such as "fight" and "demand" rather than "negotiate." The congregation-based activists seldom described their work confrontationally. Interestingly, leaders in both San Jose groups, congregation-based and ACORN, spoke more about "research" in their work than the two St. Louis groups. Both San Jose groups had strong leaders accustomed to taking the responsibility

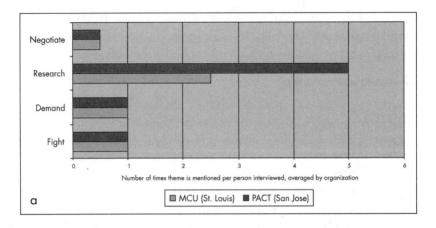

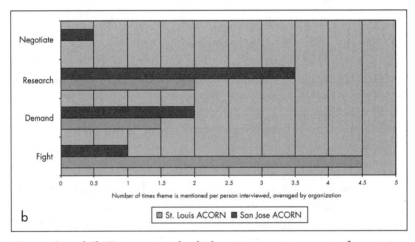

Figures 6a and 6b. Frequency with which activists mention aspects of organizing, by type of organization.

of researching issues. This may reflect better organizing conditions based on both internal and external factors: internally, effective staff members in both organizations; and externally, members who were, on average, not as poor and perhaps better able to form stable, long-term corps of indigenous leaders.

Gender and Emotion Norms of ACORN's Organizational Culture

As discussed earlier, the instrumental rather than expressive aspects of work and life are coded masculine: tasks, numbers, and strategic pursuit of power. These were more typical of ACORN. For example, anger and cynicism could be expressed publicly in ACORN while other emotion talk was rare. Rather than discussing "relationships," at one St. Louis ACORN staff meeting, organizers discussed the need to build "machines" in the wards. Organizing was about "how to understand numbers." While some ACORN methods, such as house meetings, draw on the power of social networks, the systematic development of social incentives and relationships among members was not part of staff members' frame of reference.

Gary Delgado, an African American former ACORN organizer, wrote, "In my view, ACORN reflects the shortcomings of an organization that is controlled by white middle-class male progressives."[60] In 1986, of a staff of 150, fewer than five women had access to top decision making.[61] While this study includes two significantly different chapters of ACORN, both are heavily influenced by the cultural norms disseminated by the national staff. ACORN's founder, Wade Rathke, has been its guiding force since 1970. Rathke and the majority of the national staff are white and male and have been criticized for a masculine cultural style with its roots in the New Left. For example, for a time it was common for male ACORN organizers to sport cowboy boots with their jeans, mimicking Rathke.[62] Especially before the Reagan era shrank ambitions, these organizers spoke expansively of organizing whole states or industries as a kind of conquest.[63] Especially in St. Louis ACORN, aesthetic and ceremonial dimensions were largely absent.[64] (An exception was one black organizer who was also a minister. His neighborhood groups tended to use prayer vigils frequently as a protest form.) While these qualities make ACORN an easy target for feminist criticism, they also have imparted an undeniable energy and ambition to an organization with few resources seeking to mobilize the disempowered against great odds.

Two Mobilizing Cultures

Based on their shared ancestry in Alinsky-style community organizing, ACORN and congregation-based community organizing share important similarities. Each seeks to unify its constituency under a broad umbrella that eschews racial, gender, and sexual identities in favor of a broad populist identity as ordinary working people. Each understands the importance of mobilization; each seeks to let "the people rule," and to train its members in grassroots politics through contention itself. Furthermore, their members share broad values, goals, and reasons for participation.

However, their cultures of commitment also exhibit striking differences. ACORN has an instrumental and utilitarian organizational culture in which transcendent values and beliefs are seldom articulated. Organizers point to the conditions of poor people as self-evident motivation for organizing, and the organization does not have an elaborated ideology that it teaches members. ACORN sees itself as an action organization, a band of intrepid militants. Its collective emotion work is primarily to generate excitement and anger at opponents. The utilitarian, task-oriented style of the founding national staff—mostly white, mostly male radical activists—deemphasizes attention from processes that could build solidarity in favor of more immediate results. Its militant, action-oriented approach has drawn together thousands of unrepresented Americans with serious grievances since 1970.

Congregation-based community organizing can draw on religious as well as populist or neighborhood identities. But aside from this obvious difference, CBCO differs from ACORN in the elaborated, expansive nature of its organizational culture—the discourse and practices that are developed and taught to activists. An elaborate set of concepts like power, self-interest, and values, and practices like the one-to-one interview, help produce a collective identity and a common culture. Practices that emphasize discipline and control help produce a self-image as effective, efficient, serious players in the arenas of power. At the same time, CBCOs must link these traits to participants' religious identity. Opportunities to do so include prayers, readings, and rituals during meetings and actions. Practices such as challenging one another, and concepts such as tension, agitation, and accountability, institute high expectations for members. These practices influence the organizations' mobilization capacity and depth of leadership development. They also, however, take an enormous amount of time from organizers on the theory that well-trained and dedicated leaders can conduct much of the organizing process.

Chapters 2 and 3 present and analyze each organizing approach's most distinctive contribution. Chapter 2 argues that the innovative cultural strategy of CBCO accomplishes cultural tasks that enable it to unify racially and economically diverse congregations and resolve ideological dilemmas of American political culture. Chapter 3 examines ACORN's early attempts at national organizing campaigns and identifies its innovative organizational and political strategy.

2

Religion and Progressive Politics: Congregation-based Community Organizing's Innovative Cultural Strategy

People just expected us to come and pray . . . they forgot: social change happened because of churches. Prohibition. Child labor laws. Things happened because the churches said so.

—MCU activist, St. Louis

Church-based community organizing and ACORN are both growing forms of civic engagement. In this chapter I show that CBCO has contributed a unique mobilizing culture to the repertoire of American social movements. While this culture is made up of sincerely held beliefs, it is also a strategy. I use the term "cultural strategy" in two ways. The original choice by the Industrial Areas Foundation to organize a broad-based social change movement through churches was a cultural as well as a structural strategy; that is, besides pursuing the sheer structural availability of the resources and social networks of churches, CBCOs sought their powerful cultural resources. These include their authority and legitimacy; their role in family life; their history as the primary domain of ritual, symbol, meanings, and values; and the Jewish and Christian prophetic traditions of social criticism. Also, it is a cultural strategy more narrowly understood as a set of specific ideas and practices. This distinct mobilizing culture uniquely combines religious ideas with practical organizing principles in a way that brings together cultural oppositions from the two ideal types of American social movements (see the Introduction). CBCO combines the expressive and instrumental, the moral and virtuous, with the strategic pursuit of power. It also combines inclusive democratic process with efficiency and practicality. Because church culture

45

lends itself to Ideal Type A, organizers usually must work harder to introduce the stern realpolitik of Type B to members. This chapter analyzes how CBCO ideas and practices manage these oppositions to produce a mobilizing culture that can attract the broadest possible constituency.

CBCO attempts to build a majority, cross-class constituency from a population fragmented by race and class. Scholars have documented a decline in ongoing face-to-face civic engagement. In its place more episodic volunteering has grown, along with small self-help groups, public interest groups without an active membership base, and Internet-based advocacy.[1] In an altered civic universe, American religion looms large as a source of civic engagement. Few other institutions feature powerful unifying symbols that reach such a wide cross-section of Americans. Religious participation is strongly correlated with other civic engagement. Churches are also the most stable American voluntary associations.[2] They have access to the private sphere of emotion, vulnerability, and family ties and can link them to the public sphere of political action. For better or worse, no domain has such a widespread and socially legitimate claim to individuals' private and emotional lives as religion does. Rites of passage—birth, adulthood, marriage, death—are celebrated in church, temple, and mosque; entire families participate; people light candles for their hopes, griefs, and joys and turn to clergy with their most personal problems. And yet, problematic as it sometimes is in a liberal polity, religion has a public face as well.

CBCO's cultural strategy addresses tensions in American political culture that have foiled other attempts to build unified constituencies for reform. I contend that its mobilizing culture provisionally resolves, for its own purposes, five tensions in American political culture:

1. *Bridging class and racial fault lines.* CBCO brings together racially diverse middle-class, working-class, and low-income Americans, an elusive goal for many movements.

2. *Combining participatory democracy and efficiency.* CBCO encourages the democratic deliberation emphasized in movement Ideal Type A, but combines it with the instrumental effectiveness valued in Ideal Type B.

3. *Bridging the liberal-conservative fault line.* CBCO can attract church members with somewhat divergent political views, including moderates, some moderate conservatives, and social conservatives (the latter usually from conservative African American denominations). They accomplish this partly with broad universal appeals but more specifically by combining liberal demands for redistributive policies with an

emphasis on personal accountability that is usually associated with conservatives.

4. *Bridging altruism and self-interest.* CBCO motivates participants by a counterintuitive but successful melding of two familiar ideas: self-interest and the religious values of human needs and community well-being.

5. *Integrating private life with public action.* The church has always had one face turned toward the private sphere and the other toward the public sphere. American Christianity, especially Protestantism, is historically the space of confessional narratives of sin and redemption, or pain and deliverance—from alcoholism, poverty, disease, or failure. Individual confessional narratives, whether couched in religious or secular terms, are ubiquitous in popular culture, but they are depoliticized.[3] Church-based organizing can draw on the emotional power of confession and conversion, but it is a conversion from isolation and powerlessness to empowered community action.

I argue that part of the reason reformers have had difficulty building unified constituencies, in the face of long-standing barriers that divide Americans, is inadequate cultural strategies.[4] Religion by itself is not responsible for the cultural innovations of CBCO. Only when combined with a specific set of ideas about organizing, power, and politics do shared religious ideas produce CBCO's innovative cultural strategy.

Bridging Class and Racial Fault Lines

The first tension I examine is a familiar one: the difficulty that working Americans have had in transcending barriers of race, ethnicity, and religion to win class-based redistributive reforms. In the past, region (especially North–South), national origin (WASP versus Irish, Italian, and Eastern European), and religion (Protestant nativist versus Catholic immigrant) were more divisive. Since the 1960s, progressives have often split between those who insisted that racial, gender, or sexual identities must not be subordinated to class and those who argued that economic redistribution should take precedence.[5]

The divide between white middle-class and working-class activism is at least as stark. The gradual decline of local party organizations and civic associations reduced opportunities for citizens to come together across class lines. In the sixties, the Democratic New Deal coalition of urban white ethnics, blacks, middle-class liberals, and others "ran headlong into a conflict of interest between blacks and middle-income [blue-collar] whites."[6] Urban working-class whites felt their property values were threatened by white flight and rapid racial turnover, their neighborhood schools by busing, and their economic interests by affirmative action based on race but not class. Meanwhile, the middle-class liberals who advocated these policies remained unaffected by them. This class-based cleavage among white Democrats was exploited and widened by conservative political entrepreneurs in Nixon's 1968 campaign and subsequent Republican presidential campaigns and reshaped American electoral coalitions. Republican political strategy has encouraged white workers to view themselves as victimized by minorities and welfare cheats. It has also used differences in middle-class and working-class white cultures to attack liberals as affluent cultural elitists, framing elites as cultural rather than economic.[7]

Not only do working-class Americans not participate much in cross-class movements, they often do not participate at all. This is partly due to the decline in working-class mobilizers such as local party organizations, unionized workplaces, and urban machines. These have been replaced as sources of political clout by money, experts, and media. Heightened voter mobilization in the 2004 election, the union renewal movement, including the breakaway Change to Win coalition, and newly awakened immigrant mobilization are recent exceptions to the trend, although it is too soon to judge their potential.[8] Yet working-class Americans (defined as those without a college degree) are in the majority. Even with the decline of traditional manufacturing, almost nineteen million white men are employed in manual blue-collar jobs in the United States today, compared with sixteen million in managerial and professional jobs and nine million in lower-level white collar jobs.[9] Not only are they a principal constituency that community organizers seek to empower, they are essential for a broad-based majoritarian movement.

Differences in Class Cultures

Class is more complex and confusing for Americans than race or gender, and American activists are comparatively less aware of how it affects social movement cultures. Different experiences of education and work fundamentally influence class-related attitudes and values. For example, working-class jobs are characterized by "physical labor, a relatively dangerous or dirty environment, boring or routine tasks, close supervision and limited opportunities for upward mobility."[10] There is usually little autonomy or recognition. Therefore, instead of individual achievement and career ambition, central working-class values are work, family, friends, and character. (Some argue that in 2000, George W. Bush's self-presentation as a "common man," using simple statements that appealed to these values, won the votes of white male working-class voters, whereas Al Gore's argument style, based on data and expertise, drew on middle-class sources of authority.)[11] Scholars of working-class activism characterize it as more rooted to concrete local communities—their neighborhoods, the black community, and the church—than more mobile, individualistic, middle-class activism. Middle-class people are typically college graduates, who are on average less likely to be religious than other Americans. Higher education teaches people to place a premium on autonomy, independent thinking, and self-expression, which their jobs require. Relative to working-class people, they have a greater sense of efficacy and personal mobility. The self-directed attitude that higher education imparts is evident in the plans of one PACT leader, a teacher, to interview members of her church:

> H S : What is a "quality one-to-one" versus another kind of one-to-one?
>
> ROSEMARY: Where I really thought about how I'm going to structure exactly what I want to try to get out of it. I want to definitely hear concerns, okay? I don't want to be the one doing most of the talking. I definitely want to give the credential[12] and do it well. I definitely want to be knowledgeable enough to update them by answering their questions, because if I can't answer those things, what is going to encourage them to come back?

Different social classes experience different degrees of individual efficacy in politics and efforts at social change. Blue-collar Americans may feel an overwhelming lack of efficacy, partly because they view technical expertise or skills that they lack, such as public speaking, as prerequisites to political involvement. Reinforcing this sense of resignation is a deep alienation from politics, the view that politicians are both incompetent and corrupt. Labor unions often fare no better: many see them as remote bureaucracies little different from business. Conservatives have helped promote this view and the notion that "big government" is overwhelmingly hostile to citizens' interests and primarily constrains individual rights. Experiences of impenetrable bureaucracies, ever more incompetent partly due to slashed resources, reinforce this view of government.[13]

Members of the peace, environmental, feminist, and other liberal movements are predominantly college educated and middle-class. Movement activists are often mystified by their inability to recruit working-class participants.[14] They sometimes assume that working-class Americans are prevented from joining by a lack of time or money or that they do not participate because they are unaware of social problems. However, such explanations of working-class citizens' nonparticipation often credit them with little agency and responsibility, far less than middle-class people would expect of themselves. Many working-class people have a clear sense of what is wrong in society and feel patronized when well-educated activists seek to instruct them.[15] However, while they may feel keenly that things are wrong, they may see the technical or policy aspects of governance as bewildering and "experts" as the only people qualified to advocate specific solutions.[16] At the same time, they also tend to mistrust middle-class experts—who, after all, are the professionals who have authority over them on the job. David Croteau writes:

> The professional middle class has served as a buffer between labor and capital. Workers can see benefits they get from capital, namely, jobs, and they do not see capitalist exploitation very clearly (unless a factory closes). Working people see managers and professionals enforcing the mental/manual divide but do not see benefits coming from this professional middle class. Thus, working-class resentment and anger—at least in the short run—gets channeled towards the [professional middle class]. The Right has effectively capitalized on this resentment.[17]

Their base in diverse congregations allows CBCOs to recruit an unusually racially and economically diverse group of Americans. (While about 12 percent of working people belong to a union today, according to one study, 67 percent belong to a church.)[18] Their class diversity is suggested by occupational data on the San Jose PACT citywide steering committee members. Their jobs fell into the categories shown in Figure 7. Of these thirty-two steering committee members, ten were retired, underscoring the importance of free time for civic participation.

It is challenging to bring together such an educationally diverse group without intimidating the less educated, boring the most educated, or al-

Type of job	Number of committee members
Unskilled labor	9
Skilled labor	14
Requires college degree	4
Requires master's degree	5

Figure 7. Occupational data for the San Jose PACT citywide steering committee members. Data were available for only thirty-two of the forty members.

lowing the latter to dominate the group. Several ideological tactics help bring together racially diverse middle-class and working-class Americans. CBCOs forge a common collective identity by framing themselves as *not* dilettantish, radical, elite, or ideological. Positively, CBCOs build solidarity through shared religious culture combined with a challenging yet accessible set of organizing principles.

We're Not Activists in a Movement

Chapter 1 showed that participants are taught who they are *not:* movements with activists or paternalistic agencies with clients. Instead, they are people's organizations of citizens, families, and children. One might wonder why CBCOs are so eager to distance themselves from social movements with which they share such interests as peace, clean air, and social programs. This distinction makes more sense when one considers that Saul Alinsky and the Industrial Areas Foundation always sought to build a majority coalition that would include the moderate middle of the political spectrum. Today Edward Chambers, Alinsky's successor at the IAF, still decries the tendency of movements to alienate moderates and conservatives, arguing that an "effective broad-based organization" must include them.[19] The IAF saw social movements of the sixties and seventies as strident, extreme, and unrepresentative of the silent majority of Americans.

This silent majority includes the white working class, many of whom view social movements as alien. New social movement norms are influenced by the experiences of their educated middle-class members, such as belief in the power of information to convert others, the value of individual expression, and the importance of egalitarian process.[20] In their language, self-presentation, and ideas, CBCOs both tacitly and explicitly distinguish themselves from such movements and reassure working-class church members that they belong. CBCOs do not speak of the "working class"; unlike many movements, the groups I observed seldom used such terms as "racism," "sexism," "classism," "homophobia," "oppression," or "multiple oppressions." Staff frequently allude to "racism" and use other terms among themselves and occasionally with members; however, these are not terms they typically use to frame members' problems because for CBCOs this language connotes ideological movements beyond the experience of most of their members.

Figure 8 lists some common working-class perceptions of liberal social movements and how CBCO presents itself in contrast.[21] The CBCO emphasis on leadership training assumes many participants (especially women, poor and working people, and immigrants) are inexperienced, intimidated

Some white working-class views of liberal social movements	Church-based community organizing features
• Social movement participants are hippies left over from the sixties, weirdos on the fringe, not regular people; dress and theatrical tactics seem bizarre or too radical (such as property damage).	• Organizers and participants wear conventional clothing, often business attire. Tactics—research, meetings, accountability sessions—are formal, dignified, appear conventional.
• Social movements are seen as transitory.	• Building a stable, ongoing organization is emphasized.
• Social movements are seen as naive, idealistic.	• Organizations present themselves as practical, pragmatic.
• Social movements are seen as ineffective.	• Concrete and realizable campaigns are emphasized.
• Social movement issues seem distant, unrelated to working-class life issues; middle-class activists' motivations may be more ideological, expressive, or solidaristic as opposed to protection of immediate interests.	• Issues are identified based on importance to constituents, concrete and immediate concerns.
• Language may be unfamiliar or alienating: may use sophisticated terms or technical policy-related language; may use unfamiliar terms from identity politics such as "sexism," "classism," "homophobia," "oppression," "multiple oppressions."	• Commonsense terms of identification, such as "people of faith," "children and families' needs," "ordinary people," "neighborhood needs," "working families," predominate.

Figure 8. Features of church-based community organizing that address working-class attitudes toward activism.

by politics, and feel inadequate to lead. Figure 9 summarizes research on working-class attitudes and traits that affect political efficacy and how CBCO training addresses them.

CBCOs explicitly appeal to the working-class values that undergird organizing. They appeal to personal integrity and character when they hold leaders accountable to take risks, challenge themselves, and do things they have never done before. Many educated members' sense of political inefficacy is transformed along with their working-class counterparts. Middle-class Americans who vote and feel comfortable chairing a meeting or leading a volunteer cleanup may feel incompetent as citizens pursuing urban policy reforms. College graduates from PACT and MCU, including ministers, re-

Working-class people often bring these assets to organizing	CBCO responds by
• Awareness of injustice • Skepticism toward authorities • Relational and other individual leadership skills • Social networks	• Heightening awareness of injustice and skepticism of authority • Basing organizing on developing relationships and mobilizing social networks
Working-class people often bring these challenges	**CBCO participation includes**
• Feelings of powerlessness; difficulty envisioning alternative futures • Lack of confidence in ability to lead • Lack of civic skills or experience speaking in public, chairing meetings, etc. • No feeling of entitlement • No specialized technical knowledge (e.g., of public policy); the belief that expertise is a prerequisite for participation; tendency to defer to experts	• Exercises in envisioning a just society • Extensive leadership training that addresses both emotional and cognitive dimensions (fear and shame, as well as lack of skills); imparts commonsense ideas and principles • Organizers coach members to speak in public, run meetings, plan strategy; members experience their power in small victories; organizers reinforce these experiences in one-to-one meetings after public actions with officials • "Challenging," whether aggressive or nurturing, to break down defenses against participation • "Agitation," attempts to provoke anger at status quo • Experience of conducting down-to-earth research, such as interviewing officials about issues, to demystify the process of knowledge gathering

Figure 9. Features of church-based community organizing that help empower working-class participants.

ported that before joining their CBCO they felt "very remote from the city mothers and fathers . . . that there was no real way of making a change," "ineffective," or that they "hardly had a clue." One member reported having "not much ability on the community level; I became a probation officer partly so as to make a difference, and later realized I can't really make that much of a difference." CBCOs also build shared identity and solidarity among diverse participants through shared religious culture.

We Are People of Faith

It may seem that shared liberal Christianity is enough to overcome other differences and exclude extremists. Yet among members allied in CBCOs, major differences remain. CBCOs may include Jews, Muslims, and other non-Christians. CBCOs perform cultural work to unify their members. One way activists link religion with organizing is to explicitly draw on religious social justice traditions. These include the Protestant realism of Reinhold Niebuhr, the social justice teachings of the Catholic Church, and liberation theology originally developed by Latin American Catholics.[22] Along with a shared commitment to social justice, shared personal faith and rituals produce a collective identity.

Typically, CBCOs open their meetings with a prayer or reflection that expresses values that undergird the organizing work. Other rituals include prayer. One of MCU's three component neighborhood organizations held a twenty-four-hour prayer vigil outside a U.S. senator's St. Louis office to urge him to oppose pending legislation.[23] Unifying rituals may also include secular texts and symbols. After the terrorist attacks on September 11, 2001, a Chicago-area CBCO affiliated with the IAF held a gathering for religious tolerance and unity that began with a member reading from the Declaration of Independence. The meeting ended in a ritual enactment of unity, with all four thousand participants reading the same passage in unison.[24]

Religiously divisive issues such as abortion and gay rights are off most organizations' agendas. Although CBCO includes few conservative white Protestant congregations, Catholic churches are a mainstay, and some black Protestant churches are conservative on issues of gender and sexuality. Participants unite around broad issues of public safety, housing, education, health care, jobs, and increasingly, immigrants' rights.[25] If an issue is specific to one congregation, it can be accommodated as a local church campaign. Only when an issue is a widely expressed priority, or can be made one, will it land on a group's citywide agenda.

Race and CBCO Mobilizing Culture

Race is problematic for those seeking to build majority coalitions because addressing it directly has the potential to produce backlash among whites. Politicians avoid it: of the 2004 Democratic presidential nominees, only Al Sharpton talked regularly about race. After Hurricane Katrina in 2005, black politicians resisted identifying racism as a cause of the disastrous government performance in rescuing black citizens of New Orleans. They understood that "talking race begs being labeled a racist, an agitator, or a troublemaker."[26]

CBCOs acknowledge race as a major American issue, but they do not frame racism as the fundamental social problem to address because that would highlight a cleavage among their members. Instead, they acknowledge that race is one category of political and economic domination.[27] Because black pastors often distrust multiracial or majority-white CBCOs, they frequently form their own caucuses. For example, the Gamaliel Foundation's African American Leadership Commission includes pastors and organizers within that network and aims to "train and agitate African American clergy, top leadership and their allies."[28]

Because they seek to build majority coalitions, CBCOs typically frame their goals as good education, jobs, housing, health care, and the like. The populist universalism imparted during national trainings highlights shared interests; the personal narratives activists hear in one-to-one interviews and the interaction with people different from themselves help produce sympathetic identification with members of different backgrounds. On the final day of a PICO national training, an African American female participant expressed the "high" of solidarity that the training had produced for her as "a glimpse of heaven. This is God." A Filipino man became emotional about experiencing "so many religions come together: to see black, Hispanic, Asian, Filipino all together—if we can do it here, up on this hill, why can't we do it down there?"

In summary, CBCOs partially bridge fault lines of class and race by making their organizations culturally hospitable to both working-class and middle-class members. They reinforce a common identity as people of faith who seek what is right and just for their families, neighborhoods, and city. The next section explains how CBCO mobilizing culture places a high value on deliberation and democratic process as well as instrumental productivity. This combination has cross-class appeal. It helps satisfy educated members' desires for individual expression, deliberation, and professionalism and offers working-class members a voice as well as opportunities for leadership.

Combining Participatory Democracy and Efficiency

Every democratically run SMO that seeks to influence society has to balance attention to members' interactions and deliberative processes with getting things done in the world. Francesca Polletta has convincingly argued that the two goals are not necessarily at odds: open and thorough deliberation often serves instrumental purposes essential to an organization's mission, such as building trust and solidarity in high-risk activism or hearing the greatest number of ideas and proposals.[29] However, the groups she studied in the civil rights movement and the New Left drew heavily on students and youth, a population known for its activism and predilection for "endless meetings" made possible by the lack of family and work responsibilities. In her book *Freedom Is an Endless Meeting,* she includes church-based community organizing as an example of participatory democracy.

For busy parents and workers, freedom is not likely to be an endless meeting. One white middle-class leader of MCU was "intrigued" and motivated to stay involved with her organization "because they kept meetings to one hour." A middle-class PACT member commented: "Our meetings are very timely [and] planned. I'm not a big meeting person, I want to get things done and out of there. And that's another thing, when you know you have a time frame, and everyone is busy, then you make decisions a lot faster and you're more productive that way."[30]

Yet as Polletta and others have observed, CBCO's decision-making norms are participatory and democratic. One way this is accomplished is through extensive communication in which consensus is forged informally outside of the formal venues where decisions are made by majority vote.[31] Local congregation organizing committees talk through issues, and organizers meet extensively with individual activists to deliberate strategy and develop their skills. Throughout the organization, leaders from different congregations who have worked together on major campaigns can sound each other out. While to SMOs close to Ideal Type A this may smack of backroom politicking, CBCO participants view this as a normal part of the democratic process, just as a city council or legislature operates. Substantive deliberation also occurs in formal meetings, but for a fixed amount of time. If there is a pressing issue that calls for more discussion, participants may ask for the group's consent to add ten or fifteen minutes to the agenda. This norm communicates respect for members' private time and family responsibilities.

This style of participatory democracy with efficiency is well-suited for both working-class and middle-class participants. While it is straightforward and hardly original, it places an unusual emphasis on discipline, that is, remaining faithful to a preplanned agenda and staying within allotted time limits. This differs from movement organizations more like Ideal Type A, which often feature alternative or less formal modes of conducting business. They feature a cultural style that sociologist Paul Lichterman calls "personalist," which I understand as egalitarian individualism. Its egalitarianism may hold that "the intrinsic worth of all contributions and all contributors" preempts any "standard for judging between them." This style is absent in ACORN, which seeks mainly to organize the poor and working class and effectively acculturates middle-class staff members into its norms.

However, congregation-based organizing seeks to build a multiclass movement and this cultural style can inhibit cross-class coalition building.[32] CBCO norms and practices partially accommodate personalism while avoiding some of its pitfalls.

Personalism

Personalist organizations have been part of the more countercultural wing of the feminist, peace and justice, antinuclear, environmental, and other movements. Often they emphasize participatory democracy, understood narrowly as decision by consensus, the priority of deliberation over expediency, and sometimes internal process over external impact. In some cases the hostility to hierarchical roles, even when rotated democratically, is so strong that leadership is discouraged. Lichterman's study of local environmental groups suggests that these cultural traits can undermine successful campaigns. Weir and Ganz argue that "an organizational culture suspicious of authority, leadership, and orderly democratic process" makes "collaboration across groups and levels of governance and coordination very difficult."[33] These organizations may privilege what Katzenstein refers to as "discursive politics"—internal discussion and education through community forums and the media—because tangible gains are not realizable at a given time.[34] A "prefigurative" goal of embodying a just society, such as egalitarian decision making, may become more salient when avenues for effective political action close.[35] Alternatively, activists may lack experience in running campaigns with realizable goals. The tools in their repertoires of contention may be limited to politicized personal choices (recycling or socially conscious investing), educational events, and symbolic protest. Members' value as distinct individuals can overshadow the collective good of the organization.

A related feature of movements influenced by feminism is an anxiety over power. Because power was associated with oppression, leadership was often seen as domination. Participants challenged leaders' authority, and activists took pains to avoid the appearance of leadership.[36] But since groups need leaders to help them focus, make decisions, and act, and leaders usually emerge whether they are acknowledged or not, a cultural style in which leadership is taboo can damage organizational effectiveness.

Many MCU and PACT members who are social/cultural specialists, such as teachers and social workers, may share aspects of the personalist ethos. To these kinds of participants, CBCOs need to communicate respect for democratic process and the value of all individual contributions. CBCOs accomplish this through several norms. First, the CBCO emphasis on listening and building relationships through one-to-one interviews allows participants to translate their concern for individual development into CBCO terms. Graciela, a teacher and PACT member, could interpret her school district's diversity training program this way: "That black person who is sharing their story and their struggle—I have an appreciation for that person and it's the one-on-one relationship. So it goes right along with the PICO training and the one-on-one relationships." The difference between diversity training and church-based organizing is that in the latter, listening and relationship building are undertaken to build social capital for political mobilization. In San Jose PACT, for example, organizers give painstaking attention to individual development, but in the context of goal-directed political work. Individuals' right to express themselves becomes subordinate to the group; since group goals are chosen democratically, individuals who seek to dominate discussions are seen as antidemocratic. The hierarchy of leaders and followers is democratic as well, since leadership is open to all who show the ability and commitment to lead by doing the work and mobilizing members. The ideal is to develop everyone's leadership capacity to the maximum possible, which harmonizes personal growth with organizational potential. Accountability norms are mutual and seen to serve the organization as a whole.

Thus, CBCOs recruit a wide variety of members, some of whom may bring highly educated personalist norms to their activism and others who cannot speak English or have no organizational experience whatsoever. For the uneducated, CBCOs offer a set of easy-to-grasp concepts that explain the inner workings of politics. For the well educated, they offer a high standard of productivity and efficiency, norms that are familiar to those with professional training. Their emphasis on building relationships, orderly democratic decision making, and the process of learning through action, evaluations, and individual reflection with organizers all give individual attention to activists. But meetings and actions are tightly planned and efficient, which gratifies busy family members of all classes.

The next section examines how CBCO attempts to bridge the divide between liberals and conservatives.

Bridging the Liberal-Conservative Fault Line

In addition to bridging divides of race, gender, and class, CBCO also seeks to bring members together across the fault line of political ideology. One ideological tactic conservatives have used since the 1970s to divide the Democratic Party coalition has been to counterpose virtuous self-sufficient individuals against others—the poor, the unemployed, criminals, welfare recipients—and their apologists, "big government liberals." These liberals purportedly want to "throw money at government programs" rather than hold individuals accountable for their condition. The section "Bridging Class and Racial Fault Lines" noted how conservative entrepreneurs racialized the ideology of individual responsibility versus liberal big government during the 1960s and skillfully exploited class division among whites.[37] The Republican Party was then able to recruit disaffected working-class Democrats. While this conflict among white Democrats was real, liberals exacerbated it by dismissing working-class white concerns as "racist" or "redneck" and allowing conservatives to hijack the language of values and responsibility. Working-class whites became cynical about the liberal silence on crime, and conservatives denounced liberals' preference for state intervention as a love of big government. They accused liberals of blaming the system for individual failures, while individual responsibility, character, and virtue became increasingly associated with the right.[38]

Movements such as CBCO that attempt to cross race and class lines also, then, cross political fault lines. To appeal to the constituencies they seek, they must avoid racial scapegoating and victim blaming, present problems and solutions not as personal and private but as public and social, and frame their issues as broadly shared and their policy proposals as common sense. This poses a challenge: as Stephen Hart notes, the public has responded to the conservative resurgence despite the fact that polls show no significant move to the right on issues.[39] Despite political positions that collided head-on with white working-class voters' material interests, 62 percent of voters with a high school education voted for George W. Bush in the 2004 election.[40] In 2000, more than 60 percent of white male voters supported Bush even though Democrat Al Gore's positions on major *issues* such as health care, education, and tax policy were significantly more popular with them than Bush's positions.[41] With Hart, I argue that part of the reason is the failure of American liberals to frame themselves and their political positions in terms of deeply held American values such as independence, freedom, patriotism, equality, and the work ethic.

CBCO mobilizes these traditional American political values to help reach moderates and some conservatives. As church-based groups, they symbolize tradition. A *church*-based organization, for example, can hold a candlelight peace vigil that also "honors the 28 soldiers from Louisiana and 1,500 nationally who lost their lives in Iraq" without being seen as unpatriotic. It draws on the ritual of the memorial service, which *honors* soldiers killed in the line of duty.[42]

CBCO also draws on more general ideas and norms to link traditional values to redistributive goals. The norms of *challenging* and *accountability* emphasize individual responsibility. The IAF Iron Rule—"Never, never do for others what they can do for themselves"—expresses classic American self-reliance, except it is collective, not individual. Its larger purpose is empowerment of the disempowered.

The PICO National Network organizes in areas with many working-class Republicans, such as San Diego, with its huge military population. "We're here to bring new religious voices to the public debate," said local bishop Roy Dixon, an African American leader with the Pentecostal Church of God in Christ. "We're conservatives, moderates, Democrats, liberals. I'm a Republican."[43] PICO organizing director Scott Reed argues:

> The suggestion of individual responsibility runs pretty deep in most of us, and the Republicans tap into that framework more successfully than Democrats do. . . . A lot of folks that we would end up organizing with resonate with a more moderate Republican agenda. They're concerned about entrepreneurship, they don't like a lot of paperwork and regulations, they feel strongly about individual responsibility, so they are comfortable with . . . a Republican moderate position.

People learn to be responsible and accountable in settings like families, schools, and workplaces. This ethos is less common in liberal churches, the backbone of CBCO, and social movement organizations. These churches' very liberalism suggests tolerance for varying degrees of commitment and responsibility.[44] Unlike liberal churches, strict churches with high demands of members are the fastest-growing denominations in America.[45] This is why a liberal church-based movement that imposes high expectations on participants is unusual. Institutionalizing norms of "agitating," "challenging," and "holding one another accountable"—demanding high commitment and responsibility—are innovative for a progressive redistributive movement.

However, unlike social conservatives, for CBCOs individual morality is not the basis of an adequate public policy. What makes CBCO ideology liberal rather than conservative is that it advocates not private or voluntary solutions but collective public programs. They seek action from the state: social welfare programs, redistribution, or regulation. Within an organization, staff and members challenge one another, but publicly CBCOs usually emphasize individual responsibility *on the part of authorities*. Because they apply the same ethic of responsibility to themselves as well, they seem fair and evenhanded.

One St. Louis activist illustrates this ideology:

> I feel that we the people who say we're represented by the people that we elect have held them not accountable, so if we want to hold them account-

able we need to change the political system so that we have power—either throwing out or backing up the people we've elected. Making them accountable: "This is what you said you'd do and you haven't done it." We allow them to be as corrupt as we are . . . lackadaisical, apathetic.

A San Jose activist echoes this idea: "They're only as good as the pressure put upon them from outside. And they have to be held accountable."

Another strategy that the PICO Network uses to transcend competing ideologies is framing issues neutrally as *practical problems* rather than as ideological issues. One PICO organizer stated:

> When communities come into contact with one another and race and class begin to break down, and there's a common set of concerns about youth or after-school programming, quality of schools, access to health care—Republican or Democratic ideology really doesn't matter too much. Then it's a question of how do we fix this problem.

This practical, problem-solving tone, designed to appeal to a broad majority, is evident in PICO publicity:

> In *urban, rural and suburban* communities PICO federations are discovering and refining strategies that address the most important social issues facing America. Beginning with the *concrete problems* faced by *working families* and then doing *careful research,* PICO leaders create *policy innovations* from the ground up. These solutions come out of specific places and problems, but offer models for communities and states across the United States. These are solutions that *unify rather than divide* . . . [including] Provide parents with *high quality* public school *choices;* Help people *have a say* in local, state and national decisions.[46]

Related to the "neutral problem" framing is the theme that the proposed solutions "unify rather than divide." This is especially important for issues that do, in fact, have potentially strong opposition, such as immigrants' rights. PICO presents its campaign to provide driver's licenses to undocumented immigrants as "efforts to find common ground on legislation." The PICO New Voices national campaign is "challenging our nation's leaders to find common ground on domestic policies that support families and strengthen communities."

In summary, CBCO addresses constituents' potential ideological conflict over its policy agenda in several ways. It applies the bootstraps morality of responsibility beloved by conservatives, but in the service of collective empowerment and liberal redistributive policies. It applies the same ethic of accountability to its members and to authorities outside the group. It selects issues that have wide support in order to achieve broad legitimacy. Finally, it presents its goals as noncontroversial, pragmatic, commonsense proposals based on wide research. If the issue is controversial, it seeks reasonable goals that "find common ground." These tactics, along with the fact that CBCO stays strictly away from the third rail of the culture wars—abortion and homosexuality—help CBCO surmount liberal-conservative divides among its church members.

Bridging Altruism and Self-interest through Values

One can discern two broad tendencies in the history of early American Protestantism: an optimistic and a pessimistic stance toward society and prospects for reform. CBCO rather ingeniously, if not consistently, draws on both. One tendency, known as Christian perfectionism, was based on the optimistic vision that human beings could so radically improve themselves and society as to bring about Christ's thousand-year reign of peace on earth. This expansive vision, developed in the revivals of the Second Great Awakening (1780–1830), drove nineteenth-century moral reform movements such as temperance and abolition. They created the American voluntary association as we know it, and later informed the Social Gospel movement. The more pessimistic tendency, drawing on Augustine and Calvin, holds that original sin sharply limits human potential for goodness in human society. This view may call for different responses: to withdraw entirely from society, as some Protestant fundamentalist sects have done, or to strive for God's justice in flawed human institutions.

Christian perfectionists such as abolitionist William Lloyd Garrison believed in social change by moral suasion and individual conversion.[47] Abolitionists only reluctantly entered the corrupting world of politics and parties. A similar struggle unfolded among maternalist reformers and Progressives, who shared the optimistic assumption of progress informed by reason and science.[48] However, the suffering of workers under industrial capitalism, the Great Depression, two world wars, and the atom bomb savaged the optimistic hopes of reformers—none more than the great Protestant theologian Reinhold Niebuhr (1892–1971).[49]

Twentieth-century history convinced Niebuhr that human sinfulness greatly constrained efforts for societal reform. Niebuhr's ideas are evident in Saul Alinsky's writing and in CBCO mobilizing culture. Niebuhr's Christian realism aimed for an achievable moral standard: "a society in which there will be enough justice, and in which coercion will be sufficiently nonviolent to prevent [the] common enterprise from issuing into complete disaster."[50] Justice requires either coercion or the resistance to coercion. The

Christian realist must acknowledge the reality of power and not flee from it but engage it with skill. Hence, CBCO relentlessly pressures members to acknowledge that those with the power, not the better moral claim, will win. To play the political game they need political and tactical skills.

This view resonates with those who have been on the losing end of American politics. Although Christian realism draws on the concept of original sin, nonbelievers like Alinsky could interpret sin as flawed human nature, humans as tainted by the will to power that produces domination. This implies a certain moral humility and an openness to compromise, which is reflected in the title of Alinsky's second guide to organizing. Directed at student radicals that he felt were dogmatic and ineffective (the most hostile view of Ideal Type A), it was subtitled "A *Pragmatic* Primer for *Realistic* Radicals" (emphases mine). Alinsky thought this was the basis on which to design campaigns in which many people would participate, not just the minority of idealists who will get involved on the basis of principle or solidary incentives rather than results.[51] Although self-interest was a pragmatic basis for realistic radicalism, Alinsky and his followers believed that as participants gained wider experience, they would eventually identify with other ordinary Americans' concerns across the barriers that kept them apart. But when Ed Chambers and Ernie Cortes reorganized the IAF after Alinsky's death, they sought to more explicitly link pragmatic self-interest to a moral vision—in a sense, recovering the guiding vision of Christian perfectionism. This moral vision is a touchstone that can help prevent activists from becoming like the self-seeking politicians they target. It was one of many resources for which CBCO entrepreneurs turned to the church. They began to define their members' self-interest in terms of their religious values.

One PICO organizer distinguished self-interest from selfishness by defining it as inherently relational: as one PICO organizer lectured leaders, "Self-interest is embedded in the very existence of relationship, of being true to the relationship. It stems from the Latin root *interess,* to be involved, among, between, engaged." A Gamaliel organizer taught local leaders that "Values are what people believe in, act on with regularity, and defend publicly."[52] Another organizer linked self-interest to values this way: "Spiritual life is values, social life is self-interest. We have to put flesh on the word: the word has to become flesh." CBCO thus links pragmatic self-interest and the common good. Organizers teach activists that while politicians are sure of their self-interest, church people often are not. Organizers use values as a standard with which to challenge activists: if values guide action, and members claim to value their families' well-being, then surely they must act to ensure it.

In personal interviews, organizers and activists discern the interests of both authorities and potential activists. CBCO participants learn to think in terms of the self-interest of prospective participants, churches, politicians, potential allies, and other stakeholders. One Gamaliel Foundation memo reads, "Senator Feingold found it in his self-interest to use Gamaliel Comprehensive Immigration Reform Principles."[53] A PICO organizer wrote in her weekly staff report that she "didn't know how to get to the self-interest of comfortable middle-class people who are busy at their jobs."

In practice, the concept of self-interest becomes broadened to include motivation and values. While it retains its hard-nosed realist associations, activists use it more broadly to include public-spirited, even altruistic, work. One CBCO member, Jenn, was known for tirelessly identifying and working for broad community needs. She framed her public-spiritedness in terms of self-interest: "I mean, face it, I'm in it for my self-interest. I see things that need to be done. So I go out and find people around me who feel the same way, or who I can convince to feel the same way. And then get them to come to these meetings and support this." Jenn's comment illustrates how her own public-spiritedness—seeing things that need to be done but which do not directly affect her family—gets folded into the tough-minded realism of "self-interest" that, "let's face it," is what Jenna is "in it for." She has learned to diagnose the interests of elected officials and corporations. However, she also understands self-interest so broadly that it is ultimately a placeholder for the values, selfish or social, that drive public-spirited civic engagement.

Integrating Private Life with Public Action

Although the distinction between the public and the private spheres is enduring, the exact border between them is a site of struggle. While totalitarian societies subordinate the private to the public, in Western societies capital and its political allies divert matters of public concern into the private sphere of personal consumption. David Croteau argues that for working-class Americans in particular, private life and family—not the workplace or the vibrant urban social life of the past—loom large as domains of security, control, autonomy, creativity, and love.[54] Suburbanization, television, cocooning, and watching movies at home rather than collectively in theaters have helped speed the decline of neighborhoods and social institutions.[55] Corporations and real estate developers have found it profitable to replace the public sphere with private malls and urban neighborhoods with gated developments.

Other forces reduce the scope of the public and political by framing common problems as personal and individual. Following the model of Alcoholics Anonymous, this framing draws on a secularized version of the individual confession of sin and conversion. Support groups for individual self-help make up a large proportion of Americans' voluntary activity. Often their framing of problems as personal, private, and psychological obscures the dimensions that are collective, public, and structural. The culture of personal self-help, deeply rooted in American Protestantism, can be seen negatively as a distraction from social change, or positively as a quest for community and social capital.[56] However, without a framework that links personal experiences and social systems, participants are likely to experience these small groups as communities of individuals who share a *personal* problem with private solutions.[57]

As noted earlier, churches straddle the boundary between public and private. CBCOs reach into congregations to mobilize the concerns of American families into public action. In talking so much about families and values, CBCOs offer an alternative notion of family values that mandates public provision for broad-based social needs.

Moving from Private to Public

Church-based community organizing integrates the public and private spheres by harnessing three discourses to the goal of redistributive politics: liberal Christianity, emotion, and family. It draws on Christian discourse for political action; applies the language of private emotion to public problems; and harnesses family and values to a progressive rather than a conservative politics. Its innovation is to intertwine the discourses of liberal *Christianity, emotion,* and *family values* with the discourses of *politics* and *policy* so that they seem naturally bound to each other. The fusion of these realms of meaning channels private concerns about family life and private emotions of vulnerability, pain, and anger into the public realm of policy making.

One Filipina CBCO activist named Elena was grief stricken by her daughter's involvement with drugs and gangs. Elena thought she knew how to get resources for her daughter, but she could not. She learned that her daughter had to be arrested in order to enter a public drug rehabilitation program. Elena and her husband sold their house and spent their life savings to pay $18,000 for a twenty-eight-day rehabilitation program. Elena began two decades of leadership in her CBCO that expanded to include work with city and county government. She spearheaded a campaign for a city- and county-funded drug treatment center. When asked to explain the source of her commitment, Elena said, "I think it's my belief that God and love are one and the same. That and I still have a mission to say thank you, I think. I've been given a very good life both for my daughter and my family and I can't lose. He won't let me." Elena's family, religious, and political lives are highly interwoven. Her spiritual advisor is not her own parish priest but a priest she met in her CBCO. Her personal religious concerns are inseparable from her public political work.

Christian Emotional Discourse and Gender

Part of what characterizes the private sphere is emotional expression. Because religion addresses joyful and sorrowful rites of passage, emotional expression that is suppressed in public settings such as work, school, or clubs is accepted in church life.[58] CBCO's basis in churches means that its organizational culture exhibits some traits, such as expression of emotions, that have female-gendered associations. In 1955, Talcott Parsons and R. F. Bales identified cultural traits associated with male and female roles: the male role was *instrumental,* representing the family to the outside world as breadwinner, while the female role was *expressive,* expressing and managing emotions within the family.[59] American church pews have long been dominated by women, and churches reflect cultural features associated today with women. Chapter 1 discussed how churches include some features culturally coded in the United States as feminine, such as a focus on emotional expression, relationships, and community building, and attention to interactive processes and expressive activities such as rituals. However, CBCOs link these expressive features to instrumental goals. CBCO believes in celebrating accomplishments, which takes valuable staff time without instrumentally advancing issue campaigns, because the psychological benefit is seen as critical to long-term commitment. At the same time, CBCOs help broaden the definition of "being church" to include mass-based policy advocacy. This entails venturing into the masculine-valenced world of politics, a challenging but invigorating experience for church members unaccustomed to wielding power. CBCO confronts the timidity and politeness of church culture with a self-consciously hard-nosed political realism while attempting to retain the female-coded strengths of emotional awareness and relationship building. This balancing act is expressed concisely in the PICO National Network's slogan "The power is in the relationship."

Determination and anger are permissible public emotions for activists in many organizations. However, uncovering more vulnerable private emotions, like fear, shame, and hurt, in a group setting is typically the domain of the self-help group. But finding that these emotions are shared, becoming angry and determined, and recasting personal failure as social injustice is the dynamic of consciousness-raising. The experience of risking exposure, gaining trust, and reframing the personal as political binds the sharers more closely together and broadens the range of experiences on which political work can explicitly draw. It is a sort of conversion experience to a new collective identity and political understanding.

In interviews with CBCO activists, common themes included community, faith, and love. Churches easily wove these themes into their neighborhood organizing. Staff at one Catholic church expressed their goal for the next year as "Continue the work of building a community of faith and love. . . . We need to get in touch with where people are—what are their dreams, concerns, their pain?"

Naming the emotional dimension of participants' experiences is organizationally valuable for several reasons. First, emotions that members express provide information about the organizing. After meetings and collective actions, CBCOs conduct an evaluation so that participants learn from their mistakes and successes. The initial question a Gamaliel Foundation organizer asks is "How do you *feel*?" Second, explicitly naming ignoble emotions that members might wish to hide domesticates these emotions and incorporates them into the group's identity. Being encouraged to reveal emotions and beliefs that participants think are taboo and finding them acceptable help participants feel accepted, included, approved of. Feeling that they belong builds solidarity and loyalty. Staff members model this understanding of organizing as emotion-laden in their language. Typical "emotion statements" during one CBCO training session included:

> You are dealing with an activity [organizing] that is *uncomfortable.*

> When we walk into someone's home we're not going to hear the values, we're going to hear the pain.

> Where is the pain of the community?

> [Members' testimony at a mass meeting] "got really down to the pain."

> You don't have to be wealthy to be comfortable in your pain.

> TRAINER: You have a lot of work to do! Now you'll see if you are fighters or wilters! It's anxiety producing, but it's exciting, isn't it!
> MEMBER: Yeah!

Anger can be used to provoke ("agitate") members to action, as one organizer did when he pounded a table and exclaimed, "The conditions of our community are unacceptable, and they're not going to change unless *you* make them change!"

Resignifying Family Values as Liberal

Family is still seen as the private sphere, framed as unsullied by the dirty, rough-and-tumble world of politics. For example, in one organization studied by Nina Eliasoph, "good" citizens were concerned about their families, not about "flaky" or "radical" causes. When a local antitoxics group proposed a parade float protesting a nearby toxic waste incinerator, officials forbade the float because the parade was a "family" event, not a "political" one.[60] Families and children are politically impossible to oppose, so groups on the left and the right compete to appropriate these frames. The Christian right has largely appropriated the discourse of family for socially conservative goals. Political issues inherently concern families, but that is no guarantee that organizations frame them this way or that participants understand their goals in these terms.

CBCO participants in interviews mentioned families, children, and youth repeatedly as their motivations for organizing. Activists from both CBCOs and ACORN framed their problems in terms of "family," "children," "kids," and "youth" far more than in other terms such as "rights" or "justice." This suggests not that activists were unconcerned about rights or justice but that they articulated their reasons for organizing concretely and personally rather than abstractly. Members worried about unsafe parks, dangerous abandoned buildings (in St. Louis), and gangs that might recruit youth.

Churches are respected advocates for families and children because family life has historically been their province. CBCOs frame their issues frequently in these terms.[61] For example, one CBCO worked to implement its "youth agenda" and build "safe and healthy communities for our youth and families."[62] Framing issues this way names one of members' greatest concerns, frames public expenditures as protecting families, and helps progressive organizing recapture the discourse of family and children.

The mobilization of family and emotional discourse carries risks. When women in Eliasoph's study presented themselves as "concerned moms" with personal agendas, they were seen as passionate and emotional, not rational advocates for policy change. In contrast, scientific experts were given great authority. These citizens made a distinction between emotion and reason in public discourse and devalued emotionalism, which they associated with women. One CBCO presentational tactic combines the emotional appeal of "moms" and families with the authority of researchers. PICO organizations research issues among their own members and also with experts and officials. When they present an issue to officials at a mass meeting, a few members with personal experience present the grievance in emotional personal narratives. Immediately thereafter, other activists present a formal research report that provides evidence that the speaker's problem is widespread and frames members as grassroots experts. Men and women both present personal testimony and objective research.

Conclusion

There are numerous studies of Christian conservatives.[63] However, there is very little scholarship on the ideological strategies of the Christian left. This is not because there is no liberal religious activism; its liveliest presence is felt locally in urban community organizing, which is far less visible nationally than the Right. Scholars of American politics interested in religion or civic engagement would do well to consider, in John C. Green's wording, not just the "traditionalists" (theological conservatives) but the larger number of "centrists" and "modernists" among evangelicals, mainline Protestants, and Catholics.[64]

The 2004 presidential election and the disjuncture between voters' issue preferences and their votes for president demonstrate that scholars, politicians, and civic entrepreneurs need more research on what political ideas, identities, and symbols mean to various groups of Americans. I have argued that church-based community organizing as an American social movement is a significant cultural innovation. Like all strategies, it is flawed. Because CBCO is made up of organizations, each of which makes decisions more or less democratically, uniting member churches behind an issue campaign can take time. This can frustrate coalition partners that have more centralized control and faster decision making. Churchgoers accustomed to being "nice" can restrict CBCO's range of tactics, ruling out militant direct action. Finally, CBCOs must leave divisive issues, such as abortion and homosexuality, off the table because Catholic and black evangelical churches are often at loggerheads with liberal congregations on these issues. Like all coalitions, CBCO acts only on the issues its members share.

However, CBCO's advantages—access to congregational resources, social networks, pastoral and lay leaders, legitimacy, and religious social justice traditions—have helped it sustain organizations with unusually diverse memberships and win concrete improvements. The most original contributions of church-based community organizing, I argue, are the ideas and practices that allow it to reconcile values and concepts that have frequently been irreconcilable in the logic of American political culture. Through various ideological tactics, CBCO has partially surmounted tensions that challenge other American social movements. It constructs various unities (people of faith, families, residents of San Jose, CBCO members) and op-positions (organization versus movement; leaders that deliver a following, not gadfly activists) that help forge a strong collective identity across lines of race, class, and gender. CBCO validates a concern with individual responsibility while calling for generous social programs. It pushes church members to engage in the messy world of power politics but bases the quest for power on morally defensible values. It draws on the long American tradition of participatory democracy but combines it with orderly and efficient decision making. Finally, it links narratives of private pain with public action. Church-based community organizing is just one way to address these tensions creatively, but its base in American religion lends it wide appeal and cultural resonance.

3

Experimenting with National Organizing Campaigns: ACORN'S Innovative Political Strategy

ACORN, the Association of Community Organizations for Reform Now, has represented low- to moderate-income people since its founding in 1970. From the beginning, it has seen itself as both a poor people's interest group and part of a broad populist movement for social change. I argued in chapter 2 that CBCO's most original contribution to American social movements is a unique mobilizing culture that can unite a diverse constituency and avoid political minefields common in American movements. ACORN, like church-based community organizing and all organizations that mobilize adherents, has its own characteristic norms, but its methods of mobilizing members are more familiar and task-oriented than those of the CBCOs. ACORN organizing in San Jose and St. Louis was a matter of setting goals for recruitment, fund-raising, and mobilization, as well as planning strategy and negotiations in local campaigns. ACORN's particular strength is its *strategic innovation*. ACORN's *national campaigns* use innovative tactics, which are quickly disseminated through *one centralized organization* to its thirty-five state organizations and eighty-five city chapters. ACORN had ambitions for a national presence as early as the 1970s, but lacked the organizational capacity to successfully launch the campaigns it has conducted since 2000. In part, ACORN's rapid expansion since 2000 made these campaigns possible, but that expansion was itself the result of a planned strategy.

ACORN and CBCOs both seek concrete gains and power for low- and moderate-income Americans. They also seek mass mobilization as their fundamental source of power. However, relative to CBCOs, ACORN has had a national focus for a longer period of time. The following features characterize ACORN's organizing:

1. ACORN has a unified national strategy.
2. Unlike CBCO, ACORN's long-term political strategy includes a consistent alliance with labor.
3. Unlike CBCO, ACORN's long-term political strategy includes direct participation in electoral politics.
4. ACORN combines three functions that are not usually found in one organization. These are the mass base of a grassroots organization, the services of a mutual benefit association, and the national issue advocacy of a public interest organization.
5. ACORN experiments with multiple tactics. Consistent with its multiple functions, it combines many simultaneous tactics in a given campaign.

ACORN's unified national strategy, alliance with labor, electoral tactics, and multiple roles and functions are relatively long-term and consistent. The fifth feature, ACORN's proliferation of tactics, has intensified in recent national campaigns. This has helped ACORN leverage its limited resources by multiplying its points of pressure on the target.

I consider these five aspects of ACORN's organizational strategy in turn.

ACORN's Unified National Strategy

Like Alinsky, founder Wade Rathke saw the "fundamental issue" as "the distribution of power in this country."[1] ACORN sees itself as part of a long history of American populist movements for workers, farmers, and others. Its goal was to build a national "majority constituency" of low- to moderate-income people, and that required a national movement.

Consistently National Ambitions

Since 2000, both PICO and the Gamaliel Foundation have launched national organizing campaigns. ACORN launched national campaigns as early as the 1970s. Like the CBCOs, ACORN defines its strength as its base in local communities. However, for thirty years it has also tried to batter its way into electoral and legislative politics, experimenting with one method after another. By 1975, ACORN had expanded through Arkansas and had begun expanding throughout the South. In 1976 the *New York Times* described ACORN as the "most potent organization of have-nots since the Southern Tenant Farmers' Union."[2] Figures 10 and 11 illustrate the rapid growth since 2000 that helped enable ACORN to undertake successful national campaigns.

Year	Number of states	Number of cities
1970	1	1
1975	3	8
1980	24	35
1985	27	39
1990	27	40
1995	28	41
2000	29	46
2005	35	92

*Figure 10. Growth of ACORN: number of
state and city organizations, 1970–2005.*

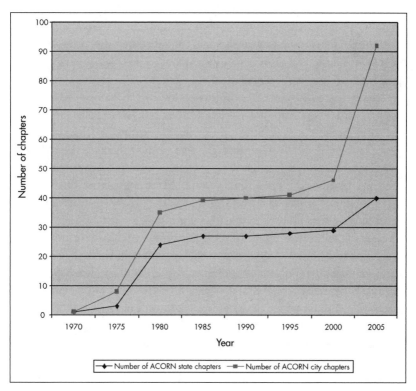

Figure 11. Growth of ACORN chapters, 1970–2005.

Under the constraints of a hostile national political environment, ACORN has developed two types of national campaigns. When no national venue is promising, it organizes a series of local campaigns that win incremental victories while helping build national momentum. When there is a promising national venue, ACORN runs a national campaign at multiple levels: its city locals, often its statewide organizations, and its national organization. Figure 12 summarizes these two types of campaigns. Both include coordinated local grassroots action in ACORN cities across the country. The difference is whether a national decision venue is open to grassroots challenges.

Incremental Groundswell: A Series of Local Campaigns

The series of local campaigns relies on fast replication to build momentum. The goal is not only to win a series of local victories but also to alter the public discourse and political climate for more ambitious campaigns. It is useful when there is little opportunity for national policy change. The classic example is the living wage movement, so-called because of its classically movement-like qualities: it began locally, succeeded, was replicated, and spread quickly across the country.

The living wage tactic was originated by the Baltimore congregation-based organization affiliated with the Industrial Areas Foundation, and replicated because it is well suited to a hostile national political environment.[3] It is important to note that it did not diffuse through the IAF—six decentralized regional organizations, each with its own powerful organizer-director—but through the unified centralized structure of ACORN.

Although the real wages of low-wage workers have declined since the 1970s, the political climate for a national minimum wage increase was hostile after the increase in 1996, from $4.25 to $5.15, far short of the poverty level for a family of four. However, public opinion polls showed consistently broad support for an increased minimum wage.[4] The living wage movement represents an incremental strategy that in itself affects only a small fraction of the working poor—those that work for private firms who hold contracts with, or receive subsidies from, local governments. Nevertheless, these campaigns often arouse strong opposition from local business. A common argument opponents make is that such a policy gives a city a competitive disadvantage. However, city contractors often supply services that are not mobile to other cities, and increasingly, other cities have a living wage policy anyway. Living wage ordinances only affect about 1 percent of a city's workers. The strategy to build coalitions and public support for higher wage standards, therefore, is primarily not economic but political.[5] Most campaigns

	Incremental groundswell— local campaigns	Simultaneous local-state-national campaign
Decision venue	Series of local or state venues, coordinated by ACORN national headquarters	Can be market-based or public: • If a corporate campaign, decision venue is corporate headquarters • If a political campaign, venues may be multiple and competing; may be played off against each other
When used	When national venue (e.g., Congress) offers little or no opportunity	When national venue offers most far-reaching result or when resolution of a local grievance requires a national corporation or branch of national government
Example	Living wage "movement"— series of ordinances passed by individual municipalities	Household Finance, one of United States' largest lenders of subprime loans
Strategy	Series of local victories creates momentum; goal is to change expectations and level of discourse. Helps create opportunity by winning incremental victories and creating broad coalitions to support more far-reaching local or national reforms, such as • Extensions of living wage ordinances to more employers • "Labor peace" provisions (business agrees to not interfere with union organizing campaigns) • State minimum wage increases	Local chapter tactics: • Identified loan victims • Documented predatory business practices • Protested at local Household Finance offices • Launched local media campaigns • Sought local legislation to curb loan practices State level tactics: • Legal: pushed state attorneys general to sue Household Finance • Legislative: sought local legislation to curb loan practices • Regulatory: pushed banking regulators to act National level tactics: • Legal: two class-action lawsuits • Pressure through allies: AFL-CIO, which had contracts with Household Finance to provide discounted loans to union members, lobbied Household Finance • Shareholders: resolution introduced at Household Finance shareholders meeting, which in 2001 received 30 percent support • Media campaign about loan practices directed at Wall Street analysts

Figure 12. Two types of national ACORN campaigns. •

feature broad religion-labor-community-based coalitions. The movement has helped reframe the public discourse about wages, bringing into focus the fact that the legal minimum wage is well below the poverty level. It has built a national movement in which 140 city and county living wage policies were enacted, and more by colleges, universities, and school boards.[6]

ACORN has led or helped lead only about 14 of the 140 successful local campaigns; helping lead the national living wage movement is nonetheless a national ACORN strategy. ACORN staffs a Living Wage Resource Center that provides technical assistance to living wage campaigns, has organized national conferences open to all to share strategies, monitors the growing number of ordinances, and has led local campaigns as part of a comprehensive effort to raise wages nationwide at whatever political venue seems most promising. Chapter 5 shows how ACORN began its search by launching a campaign through Missouri ACORN in 1996 to raise the Missouri state minimum wage. When it failed resoundingly but won overwhelming support in the city of St. Louis, the organization lowered its sights to the city level.

A series of local campaigns may even include some political work in Congress or with federal bureaucrats; for example, although a national minimum wage increase was unlikely, ACORN worked for years with Senator Ted Kennedy's office on national legislation during the George W. Bush administration. ACORN also formed an alliance with 2004 vice presidential candidate John Edwards to support state-level minimum wage increase campaigns in Ohio, Michigan, and Arizona. In June 2005 Edwards, ACORN President Maude Hurd, and others appeared together at rallies in the targeted states to build support for the campaign.

This incremental strategy resulted from the fact that the presidency and a Republican Congress were hostile to raising the federal minimum wage. But this strategy also helped expand opportunity by (1) framing the issue of wages as an issue of economic justice and (2) building broad coalitions that can exert pressure from below for state wage increases.[7]

Simultaneous Local-State-National Campaign

The local-state-national campaign operates in many venues at once, with the goal of building pressure at the highest level of decision venue: a corporation's national office, one or more national branches of government, or both. While the incremental groundswell campaign can be thought of as horizontal, this kind of campaign features a kind of vertical integration in which tactics aimed at all levels of the target are employed simultaneously. Some of the first attempts by contemporary community organizations used the Community Reinvestment Act (CRA) as a wedge to pry open major banks to demands for investment in inner-city communities. The 1990s saw a massive wave of bank mergers and acquisitions. Frequently these mergers made capital for urban communities even less accessible. However, the CRA made federal bank regulators' approval of these mergers conditional on investment in local communities. By filing challenges to banks who applied for merger and acquisition approval, ACORN could force banks to the bargaining table. These financial institutions typically prefer a settlement with ACORN to full-scale review by one of the four federal supervising agencies: the Federal Reserve, the Office of the Comptroller of the Currency (OCC), the FDIC, or the Office of Thrift Supervision.

ACORN filed its first CRA challenge in St. Louis in 1985. A 1991 ACORN campaign illustrates the process well. That year, North Carolina National Bank planned to merge with C&S/Sovran to create NationsBank. According to an ACORN report to the Annie E. Casey Foundation, the merger would have created the fourth largest financial institution in the country.[8] However, North Carolina National Bank had a record of taking local deposits but *not* making local loans, instead sending profits back to its headquarters in Charlotte, North Carolina. One risk of bank mergers is that small local banks with relatively good local lending records get swallowed up by larger entities that do not make capital locally available. ACORN saw this risk and also saw the potential of gaining access to what would become the largest bank in many southern cities where ACORN had a strong presence. ACORN conducted research and discovered that North Carolina National denied black and Latino loan applications far more than white loan applications, even controlling for income: "Middle income Black applicants were seven times as likely to have their loans denied as middle income white applicants." ACORN enlisted community allies and elected officials, including House Banking Committee chair Henry Gonzalez and Senate Banking Committee chair Donald Riegle, to call for public hearings by the Federal Reserve Board. At this point in a campaign, ACORN typically launches a spate of tactics to create publicity and pressure, in this case for the bank to submit a plan for community investment to the Federal Reserve as part of its merger agreement.[9] The Fed approved the merger but included an agreement between NationsBank and ACORN in which the bank funded ACORN Housing Corporation to recruit, screen, and counsel low-income and minority applicants for a new low-cost mortgage product. The interest was at 1 percent below market rate, which ACORN claims "alone was worth hundreds of millions of dollars to AHC borrowers."[10]

ACORN has made over forty-five such agreements with banks, as well as many other agreements with companies providing ancillary products such as home insurance and secondary mortgages. In 1992 the Federal National Mortgage Association (Fannie Mae) agreed to a $55 million pilot program to purchase mortgages from banks that had agreements with ACORN. The program adopted the kinds of terms that make mortgages possible for ACORN borrowers: down payments as low as $1,000 or 3 percent of the sale price, and the use of nontraditional proofs of credit-worthiness, such as rent or utility payment records.

Bank campaigns and other multilevel national campaigns employ a wide variety of tactics at all levels to meet their goal. A good example is ACORN's campaign against predatory lending by Household Finance. Predatory lenders offer subprime mortgages to borrowers who are poor credit risks, including low-income borrowers. They often have hidden costs and astronomical interest rates. ACORN claims one-third to one-half of these borrowers are actually eligible for "A" loans (the best class of loans).[11] ACORN organizer Lisa Donner and president Maude Hurd wrote:

> We learned over time that Household was regularly extending extremely high rate second mortgages to borrowers along with their first mortgages. Between the two loans, borrowers frequently owed Household more than their homes were worth, and were thus effectively trapped. In addition, the combination of the extremely high rates and the way they were amortized meant that borrowers were making virtually no progress in paying them down. Some borrowers were even seeing their balances increase over time, despite making their monthly payments.[12]

ACORN used a dizzying array of simultaneous local, state, and national tactics to build pressure on Household Finance. By May 2002, banking newsletter *Retail Banking International* reported:

> Household Finance, one of the leading US specialists in consumer credit, appears to be losing the battle to clear its name. Already under attack on several fronts for alleged predatory lending practices, it now faces a new and alarming adversary. Carl McCall, the man in charge of the finances of New York State, has called on Household to take drastic action to reform its business practices. McCall controls the state's retirement fund, which holds shares in Household worth over $100 million. His remarks, which include a clear threat to sell the shares if things do not improve, are likely to make ethical funds and other socially aware investors take notice. And if they start selling it will put further pressure on Household's share price.[13]

In the absence of national government support for reform efforts, individual corporate campaigns help build a broader constituency for regulatory reform at the state and national levels.

ACORN's 2004 education campaign attempted to unify and nationalize the organization's many local school campaigns through the vehicle of the No Child Left Behind Act (NCLB). ACORN, teachers, and other allies had mixed views of the NCLB, but united in a national campaign to fully fund it. The 2004 national campaign included ACORN, the National Mobilization for Great Public Schools, along with the National Education Association, MoveOn.org, Campaign for America's Future, the NAACP Voter Fund, and U.S. Hispanic Leadership Institute. In September 2004 the campaign held close to four thousand house parties whose goal was to make the issue of education an election priority.[14] ACORN locals in forty-eight cities held rallies and events to demand full funding for low-income schools. Figure 13 is a list of recent or current national ACORN campaigns of each type. These two kinds of national strategy are successful adaptations to formidably difficult conditions for redistributive movements. Having few elite allies and accelerating threats to working-people's interests challenged ACORN to search for venues where limited but significant gains were possible.

Senior organizers developed its national campaigns guided by a vision of national visibility and impact for ACORN. However, implementing this vision was made possible by an organizational structure significantly different from the CBCO networks.

Incremental groundswell— local campaigns	Simultaneous local-state-national campaign
Maintain charity or reduced-price care in hospitals—seeks individual agreements with hospitals as well as ordinances	Bank campaigns using the Community Reinvestment Act: ACORN has won agreements with over forty-five banks
Inclusionary zoning includes affordable housing provisions in new developments	Predatory lending: • Ameriquest • Citigroup, two campaigns • H&R Block • Jackson-Hewitt • Wells Fargo
	2004 Voter Mobilization Campaign
	2004 Education Campaign

Figure 13. Examples of ACORN national campaigns of each type.

ACORN's Structure: One Centralized National Organization

Unlike the CBCOs, ACORN is not a network or federation of affiliated but legally distinct organizations. It is one national organization with local and state chapters. This structure makes it far easier than for CBCOs to mobilize coordinated national campaigns. The national networks that conduct CBCO are organizationally and legally decentralized: they are networks of independent 501(c)(3) nonprofit organizations, each of which has its own board of directors that is accountable to that specific organization, such as PACT or MCU. (Churches and CBCOs are both classified by the Internal Revenue Service as 501(c)(3), able to receive tax-deductible donations.) PICO, the IAF, the Gamaliel Foundation, and DART are also separate 501(c)(3) organizations. Their local affiliates have the authority to choose their own campaigns. In practice, authority is shared among local leadership, local staff, and national network staff, and the balance of power among them varies.

The democratic decision-making process of local CBCOs means they are slower to coordinate as a group. They have more institutional layers than ACORN: while ACORN members are individuals and families, each legally independent CBCO is a federation of *other* nonprofit organizations— its member congregations. Each congregation has a local organizing committee that may agree or disagree with a given course of action. A CBCO's board of directors may resist coordination from the network it consults with. As an independent organization, its own identity may be stronger than its identification with the IAF, PICO, Gamaliel, or DART; indeed, it may have switched from one network to another over its history.

In contrast, ACORN's centralized direction allows it to quickly launch nationally coordinated campaigns. While the boards of directors of ACORN locals set local policy, crucially, the national head organizer (since 1970, Wade Rathke), not the elected local ACORN boards, has the ultimate authority to hire and fire *all* staff, including local organizers.[15] Therefore, organizers primarily report to the ACORN national office and only secondarily to the local board. In contrast, most local CBCOs, even if affiliated with a national network, can hire and fire their own staff. In ACORN, national decisions (except staffing) formally rest with the national board of directors, and local boards choose local issues and approve participation in national campaigns.

ACORN senior national staff wield enormous influence in choosing campaigns and strategies. The national executive director of ACORN is Steve Kest, and his brother Jon is the director of one of ACORN's most powerful city and state organizations, New York ACORN. One local organizer commented admiringly that at the annual all-staff retreat held in December, "the Kest brothers will just say, 'Now we're going to do this.'" He was not criticizing top-down control; ACORN has a strong collective identity as a democratically governed membership association, and elected local and national boards of directors formally approve all issue campaigns. Nor do the Kest brothers develop strategies in isolation; they are part of a corps of national staff who work closely together as well as with city and state organizing directors. Rather, he expressed organizers' admiration for these experienced strategists' creativity in developing local campaign strategies that can be replicated nationwide or national campaigns that draw simultaneously on local, state, and national tactics.

ACORN's Long-Term Alliance with Labor

An important aspect of ACORN's political strategy that distinguishes it from CBCOs is its consistent relationship with the labor movement. A classic maxim of CBCO organizing is "no permanent friends, no permanent enemies." CBCO inherited from the Industrial Areas Foundation a reluctance to work with existing groups and a pragmatic, situational view of allies. This is largely true of ACORN as well, with one major exception: while CBCOs have often collaborated with labor on a case-by-case basis, ACORN sees labor as a "permanent friend." ACORN sees long-term shared class interest with labor on wages, social welfare programs, and services to poor and working-class communities. ACORN executive director Steve Kest argues that ACORN and labor are natural allies because they share the same constituency; they are not just advocacy or policy organizations but membership organizations that can offer each other the ability to mobilize a mass base, and both seek long-term power for political and social change.[16] In the 1980s, ACORN itself organized low-wage fast-food and home health-care workers in what it called the United Labor Unions. These unions were ultimately turned over to the Service Employees International Union (SEIU). Two ACORN-founded unions, SEIU Locals 100 and 880, are still allied with ACORN and often share office space.

Labor is an essential ACORN ally for many campaigns, such as minimum-wage increases. In 2003, a coalition led by ACORN, SEIU Local 880, and the AFL-CIO won an Illinois state minimum-wage increase.[17] ACORN and labor also allied in successful campaigns in New York and Florida.

Sometimes this labor-ACORN alliance is formally institutionalized. For example, the San Jose ACORN and the South Bay AFL-CIO Labor Council signed a memorandum of understanding in 2003. The Central

Arkansas Labor Council established a formal partnership with ACORN that has conducted successful campaigns to curb lending abuses and raise taxes to fund Medicaid. The partnership also benefits by being able to jointly offer membership training, voter registration, and precinct worker development. These partnerships contribute to social movement unionism that uses lively grassroots tactics and addresses a more comprehensive program of workers' job, school, and neighborhood issues. They also provide ACORN with campaign activists and money to support the innovative ideas ACORN develops but cannot fully fund. For example, one victory snatched from the jaws of Democratic presidential defeat in 2004 set a precedent: the first time a minimum-wage increase was passed in a Southern state. Florida ACORN collected close to a million signatures to place its wage increase on the November 2 ballot, partly as a strategy to boost low-income voter turnout for the presidential vote. Florida ACORN director Brian Kettenring proposed the campaign, but his organization lacked the ability to fund it.[18] However, by enrolling labor unions (particularly the National Education Association) and the Florida Democratic Party, the Floridians for All Campaign received the funds and volunteers it needed. The measure passed by 72 to 28 percent and raised the minimum wage to $6.15, indexed annually to inflation. About 850,000 workers each gained $2,000 of additional annual full-time income in May 2005.

Because public opinion polls showed wide support for minimum wage increases, before the national minimum wage was increased in 2007, state ballot initiatives were effective in bypassing hostile state legislatures. In California, the legislature passed a wage increase from $6.75 an hour to $7.75, but the bill was halted by Governor Arnold Schwarzenegger's veto, his second rejection of a wage increase. Schwarzenneger then reversed his position and proposed a weaker measure in order to pre-empt a stronger ballot initiative.[19]

Like the labor movement, ACORN sees direct engagement in electoral politics as an inescapable route to achieve its goals.

Acorn's Long-Term Commitment to Electoral Politics

All community organizations that challenge authorities for policy changes address the political system, at least as pressure groups. With the implicit threat of electoral retaliation, they pressure their representatives for concessions and develop collaborative relationships with city, state, or national representatives. They provide data from their communities, testify at hearings, and influence and even draft legislation. However, organizations (including churches) that are classified as 501(c)(3) nonprofits are legally able to accept charitable donations only under certain conditions: they are permitted unlimited "educational" activities but only a specific amount of "lobbying" activity. They cannot make partisan endorsements or run candidates, but they can educate and organize on the basis of issues. There are other reasons CBCOs are officially nonpartisan: they often have a more politically and economically diverse membership than ACORN, and although they regularly take stands on issues, officially taking positions on candidates would be divisive. Furthermore, in Congress and state legislatures that are closely divided, organizations need the support of both Democratic and Republican politicians to pass legislation. The PICO Network's national New Voices Campaign has adopted a bipartisan national lobbying strategy for this reason. Some argue that the legal inability of 501(c)(3) organizations to openly campaign for political allies and deliver votes, as labor does, is a source of weakness for CBCOs.

In contrast, ACORN has no IRS status that limits its involvement in politics. It endorses and even runs candidates for office and has played a major role in founding a successful third party, the Working Families Party, in New York State and Connecticut. ACORN has sought to engage the political and electoral systems from the very earliest days of its existence. Quite early, in 1971, ACORN made its first venture beyond the traditional pressure group model into the formal political system. With a membership of only one thousand, ACORN registered as a special interest lobbyist for poor people. Perhaps it was a combination of hubris and naiveté that led ACORN to target the 1980 presidential election when it was only six years old. In 1976 founder Wade Rathke proposed a plan to expand ACORN from three to twenty states by 1980, run delegates in caucus states, and influence the national Democratic platform. The 20/80 Campaign sought to break down ACORN localism, build ideological coherence, and ultimately build a national social movement. By not endorsing a candidate, it lost potential allies such as labor, which ran into the arms of the Democratic Party after Reagan's 1980 victory and the decline of opportunity for progressive groups.[20] ACORN failed in its attempts to influence the Democrats but succeeded in expanding to twenty states. This grandiose ambition, combined with dogged determination and a willingness to learn from its mistakes, has been an asset for ACORN.

ACORN has continued to run and endorse candidates and place initiatives on the ballot and was a major force behind both the New Party and the Working Families Party. Both third parties relied on the strategy of fusion, which means that more than one party can nominate the same candidate. A third party can nominate its own candidate *or* use its ballot line to endorse the candidate of another party. Fusion enables minor parties to attract voters because they can support their candidates without "throwing away their vote." For example, New Yorkers could vote for Hillary Clinton for senator on either the Working Families line or the Democratic line. This allows third parties to expand their base of voters and achieve the vote totals required to retain a spot on the ballot, which ensures their ongoing ability to participate in electoral politics.[21] The third party strategy broadens ACORN's tactical options at the state and local levels.

Nevertheless, groups whose base of strength is grassroots and local, not financial and national, are better suited for tactics that rely on mobilizing the grassroots. In 2003, ACORN assumed management of Project Vote, a leading voter mobilization organization since 1982. From 1982 until the 2004 election, Project Vote claims to have registered and mobilized over three million new low-income and minority voters.[22] In preparation for 2004, using ACORN's network of neighborhood chapters, Project Vote mounted a massive voter mobilization campaign in fifty-one cities, located in fifteen of the seventeen presidential battleground states. It claims that over ten thousand workers and volunteers registered over 1.12 million new voters in low-income African American and Latino neighborhoods. They contacted a similar number of registered but new or infrequent voters during November and a total of 2.2 million voters on Election Day.[23] The CBCOs also registered and mobilized voters in 2004, but not at the same scale (see chapter 9).

ACORN's use of electoral tactics is part of a history of tactical experimentation. Another part of this history is a combination of roles and functions that are not usually found in the same organization.

ACORN's Unique Combination of Functions

ACORN has continuously experimented with new organizational forms. It has been a pressure group, a labor union, a voter registration organization, a series of local political action committees, a housing developer, a low-income financial services broker, a charter school founder, and a leadership training institute—among other functions. Its related organizations include ACORN Housing Corporation, which is a housing developer, loan broker, and counselor; the American Institute for Social Justice, its separate tax-deductible 501(c)(3) education and training arm; APAC, the ACORN political action committees that endorse and run candidates in local and state elections; and Project Vote. It uses multiple tactics, including protest, candidate endorsements, third parties, voter mobilization, litigation, and policy research. In New York City alone, ACORN Housing has helped develop about five hundred housing units, a local ACORN Schools Office helps plan community-controlled charter schools and directs education campaigns, a Community Jobs Hiring Hall has channeled low-income local residents to jobs, and a Workers Organizing Committee has organized workfare participants.

New ACORN-affiliated organizations often emerge from issue campaigns. For example, in 1979 ACORN began dramatic, well-publicized squatting campaigns in vacant houses in Philadelphia. In 1982 it set up a squatters' tent city behind the White House. This campaign led to the ACORN Housing Corporation, which operates in twenty-seven cities. ACORN has continued to experiment with multiple organizing vehicles: an ACORN Tenant Union for public housing tenants, first-source hiring agreements and living wage agreements, union organizing campaigns, voter registration initiatives, organizations of parents who have won charter schools in New York and St. Paul, and many more. Many experiments fail, but ACORN learns from both its failures and its successes.

Part of ACORN's motivation for experimenting with new functions and tactics is the imperative of identifying new sources of funds. To some extent, creative resource mobilization and tactical and organizational innovation have gone hand in hand.

Sources of Funding

ACORN's structure as a direct membership organization of poor people, rather than as a group of existing organizations such as churches, has direct consequences for available sources of funding. Yet its budget is over twice that of PICO—while PICO raised $18 million in 2006, ACORN's budget that year was a full $37.5 million, supposedly not including ACORN Housing, a startlingly large figure for a poor people's direct-action organization. According to the *New York Times,* only $3 million of this total, 8 percent, comes from membership dues. This section examines ACORN's ingenuity in mobilizing resources as an integral part of its issue campaigns. Using multiple sources of leverage to extract concessions from private corporations has partially made up for vanished federal funds.

Requiring membership dues provides some measure of self-sufficiency and a sense that the organization belongs to its members.[24] However, since recruiting dues-paying members from ACORN's low-income constituency is a significant challenge, ACORN must mobilize external resources as well. Its dues-paying membership gives ACORN legitimacy in the eyes of foundations that support poor people's political organizing, but foundation funds for confrontational organizations are extremely scarce.[25] This has motivated creative methods of fund-raising, such as campaigns that pressure banks and other lenders to provide below-market home loans to low-income borrowers. Because banks seek these new customers, they pay ACORN to screen and counsel loan applicants from ACORN neighborhoods. These campaigns fulfill multiple goals. First, they extract resources for poor and working-class people—over $4.6 billion in home loans from 1995 to 2004.[26] They also increase ACORN's visibility and value to constituents, use selective incentives to recruit new potential members, and fund the ACORN Housing Corporation. Some of the ACORN Housing budget supports ACORN's issue organizing. Corporate campaigns mobilize resources while also winning gains for low-income people, making new potential members aware of ACORN, and building support for investment in inner-city communities.

ACORN used a similar tactic in its earned income tax credit campaign but with a difference: instead of mounting an issue campaign to extract concessions from a corporation, it won a private foundation grant to help eligible low-wage workers apply for the tax credit. The earned income tax credit is now the largest remaining federal entitlement for income support and lifts more children out of poverty than any other government program.[27] In 2003, the Marguerite Casey Foundation awarded ACORN a two-year $1.5 million grant to recruit low-income families to apply for the credit in three pilot cities with large low-income populations. ACORN's unlikely partner was the Internal Revenue Service. ACORN was one of hundreds of community-based organizations that collaborated with the IRS's Community Partners Program, which aims to recruit the 10 to 20 percent of eligible families unaware of the tax credit. This program occupies what must surely be the narrow ground of shared interest between ACORN and the IRS. The Marguerite Casey Foundation funded ACORN's participation because, unlike service organizations, it could mobilize its extensive grassroots network of neighborhood chapters door-to-door. In 2003 this allowed ACORN to exceed its goal and direct $3.8 million in earned income and child tax credits to new applicants, reaching far more people than most volunteer groups.[28] The IRS found ACORN so effective that it expanded ACORN's participation from three cities in 2003 to forty-five in 2004 and eighty in 2005.[29]

This ACORN campaign exemplified synergy: it performed multiple functions, each of which reinforced the others. It mobilized resources for itself and won gains for constituents. It funded delivery of a service that was *both* a selective incentive for prospective members and a goal consistent with ACORN's ultimate mission: political and economic gains for lower-income Americans. Organizers conducted door-to-door education about the tax credit in multiple languages, for example, English, Spanish, and Haitian Creole in Miami. ACORN staff and members with handheld electronic devices could immediately determine a person's eligibility while on their doorstep. They staffed free tax preparation centers, which are a part of the IRS outreach program, and recruited more applicants through media coverage, signs, billboards, phone calls, and word of mouth. Free tax preparation saved applicants tax preparation fees as well as the high-interest refund anticipation loans (RALs) that commercial tax preparers offer. ACORN is fighting RALs as part of its campaign against predatory lending.

The role of external resources for ACORN raises questions about whether they might co-opt the organization. According to William Gamson's definition of co-optation—acceptance in the political system at the price of concrete gains—ACORN is not co-opted; it continues to launch campaigns and win concessions.[30] However, does dependence on agreements with banks and grants from foundations blunt its tactical militance? Funding to provide services may induce ACORN to turn more staff time to delivering services instead of campaigns to win collective benefits and political power, which often require contentious tactics.

The evidence suggests that ACORN has not succumbed to such pressure, if it exists. ACORN Housing has been active since 1985, and ACORN's use of disruptive protest is still a staple of its repertoire of contention.[31] ACORN has retained its autonomy, grown rapidly, and won major concessions. Several reasons may explain why ACORN has been able to accept resources from foundations and banks while continuing to build organizational capacity and win gains. First, funding from banks for ACORN Housing Corporation primarily supports a specific mission: service provision (loan counseling and community development) that serves the interests of *both* banks and ACORN. ACORN Housing is legally distinct from the rest of ACORN—it is an affiliated organization, and its service delivery function is thus set apart in a separate organization with its own budget. Some ACORN Housing chapters receive city funds for community development as well. Second, its diverse funding base, including membership dues, other internally raised funds, and foundation grants, insulates ACORN from vulnerability to any one external source (see the budget for St. Louis ACORN, chapter 4). Finally, sometimes the desire to use tactics in keeping with a group's identity can trump the goal of tactical effectiveness (see the Introduction).[32] ACORN's very identity, detailed in chapter 1, is based on organizational autonomy and an oppositional, challenging stance and ideology. The need to instill this identity in its members, as well as to pressure opponents, motivates ACORN to use nonviolent but disruptive tactics that force a confrontation.[33] Indeed, some argue ACORN may use such tactics even when less confrontational methods would produce the same results.[34] In any case, not tactical changes in themselves but the loss of autonomy, influence, and new gains should indicate co-optation. If anything, the opposite has occurred. ACORN is a pragmatic poor people's interest group with a strategy of incremental gain, not a radical outsider to the polity. While its leaders may have private visions of democratic socialism, the organization is populist and functions within American capitalist democracy. To redistribute resources, one of its tactics has been to find, and sometimes help *create,* areas of mutual interest for itself and powerful establishment members such as banks and the Internal Revenue Service. It helped develop a new market of lower-income and immigrant first-time homebuyers that created a new source of profits for banks while also creating assets for predominantly African American and Hispanic citizens. Blacks in particular suffer a historic disparity in wealth relative to whites. Increasing their access to capital helps break the cycle of racial inequality.

ACORN's Tactical Experimentation

ACORN has always tried to identify new tactics and sources of leverage, but as it has expanded its national organizing, its use of multiple tactics has intensified. A good example is its successful campaign against predatory lending by Household Finance. The campaign had multiple goals: directly help prevent lending abuses; build the organization and an organizing campaign; put the issue on local, state, and national agendas; and ultimately win regulatory reform. Methods ran the gamut from classic outsider tactics (pickets, protests, the visit of two thousand ACORN members to confront Household executives at their homes) to a full array of insider tactics including shareholder resolutions, studies, media campaigns, legislation, lawsuits, and lobbying.

While movements typically include diverse organizations using varied tactics, it is less common for one organization to do so. Using numerous tactics builds a synergistic effect, creating many more pathways of pressure and allowing tactics to reinforce each other. To take one case, all Household campaign activities helped generate publicity, which built pressure in multiple ways. For example, publicizing Household's abuses helped ACORN identify more borrowers who were victim to predatory loans, which helped document abuses, which helped make the legal and political case for reform—and it also provided another vehicle to recruit new ACORN members, which built the campaign's mass base, built pressure on government officials and corporations for reform, and provided more data and individuals for reporters to interview for more news stories. Yet another effect of news stories is to reframe what many borrowers experience—from shameful personal failure to collective, political injustice. This builds solidarity and participation and recruits activists for other battles.

Part of ACORN's use of new tactics includes an openness to new coalition partners. As it has dramatically increased its number of new organizations in the 1970s and 1980s and especially since 2000, ACORN became more creative in forging coalitions. For example, in its 2004 education campaign, a national campaign to fully fund No Child Left Behind, ACORN went beyond its usual alliance with the teachers' unions. In campaigns against racial and ethnic disparities in lending, ACORN enlisted community allies and elected officials including House Banking Committee chair Henry Gonzalez and Senate Banking Committee chair Donald Riegle.

Like many community organizations, ACORN has a long history of organizational chauvinism, justified by the need for self-preservation. This allowed ACORN to justify competition with other organizing groups when an organizational fight may not have been in the best interest of constituents. Rathke and other top leaders saw coalitions as "not a path for power for ACORN" unless they were ACORN-led and developed.[35] In its early history, building a grassroots people's movement was synonymous with building ACORN, even if it alienated potential allies. However, ACORN began to realize that to win major national campaigns it would have to recruit more allies. As ACORN builds capacity through alliances, it sees its interest as disseminating skills and tactics, such as supporting the spread of living wage ordinances with its Living Wage Resource Center, which supports activists both in and outside ACORN.

This chapter has analyzed ACORN's organizational and political strategy based on its organizational form, national focus, and tactical innovation. As ideal types, ACORN and the CBCO campaigns have different strengths and innovations. Yet despite their differences, the CBCOs and ACORN share many important features. All share the advantages of vertical linkage between the local and national organizations. While not all the national organizations have a fully national presence, they strive for one. They have made strategic decisions to directly engage the electoral system (ACORN) or to remain outside it but use their numbers to influence it (CBCOs). All espouse the goal of empowering ordinary American citizens, including the most disenfranchised, to exercise power in public life. All select broadly unifying issues such as wages, public safety, housing, schools, and the like. They avoid issues that could create cleavages of race and gender, such as day care, equal wages for women, and reproductive rights. However, they differ in a number of ways. While none of the four organizations in this study has an abundance of resources, some are more secure than others. Furthermore, the amount of staff time devoted to fund-raising varies significantly between ACORN and the church-based organizations.

Chapters 2 and 3 have examined what makes CBCO and ACORN unique and distinct. However, local examples of both types are inflected through different urban contexts. Urban economic capacity and political institutions influence the resources available from community foundations, churches, and individuals; the degree of poverty and the nature and type of grievances; the availability of allies, both grassroots and official; and the institutional openness and capacity to respond to citizen challenges. Internal organizational factors, such as availability of skilled organizers and a recent history of successes or failures, also leave their mark on an organization. Chapter 4 analyzes how internal and external factors influenced the organizing of St. Louis ACORN.

4

Organizing Is a Numbers Game: St. Louis ACORN

I spent most of my life hating white people with a passion! But I sat back and looked around . . . and I realized that it doesn't matter if you're black or white; if you're poor in America, your ass is in a sling. I watched black and white people work together very sincerely. I never thought I'd see this in this country.

—ACORN organizer, St. Louis

On a January day in 1998, several people gathered surreptitiously in the cavernous rotunda of St. Louis City Hall. They waited for other carloads of people to arrive. One young woman asked an organizer, "We gonna get locked up?" Jackson,[1] the ACORN organizer, said firmly, "No! We're taxpayers; we have a right to visit the mayor." When the others arrived, the sixteen young black city residents and the three organizers, Tony, Bill, and Jackson, took the two elevators to the second floor. In the elevator, Jackson asked Bill, "What are we going to chant?" Bill thought a moment and said, "What do we want? Jobs! When do we want them? Now!" Jackson said, "I think we need a spokesperson."

On the second floor, Tony gathered everyone together and quietly briefed them on the living wage issue and ACORN's demands. ACORN wanted the city to require the developer of a new hotel to pay a living wage for its permanent jobs: $7.70 an hour.[2] Mayor Clarence Harmon had previously canceled two meetings with ACORN, but after ACORN organizers confronted Harmon at a neighborhood meeting, he said he would meet with ACORN. He had not yet done so, and this protest outside the office aimed to force the mayor to meet.

When an organizer opened the door to the mayor's office, a security guard barred the group from entering.[3] Some protesters quietly slipped off, afraid they would get in trouble. Bill started leading the group in the call-and-response chant, "What do we want?" "Living wage!" "When do we want it?" "Now!" and "The people—united—will never be defeated." While one organizer was invited in to meet with the mayor's secretary, the group chanted loudly to keep the pressure on. The protestors were orderly, but the noise just outside the office was disruptive enough to prevent office staff from answering telephones.

While waiting, the other two organizers rounded up the group to discuss strategy. Tony prompted, "What is our demand?" and one woman said, "A meeting with Mayor Harmon!" Tony asked, "How soon do we want to have it?" Silence. "Maybe in the next two weeks?" he prompted, and people agreed. "They're going to say the mayor's a very busy man, he doesn't have time to meet with you. Do we want to meet with anyone else?" The group looked dubious. "OK, so it has to be with Harmon," Tony confirmed. He warned them, "They're going to be very nice and say things like, 'Don't I know your cousin?'"

The mayor's press secretary, a slim, polished African American woman of about forty, emerged friendly and smiling. She explained cordially that the mayor was at a meeting with his cabinet, but she could write down the group's concerns and take them back to him. A few protestors promptly responded, "A living wage." When asked about other concerns, someone mentioned abandoned buildings. A highly charged discussion followed, with organizers and members making angry accusations. Bill charged that Harmon had walked around with a "bunch of white yuppies" to promote downtown revitalization, and Tony repeated, "We just need a half hour of his time for a productive meeting."[4] He noted (accurately), "We weren't making any noise until they refused to let us in his office." The *St. Louis Post-Dispatch* reporter assigned to the City Hall beat jotted notes furiously. While Tony politely repeated, "There's no way you can contact the mayor?" Bill charged, "The mayor came down to meet with us when he was campaigning, but not now! He can take a long walk with those white yuppies, but he's turned his back on north St. Louis! What about all those bodies turning up in abandoned buildings! And he can't get his ass down to north city—sorry."

Finally the press secretary offered the group a meeting with Mike Jones, the mayor's chief of staff. Tony said the group would consider it and told the protesters, "Let's caucus." He gathered them together and told the group encouragingly, "We got a meeting! You should give yourselves a hand." The protestors looked uncertain. Tony then set up the meeting with the mayor's staff, and the group retreated. After leaving, he invited all present to the meeting with Mike Jones the next week, and all but one said yes.

As the group retreated, Jackson, buoyed by the agreement to meet, said excitedly, "We got everyone to come down, and we got a win! We got a meeting! See, you just have to have bodies, you have to have numbers."

The next week, the group that met with Mike Jones, the mayor's chief of staff, included Tony and another ACORN organizer, two job seekers who had signed up with the ACORN Hiring Hall, and a representative from the hotel and restaurant workers' union (HERE) allied with ACORN. Jones agreed that $5.15 was not a livable wage, but argued that with only one bidder for a convention center hotel and an economically vulnerable downtown, the city was in a poor bargaining position. He argued that a larger issue was that while entry-level workers lived in north St. Louis, the entry level jobs were in the suburbs. The transit system that workers needed to get to jobs was inadequate because the county reneged on its commitment to contribute $40 million to it. Jones, intransigent, argued the point with Tony until the union representative offered a compromise: support three of their demands, and ACORN and HERE would approach someone else, a sympathetic alderman, to introduce a living wage ordinance in the Board of Aldermen (city council). The debate continued, Jones arguing that for low-wage and workfare workers critical issues such as transportation and child care were not city but county services. The meeting ended with an impasse.

These two related episodes of collective action illustrate many features of ACORN as it operates in St. Louis. They illustrate the types of issues it seeks to advance, its direct action tactics and what these tactics can and cannot accomplish, its norms for working with members, norms for interacting with authorities, the kind of allies it has, and the influence of a context in which the city is a weak partner of its sprawling suburbs.

ACORN's local living wage campaign was part of a comprehensive national ACORN initiative. Tactically, it began by simply requesting a meeting but did not hesitate to engage in disruptive protest. Even small protests can pressure an authority to meet, but without the perception of organizational power, they cannot win much. (ACORN is increasingly holding larger local actions by busing in participants from several cities for mobilizations of four hundred or more; the largest locals can easily exceed that.)

As the episodes illustrated, ACORN often trains new recruits on the fly, in the thick of action.

What this episode does not directly illustrate is less visible at the local level: that each city chapter is affiliated with a centrally coordinated campaign by ACORN's national office, and together, local campaigns add up to more than the sum of their parts. While its campaign was trial-and-error and full of detours, St. Louis eventually won a living wage ordinance through the Board of Aldermen in July 2002. It was one of fourteen successful city living wage campaigns in which ACORN played a part.[5]

This chapter examines St. Louis ACORN's structure and operations, campaigns and results, and impact and potential. The casual observer of the protest and meeting that open this chapter might conclude that St. Louis ACORN is an annoying but inconsequential gadfly in St. Louis city politics. Why bother to consider it? There are several reasons.

First, ACORN's ideas about grassroots empowerment, its tactics of surprising opponents with unexpected disruption, and its methods of organizing exemplify many aspects of Alinsky-style organizing of poor and working-class Americans. The 1997–98 period was a low point in the organization's twenty-year history when, exhausted after several major failed campaigns, it was riddled with problems and conflicts. In 1996, national ACORN attempted its first statewide minimum wage increase in Missouri, and it failed. The next year, the organization's bid to keep the city's last charity hospital open also failed. But four years later, it went on to finally win an ordinance requiring that businesses with city contracts, including retailers at the airport, pay at least $9.79 an hour with health benefits or $12.15 without (in 2004), the amount sufficient to lift a family of three above the food-stamp-eligibility level. Although the organization and this campaign were flawed, it finally won, and it contributed to strategic learning for future campaigns.

Second, ACORN is one of the few *national* organizations that mobilize poor Americans to advocate for their own interests. St. Louis exemplifies the dynamic of white suburban flight and black inner-city poverty in a region with low economic growth. The city poverty rate is 24.6 percent. More than 97 percent of families on federal TANF assistance are female headed, 86.5 percent are black, and more than a third have received assistance for over five years. A young black male in St. Louis has a 70 percent chance of involvement in the criminal justice system.[6] ACORN is one of the few organizations that represents these low-income citizens' concerns locally and nationally.

Third, St. Louis ACORN and ACORN as a whole have impressive

achievements to their credit. St. Louis ACORN alone has made agreements with banks totaling $200 million for community investment.[7] Nationally, ACORN has negotiated landmark agreements with banks all over the country, making over a billion dollars available for loans in low-income neighborhoods. It helped preserve the federal Community Reinvestment Act that made these agreements possible.[8] Chapter 3 shows that ACORN's method of combining seasoned national strategists and local grassroots organizing brings some of the advantages of national expert-led interest groups to traditional community organizing. ACORN consistently tries out new tactics and collaborations between community organizations. It is also notable for bringing together a largely minority constituency on the basis not of race but of class. Finally, ACORN has a history of continuous, ongoing activism since 1970. As other grassroots organizations faltered and collapsed during the retrenchment of the 1970s and 1980s, ACORN persisted, survived, and grew.

St. Louis ACORN's Structure and Operations

The St. Louis chapter was founded early in ACORN's history, in 1976. (For brevity, I will refer to the St. Louis chapter as SL ACORN.) Twenty years later, SL ACORN and its affiliates, SEIU Local 880 and ACORN Housing Corporation, occupied three floors in a dilapidated brick building in a run-down St. Louis neighborhood. Rooms were crowded with file cabinets and desks covered with stacks of papers and telephones. The walls featured posters and bumper stickers for the Justice for Janitors union campaign and Amnesty International and others reading "Bankrupt the CIA, Boycott Cocaine!" and "Kick Right Wing Butt, Work for the New Party." Local ACORN campaigns were represented with posters reading "Bosley Mayor, '97" and "Why does Mommy need two jobs? Reward hard work, responsibility, and family. Raise Missouri's minimum wage! Vote $6.25 on November 5th! Proposition A." Monthly computer printouts listed national ACORN statistics: under "Individual Organizer Performance," a memo recorded the name, city, and amount of dues raised by each of ACORN's then fifty-eight field organizers nationwide.[9]

SL ACORN includes a number of related entities. First, it is a citywide community membership organization that undertakes neighborhood, city, and statewide issue campaigns. Each ward chapter has locally elected officers and tries to hold monthly meetings. It has a citywide board that meets monthly, drawn from officers of the ward organizations. It also includes an office of the national ACORN Housing Corporation, which secures agreements with banks to provide low-interest loans to home buyers, and recruits, screens, and counsels first-time buyers. SEIU Local 880, which organizes home health-care workers, shares ACORN's office space. Finally, SL ACORN includes the ACORN political action committee, which endorses candidates for state and local office and provides campaign support. The director is constantly in contact with ACORN's national research and policy staff.

Constituency

Nationally, ACORN's membership is primarily poor and working-class, African American and Latino. SL ACORN's membership is largely poor and virtually all black, with many active members on public assistance. ACORN members' north St. Louis neighborhoods are seriously distressed. The median family income for this area was only $18,336, and the percentage of residents under the poverty level was 35 percent.[10] However, some of these neighborhoods have long histories and proud identities as well-kept working- and middle-class neighborhoods. Some skilled tradespeople and professionals have lived there for decades. SL ACORN draws some long-term, stable members from among this group, including a retired truck driver, a disabled former meat cutter and lay minister, retail and office workers, a social worker, and an attorney.[11] The organization claimed eight thousand members, but this number included former members whose dues had lapsed (see "Resources," following).[12]

Resources

Little is known about how social movement organizations, especially poor people's organizations like ACORN, survive through downturns in national movement mobilization. A detailed look at SL ACORN's funding sources provides a valuable glimpse of how such groups, and ACORN as a whole, mobilize resources. (Little information was available on San Jose ACORN's funding.) It illustrates both ACORN's resourcefulness and the severe constraints a poor people's organization faces—especially considering that the St. Louis chapter is one of the better-funded ACORN organizations, "self-supporting," as local organizers pointed out proudly. Many other ACORN chapters are subsidized by the national office.

ACORN supports itself largely through grassroots fund-raising, including membership dues. In the standard ACORN model, organizers recruit members by going door to door, or door knocking, from 3:00 to 7:00 p.m. The method requires a constant flow of new "customers," just fifteen minutes talking to one person before moving on to the next. Locals like SL ACORN, which include branches of the ACORN Housing Corporation or Hiring Hall,

Table 2. Income and expense figures for St. Louis ACORN, based on a sample of five months in 1997–98

Total for office	Monthly	Annual estimate
Average income	$19,707	$236,484
Average expenses	$18,987	$227,844

boost their income through "selective incentives," or individual benefits—they recruit members from those who apply for low-cost home loans or job refer-rals. This helped SL ACORN overcome the fact that, during this time period, its organizers did far less door knocking than the model requires. Still, they almost never reached the dues collection goals that they set each week.[13]

Resources are scarce for SL ACORN, mostly due to their limited sup-ply but also partially because organizers during the observation period did less dues solicitation than necessary. While many ACORN locals compete effectively for the very limited foundation monies dedicated to commu-nity organizing, grants provide only a small part of the income. During 1997–98, ACORN had at least three foundation grants, but they made up only 16 percent of a typical monthly budget. SL ACORN raised 80 percent of its funds from grassroots fund-raising (see Table 2 and Figure 14).[14] Dues were $60 per family per year (as of 2005, $120). The organizers' goal is to raise their own salaries in dues collection.

Dues income probably ranges from one-quarter to one-third of total monthly income. Ideally members pay dues by automatic monthly bank withdrawals, which provide regular, reliable income. However, many ACORN members are too poor to have bank accounts and often pay their organizer

Membership dues	36%
Fund-raisers	21%
Church-related foundation grants (Catholic and Unitarian)	16%
Other	12%
Door-to-door canvass	12%
Street collections	3%
Total	100%

Figure 14. Average sources of income for St. Louis ACORN during 1997–98.

one month at a time—a laborious way to collect dues. In the door-to-door canvass, canvassers from ACORN neighborhoods solicit contributions in affluent suburbs, using favorable news coverage of ACORN protests.[15] During street collections, or "tags," youngsters collect donations with canisters at intersections where they approach stopped cars. But together, the canvass and tags produced only about 10 to 15 percent of the budget. Other grassroots fund-raising provided about 20 percent of ACORN income, and each organizer had a $300 monthly quota from such fund-raisers.[16] SL ACORN had little cushion for months that had shortfalls, which was extremely stressful for staff. The director was ultimately responsible, but all organizers helped raise the money needed.[17]

Authority and Control

A constant theme in ACORN ideology is that members, not paid staff, should lead the organization in selecting issues. However, ACORN is also a highly centralized national organization. Despite the dogma that the members and not staff should lead, authority is fluid and dynamic, influenced by local factors such as organizers' commitment to membership empowerment versus expediency and the capacity of local members. Unlike San Jose ACORN, SL ACORN had weak grassroots leadership during the low period of 1997–98. When it came to selecting issues, organizers followed members' lead in selecting local neighborhood issues such as abandoned houses, dishonest local merchants, or junk-strewn alleys. On city and state issues, the director and national ACORN priorities had more influence.[18] The St. Louis director consulted closely with national staff members in making decisions, including hiring and firing staff.[19] The expertise of ACORN's national staff members was invaluable in providing research on such matters as banks' patterns of lending discrimination and federal workfare regulations, which helped the director evaluate local bureaucrats' claims.

Those who champion pure participatory democracy or procedural formality might have been dismayed by SL ACORN. However, its grassroots participation was authentic and allowed for genuine power struggles. The St. Louis city board, composed of the presidents of the ward organizations, generally approved the director's proposals for issue campaigns. These decisions were formalities; during this observation period, there was no secretary at board meetings and minutes were not regularly taken. Contradicting ACORN's bylaws, there was no active finance committee to oversee the budget, and the staff did not create one. This allowed the director to take more control over such matters as finances until he was challenged by a strong new leader. This newly elected president with experience in unions and other voluntary associations learned that this contradicted ACORN bylaws when he met ACORN leaders from around the country at a national leadership training. In summer 1998 he formed a finance committee that challenged the director for the authority to approve monthly budgets.

SL ACORN's Community Jobs Hiring Hall and living wage campaign were part of national ACORN initiatives and took advantage of national research and strategy ideas. National strategy sometimes conflicted with local members' priorities; for example, ACORN pursued a living wage campaign even though several organizers insisted that members were more interested in halting neighborhood decline (abandoned buildings, street crime, inadequate city services) than gaining a living wage agreement with the city.[20] City officials and labor leaders saw downtown St. Louis as unlike booming cities such as Boston and Minneapolis, too economically vulnerable to impose conditions on new development.[21] Nevertheless, the director, with the local board's approval, launched a living wage campaign, which took seven years to win. Tradeoffs between national and local priorities are inevitable.

Organizers maintain a delicate balance between thrusting leaders forward and taking over when necessary. Especially in local ward campaigns, organizers often pushed leaders to speak to media, contact authorities, chair meetings, and the like. SL ACORN actions could be spontaneous and chaotic, especially when leaders became unpredictable.[22] To avert surprises in actions with new recruits, such as the living wage protest at the mayor's office, members participated while staff generally made the decisions. In campaigns with more experienced leaders, the director and leaders worked cooperatively as a team. In a meeting with a bank to negotiate a lending agreement, local leaders had years of experience with ACORN's bank agreements and participated fully in the negotiations.

Recruiting and Retaining Staff

Because ACORN offers low pay for very hard work, it has extremely high staff turnover.[23] The director (head organizer) was there for eight years, but field organizers usually come and go more quickly.[24] From September 1997 to March 1998, staff included the director and three organizers; at least six others began and quit during that time. Of the four organizers (all male), two were white and two were black. The director supervised them and directed city and statewide campaigns. Two staffers organized neighborhood groups and the third directed the Hiring Hall in the office. Wages are low, but have greatly improved; in the past, ACORN often came under fire for not paying its *own* organizers a living wage. In 1997, they began at $1,000 per month, or $14,000 the first year for those who stayed. By January 2005, entry-level ACORN organizers made $23,285.[25]

In response to criticism, ACORN argued in the past that its jobs are movement jobs that require sacrifice. Although this message may be palatable to the white organizers from affluent backgrounds that were its former mainstay, people of color were drawn to jobs with clear boundaries and set hours. The director said, "Five years ago ACORN was mostly young white college kids wanting to do good in America. Partly we got fed up with seeing someone stay for six months and then leave." While ACORN's staff was 90 percent white in the 1970s and 1980s, since 1980 ACORN made a concerted effort to recruit staff of color—63 percent of the staff as of 2003.[26] St. Louis still grappled with high turnover, but the office adapted by generating a high volume of organizer-trainees for a low yield of lasting organizers.

Recruiting and Mobilizing Members

St. Louis ACORN carried out four six-week ward-organizing drives in 1997. In theory, field organizers raise dues primarily from door knocking in their wards from 3:00 to 7:00 p.m. St. Louis organizers did less of this grueling work because they could partially compensate using the incentives of low-cost home loans or job referrals, advertised in flyers aimed at people in targeted neighborhoods.[27] A typical "rap" (sales pitch) to recruit participants to actions was: "Do you have a job? Do you want one? The city has $9 million [of federal workfare funds], and we want to make sure they do with it what they say they will." The pitch initially advertised an individual incentive (a job) but then reframed it as a call for collective action. This method brought many new people into contact with ACORN, but distributing hundreds of flyers to recruit thirty people was a scattershot method: as one organizer noted, people interested in housing and jobs "are not necessarily interested in [political] actions." In one ingenious maneuver, registration forms for job referrals were required to be turned in at protest actions, which produced higher than usual turnouts for the actions during this observation period. In the vignette that began this chapter, most of those protesting at the mayor's office had never been to an ACORN action. They were recruited by a flyer reading "Need a Job?" urging them to contact ACORN's Community Jobs Hiring Hall. When they called, they were scheduled for an intake meeting timed to directly precede the protest at the mayor's office. The "intake," a term familiar to social services clients, was a meeting that introduced them to ACORN, the issue of the new convention center hotel, and ACORN's rationale for a living wage of $7.70 an hour.

When Jackson, the organizer, asked the group of twenty whether anyone earned that wage, no one raised a hand; when asked if they supported a living wage, all did. Jackson said, "If you want a job right away, go on down to McDonald's or Burger King. If you want a *real* job, become part of the fight." This move ingeniously attempted to convert individuals seeking services into activists fighting for issues.

More experienced local ACORN activists were deeply involved in campaigns with Mercantile Bank and St. Louis University Hospital and in neighborhood issues. Most job seekers and welfare recipients have more pressing priorities than becoming activists, so it was harder to recruit them. Actions usually attracted either a small number of long-time regulars or a larger number of one-time participants. Selective incentives did not produce the solidarity necessary for ongoing participation.

Weekly staff meetings began with the organizers' reports to the director on dues collection and other fund-raising, followed by goal setting for the coming week. Fund-raising totals fell far short of their goals—sometimes by one-fourth to one-half.[28] Discussions of how to improve dues collections, raffle ticket sales, or member participation focused on technical matters, in particular how to design a rap that would work.[29] SL ACORN understood organizing as a numbers game: "to turn out 400 you have to get 1500 yeses." The director described ACORN's model of mobilization as "organizer-centric": "If you [the organizer] want 50, you get 150 yeses, and figure out how many you need to get per day."

The view of organizing as a short-term, high-volume numbers game rather than as a long-term process of building social networks may be adaptive for staff with high turnover and a very low-income constituency without many ties to neighborhood institutions. (San Jose ACORN's better-off members provided more stable leadership and social networks.) However, SL ACORN norms also contributed to its unstable leadership networks. When one successful organizer left ACORN, he did not inform a new ward chapter he had organized, and this active, optimistic group of stable and committed leaders became demoralized and inactive. When another organizer left, no one informed the chapter he organized; neighbors only found out he had left when they called the office asking how to pay their monthly dues. Poor communication sometimes produced inefficiency and confusion, such as the time that two unrelated actions were accidentally planned for the same day, competing for media attention and member participation. Poorly organized fund-raisers frustrated members. Meetings often did not start on time; one long-time member said she was used to waiting with ACORN. Meetings that start late can discourage stable members with jobs and commitments from participating. These practices tended to favor those with free time who were retired or on fixed incomes, who were professional meeting goers rather than effective leaders.

Racial and Religious Identities in SL ACORN

In 1986, sociologist and former ACORN organizer Arlene Stein observed that ACORN attempted to transcend its constituents' racial, gender, religious, and other identities to form an inclusive populist organization.[30] She saw this as a legacy of Saul Alinsky's reaction against 1960s movements and criticized ACORN for lacking a well-developed collective identity that could motivate long-term commitment. ACORN still fits her 1986 description of an inclusive populist organization not based on identity politics. However, the organization's collective identity draws informally but significantly on members' racial, class, and to a lesser extent religious identities. SL ACORN's African American homogeneity allowed black ACORN organizers to draw on members' shared legacy of black civil rights struggle and the black church.

The black organizers saw ACORN as simultaneously a poor people's organization and a black people's organization—an organization for all poor and working people, who in St. Louis happen to be largely black. These comments by one organizer are typical:

> The older people are my biggest concern. . . . I've gone in homes and they've shown me the bullet holes. Some people have had to move out who didn't even want to. This is our [African Americans'] political base, the city is. If we continue to move out, if blacks move from north city to south city, and from south to the county, we won't have a base—poor people in general.

> ACORN is colorblind—if we get behind someone it's because of their commitment to poor folk.

This was borne out in practice. ACORN endorsed Freeman Bosley Jr., who became St. Louis's first black mayor in 1993. However, Bosley lost ACORN's support over two issues: his lack of support for keeping the public Regional Hospital open (it closed in 1997), and his support for a golf course and gated community that might have displaced black neighborhood residents. One black organizer commented, "It was personally very painful to see Freeman Bosley go down. Some [blacks] viewed us as traitors." ACORN's refusal to endorse Bosley for a second term was politically uncomfortable, but it was consistent with its positions on issues that affected its membership. This colorblindness gave one organizer, Bill, a sense of hope:

When you can organize in ACORN and tear down an abandoned building so an old lady can sleep at night . . . you have some power. I watched
black and white people work together on this Regional [hospital closing]
thing very sincerely. I never thought I'd see this in this country.

However, black ACORN organizers and members viewed the white director with suspicion, and the organizers became cynical about the number of
whites in top positions in national ACORN. A staff conflict caused relations with the white director to deteriorate. Trust declined, and a racially
polarized view of the organization grew.[31] This hurt morale and may have
affected productivity in recruiting members and raising funds. Yet despite
this conflict, two staff members, one white and one black, were united by a
powerful shared lifetime commitment to ACORN. Bill, a black organizer,
described the conflicts but explained, "I love Rich" because of Rich's commitment to ACORN and social justice. (Bill was a minister and his statement must be understood in a Christian context.) Both had a passionate
commitment to ACORN, and both have advanced in ACORN's national
staff and remain dedicated organizers. ACORN's powerful identity as the
vehicle for social justice can generate a solidarity that helps organizers survive both internal and external challenges.

Bill's church involvement and identity was common among African
American members and staff of SL ACORN—part of their private identities, which were publicly yet unofficially expressed in ACORN. In 1998,
the lead organizer and board president were both African American ministers. The organizer considered his work "spiritual," explaining, "I believe
Scripture tells us to remember the poor. ACORN has adopted that belief."[32]
He capitalized on his clerical status at media events, and usually appeared
at actions in a clerical collar, noting, "The media doesn't care whether you're
from this church or that church, as long as it's a black preacher." He went
on to explicitly organize black preachers, and personally knew seven in
the twenty-sixth ward alone. Some actions took a religious form, such as
a prayer vigil commemorating the murder of a woman in an abandoned
building. But while the church informed *individuals'* motivations, language,
and tactics, it did not inform the *organization's* official culture.

St. Louis ACORN Issues and Campaigns

In the mid-1990s, SL ACORN undertook major campaigns that it lost,
and the struggles depleted its energy for several years. In its statewide campaign to raise the minimum wage, polling data showed that Missouri voters
would not support a proposed hourly wage increase from $4.25 to $6.25,
with annual increases. The campaign had few powerful allies—organized

labor declined to get involved, and the opposition vastly outspent ACORN. Subsequent campaigns to maintain the last remaining public hospital in the city and an attempt to prevent the sale of St. Louis University Hospital to a for-profit operator were no match for the market conditions facing American health care.

Some would argue that the organization chose issues that it could not possibly win given its existing resources. Others would counter that selecting safe issues is inherently conservative and ducks the most fundamental issues. While the manifest goal was to win, SL ACORN also needed to raise its profile with its target constituency, gain members, raise funds, and thereby build the organization.[33] If it failed to advocate on the issues of greatest concern to north St. Louis residents, it risked damaging its reputation with its base. Conversely, undertaking too many campaigns it could not win would alienate potential allies and ultimately disempower its members. Staff members in the late nineties knew that the organization needed a win.

However flawed a local campaign is, as part of a national organization local campaigns provide lessons for other ACORN chapters. ACORN learned from the 1996 Missouri Campaign to Reward Work (the proposed statewide minimum wage increase) that a better strategy was to shift venues from the state to the city level in living wage campaigns that applied to a limited group of employers. SL ACORN won its much-needed victory in 2002. Once the living wage movement won scores of local ordinances, it built the grassroots support necessary to win subsequent state minimum wage increases in Illinois, Massachusetts, New York, and Florida.

Earlier in 1994, one St. Louis neighborhood chapter prevented a medical waste incinerator from being built in a residential neighborhood. Another success was the Second Ward chapter's anticrime rally and demands to its alderwoman to help residents prevent crime, install signs, and the like. In 1998, ACORN succeeded in obtaining a jobs-referral agreement from a new drugstore in north St. Louis.

The office experienced more steady achievements in the area of low-cost mortgages. SL ACORN negotiated agreements with Boatmen's, Landmark, First Bank, First Nationwide, Allegiant, Roosevelt, Magna, Nationsbank, Firststar, and other banks.[34] By 2000, St. Louis's office of ACORN Housing Corporation, which opened its doors in 1991, had matched over nine hundred low-income home loan applicants with borrowers.

St. Louis ACORN's Tactical Repertoire: The Drama of Direct Action

ACORN emerged from the National Welfare Rights Organization, which relied on tactics of mass disruption. Since nonviolent protest has become routinized in the United States, it allows activists to experience the thrill of momentarily disrupting powerful institutions with relatively little risk of reprisal. It also gains publicity—a critical resource for grassroots challenger organizations. SL ACORN often successfully leveraged a small number of participants into coverage by the *St. Louis Post-Dispatch*. Militant direct action is still a major element of ACORN's identity, public image, and tactical repertoire. SL ACORN's standard tactic, illustrated in the opening narrative, is to arrange a meeting with the relevant authority and issue a list of demands. When an authority will not meet, ACORN will occupy private offices, picket, and chant to force a meeting. Neighborhood chapters might conduct protests or media hits designed to leverage small numbers into wide visibility. ACORN's demands are usually greater than it can win, but they provide a basis for negotiation. While these tactics usually push the authority to meet, they provide internal benefits as well: dramatic and memorable experiences for members that make them feel their own power. More fundamentally, confrontation forces a target to respond, which helps reveal for activists the conflicts of interest, which these powerful actors would rather obscure, between powerful institutions, corporations, and politicians and working-class Americans. They are sites of political education, as when the organizer Tony advised picketers that the mayor's staff would try to befriend and co-opt them. For many SL ACORN leaders, their most memorable ACORN experience was a dramatic confrontation.

ACORN's nonviolent direct action intimidates new or inexperienced activists, but ongoing participants either find it inherently rewarding or become acculturated to it. Others stay away or drop out, like one now-inactive member who commented on an ACORN protest of a bank: "I don't play that game. Now I know that the banks are treating most of the lower income and blacks unfair. But I don't think standing up in the middle of the bank with a sign is . . . going to affect [the banks]." This member suggested that organizing large depositors to withdraw their money would be more effective. However, in the short term, even if ACORN's tactics produce no tangible results (a frequent outcome), they help produce a proud, militant collective identity as courageous, combative, and unruly.

Ballot Initiatives

SL ACORN frequently attempts to make up for small numbers and scarce allies by turning to direct ballot initiatives, beginning in 1976 with a successful measure to remove the Missouri sales tax on food and medicine. In the mid-1990s, SL ACORN launched two ambitious statewide initiative campaigns. One, a campaign finance reform initiative, was rejected by the

U.S. Court of Appeals as unconstitutional; however, its placement on the November 1994 ballot resulted in state legislation designed to undercut it. This Missouri legislation, which set a $1,075 limit on individual contributions to statewide candidates, was upheld by the U.S. Supreme Court on January 24, 2000.

The 1996 initiative to raise the Missouri minimum wage from $4.25 to $6.25 failed statewide but drew over 70 percent of the St. Louis vote. Then ACORN placed a local living wage initiative on the St. Louis ballot, which passed overwhelmingly but was defeated in court (the winning campaign is described later). The ballot initiative tactic is appealing because it is low cost and relies on ACORN's greatest resource, mass volunteers or minimum-wage workers. Without a large budget, ballot initiatives can win at the polls if the issue is sufficiently popular. However, they must be well crafted or opponents can block them in court.

Allies and Coalition Building

Though it has sought to form coalitions for city and statewide campaigns, SL ACORN has had difficulty finding powerful allies. The local American Friends Service Committee, which advocates on issues of poverty, and the Reform Organization of Welfare (ROWEL) are allies, although neither has a mass base. The campaign to save Regional Hospital was endorsed by many organizations but failed to attract significant support from organized labor.[35] The 1996 minimum-wage initiative relied on the promise of significant union contributions, but unions stayed out of the campaign. Labor leaders thought SL ACORN presented campaigns to potential allies only after it had already made the key decisions: the president of the St. Louis Labor Council commented, "They have a roomful of good ideas and about $1.75. If they're going to send letters to the labor unions you'd like to be in on the planning."[36] The campaign's former manager, a liberal campaign consultant hired by ACORN, argued that a winning campaign would have had to start six months earlier, and its proponents would have had to work collaboratively to build the coalition necessary "to develop the broad-based support it takes to withstand a multimillion dollar campaign by the bad guys."[37]

How St. Louis ACORN Finally Won a Living Wage Ordinance

SL ACORN attempted to reopen the wage-increase issue locally after the state wage-increase ballot initiative failed. With no ally in the mayor's office, ACORN turned next to the Board of Aldermen, St. Louis's city council, and recruited two aldermen to sponsor an ACORN-drafted ordinance. After "much fruitless action and negotiating," the board tabled the ordinance in the spring of 2000.[38] At about this time, national ACORN placed an experienced organizer from another chapter in the St. Louis office to help the chapter build capacity. ACORN also gained an ally in the SEIU, on whose State Council sat an ACORN ally, a former organizer with SEIU local 880, which shared the ACORN office. In only two weeks, ACORN and the SEIU collected the 20,000 signatures needed to place a living wage initiative on the August 2000 primary ballot. Support was high, especially in ACORN's north St. Louis neighborhoods. An initiative passed with 77 percent support. It required city contractors, subcontractors, and companies with economic development help from the city to pay $8.67 an hour, $9.62 if there were no health benefits.

Unfortunately, the ordinance ACORN drafted included features that made it vulnerable, such as neglecting to exempt nonprofit organizations with scarce funds from the higher wage standard. The mayor exploited this opportunity by declaring that downtown businesses were exempt from the law, but paradoxically, nonprofit organizations such as homeless shelters were covered by it. The nonprofits, who pleaded that salary hikes jeopardized basic services, joined the Missouri business lobby in fighting the law. Business groups won a temporary restraining order blocking the ordinance, and ACORN sued to force implementation.[39] New York University's Brennan Center for Justice supported the initiative and later became a key legal resource for other ordinances. A circuit court judge's decision in July 2001 was positive for ACORN in that it threw out a 1997 Missouri law that prevented cities from raising the minimum wage. However, the judge found the St. Louis ordinance "fatally vague," possibly catastrophic for nonprofits, and too far-reaching.[40] On this basis he struck down the entire law.

In 2000, the pro–living wage mayoral candidate that ACORN endorsed, Francis Slay, challenged incumbent Clarence Harmon and won. However, no Board of Aldermen committee had a majority in favor of a living wage ordinance. But in early 2002, a political opportunity emerged. Board president Jim Shrewsbury, running for reelection that September, told the SEIU he would support a living wage bill. Shrewsbury needed labor support and had the power to move the bill through the board. With the Brennan Center's help, ACORN redrafted the bill. With SEIU's help, the new living wage coalition won the first St. Louis Central Labor Council endorsement of a living wage policy. Bob Kelly, the skeptical labor council president, advocated for the bill with the mayor and board members and drew SEIU locals further into the campaign.[41] At one point a local business group, the Downtown Partnership, exerted counterpressure on the mayor to weaken the law and reduce the living wage rate to what would have been the lowest in the country. Although Alderman Shrewsbury was not swayed, the mayor bowed to pressure and weakened the bill. ACORN went public, threatening a new ballot initiative with all of the features compromised away during negotiations restored. The mayor became more receptive, and when he backed Shrewsbury's opponent for board president, Shrewsbury lost any commitment to supporting the mayor's version of the law. Because ACORN sought to keep the mayor's support, it kept some concessions to the mayor while dropping most of the business lobby's proposals.

The ordinance passed easily. ACORN had sacrificed some of the law's reach to firms receiving economic development aid—not surprising, given St. Louis's economically vulnerable competition for scarce business investment. However, unlike many such ordinances, the law extends to concessions at the city's airport. As of July 2004, the St. Louis living wage was $9.79 an hour with health benefits and $12.15 without, the amount sufficient to lift a family of three above the food-stamp-eligibility level.

St. Louis ACORN's Impact and Potential

SL ACORN in the late nineties expended energy on two major campaigns and initially won neither of them. It had weak local leaders and staff, it chose some major issues without careful analysis of whether it could win, and it alienated some possible coalition partners. SL ACORN's tactics could not make up in disruptiveness for what the organization lacked in numbers. Unless a group is willing and able to command ongoing major disruption without regard for reprisals—only likely in exceptional times for drastic grievances—it must rely on more conventional sources of leverage, such as the capacity to deliver (or withhold) votes, allies, policy expertise, or knowledge of community needs. It must also be able to assess the political landscape, its own resources, and what is achievable. Above all it needs flexibility and the vision to see new possibilities, allies, and issues suited to its context. It is difficult to produce ongoing networks of talented leaders from the distressed neighborhoods where ACORN organizes, but it is possible. A number of SL ACORN leaders were well-employed or retired blue- or white-collar workers and stable homeowners or residents with a stake in their neighborhood. Some had long histories with ACORN (memberships for twenty years or more), extensive experience in other organizations, deep concern for their neighborhoods, and civic skills.

The case of St. Louis shows how being part of a national organization can enable a local community organization to renew itself, win a much-needed victory, and move on to new challenges. First, the organization benefited by the addition of an expert ACORN organizer to the staff in 2000, who helped with management and organizing. National ACORN's many city offices enable it to shift staff, providing new challenges for experienced staff and opportunities for advancement for junior staff. St. Louis was able to promote an African American organizer to the position of director, a long-term desire of many active members. National ACORN added a new layer of management in order to better assist locals with conflicts, growing pains, and everyday management challenges. It introduced six regional directors, who supervise the head organizers in each region. ACORN also created the position of full-time national field director, who helps head organizers conduct training and supervision and works with the regional directors. Finally, St. Louis staff have all the benefits of issue expertise from ACORN's national staff of specialists.

ACORN also delivers local benefits from national campaign successes. Centralized structure and campaigns benefit SL ACORN. In 2000, ACORN won a national campaign against predatory home loans by the mortgage company Ameriquest and signed an agreement in which the company committed $363 million in home loans for low-income families in ten cities with ACORN locals, including St. Louis.[42]

As for the St. Louis Living Wage Campaign, according to Jen Kern, the "biggest learning experience there was that we need lawyers" to help write ordinances that avoid legal pitfalls. Since 2002, ACORN and its allies increasingly moved on to state legislative or ballot referenda battles. Said Kern: "We definitely raised the bar and changed the way people talk about low-wage work and about development. Our goal is to make sure you can never talk about economic development without talking about wages and benefits. That's been a great accomplishment."

A Seat at the Regional Table: Metropolitan Congregations United for St. Louis

I'm capable of a lot more than I thought. We used to be typical church people and do-gooders: we just wanted to do nice things and hoped you changed the world that way. And now we realize the only way to change the world is to go out into the world and turn it upside down.

—MCU activist

On September 28, 1997, in St. Louis, 750 church members sacrificed their Sunday afternoon to attend a "Public Meeting on Smart Growth" in the echoing gymnasium of the University of Missouri at St. Louis. Their program included a "theological statement on smart growth." Two children, one black and one white, recited "prayers for their future." Then the president of Metropolitan Congregations United for St. Louis (MCU) took the podium. The Rev. Sylvester Laudermill Jr., African Methodist Episcopal (AME), led the crowd in a song he wrote:

> God made this world and we are God's people
> We've been entrusted—this land is in our hands;
> We must live together—our children are calling
> Black, white, rich, or poor—for our future, let's do more.

(Laudermill confessed, "You can't really sing 'control urban sprawl.'")[1] In a reflection, Monsignor Ted Wojcicki recalled the church's commitment to "the poor and marginalized" and reminded the crowd that "the Book of Nehemiah says, 'Let us rebuild the wall of Jerusalem!'" Wojcicki spoke of the need to preserve St. Louis's inner core and its Catholic parishes.[2]

Reverend Laudermill reviewed MCU's efforts on urban sprawl and ended by thundering, "We demand smart growth in the St. Louis region! Are you with me?" to applause.

MCU's vice president explained that taxpayer-funded federal subsidies of highways and new suburban housing had disadvantaged racial minorities and older neighborhoods. The program ended with a proposal of "smart growth boundaries" as the remedy for urban decline. Two MCU ministers, three state representatives, and two state senators rallied the troops. This ritualized expression of political will sought officials' commitment to two proposals: the state legislators agreed to sponsor MCU's urban growth boundary legislation, and MCU sought $10,000 each from St. Louis County and City for a study of St. Louis sprawl. The county executive sent a letter agreeing to seek the money.[3] The meeting's achievements, though modest, were impressive for a new federation of churches. This was the first time a large group of citizens assembled to challenge unrestricted development in the St. Louis region.

Members of MCU had experienced many aspects of neighborhood decline. While the eleven-county St. Louis region remains roughly constant in population, the once-bustling city of St. Louis is losing population rapidly to the suburbs.[4] Church members had witnessed both white *and* black flight to the suburbs and the loss of businesses, churches, hospitals, and schools that followed. This concentrated crime and poverty in the city. Some of their churches had lost members, and houses had lost value. The loss of tax revenues to St. Louis and its inner-ring suburbs meant that the schools and public services declined. Other public monies were diverted to build new suburban roads and sewers.[5] Through national training sessions with the organizing network to which they belonged, the Gamaliel Foundation, MCU activists met organizers and activists from other cities and learned that St. Louis's problems were not unique.

The attempt to link religious faith with regional development policy surely poses special challenges. American churches are better known for taking on straightforward human rights issues of poverty, hunger, or peace. This chapter examines how the church-based MCU came to address the complex issue of urban sprawl in the St. Louis area, why it chose the remedy of urban growth boundaries, and what it learned from the campaign.

MCU's Structure and Operations

The fifty-six-church organization Metropolitan Congregations United for St. Louis was formed in 1996–97 by combining three smaller church-based community organizations, each of which organized in a different section of

St. Louis. (See Table 3.) All were affiliated with the Gamaliel Foundation, a Chicago-based organizing network of about fifty organizations.

The Gamaliel Foundation's mission is

> to be a powerful network of grassroots, interfaith, interracial, multi-issue organizations working together to create a more just and more democratic society. The organizations of the Gamaliel Network are vehicles that allow ordinary people to effectively participate in the political, environmental, social and economic decisions affecting their lives.[6]

Sixteen churches in the northernmost tip of St. Louis and north St. Louis County composed CUCA (pronounced "kooka"). Individual CUCA churches took on local issues such as neighborhood watch programs, opened a police substation, pressured authorities to evict problem tenants and close drug houses, lobbied local realtors to stop negative sales tactics, pressured the St. Louis Airport Authority to soundproof a church and school, and forced Shell Oil to relandscape an abandoned gas station. CUCA's first major campaign, to keep a department store chain from closing its local store, failed. However, a major campaign to keep a local hospital open fought the University of Missouri, the Washington University hospital, and the state of Missouri and won.

When a priest who helped found CUCA was moved by the diocese to a parish in south St. Louis, he helped found C4. C4 includes twenty-two churches in traditionally white working-class (but increasingly black) south St. Louis. Its member churches have taken on landlords in local campaigns, and a team of three churches led a successful campaign to redevelop a vacant Sears building into thirty-five housing units. C4 also pressured the St. Louis School Board and the judge presiding over St. Louis's desegregation plan to keep four local schools open and remodel them. C4 has strong working relationships with four local aldermen and women, and local neighborhood associations as well.

CACI (pronounced "casey"), founded in 1993, includes eighteen churches in mostly black north St. Louis, the area where St. Louis ACORN organizes. Of the three groups that formed MCU, CACI has had the most troubled history, for several reasons. It seeks African American organizers to effectively recruit black churches and mobilize their members, but has had difficulty locating black staff members who were both talented and committed to organizing. For over a year, CACI was without an organizer-director; activity diminished so that in 1997–98 only four of CACI's sixteen churches had active organizing teams, called core teams in the Gamaliel Foundation.[7] Member churches are either African American or have a siz-

Table 3. Component organizations of MCU for St. Louis

Year founded	Acronym	Full name of organization; area it organizes	Constituency
1991	CUCA	Churches United for Community Action; northern fringe of the city and bordering county suburbs	Largely white, working class, and middle class
1992	C4 (CCCC)	Churches Committed to Community Concerns; south St. Louis	Largely white, working class and middle class
1993	CACI	Churches Allied for Community Improvement; north St. Louis	Largely black, working class
1996–97	MCU	Metropolitan Congregations United for St. Louis; formed by the three organizations above for citywide and regional campaigns; each of the three also remains separate; after 2000, Joshua and MCU-ISAIAH were added to MCU	Combined constituencies of all member groups
2000	none	Joshua; north St. Louis County; merged in 2002 with CUCA	Largely white, working class and middle class
2001	none	MCU-ISAIAH; south St. Louis County	All constituencies combined

able black membership. One AME minister and former president of CACI, Sylvester Laudermill, went on to become the respected president of MCU. Because CACI is integrated, it has trouble gaining the trust of black ministers, who are reluctant to join an organization that they fear whites might dominate. CACI has had difficulty recruiting black Baptist churches, which form the bulk of the black church power structure. Despite these limitations, CACI churches have shut down drug houses, forced a major bank to provide armed security guards at all bank branches, pressured the U.S. Post Office to keep a branch open in a high-crime neighborhood, and helped pressure the St. Louis School Board and the judge overseeing St. Louis school desegregation to open the only four-year vocational high school in the city of St. Louis. CACI also helped bring together the mayor and a local alderwoman, who were feuding, in a compromise that would allow a new shopping center to break ground in north St. Louis. The center was to include north St. Louis's only twenty-four-hour supermarket.

The Gamaliel Foundation encouraged their affiliated groups to combine to form larger regional federations like MCU. CUCA, CACI, and C4 began working together before they formed MCU, when they founded a separate but related nonprofit organization in 1995, the St. Louis Reinvestment Corporation. Like the ACORN Housing Corporation, it works on neighborhood reinvestment by brokering low-interest home loans to families who would otherwise be ineligible. By May 2001, the Reinvestment Corporation had provided seven hundred home loans to low- and moderate-income St. Louis residents. The three groups gained more experience in 1995 when the federal Community Reinvestment Act (CRA), which is essential to the Reinvestment Corporation's work, was threatened with crippling revisions. The three groups held a joint meeting of two thousand people to lobby their elected officials, including U.S. representative and then House minority leader Richard Gephart, against the proposed revisions.[8]

The Gamaliel Foundation's Regional Organizing Strategy

The Gamaliel Foundation discovered that inner-city problems cannot be solved in isolation from their surrounding regions. The flight of middle-class residents, businesses, and low-wage jobs to suburbs means that regional transit, employment, and inner-city decline are impossible to address without suburban resources and cooperation. Gamaliel began to organize metropolitan-wide federations.

In addition to forging the broadest possible regional federation of churches, MCU and its member organizations form coalitions outside of the Gamaliel network if these might further their goals. For example, to redevelop a vacant Sears building, C4 helped organize local neighborhood organizations, business associations, and area aldermen and alderwomen as the "South Grand [Avenue] Team." This is notable, as Alinsky-influenced community organizations often fear their militance will be undercut by groups that are less savvy about power politics.

MCU Organizing Tactics

Deliberation in Meetings and Actions

MCU and the Gamaliel network teach members to conduct one-to-one interviews; select concrete, immediate, and winnable issues; learn from evaluations; and train new leaders, just as all CBCOs do (see chapter 1). However, each network is somewhat different. The Gamaliel Foundation has an ongoing consulting relationship with several "Strategic Partners" who have guided its "metropolitan analysis" and who consult with Gamaliel locals and the national staff. Because Gamaliel locals such as MCU place such emphasis on regional policy reform, they see town meetings and other efforts to educate members, the public, and authorities about their proposed policies as essential. Metaphors of deliberation and discussion are prominent and influence participants' understanding of tactics.[9] Like most CBCOs, MCU's signature tactic is the mass public meeting or action. The meeting that opened this chapter featured a lot of talk about the causes of and remedies for sprawl. Both public and private deliberation loomed large as a way MCU staff and activists understood their work. They often referred to significant conversations they had had with officials or allies. Authentic democratic deliberation and debate take place among MCU leaders informally, at sessions with expert consultants, and especially at their board meetings. MCU leaders selected urban growth boundaries from among various policy alternatives only after extensive deliberation.

Another key element of MCU's strategy was discursive—a 1999 study of sprawl in the St. Louis region. ACORN's national office has produced many studies that its locals used in immediate, tactical ways, such as in news releases to gain media coverage and launch campaigns. In contrast, MCU planned to use the study internally to educate churches, recruit them, and slowly build its base. The risk of these deliberative tactics is that education can become an end in itself, in lieu of politics.

Symbolic Tactics

MCU uses religious symbols and ritual in its internal meetings and events, as well as in its public actions. Whether these elements are collective expressions of identity or instrumental media strategy is often ambiguous—and they are probably both.

When the three local groups that made up MCU collaborated to help save the CRA, they targeted U.S. senator Christopher (Kit) Bond, a possible swing vote on the Senate Banking Committee. At one point activists held a prayer vigil at Bond's local office. One leader, a priest, reported:

> Surprisingly enough, people [MCU leaders] thought that was a good tactic, because we were churches. So sitting outside his office and praying to God for an answer, praying to God for guidance . . . praying for Bond's heart to change—people could relate to that.

Activists chose the prayer vigil not so much as a canny media strategy but out of a feeling of impotence: at a meeting, one frustrated activist said, "We can at least pray." Yet such tactics express *both* earnest sincerity and strategic calculation. They are familiar and appeal to church members and appear morally irreproachable by authorities while casting their opponents in a negative light.[10]

Some symbolic actions are directed not outward but inward, to build collective identity and resolve. When a bridge connecting (white) south St. Louis with (black) north St. Louis was rebuilt, C4 and CACI organized a walk from their respective neighborhoods. It culminated when they met on the bridge for a joint religious ceremony symbolizing racial cooperation. Another popular type of event was prayer walks highlighting current problems and victories, described in chapter 1.

Confrontational Tactics

It is hard to predict when church members will be willing to break the rules of polite and orderly conduct. CBCOs have typically used disruption or confrontation only to force authorities to meet with them or when other tactics have not worked.[11] Once organizations have regular access to authorities, their shows of force are usually restricted to mass meetings. Early in its history, when a slumlord refused to meet with C4, one hundred chanting members with signs invaded a meeting of the St. Louis Association of Apartment Owners where the slumlord was present. When he tried to escape, he was cornered by media and forced into a discussion with C4 leaders. He granted their demands. In another case, a local bank manager refused to meet with CACI leaders from a small black church whose treasurer had been robbed outside the bank. CACI sought to have armed security guards stationed at all bank branches. Members had learned from their training that they had to achieve recognition before they could win concessions, so when the bank manager refused to meet with them, they entered the bank and sat in until the manager granted a meeting.

If an official who committed to attend a CBCO meeting does not show or sends a poorly prepared representative, activists are comfortable using the official's absence against him or her. When a representative from Shell Oil did not attend a meeting with one Catholic church to which he was invited, the chair of the meeting conspicuously pointed out his empty chair, and local media featured it on television news. Shell representatives never missed a meeting again.

MCU's culture was heavily informed by Gamaliel Foundation norms. The notions of power, self-interest, challenging, and agitation (described in chapter 1) helped politicize inexperienced church members and provided norms for high standards and commitment. Employing ritual and naming emotions helped build solidarity. However, understanding its campaign against urban sprawl too exclusively in terms of conversation, education, and relationships overshadowed a much-needed analysis of the power and self-interest of its opponents.

MCU's Campaign against Urban Sprawl

St. Louis and Urban Decline

On March 9, 1997, the *St. Louis Post-Dispatch* published "A Call to Action," by urban commentators Neal Peirce and Curtis Johnson. The report was a wake-up call to a city poised to become the next Detroit: a destitute inner core with thousands of empty and crumbling buildings abandoned by business and the middle class. Writing that the "area's problems demand a reality check," Pierce and Johnson outlined the region's sobering challenges, along with its assets. They told city residents what they already knew: since 1990, St. Louis had experienced the most severe population decline among thirty-five leading metropolitan regions (12 percent). Since 1950, the city's population had declined from 850,000 to less than 350,000. Why had this happened? What were the consequences, and what could be done about it?

St. Louis is an extreme example of what has befallen other industrial cities of the Northeast and Midwest. The reasons are complex and include economic globalization, a severely fragmented political system, a stark racial divide, and few restrictions on sprawling development. The metropolitan area's population has remained steady (it grew 4.5 percent from 2.5 to 2.6 million since 1990), and the rich historical and cultural resources and low cost of living contribute to a high quality of life for many. However, the city's core is in a spiral of decline.

Clearly, incentives lead actors such as corporations and middle-class residents to leave the inner city. However, even if the public and political will were united, the twelve-county region's fragmented political system would impede coordinated policy responses. The region includes 91 municipalities and 771 units of government, more per person than any major region except Pittsburgh.[12] This fragmented authority yields political stalemate in critical regional issues such as mass transit and development policy. The city of St. Louis itself has a weak partisan mayoralty in a system of fragmented city authority. When the city of St. Louis "seceded" from St. Louis County in 1876, it gained its own structure of "county" functions separate from city offices. Control of the city budget is shared by the president of the board of aldermen and city controller. The police department is state controlled, a legacy of the Civil War. Thus, St. Louis's mayor is weak and shares power not only with a board of aldermen but other bodies as well. Despite the city's more than 60 percent population loss since 1960, there are still twenty-eight aldermen, each now representing fewer than 15,000 citizens. For these reasons, coordinated initiatives are quite difficult. While many privately acknowledge the need to revise the city charter, this has not yet been politically feasible. Observers also claim that a culture of civic timidity contributes to the inability to solve problems. While St. Louis avoided riots in the sixties, local activists claim the black community is also quiescent in more constructive forms of civic engagement.

The result of this political stalemate is that constructive urban initiatives must detour around the political structure. One way this happens is through innovative city-county special districts for specific purposes, including a sewer district and a zoo-museum district. The latter includes the city's science center and nationally recognized botanical gardens, art museum, and history museum. However, more significantly, "What the formal political structure separates, the business community unites."[13] Although the mayor, county executive, and their allies are significant power holders, and the newspaper and television stations are influential, "everybody thinks there's a shadow government."[14] Most think it consists of Civic Progress, a private organization of CEOs of the region's top twenty-nine corporations, and the interlocking Regional Commerce and Growth Association, the city's chamber of commerce.[15] Local developers are less visible but also influential.

Race, specifically racialized poverty, is a deep-rooted problem. Many claim St. Louis's racial quagmire predates the Civil War. It was in St. Louis that Dred Scott sued for his freedom from slavery. Today, both black and white residents believe race helps drive sprawl development, high private school enrollments, and suburban resistance to funding light-rail that would make suburbs more accessible to inner-city workers. If wide-open spaces and large homes pull the middle class to the suburbs, poor schools, inadequate housing stock, and a strapped city budget push them there. Relative to other cities, St. Louis has few community development corporations. Unfortunately, the 1986 federal tax reform removed historic renovation tax credits that had spurred redevelopment of twelve thousand historic city housing units in just ten years. Poverty is increasingly concentrated, especially in the northern half of the city: the number of census tracts with more than 20 percent of residents in poverty increased from fifty-one in 1970 to seventy in 1990.[16]

The mismatch between inner-city workers and suburban job growth is part of the problem, although Metrolink, the light-rail system developed in the 1990s, is an important intervention. But wages for entry-level jobs have declined, and there are still more low-skill workers than jobs.

Consulting with Experts

Through the Gamaliel network, MCU learned of the work of urban policy consultants David Rusk, Myron Orfield, john a. powell, and others.[17] With Rusk and Orfield, MCU began to investigate the causes of St. Louis's decline and concluded that the primary cause was new sprawling development. While St. Louis's urbanized population had grown only 17 percent over three decades, urbanized land had grown 125 percent. On this land, developers had built 325,000 new housing units—more than twice as many new units than were needed: "a formula for guaranteed abandonment of older housing in the city and older suburbs."[18] Critics charge that sprawl produces congested freeways and exploding infrastructure costs for new schools, firehouses, police stations, roads, and sewer networks. The rest of the region is adversely affected by higher taxes, utility fees, loss of industry, pollution, and congestion. Highway budgets are one example: from 1998 to 2015, the area will need $3.4 billion just to resurface and repair its road and bridge networks; new freeways and local roads will bring the total to $6.7 billion. However, highway revenues are expected to reach only $3.7 billion.[19] Black inner-city poverty becomes more highly concentrated, and poverty, drugs, crime, and poor schools drive out middle- and working-class whites and many blacks. In turn, sprawl further isolates and impoverishes the inner city.

Critical to MCU's analysis was David Rusk's argument that inner-city redevelopment cannot reverse poverty and decline. Only expanding city boundaries (through annexation or city-county consolidation) can recapture the suburbs and their tax base. But St. Louis's antiquated city charter keeps its original boundaries in place. Since local governments almost never initiate regional growth management, revenue sharing, or equitable housing policies, state legislatures are the preferred arena for such major reforms.

In August 1996, CACI, C4, and CUCA invited Rusk and Orfield to teach their leaders about regional issues. They organized twelve educational forums that targeted their constituents, officials, the media, and the public. Activists learned that the sprawling, oversupplied housing market had caused the average regional home value to increase only 29 percent (versus 36 percent nationally). While black St. Louis residents' properties had gained *no* value, property values in Albina, the poorest neighborhood in Portland, Oregon, doubled in five years after Portland instituted urban growth boundaries.[20] Rusk strongly advocated the urban growth boundary tool for its comprehensive approach. As the poor left the increasingly devastated inner

city, the number of *suburban* neighborhoods with at least 20 percent poverty
had grown from five to nineteen. Orfield asked the group:

> Are these natural growth patterns ordained by God and Adam Smith?
> They're not. Metro development patterns are shaped by major public
> policies—the federal interstate highway system, preferential financing for
> suburban subdivisions, tax policies that favor buying higher and higher
> priced new homes, dozens and dozens of hidden and not-so-hidden
> subsidies—a Marshall Plan for the rich.[21]

The consultants suggested that the decline of inner-ring suburbs might motivate them to ally with MCU's urban constituency.

MCU's grassroots leaders were jolted by this policy analysis, which convincingly linked many different urban problems. According to one leader,
the workshop with Rusk and Orfield "opened our eyes." Leaders met one
night at CACI president Sylvester Laudermill's inner-city church and narrowed down possible campaign issues to three: tax-base revenue sharing,
mandated mixed-income housing, and urban sprawl. They decided urban
sprawl was the most inclusive, and therefore best, issue. According to one
leader, members of her suburban church don't easily embrace political issues, "but they've latched on to urban sprawl. . . . I had several older ladies
say they were worried about losing farmland. And they worry about losing
younger families."

On February 8, 1997, the MCU organizations held the first Metro-
politan Summit at St. Louis University with three hundred people. Fol-
lowing other regions, MCU framed the issue positively as "smart growth."
MCU began working with two St. Louis state representatives and one state
senator to draft legislation for urban growth boundaries. State Senator
Ron Auer, himself a member of a C4 church, introduced the bill in 1997.
It failed to get a committee hearing, but gained some St. Louis publicity.
Environmentalists and local municipal leaders began attending public
MCU events. Aware that they would need a wider coalition to effectively
oppose sprawl, one MCU organizer pulled together the Smart Growth
Alliance. The coalition brought together the MCU churches, environmen-
tal groups such as the Sierra Club and Coalition for the Environment, the
Urban League, transportation policy makers, mass-transit advocates, and
the St. Louis County Municipal League (representing the inner-ring municipalities most threatened by sprawling newer suburbs).

On June 9, 1997, MCU held its second Metropolitan Summit on
Urban Sprawl, with five to six hundred church members present. MCU
drew its first official response in the urban sprawl campaign: the Missouri

State Assembly formed a Special Legislative Interim Committee on Urban Sprawl.[22]

Three months later, MCU held the September 28 public meeting described at the beginning of the chapter. Organizers were disappointed with the attendance of 750 (the largely white crowd was far smaller than MCU's goal of 2,500) though the event mobilized previously uninvolved church members and advanced the goal of funding a study of local sprawl. Growing coverage of the sprawl meetings in local media laid the groundwork for the controversy that broke out the next month. When the state assembly Committee on Urban Sprawl held hearings in St. Louis, they made the front page of the *Post-Dispatch,* and the contentious public debate alarmed public officials.[23] MCU leaders were exhilarated.

However, in response to the controversy, allies' support for urban growth boundary legislation dwindled. MCU organizers feared that pressure from business and development interests was forcing legislators to back down. Legislative sponsors suggested that MCU pursue a more incremental strategy and intermediate goals such as tax-increment financing reform and brownfields legislation. As it happened, another issue temporarily distracted MCU from urban growth boundaries.

The Page Avenue Freeway Campaign

In 1998 the sprawl debate became focused on the Page Avenue Extension, a long-pending $550 million highway extension and bridge that would add ten freeway lanes from St. Louis County to St. Charles County.[24] Opponents saw the freeway extension as a costly boondoggle that would facilitate further sprawl. Supporters, chiefly developers, road builders, businesses, and other St. Charles interests, framed the project as necessary to ease traffic congestion and enhance economic development. Opponents placed a referendum blocking the extension on the November 1998 St. Louis County ballot. Because of the alliances forged in the Smart Growth Alliance, MCU joined the coalition. The referendum provoked a countermobilization of developers, road builders, engineers, construction unions, and real estate, financial, and other interests.

The ballot measure to block the Page Avenue Extension was defeated by a 60 percent majority in November 1998. The Page Avenue fight helped MCU clarify the identity and strength of their opponents. St. Louis's business elites refused to oppose unplanned growth and donated heavily to the pro–Page Avenue campaign. Poll data suggest the race was extremely close, although the anti-Page forces, including MCU, were outspent eight to one.[25] The divisiveness and conflict led the region's metropolitan planning organization, the East-West Gateway Coordinating Council, to back away from the issue. Politicians representing suburban districts refused to oppose the freeway, instead supporting a massive elite-led urban redevelopment project—a strategy that Rusk argued could not make the city competitive enough to stem flight to the suburbs.[26]

The defeat of the referendum to stop the freeway extension added a note of urgency to the *St. Louis Post-Dispatch*'s editorials against sprawl but made no lasting change in their position against growth boundaries. In February 1998 legislative sponsors Senator Wayne Goode and Representative Ron Auer recommended a slowdown on the legislation, but MCU's board and staff still resisted retreat. Finally, they were convinced to back off growth boundaries or be ignored. MCU's stripped-down bill removed growth boundaries, reduced its scope from statewide to the St. Louis region, and turned to the area's metropolitan planning organization, the East-West Gateway Coordinating Council, to set up a land use commission.[27] MCU retreated from the growth boundaries issue and repositioned itself for a much longer campaign. It added staff, completed a $40,000 study of the costs of St. Louis sprawl, and turned its attention to more specific and manageable land use and transportation issues.

MCU organizers and leaders learned from experience that urban growth boundaries were politically unfeasible:

> MCU ORGANIZER: The growth boundary piece is not winnable right now; we realized [that] when we saw the magnitude of the opposition that was lining [up] against us. Some of our allies were running from the urban growth boundaries piece, were backpedaling on it. . . . I think we realized some of the reasons. That led us to understand who's profiting. We also realized how this is going to be spun in the media and what it's going to take to win. . . . Right now we're not prepared to do a referendum or ballot initiative. It helped us to do a power analysis.
>
> HS: What would you do differently in hindsight, on this issue?
>
> MCU ORGANIZER: Have a hell of a lot more money in the bank; have more organizers on board; I think having this . . . study done. It's very much geared toward winning the allies, first- and second-ring suburban people.

An Unfavorable Political Context

While widely shared grievances related to sprawl impelled MCU to select this issue, the political context was unfavorable. On its fundamental

challenge—passing urban growth boundaries—MCU discovered that political and economic elites were unified against them. Local public officials
opposed development limitations based on suburban constituents' interests.
While business interests supported the antipoverty and antiblight measures
that would benefit them or their workforce—school desegregation, better
education, urban revitalization, and mass transit—they refused to support
restrictions on development.[28] A cleavage between downtown and suburban
business interests is unlikely, not only because of the impulse of businesses
to ally against restraints, but because many downtown business owners' loyalties are divided between downtown preservation and suburban growth.

MCU had access to the mayor, some aldermen, and a few state legislators, and had many bureaucratic allies. However, this was not enough
to make a difference because their primary allies, city officials, lacked the
authority to address regional issues. The city of St. Louis is a small part of
the greater region. Thus it was not enough for MCU to gain the allegiance
of the St. Louis mayor or any number of city aldermen since the decisions
that affected the city's fiscal health were dispersed among ninety-one local
governments (as well as businesses and state and national governments).
Any campaign for growth restrictions must be regional, including both
Missouri and Illinois suburbs. The *St. Louis Post-Dispatch* offered worried
editorials, but presented sprawl as a technical rather than a political problem. It clearly spelled out its costs, but was unwilling to use investigative
reporting to identify those who profit from sprawl.[29]

In St. Louis and Missouri in general, electoral competition has not
yet provided political openings for smart growth advocates. They are out-
numbered in the conservative state legislature, and suburban legislators have
seized the opportunity to oppose measures that smack of regulation—even
freeway carpool lanes.

Issue Selection and Framing

As a church-based organization, MCU perceives and frames its issues as
values- and faith-based. It views the issue of sprawl development as *unjust* to
the people and communities left behind. This made sense as a strategy for
recruiting inner-core churches. The injustice frame was complemented by
the framing of sprawl development as *irrational* and *wasteful*. However, the
highly complex regulatory issue of urban sprawl and growth boundaries is
very difficult to present as a valence issue—an issue with only one legitimate
position that elicits "a single, strong, fairly uniform emotional response and
does not have an adversarial quality." Findings that cognitively easy issues
win more favorable media attention and electoral results than complex ones

help explain MCU's difficulty in promoting the sprawl issue.[30] With the freeway extension issue, both sides could make a legitimate case: proponents of Page Avenue claimed it was necessary to *prevent* traffic congestion, while opponents made the less intuitive argument that ultimately it would *produce* congestion.

Why Initiate a Campaign for Urban Growth Boundaries?

One might assume that a CBCO in a network with experience in similar cities would have expected powerful opposition to an ambitious challenge and hesitated to embark on it. Both external and internal factors explain why MCU made this choice.

Competition among Organizing Networks

Competition among networks creates incentives to protect and expand their market share, especially when it may be threatened. The Gamaliel Foundation is headquartered in Chicago. Several years ago the Industrial Areas Foundation returned to Chicago, its original home base. The IAF's return to Chicago from Long Island heightened competition between these two networks for dominance in the Chicago area. The IAF, PICO, ACORN, and others compete for scarce foundation funds, choice organizing sites, and among CBCOs, the allegiance of pastors and churches. They seek to protect and expand their organizations, and the national demand not just for funds but for experienced organizers far outstrips the supply. But this structural context does not determine how strategic actors respond to it. Many observers believe that Gamaliel may have expanded too rapidly for its limited staff and financial resources.[31] Young Gamaliel affiliates like MCU may need more supervision and resources than are available.

A Young Organization

In 1997 MCU was a new organization and its three constituent organizations were only about five years old. One of MCU's two staff members was a novice organizer, while the other had experience with only one prior organization in a much smaller city. Neither had directed a large community organization in a major city before, much less a regional campaign for state legislation. Members' experiences were primarily with local neighborhood issues. They turned to their urban policy consultants for their expertise on policy, not politics. The organization learned from experience that the issue of urban growth boundaries was not realizable.

However, all community organizations have failures, and these are indispensable experiences in political education. Like MCU, San Jose PACT, probably the most successful of the four local organizations in this study, embarked on a similar sweeping but unrealizable challenge early in its history (see chapter 7). But the urban growth boundary campaign illustrates typical pitfalls a young organization faces. MCU leaders were justifiably convinced that combating urban sprawl was the best way to address urban blight, racial polarization, and segregated black poverty. Their strategy was local public education to build support for state urban growth boundary legislation. However, it was a local strategy to win a statewide goal, and MCU lacked state-level organizational capacity. At the time, MCU was the only Gamaliel affiliate in Missouri; the only CBCO in Kansas City belonged to the PICO network, and organizations from rival networks almost never collaborate. Yet winning state legislation almost certainly would have required a base of support in the other large city in Missouri.

Most Americans have little experience assessing political power, and community organizing both requires and develops this skill. Like Progressive-era reformers, MCU's emphasis on public education tacitly addressed the problem as one of *knowledge* rather than *power* and conflicting interests; hence, it was approached primarily as a task of education rather than political battle. Both organizers and leaders were swayed by the righteousness of their cause. Typical comments from leaders included the following:

These people in Jefferson City [state legislators] absolutely do not get it. They can't even speak the language.

We're leaps and bounds ahead, on growth boundaries. They have no idea what we're talking about.

We need to set up a meeting with [one legislative sponsor] and ask why he's waffling. . . . Maybe he hasn't educated himself enough.

These leaders lacked a detailed analysis of politicians' interests, such as political contributions from highway construction firms and developers. MCU leaders had had enough local successes to believe that, in one member's words, "most of the barriers people believe exist, to change, are . . . not as big and strong as they think. They can be overcome." Flush with the accomplishment of gaining access they never dreamed they could have to public officials, activists had to learn from experience the limits of their power.

MCU's Continuing Impact and Potential

Saving the City Bit by Bit

Since 1998, MCU expanded as a regional organization from forty-three to seventy-six congregations, adding area "clusters" of churches from the St. Louis County suburbs. The group has amassed far more experience with the Missouri state government, winning state as well as county funds for roads and highways, measures to aid community development, and protections or expansions of health-care programs for low-income Missourians. Appendix C lists major MCU accomplishments. MCU also collaborates with a new Gamaliel affiliate, United Congregations of Metro-East, across the Mississippi River in Illinois, in national transportation policy lobbying and helped win redistributive provisions in the national transportation bill of 2006.

Because MCU's church-based structure allows it to recruit black and white churches from all over the region, in theory it has the potential to build a broad, cross-racial constituency. Barriers to a strong biracial constituency include black pastors' fear of white control. Also, difficulties in recruiting black organizers who would stay for more than a year or two have inhibited its ability to organize black churches. Nevertheless, probably no institution offers more potential to unite St. Louis's diverse residents than the church.

A more fundamental problem than bridging the racial divide is scarce resources, especially in urban churches. MCU's expansion in St. Louis County in theory will both bring in dues from inner-ring suburban churches and help insulate MCU from being painted as a special interest defending a few particular neighborhoods. Its church base allows it to recruit suburban churches on the basis of both long-term self-interest (efficient use of taxes, reduced congestion, preserved open space) and ethical and religious appeals to social justice.

But perhaps the most important achievement of MCU is not a policy outcome, but a pattern of civic participation. MCU activists are empowered by working with organizers and national policy experts and have learned to apply new ideas to old problems. MCU has drawn a core of dedicated activists into sustained political engagement and, through them and their churches, thousands of St. Louis citizens as well. It has not only drawn them into action on immediate neighborhood issues but challenged them through an ongoing deliberative process to understand these issues as local manifestations of a larger problem: middle-class flight and sprawling development that is eviscerating the city of St. Louis.

6

La Puebla Unida: ACORN in the Sunbelt

My parents . . . came over here to the United States because they wanted something better. Since they wanted something better, and we are stuck in this neighborhood, we have to make it better.

—San Jose ACORN activist

On a warm May evening in 1998, over ninety people filled the large meeting room of the Hank Lopez Community Center on San Jose's East Side. The meeting's leaders—five Hispanic women, one Hispanic man, and one black man—sat up front behind tables, against the backdrop of a large ACORN banner and logo. Half of the crowd consisted of Hispanic women, most middle-aged or older, but some were in their teens and twenties. Another quarter was made up of Hispanic men and a few children, with the remaining quarter divided evenly between blacks and whites.

The meeting served two purposes: it was the Hillview chapter's monthly meeting, and it fulfilled the city manager's and city council member Manny Diaz's agreement to attend an ACORN community meeting. It was also a recruitment ground for new ACORN members, whose dues are a major source of income. Before the city officials arrived, the meeting's leaders made a pitch to recruit new members and announced one of the popular monthly neighborhood cleanups. Members distributed ACORN application cards while others signed up new members. Sarah,[1] San Jose ACORN's sole organizer, scurried around the room assisting and prompting the leaders.

At about 7:00 p.m., the formal community meeting with city officials began. James, an African American man of about sixty, dressed in overalls

127

and seated at the front table, asked, "Will all city officials come to the front please?" A representative of the Office of Code Enforcement, the city manager of San Jose, and a police officer took chairs at the front of the room. James asked, "Who is the spokesperson for the city?" Diaz, already standing, said, "I will be." He began to preside, saying, "First of all I'd like to thank all of you for coming to this important meeting. I said I would bring our city manager." He reminded the crowd of his work in expanding the community center, commended the police department for capturing a serial rapist, and checked whether everyone had received the agendas his assistant was passing out. The first power play of the meeting had occurred.

The organizer crouched, whispering to her leaders. James interrupted, "Excuse me, Manny, we have our own agenda. If you could introduce who's here . . . " Diaz quickly said, "Okay," and fell into line with ACORN's plan for the meeting. Estella, a young Hispanic woman, stated the meeting's purpose: to demand participation in the city's selection of a new police chief. The other women on the panel spoke in Spanish (later translated) about children in traffic accidents, graffiti, attacks by dogs, and rude treatment from police. ACORN wanted a community forum with all the candidates for police chief and for an ACORN member from each of the three ACORN chapters to join the city hiring committee. Estella asked city manager Regina Williams to sign a statement granting these demands. Williams "respectfully declined" to allow community members to meet with job candidates "to protect their privacy," but committed herself to community participation. Estella seemed paralyzed, unsure how to respond to this compromise agreement. Again, Sarah the organizer conferred with Estella, reminding her that members had agreed that the demand for three community representatives was an initial bargaining position; the real goal was just one ACORN representative.[2] Estella recovered and said, "Okay, we have one more thing to ask: if you agree to put just one member from Hillview, Tropicana, or Mayfair ACORN on the committee." Williams agreed as long as she was given several names from which to choose and signed the commitment form members had prepared. The main demand of the action had been proposed and agreed to. Williams said, "Let me confess. It was easy to commit to having one ACORN representative; I had a list of groups to consult and ACORN was on that list."

The meeting concluded with questions to city officials about neighborhood services. The city's director of Parks, Recreation, and Neighborhood Services asked people to call his private line if they didn't get a response in forty-eight hours, closing with "Thank you very much. I like to work with people who care about their community."

The description above of the community meeting appears routine, with little at stake and even less drama. City officials seem agreeable to a fault. The city manager consented to include an ACORN member in the selection of a new police chief. One might argue it was a largely symbolic inclusion in governance that would have taken place whether ACORN had insisted on it or not. However, this would overlook not only what ACORN accomplished but the neighborhood organizing that made its participation in the hiring committee a foregone conclusion. Furthermore, it would assume that grassroots politics, to be genuine, must be overtly contentious—or that grassroots participation and access is granted routinely, without organizing effort. In fact, the meeting illustrates the opposite. San Jose ACORN's hard-won access was a product of local activism, along with the advent of a new kind of San Jose politician who emerged from the city's neighborhoods.[3] But these grassroots politicians typically came from organizations that represented middle-class and affluent neighborhoods not from the disenfranchised East Side and downtown where ACORN organizes. ACORN, PACT, and before them the Community Service Organization (the forerunner of the United Farmworkers' Union) organized by Fred Ross Sr. and Cesar Chavez all helped give San Jose's Latino East Side a voice. This meeting demonstrated that San Jose ACORN had achieved recognition. It had robust local involvement and gave previously uninvolved citizens opportunities to exercise civic skills such as public speaking, chairing a meeting, making demands of authorities, and the deceptively easy-looking task, in this case, of regaining control of the meeting from an elected official in front of ninety people. This chapter explores why San Jose ACORN (for brevity, SJ ACORN), with a staff of one and limited experience, was surprisingly effective.

San Jose Acorn Structure and Operations

In the window of a one-story outbuilding of a Methodist Church, a small sign reads "ACORN office." The tiny office of two narrow adjoining rooms is crammed with desks, bookshelves, a coffeemaker, and a small, worn couch. The walls are covered with charts and lists, flyers, a map of San Jose council districts, a list of "housemeetings/juntas de casa" listing eight Hispanic names, a poster opposing alcohol sales that reads "Cinco de Mayo/Our Cultura is Not for Sale," a schedule of volunteers for cleaning the office, a red ACORN T-shirt, and a "No on 227" sign. A United Farmworkers

Union red and black flag with the slogan "Si se puede" (Yes, it's possible) seems fitting here in the neighborhood that produced Cesar Chavez. A thermometer drawn in black marker on butcher paper, the "Milwaukometer," measured SJ ACORN's progress toward raising $10,000 to send twenty-five members to the biannual national ACORN convention in Milwaukee. The office's sole organizer, Sarah Rosen, was in her early twenties and dressed in jeans and a T-shirt. Sarah was interviewing a woman, who spoke only Spanish, for a position as an apprentice organizer.

SJ ACORN was founded in the summer of 1993 by a young woman who eventually became the California ACORN director, based in Los Angeles. After she left, the office was without a director for almost a year. Sarah Rosen, a recent graduate of the same highly selective college as the first organizer, had been organizing in San Jose for only ten months and was planning to leave the San Jose office soon to start an ACORN chapter in Sacramento. In spring 1998, hiring a replacement organizer and raising travel funds for the national ACORN convention were higher priorities for Sarah than organizing issue campaigns.

Constituency

SJ ACORN has chapters in three east San Jose neighborhoods: Mayfair, Hillview, and Tropicana.[4] Mayfair and Hillview fall within city council District Five, represented by council member Manny Diaz. Tropicana ACORN is within District Seven, represented by council member George Shirakawa Jr. Each chapter had a varied, sometimes stormy history of interaction with its city councilman.

The largely Hispanic population of these three areas is significantly poorer than that of Santa Clara County as a whole, as seen in Table 4. In 1999 the Latino graduation rate in the county was only 56 percent and only 19 percent complete basic courses required for college entrance compared to the national average of 42 percent. By 2007 the situation was little changed: Latinos have the highest dropout rate of any ethnic group and only 22 percent of Latino graduates met University of California/California State University requirements, compared with 53 percent of whites and 65 percent of Asians.[5] SJ ACORN reflected its neighborhood demographics, with an estimated 80 percent Latino membership. African Americans made up perhaps 10 percent, with the rest divided between whites and Asians.[6] Many members are bilingual, but a sizable number are monolingual Spanish speakers. Members typically rent or own one-story tract houses built in the 1950s. One typical member's small, crowded house sheltered three generations. Lupe wished that her son, daughter-in-law, and three grandchildren could move into a home of their own, but the hyperinflated housing market made that impossible.

Table 4. Ethnicity and income: comparison of San Jose ACORN neighborhoods to Santa Clara County, 1990 and 2000

	East San Jose tracts 1990	Santa Clara County 1990	East San Jose tracts 2000	Santa Clara County 2000
Median family income	$33,854	$48,115	$55,987	$81,717 (for U.S., $50,046)
Persons below poverty level	20%	7.5%	13.5%	7.5%
Hispanic	65%	21%	68%	24%
Female head of household	26%	10.3%	27%	(unavailable)

Note: The data for east San Jose for 1990 are drawn from six census tracts, which include the Mayfair, Hillview, and Tropicana neighborhoods, each of which have ACORN chapters. Values are the means of the median value for each census tract. Figures for 2000 were derived the same way, but the specific census tracts differ. Census data for East San Jose are from Center for International Earth Science Information Network, online at http://www.ciesin.org. Data for Santa Clara County are from http://factfinder.census.gov/servlet (accessed February 10, 2004, and October 27, 2005).

While ACORN members are disadvantaged relative to San Jose as a whole, they are better off than many east San Jose residents, and even more so relative to north St. Louis residents. The activists interviewed were all either retired or employed blue- or pink-collar workers; none were on public assistance, and several said they knew no one in their neighborhood on welfare. A majority were homeowners. One noted that a special East Side problem was the illegal immigrants who were "afraid to speak up," and she saw her role as their spokesperson.

ACORN members said that their neighborhoods used to be "terrible" due to drugs and gangs, but had improved. The chair of one chapter noted that the rampant drug dealing and burglaries that had plagued her neighborhood had abated, partly due to greater police enforcement. However, she had still seen her community decline: "If you knew this community before, it was a lot of nice people with kids. The whole street was kids playing baseball in the street. You can't do that anymore." Another said, "Honestly, I've been living here for two and a half years and I have never had any problem . . . your neighbors usually sit outside . . . in this area it's very safe." This leader estimated that her street included mostly homeowners who had lived there for thirty or more years. Another activist said, "I love my community. It's very safe, and it's like my own town. It's like a home. You know your neighbors."

Social ties in the ACORN neighborhoods are often formed through neighborhood proximity but are reinforced in church, since Catholic parishes overlay neighborhood boundaries. One member said, "I know almost everybody that lives around here because they go to church." Of the nine leaders interviewed, six had lived in their neighborhood for twenty-one or more years.

Active members exhibited a robust commitment to their organization. SJ ACORN sent twenty-five members to the 1998 ACORN national convention, a formidable achievement for the limited-income members, who spent spring and summer 1998 raising the $10,000 needed to supplement their personal funds. The cost for airfare and convention registration was $390 per person. Members sold chocolate and held a raffle, dances, carwashes, and tamale sales. Individuals also obtained sponsorships from favorite local businesses, and teenage members sold food at the dances.

Resources

Although the south Bay Area political economy is significantly healthier than the St. Louis area, only a tiny fraction of philanthropic dollars makes its way to organizations like ACORN. For example, the William and Flora Hewlett Foundation granted $4.6 million to fund the Mayfair Collaborative, a resident-driven community development project in the Mayfair neighborhood. Such projects may or may not pursue a constructive development agenda, but they do not encompass political organizing that directs residents *against* authorities, challenging business and government elites.

Information on SJ ACORN's budget was not available, but it must have been a fraction of St. Louis ACORN's estimated $240,000 annual budget. While St. Louis ACORN had at least four full-time organizers plus part-time clerical support and paid canvassers, SJ ACORN had only one staff member.

Authority in San Jose ACORN

Most leaders and organizers of community organizations experience some conflict over issues, strategy, and tactics. However, SJ ACORN had a relatively harmonious mix of local and national direction, based on the mutual respect between local leaders and organizers. Leaders held their past and current organizers in high esteem, while organizer Sarah Rosen was "shocked" by how dedicated and responsible the local grassroots leadership was. The organizers supported members' choices of local issues, and members welcomed organizers' guidance on citywide issues.

The president of one chapter explained that in ACORN the phrase "coordinated autonomy" meant that all the money—dues, salaries, etc.—is channeled through ACORN's central office in New Orleans. The central office approved all expenditures, which one leader said sometimes caused "a lot of problems for the local organizations." Local staff had to supply weekly income statistics or they would not get paid. While this was an annoyance, tensions between the local and national organization did not seem to play a major role in SJ ACORN.

Member Recruitment and Mobilization

One of SJ ACORN's strongest leaders described how she was recruited. The founding organizer knocked on her door:

> I said I've got a lot of things to do and I don't have time to be going to meetings. . . . She goes, okay, what is it that you would like to really see change in your neighborhood? I said, the drugs. I want to be able to go out and make sure that my house and everything that's in there is still here when I come back. I don't go out at night, I don't go anywhere because of that. . . . She says, what if I guarantee you'll be able to do that? But you're going to have to work with me. And I say, yeah, after something happens, you'll back out. She says, no, I'll be here, I'll give you my word. . . . Right now all I'm asking is for you to come to our house meeting, see what we're about, and if you don't like it, fine, if you do, okay. So I went and there was about seven of us. We got the police to come out, we got direct lines to the captain who was in charge in the neighborhood . . . and we started to make a difference.

In Mayfair ACORN, members achieved some local improvements simply by inviting police to regular meetings and requesting better enforcement and regular reports.

SJ ACORN's strength has been its organizers' adherence to the ACORN model, particularly regular, intensive door knocking. Nationally ACORN has also used house meetings, like the one the member described above, which use preexisting social networks to recruit new members. The ongoing, labor-intensive recruitment and mobilization contrasts with St. Louis ACORN, which relied heavily on flyers advertising inducements such as jobs or home loans. While flyers were less time-consuming and more efficient in the short run, individuals recruited with one-time incentives were less motivated to get involved in political work than those who were recruited explicitly on that basis. SJ ACORN recruitment relies heavily on the organizer, but less than in St. Louis. San Jose members take more responsibility for mobilization—for example, many blocks in Tropicana ACORN have block captains who pass out flyers and make phone calls.

Leadership

A senior ACORN staff member cited San Jose as having one of the most stable, dedicated leadership networks. One chapter president was on the California state board and was ACORN's national vice president. Although the office had no staff for nine months during 1996–97, leaders applied by themselves for a city grant to organize neighborhood cleanup days and attended other neighborhood and coalition meetings. It took only three months after a new organizer joined the staff in 1998 for the three local chapters to be reactivated.

It is hard to measure how much the committed and effective leadership is due to activists' inherent skills and advantages, such as organizational experience, social embeddedness, and employment, and how much is due to the quality of supervision from their organizers. Data, interviews, and observation suggest that both were significant.

Quality of San Jose Organizing

SJ ACORN organizers were diligent and skilled. They worked closely and often with members, provided frequent training, and prepared them carefully for actions. For example, one chapter conducted a surprise occupation of its city council member's office because he had refused to meet with ACORN. The organizer had a preparation meeting with leaders with a printed bilingual agenda that included background on the grievance, plan of action, and song and chant practice; a section on what to do if the city councilman was absent, they were locked out, or the police were called; and how to react to three possible responses by the councilman. San Jose leaders frequently praised their organizers for motivating them and teaching them skills such as how to chair meetings.

SJ ACORN's wary, oppositional approach to authorities, and activists' opportunities to interact with them, made members less vulnerable to intimidation or manipulation. During an April Fool's action against George Shirikawa, their recalcitrant city councilman, an ACORN organizer posed as a student and set up a spurious research meeting with him. Then about twenty members burst into his office, chanting loudly and waving signs. Shirikawa, furious, asked the protesters why they were using such tactics and "dividing the neighborhood."[7] Less confident leaders might have been immobilized by his charges. One particularly strong leader who was offended by his refusal to meet was not confused or intimidated, and she stuck to the ACORN demands: that he meet with them and help get better neighborhood lighting, stop signs, and funding for neighborhood cleanups. Shirakawa met with ACORN and became more responsive, especially to this stubborn leader, but she was canny enough to interpret his actions strategically: "I think he's just trying to make friends."

When asked if they had been "challenged" by their organizer, the most senior leaders all understood what it meant—challenged to take on greater leadership or visibility or to try a new skill—and all said they had. In contrast, St. Louis ACORN leaders either said no or did not understand the question, assuming that it meant something negative such as "chastise" or "criticize." Top San Jose leaders had participated in national ACORN trainings. Leaders actively researched issues and sought information in many meetings with local officials, as both church-based organizations in this study do. After becoming involved in ACORN, three of ACORN's top leaders became leaders of the Mayfair Collaborative community development project, and many of the Collaborative's subcommittees are made up of ACORN members.

Staff Recruitment and Retention

San Jose was a difficult context for recruiting organizers. The local culture is influenced by hi-tech industry and lacks the strong counterculture of San Francisco, Oakland, and Berkeley. The cost of housing also discourages low-paid movement activists from living in the area.[8] Eventually, California ACORN had to assign an Oakland staffer to the San Jose office. Some members cited the staff shortage as an organizational weakness. One said, "If we had money we could get some organizers, but then we'd probably get a different kind of organizer. These organizers are like priests and nuns—they hardly get any pay. I, in the National Board, have brought proposals to try to raise their salaries so they could afford to live in California or New York."

San Jose Acorn Campaigns and Results

East Side neighborhood issues include local safety and maintenance, greater police patrols, adequate lighting, traffic safety enhancements, parks and recreation, and schools. The cost of housing is a major issue that neither PACT nor ACORN addressed significantly during the 1990s. However, after 2000 ACORN did pursue a campaign on housing in collaboration with PACT, San Jose's church-based community organization (see chapter 7).[9] Mayfair ACORN, the first chapter established in San Jose, began by addressing the extraordinary conditions at the local Cesar Chavez Elementary School. Traffic was unsafe for children, grounds were littered with glass and

trash, and the school of three hundred children had no working water fountains and only two bathrooms. ACORN won traffic safety enhancements,
a school cleanup, repair of the water fountains, additional bathrooms, and
community participation in hiring a new principal. Mayfair also won the
Police Athletic League's help in setting up a soccer league for local children. Tropicana ACORN's accomplishments included a $125,000 street
lighting project, trees trimmed, greater police patrols, and lights for a gang-
infested local park. The chapter pushed the city to install speed bumps to
prevent dangerous speeding, and initiated a citywide speed bump program.
ACORN's Hillview chapter won portable bathrooms and a grounds cleanup
at a new elementary school, neighborhood cleanups, repaved streets, and
upgraded streetlights.

Beyond the Neighborhood: Citywide ACORN Campaigns

By 1998, SJ ACORN's three chapters had collaborated on three campaigns,
of which one was successful. In its antiliquor license campaign, what began
as a local Tropicana issue developed into an all-ACORN campaign for a
moratorium on liquor licenses within a one-square-mile area. Tropicana
ACORN fought a proposed nightclub on the site where a previous club had
episodes of drunk driving, stabbings, and murders. ACORN strongly opposed more liquor sales because members saw alcohol as a major community
problem. The mostly Latino membership was sensitive to liquor companies'
exploitation of their community. ACORN leaders believed large corporations as well as local Hispanic businessmen exploited Hispanic communities where they did not have to live. Neighborhood clubs and associations
took large donations from liquor manufacturers or breweries in return for
selling alcohol there.[10]

Behind the issues of public health, crime, and drunk driving also lies a
women's issue: domestic violence. One member explained, "A lot of people
don't stop to think that if they start drinking . . . they keep drinking more
and more. Especially our culture [Mexican], they drink, and they drink,
and they drink. They go home and they beat their wives." Another leader
commented, "Everybody in this community has been affected by the alcohol or drugs in this community. . . . We have very high domestic abuse
here and it's all because of alcoholic drinks." This issue is publicly framed
as a community issue, not a feminist issue, because community organizations like ACORN do not frame issues along the potentially divisive axis
of gender.

Members conducted a survey and discovered that 120 establishments
served liquor in a one-square-mile area.[11] While many ACORN neighbor-

hood campaigns demanded services from city government, this one took on the liquor business and its political allies, the area's two city council-men. Council members Diaz and Shirakawa strongly opposed ACORN's efforts, citing the need for business to bring revenue to the community. One of the councilmen even brought the nightclub entrepreneur to meet with ACORN and, said one leader, "put money here and kind of tried to buy us out." ACORN refused and pursued a comprehensive ordinance ban-ning all new liquor licenses in the square-mile area. When Diaz refused to sponsor it, ACORN leaders researched the process of placing an item on the city council's agenda themselves. After producing large turnouts and testi-mony at two city council meetings, the ordinance passed unanimously. In 1997 it was extended to cover twenty-four census tracts—most of east San Jose. ACORN continues to fight increased alcohol sales in east San Jose. In 1998 Diaz attempted to circumvent the new city ordinance on behalf of the Mexican American Heritage Corporation, a nonprofit organization that built a major new community center with city redevelopment help. ACORN opposed its alcohol license.

Hillview ACORN's biggest campaign targeted noise and safety risks from a local airport. This became an all–SJ ACORN campaign before it was ultimately defeated. When an environmental impact report pronounced it safe, the Santa Clara County Board of Supervisors unanimously reversed their opposition and allowed the airport to stay open.

The other major East Side campaign involving all three chapters ad-dressed the terrible local schools and unresponsive school board. Hispanic East Side residents have extraordinarily low rates of high school graduation. One ACORN leader commented:

> I had a nephew that was going there. My son was five and was reading in-structions for a game to him. He didn't know how to read. Consequently, he's in prison right now. He never learned how to read, so he couldn't apply for a job. . . . I have friends right now that . . . can't even fill out an application, their family members have to do it for them. . . . We've lost too many kids to drugs because of the frustration of not knowing how to read, not being able to get through high school, through junior high.

Mayfair and Tropicana ACORN first got involved in this issue in 1997 in response to calls from parents. Their children's schools had no planned cur-ricula, inadequate materials, no working water fountains, no writing ma-terials, and few or no books. They learned that by the time they reached high school, 50 percent of area children were reading below grade level. At a school board meeting, about twenty ACORN activists demanded more books, daily periods dedicated to reading, and regular progress reports on program improvements. The board deflected the demands by asking ACORN to write a proposal. The activists researched other schools and wrote a proposal, which the board rewrote. The revision was unacceptable to ACORN, and the campaign remained at an impasse.

Forcing the school board to be accountable and improve the schools was a daunting issue with enormous community and social implications. It sought to arrest spiraling Latino illiteracy, poverty, crime, delinquency, and a growing Latino underclass. While ACORN supported the respected district superintendent, it targeted the corrupt and unaccountable elected school board. Reform of the Alum Rock School District required broad alliance building.

Participation in National ACORN Campaigns

From 1991 to 1997, the poorest 20 percent of Silicon Valley households saw real income fall 8 percent, while the wealthiest 20 percent saw income increase 19 percent.[12] SJ ACORN's citywide issues were redistributive responses to working-class impoverishment, coordinated by national ACORN. These included jobs, a higher minimum wage, and community reinvestment. SJ ACORN was part of national ACORN's nationwide push for living wage ordinances, though unlike St. Louis, it was one among many organizations in a coalition led by the South Bay Labor Council.[13]

Rather than pursue a living wage campaign on its own, ACORN pursued a first source hiring agreement with the San Jose Redevelopment Agency and major corporate recipients of agency subsidies. About thirty-five ACORN members crowded into the Redevelopment Agency headquarters on March 3, 1995, with children and picnic baskets, chanting "El Pueblo unido jamas sera vencido, the people united will never be defeated," and insisted on an appointment with agency director Frank Taylor. They demanded that all companies receiving financing from the Redevelopment Agency give preference to local workers, subject to penalties, and pay a living wage. ACORN, making good use of its research on state redevelopment law, pointed to a little-known feature of state law mandating that all redevelopment agencies expand opportunities for "jobless, underemployed, and low income persons" and "insure training and employment opportunities for lower-income project area residents." ACORN charged that the Redevelopment Agency had no such local hiring preferences and that funds went instead to "subsidizing fancy buildings."[14] At first, Mayor Hammer appeared sympathetic, but then eventually preempted the campaign by producing a toothless program for voluntary participation.

SJ ACORN also participated in ACORN's ongoing national campaign to combat discrimination in lending and to redirect investment into inner-city communities. It did not lead any challenges to bank mergers, but conducted local pickets as part of national ACORN challenges to Price Waterhouse, First Interstate Bank and Wells Fargo Bank, Citibank, and Travelers Insurance. ACORN also held an annual bank fair that drew about two hundred East Side residents seeking home loans to meet local banks.

Strategy

SJ ACORN provided members with experiences of success by following their lead on local issues that were pressing and realizable. Like St. Louis ACORN, members led on choosing local campaigns, while city and national campaigns are influenced by national ACORN priorities. SJ ACORN's organizers invested a great deal of time in recruiting members and building local leaders' capacity to pursue the issues of their choice. Due to the then-thriving economy—Santa Clara County's unemployment rate for 2000 was 2.6 percent—as well as a membership that was either retired or working, SJ ACORN did not address welfare issues.[15] They focused on schools with third world conditions, dark unlit streets, drugs, crime, a high concentration of beer and liquor outlets, and poor or few neighborhood services.

Tactics

San Jose ACORN's tactics ranged from the polite to the disruptive in a predictable pattern. First, ACORN would request a meeting with the relevant official or authority. If that authority agreed to meet, ACORN put its energy into producing a good showing and bringing in trained leaders to articulate its demands. Sometimes meetings took a creative form, such as the "flashlight tour" for Tropicana officials to demonstrate the need for more lights and better services. If the authority refused to meet or to grant demands, SJ ACORN could be relied on to initiate a disruptive protest, either a picket or occupation of an office. These tactics were rational in that they typically produced the results ACORN wanted: an agreement to meet. However, one-size-fits-all tactics were sometimes inadequately calibrated for local settings. For example, SJ ACORN took people to city council to support the proposed ordinance banning new liquor licenses in the King and Story roads area. At the first hearing, sixty to seventy-five ACORN members, who had waited for hours and were frustrated with the delay, marched into city council chambers "chanting, doing our normal ACORN stuff," and disrupted the hearing. Mayor Susan Hammer, a product of San Jose's participatory political culture, became angry and called them "rude."

When the vote was scheduled, nearly one hundred members attended but switched their tactic to a silent procession. SJ ACORN members adapted their tactics to the more decorous environment of San Jose's reform political culture when it was in their interest to do so.

In another instance, Tropicana ACORN staged an action against its councilman, Shirakawa, with whom it had a "difficult" relationship. Since he was running uncontested for reelection, "he forgot he needed to come to the neighborhood."[16] After several unsuccessful attempts to get him to meet, ACORN staged their April Fool's action on April 1, 1998, in which they tricked him into letting members burst into his office. The action, "a great press hit for us," was covered by a Spanish-language weekly, an English-language television station, and two Spanish stations. The action achieved its goal: Shirakawa was embarrassed and furious, but he agreed to meet with ACORN leaders.

Political Activism versus Social Capital as an End in Itself

In keeping with ACORN's ideological commitment to politics rather than service provision or mutual assistance, organizer Sarah Rosen found leaders' desire to organize local neighborhood cleanups faintly embarrassing and counter to ACORN ideology. Nevertheless, she supported leaders when they organized the cleanups, since part of empowerment and mobilization is encouraging residents to define their own issues. But neighborhood cleanups lack a political edge; they do not challenge the status quo or win political gains. Residents' pragmatic desire for the cleanups clashed with organizers' radical vision of political empowerment. On this issue, residents displayed a volunteer rather than a political activist orientation.[17]

However, the neighborhood cleanups also perform an organization-building function: they strengthen collective identity and social networks as well as community solidarity. One member cited a cleanup as her most memorable ACORN experience:

> I volunteered for that . . . since 6:30 in the morning till close to 2:00 in the afternoon, and it was really nice to be there and help organize. . . . A lot of people participated, we had a lot of volunteers. It was kind of neat seeing a lot of people out there.

San Jose Acorn's Impact and Potential

San Jose ACORN has won local neighborhood improvements. It organized many east San Jose residents who lacked a collective voice, trained and encouraged them, and retained effective local leaders with deep roots in their community. Some members became recognized leaders in national ACORN; one became the national ACORN vice president. SJ ACORN has sought not to build a broad-scale multiracial, multiclass coalition but to build its base in a relatively disenfranchised community, the Hispanic East Side. It represents the *local* concerns of working-class residents. It has gained recognition and access to a range of local city officials. In 1998 its small size limited its power to win on the more fundamental citywide challenges it launched.

In SJ ACORN, staffing difficulties may be remedied as the strong corps of leaders continues to learn through experience. Indeed, since 1998 SJ ACORN mounted an electoral campaign to unseat several local school board members and helped unseat three of the four candidates they targeted. Perhaps the biggest challenge SJ ACORN faces is to attract and retain skilled organizers. It demonstrated strong local leadership; with adequate resources, staff continuity, and political experience it may achieve greater local successes. Limited resources may hinder it from making a citywide impact unless it adopts a strategy ACORN has used successfully in other cities: forging broad coalitions.

Chapter 7 describes and analyzes the final organization considered in this study, People Acting in Community Together, or PACT. PACT members share many of the same concerns as SJ ACORN members, but their resources, ideas, norms, methods, and results are strikingly different.

7

The Power Is in the Relationship: San Jose PACT

I am very happy for the leaders because they had a great action. There were things that could have been a lot smoother, like having the pins be stronger. . . . Nothing beats Guillermo going at it with [a city council member] and Lucy holding her ground when he came at her. Guillermo was a warrior that night. Mike and Eduardo, those two have learned so much. Eduardo wrote that research report and organized that prayer service. Mike was invaluable and has begun to internalize the work. That's leadership.

—from PACT organizer weekly report

Among the groups that will be pushing a political agenda on San Jose mayoral and city council candidates this spring is a faith-based, grassroots organization that will neither make endorsements nor contribute to campaigns. But wise candidates will be listening.

—*San Jose Mercury News,* February 2006

On May 18, 1998, PACT held its largest annual action (mass meeting) with the mayor. For the first time the event was held not in a church but in the San Jose Civic Auditorium, to symbolize that PACT's domain was not just the church but the public arena. The action was a mayoral candidates' forum at which PACT sought commitments from the three candidates in the Democratic primary to support increased neighborhood services, after-school programs, and affordable housing. In the tightly scripted event, PACT leaders acted as bus coordinators, greeters, ushers, troubleshooters, and media liaisons. A mariachi band performed while the PACT action team met for final preparation. Clergy processed with church banners. PACT members testified emotionally to experiences with unaffordable housing and terrible schools, and others presented research on each issue. Closed-circuit television projected huge close-ups of the candidates. All three candidates signed PACT's 1998 platform.

Afterward, PACT organizers and leaders evaluated the event's strengths and weaknesses. Only about nine hundred people came, not the thirteen hundred to which leaders had committed. They guessed that no single burning issue motivated members, as gangs, drug sales, and youth crime had a decade earlier. Activists were tired from four other actions in April and May, including two local church actions, the PICO California statewide mass meeting in Sacramento and a subsequent news conference, and visits to lobby state legislators for a $9 billion state bond act for schools. Also, numerous screwups had undermined the May 10 Sign-Up Sunday in churches: a church was preoccupied with Communion Sunday, or the priest didn't make the announcement, or there were no pencils for members to fill out commitment cards. Not even the Filipino priest who said that not attending the action was a sin could make up for everything. But in her report, PACT director Kathy Samuels wrote, "Overall I felt good about the action: well-executed agenda, solid leadership team, good press, got some solid wins, kept our face in the power arena. Took some risks. Need to look deep and hard at turnout and how we had thirteen hundred committed and only eight hundred plus showed up."[1]

Yet the event was by far the largest candidates' night held in San Jose that year. All three candidates affirmed their support for PACT's platform. While promises from candidates are cheap, the organization had a solid record of achievements. It had established working relationships with the mayor and city council and by that time had won $45 million in redistributive programs and services. These included major new building projects, youth programs, traffic and safety improvements, and three city programs that were replicated throughout California. One program alone funds thirty-one separate youth crime, drug, and gang-prevention programs. PACT also trained a large cadre of neighborhood leaders to influence city governance. In the 1980s, city departments ignored PACT and the mayor dismissed its demands. But since 1996, politicians usually attend PACT's annual fund-raising luncheon themselves rather than sending their staff. (In 2004, PACT grossed over $100,000 from the event.) A 2006 *San Jose Mercury News* article commented:

People Acting in Community Together enters its third decade with an impressive list of accomplishments and a membership that has grown from 12 churches in East and downtown San Jose to 20 citywide congregations representing 50,000 people. The collection of Catholic, Protestant and Jewish congregations has matured into a force that has little difficulty getting meeting time with officials, can gather 1,000 people at the drop of a hat and is getting sizable grants from foundations and corporations to support its $1 million budget.[2]

This chapter illustrates the structure and operations, organizing practices, and political context that allowed PACT to evolve from an outsider to a grassroots organization with standing in local policy making. It has introduced innovative new programs, gained respect as a partner in policy making, and trained scores of unconventional leaders in urban politics.

PACT's Structure and Operations

PACT mobilizes pressure from San Jose neighborhoods to redirect city monies to human needs. As a member of the PICO National Network, PACT participates in PICO California, which included fifteen California community organizations in the late 1990s (twenty in 2006).

In 1998, PACT occupied two rooms in the office quarters of the First United Methodist Church in downtown San Jose. The office was cluttered but organized. The full-time development director's file cabinet reflected the scope of any sophisticated nonprofit fund-raising operation: foundation and corporate grant proposals, individual and major donor campaigns, and PACT's annual fund-raising luncheon.

PACT's history really began in 1977, when several Catholic priests in downtown and east San Jose started a church-based community organization to advocate for their low-income parishioners. Directly inspired by COPS, the IAF's successful church-based organization in San Antonio, Texas, they founded the Eastside-Downtown Organizing Project (EDOP). EDOP included the six large Catholic parishes that still make up the backbone of PACT. When EDOP went defunct, the churches reorganized themselves as the Ecumenical Sponsoring Committee (ESC), which raised seed money to hire organizers. In 1982 the group began to mobilize mass annual meetings with the mayor or mayoral candidates. In 1985 the ESC held its official founding convention and renamed itself People Acting in Community Together. PACT affiliated with the PICO Network so that it could send members to leadership trainings.[3] The ESC and then PACT has had a full-time director since 1981.

PACT's structure is typical of congregation-based organizations. It is funded by a mix of private foundation grants, small local corporate grants, church dues, and grassroots fund-raisers. Each of its member churches has a local organizing committee (LOC, which MCU and the Gamaliel Foundation call a "core team"). The LOC functions democratically, either by informal consensus or vote. Issues can originate in a member church or the all-city organization, which is led by a steering committee (board of directors) chosen from member churches. Each LOC selects several members for the steering committee, which elects an executive board. As in other nonprofit organizations, the steering committee hires and fires the director, who hires the other staff. PACT is unusual in employing a full-time fund-raiser, as well as four full-time organizers (including the director). The 1998 staff included a forty-five-year-old white woman director-organizer, a Hispanic organizer in her fifties, two young male Hispanic organizers in their twenties, a white female organizer in her thirties, and a half-time white female fund-raiser in her thirties. Organizers' salaries were consistent with other Bay Area nonprofit organizations: they ranged from $25,000 to $30,000 for beginners to $50,000 for the director, with medical benefits.

PACT's federated structure is flexible and encourages innovation by individual LOCs. Many major PACT initiatives begin at the local church level. While all CBCO member churches in theory can initiate local church campaigns, to succeed they need strong leadership, wide participation, and experience. Strong local organizing is a hallmark of the PICO Network, to which PACT belongs.[4] In 1998, of seventeen member churches, PACT had only thirteen active LOCs. But many of these had over a decade of organizing experience, and they had extensive training and support from PACT organizers. Each PACT organizer is responsible for two to five churches. The organizer meets at least monthly with the LOC, and far more often with individual activists and pastors to plan campaigns.

Constituency

PACT's membership is diverse, but includes working- and middle-class whites/Anglos, and poor to middle-class Hispanics. Seven churches were Catholic and ten Protestant. The Catholic churches are large, ranging from three thousand to over five thousand families each, while nine of the ten Protestant churches include only eighty to two hundred families. PACT claimed to represent thirty-five thousand families; however, the number of families each church actually claimed was less, as shown in Figure 15. PACT's Protestant churches are predominantly middle-class and Anglo, while its Catholic churches are more working-class and poor. Of the Catholic

Catholic	23,014
Protestant	1,865
Total	24,879

Figure 15. Number of families represented by PACT in 1998.

churches, only one has an Anglo majority and only one has a middle-class majority (of only 65 percent). The other six Catholic churches are respectively 100 percent, 99 percent, 80 percent, 75 percent, and 60 percent poor and working-class. Several are mostly monolingual Spanish speakers and undocumented immigrants.

A local church organizing committee includes from four to twenty members (ACORN and the CBCOs all refer to their leading active members as "leaders") who mobilize church members. PACT's constituency also includes the staff and beneficiaries of the many social programs PACT has pressured the city to provide, including students, parents, teachers, neighborhood residents, and staff and clients of programs funded due to PACT campaigns.

Resources

During the 1990s, PACT's budget was approximately $250,000 to $300,000, slightly more than St. Louis ACORN's budget. PACT is unusually successful in winning corporate and foundation grants, probably due to its Silicon Valley location and history of accomplishments. Church dues, though significant, make up only 15 to 20 percent of the budget. Catholic churches provide about two-thirds of the dues, even though their members are poorer.[5] The sheer number of Catholic members (and presumably diocesan resources) helps compensate for their relative poverty. Silicon Valley wealth trickles down to PACT through family and community foundation grants and the relative ease with which PACT attracts politicians and corporate supporters to its annual luncheon, which regularly draws five hundred Silicon Valley businesspeople, educators, bureaucrats, and others at $50 per person.

Authority and Control

Members of PACT have significant authority. PACT leaders take for granted their authority to hire and fire staff and to choose issues. While pastors play traditional roles in PACT meetings and actions, such as giving prayers, laypersons dominate the PACT leadership. PACT and PICO place an extraordinary emphasis on leadership training for average citizens. The most legitimate rationale for selecting an issue was that it had emerged widely in interviews with members. PACT activists learn to frown on "lone rangers," or activists without a constituency. A PACT organizer explained that one such lone ranger periodically tried to pursue his pet issue with PACT, but "he has no respect for PACT or the PACT process," and she must remind him that "we have to take it through the PACT process," meaning "do some one-to-ones." An issue is legitimate if it has "come up through the grassroots." A leader explained:

> Every LOC meeting we report out on our one-to-ones. . . . like this affordable housing issue that seems to be coming up more. If we see a whole bunch of people keep saying that, we look at it: is it universal within our LOC, or does it seem federation-wide? If it's across the LOCs, then the executive steering committee makes the decision to work on it. If it's just a local LOC, then the local LOC makes the decision by a vote to work on it.

For example, First Congregational Church carried out 200 to 250 interviews with church members that provided clear evidence that members' priorities were the needs of youth and the elderly. Having learned about after-school tutoring centers from the San Diego Organizing Project, they nevertheless confirmed their issue through more one-to-ones.

Mobilizing Members

PACT mobilizes as all CBCOs do. Organizers and leaders set quotas for turnout and internalize the expectation that they will be "held accountable" for them. If its leaders are experienced and well connected, even a small LOC can mobilize large numbers. One LOC in a Protestant church with only four leaders could regularly mobilize one hundred people from church and community. The leaders were experienced, respected, and belonged to overlapping social networks of church, neighborhood, and other voluntary associations.

Training Leaders

PICO organizations emphasize "developing people" as an end in itself as well as a means to winning campaigns. Like any CBCO network, they send leaders to a weeklong (five-day) training and emphasize learning through campaigns. But organizers spend an unusually high proportion of their time with activists individually, challenging them and discussing their progress. Even ordinary committee meetings regularly include a training item, a short module on some organizing skill. Leadership assessment is broad and holistic. Leaders learn to conduct meetings democratically yet efficiently. One activist described PACT meetings as

> a real good process [with] a lot of integrity . . . but if they didn't finish something, so be it. One of two things would happen: they would say, "Do we have the group's permission to extend the meeting X number of minutes, or do we want to stop?" and they would take a vote on it, and they would honor whatever the vote turned out to be, and not have a loud voice in the crowd push the agenda.

Training and Managing Organizers

PICO and PACT put a similar emphasis on training and development for organizers and general awareness of organizational processes. PACT held two one-and-a-half- to two-hour staff meetings per week. These began with a check-in from each staff member that could include personal, emotional, and work-related concerns. Staff shared information, got advice, made commitments, and planned together. Thursday meetings featured a reflection by a staff member, religious or secular, to link organizing to values. Staff took turns distributing readings on work-related topics, and each met with the director weekly for individual supervision. All staff wrote detailed weekly reports, which included the number of one-to-one interviews conducted with activists, officials, and community members.

PACT Issues and Campaigns

Strategy

Like MCU, PACT and its churches' status as 501(c)(3) nonprofit organizations legally restricts them from directly endorsing candidates for office. Therefore PACT is limited to exerting pressure with its mass base. As it has matured, PACT has gained leverage as a member of broader coalitions in San Jose, Santa Clara County, and California.

Strategic Framing

PACT frames its challenges to authority as the exercise of democracy. In 1991, the deputy city manager challenged PACT's access to city officials by circulating a memo to department heads informing them that PACT was a "Saul Alinsky-type organization" and that from now on he would control its access to officials. In a response to the mayor, PACT did not frame the policy as a challenge to its *power* or *rights* or as a cause of *outrage* or *anger* as ACORN might have.[6] Instead, the anti-access policy was couched as *harm* to *democracy* that *frustrates* well-intentioned citizens. PACT's letter to the mayor politely expressed concern for democratic values: "In a democracy, it is essential that the government encourage input from the families and neighborhoods that are the lifeblood of a city's vitality." PACT needs to "freely gather information and develop relationships with the appropriate city official responsible for a given area of concern." Access to authorities on PACT's terms was presented as an essential democratic right, and the mayor needed to make a "public repudiation of this anti-democratic policy."[7] And she did.

The Evolution of PACT Tactics

One church newspaper defined PACT's "typical, sometimes controversial, approach" this way:

> Instead of complaining to elected officials, propose realistic solutions which will solve specific problems. Do your research carefully and then invite decision-makers to discuss and debate specific issues and answer questions. Attend legislative meetings in force. *Never* boo a politician or treat him or her with disrespect. But confront office holders and speak the truth about neighborhood problems and solutions as forcefully as you can.[8]

PACT's "courteous contention" evolved from a stormy beginning. Its predecessor, the Ecumenical Sponsoring Committee, used confrontational direct action, which gave way to mass meetings coupled with informal collaboration and negotiation. Through the 1990s, PACT's relations with the mayor, city council, and bureaucrats became familiar and even cordial. PACT appears "too polite" and "nice" to ACORN leaders, who are accustomed to demonstrations and office occupations. But PACT's tactical evolution does not necessarily limit its effectiveness. It was historically more restricted by its localism and limited capacity than its polite self-presentation.

In a campaign against crime-ridden flophouses from 1982 to 1984, the ESC, then trained by the IAF rather than PICO, used guerrilla-like tactics that worked but backfired against its Catholic churches. This turned some PACT priests away from the kind of "tactical jujitsu" Saul Alinsky recommended. In 1982, staff at the soup kitchen of an ESC member church learned that nine squalid flophouses in downtown San Jose were severely abusing their mentally ill, addicted, and retarded residents, who patronized the soup kitchen. There had been several rapes and a murder. The properties' absentee landlord was said to be a loan shark involved in organized crime whose family lived in a gated estate. Not only was the family a major donor to Catholic Charities, but the owner's wife ran the annual fund-raising ball.

When direct appeals to the city failed and the landlord refused to meet, the ESC organizer followed the classic technique of escalating, personalizing, and polarizing the issue.[9] The tactic that finally worked was a threat to publicly embarrass the landlord's wife at a Catholic Charities ball. At the last minute, the landlord met with the ESC. However, he had already filed a $25 million lawsuit for defamation of character, $5 million each against an organizer, two priests, and two leading activists. The Catholic diocese settled the suit for $50,000. The flophouses were shut down and replaced with city-funded affordable housing, which opened with a ribbon cutting by the mayor.

The flophouse campaign impressed upon the city the ESC's determination, but it also impressed upon the bishop and diocese the risk of tactics that crossed the boundary from public to private—such as picketing a home or targeting family members. In 1985 PACT joined the PICO Network. One of the founding priests observed, "PICO has a gentler approach. After IAF, I thought, 'These guys are too gentle, we're gonna get killed.'" However, he came to believe that PICO's style was more moderate but "not weaker."

PACT's guerrilla-style tactics were abandoned partly due to the flophouse lawsuit and partly because with growth, PACT had more clout and didn't need them. PACT has avoided personal attacks and pursued power through mobilizing large numbers and effectively researching its demands. The tactics of the flophouse campaign are better suited for those without other levers of power, or those like ACORN who use confrontation to produce political education and a unifying, oppositional collective identity. By 1998 the city saw PACT's value as a gauge of grassroots sentiment and a source of policy ideas with the constituency to support politicians who advanced them. Once officials learned that organized communities kept out crime and drugs, the city went so far as to fund its own community organizing. One PACT president commented that PACT had become "stronger, different . . . we're more collaborative, and that was my goal. Not that we're not confrontational with the city, figuring out how to get what we want. The city can be on our side—they're working for the citizens."

Through their eight-year relationship with Mayor Susan Hammer (1990–98), PACT learned that she hated to renege on promises and frequently refused PACT requests only to agree to them later. "She says no all the time," said one PACT leader, but "there's a joke: we say every time she says no it costs her a million dollars." In return for her support, PACT recognized Hammer at annual celebrations and fund-raisers. However, mayor Ron Gonzalez took office in 1998 and PACT again had to struggle for recognition and access. Despite PACT's well-mannered contention, some officials still find it threatening because the CBCO method unilaterally alters the rules of engagement between politicians and citizens.

Media Coverage

The formal and professionally run actions typical of CBCO may actually harm its ability to gain publicity because they appear staged and unexciting. When PACT was new, it got frequent press exposure. Later, publicity was harder to get. When the *San Jose Mercury News* told PACT it doesn't like to cover "theater" or "staged events" and "doesn't cover meetings," CBCO activists became frustrated because they see the mobilization of one thousand to five thousand citizens in political engagement as newsworthy in itself. One PACT member expressed frustration that ACORN gained more publicity because its comparative lack of preparation made it look more unrehearsed and therefore more grassroots. However, as PACT gained victories and credibility, *Mercury News* coverage became consistently respectful.

Use of Coalitions

Like most CBCOs, PACT works pragmatically issue by issue, in coalition with allies. In addition to its sister organizations in PICO, it works with politicians, corporations, labor, neighborhood associations, local businesses, schools, and parent-teacher organizations. When a nonprofit hospital converted to for-profit, PACT joined with the California Nurses' Association and local officials, mobilized 350 people for an event with the attorney general, and helped win a $12 million set-aside for indigent medical care.

First Congregational Church PACT illustrates PACT coalition building. The church pioneered the first two homework centers, city-funded afterschool tutoring centers open until 6:00 p.m. in local schools. The schools became immediate allies. A new principal who sought more community participation hired the PACT organizer to train teachers to interview parents. In turn, when First Congregational PACT and this school undertook a joint campaign for a stoplight near the school, the teachers mobilized one hundred parents and other residents to an action, while the students held a protest during recess to gain media coverage.

Because PACT's primary strategy has been to propose, win, and expand new city programs, the staff and beneficiaries of these programs become allies that PACT targets for mobilization. But the backbone of mobilization is by far still the churches, where PACT organizers concentrate their leadership training and organizing.

PACT Issues and Campaigns

The Challenge to Downtown Redevelopment

PACT and its predecessor organizations are much older than MCU, the other church-based organization in this study. Many PACT churches have been members for over two decades.

Between 1981 and 1984, PACT's predecessor, the Ecumenical Sponsoring Committee, cut its teeth on typical neighborhood issues. It tried unsuccessfully to challenge sprawling development in the Evergreen Valley but was more successful addressing typical neighborhood complaints. The ESC won $2 million in street, sewer, and traffic improvements; $1.5 million for a community center in a Hispanic neighborhood; had a drug house demolished; temporarily prevented the expansion of a local airport; replaced nine dangerous flophouses with affordable housing and resettled the residents; and preserved thirty downtown houses from destruction. During this time, its membership grew from five to fourteen churches.

Since the 1980s, PACT has pressured the city to reallocate Redevelopment Agency monies from massive downtown building projects to affordable housing, neighborhood needs, and social services. Unlike St. Louis, San Jose was never a major manufacturing center. But with the rise of Silicon Valley, it competed for business development with suburbs like Santa Clara, Mountain View, and Cupertino. San Jose sought not to reclaim old glory but to gain standing for the first time as a major city, not a cow town surrounded by hi-tech suburbs. Mayor Tom McEnery and his protégé and successor Susan Hammer believed that to do this, the city needed to build a real downtown with museums, hotels, corporate offices, athletic stadiums, and parks. McEnery and Hammer were of one mind with Frank Taylor, the ambitious director of the San Jose Redevelopment Agency.

The San Jose Redevelopment Agency has few checks on its power and authority. Its board consists of the San Jose City Council—the same city council that oversees the Redevelopment Agency. Since the Redevelopment Agency board has no separate oversight, it has tended to support the mayor-appointed director's priorities. In Santa Clara County, 9 percent of the property tax went to redevelopment, the highest of any urban county in California.[10] While other redevelopment agencies channel some tax income to counties and schools, the San Jose Redevelopment Agency avoided doing so.[11]

Through the late 1980s and 1990s, PACT mounted one challenge after another to this pro-growth coalition to reallocate funds for social (neighborhood) needs. PACT sought to convince city officials that it was the legitimate bargaining agent for thousands of San Jose voters and must be recognized and taken seriously. While it failed in its early, most sweeping proposals—diverting 30 percent of new Redevelopment Agency income to youth programs and emphasizing job creation—it developed an alliance with mayor Susan Hammer, who shared PACT goals for education, youth, and neighborhood services. This allowed PACT to propose and win significant new city programs addressing youth, drugs, crime, and neighborhood needs.

Every spring at its largest annual action, PACT presses the mayor (in an election year, candidates for mayor) to adopt its agenda for the year. In election years the meeting precedes the Democratic primary; in nonelection years, it precedes the city's budget adoption.[12] In 1987, PACT was new and Mayor Tom McEnery refused to accede to its demands. At the PACT meeting McEnery stonewalled, arguing that the people "didn't understand the significance of redevelopment and how it was helping the city." Although McEnery was taken aback by PACT's direct challenge and firm control of the meeting, he had to acknowledge the huge crowd of church members present. One leader noted, "McEnery was probably one of the strongest mayors we ever had, and we set him back on his heels." Another said the 1987 action "changed the political landscape of the city of San Jose" for PACT. PACT then turned to the city council, which endorsed all the PACT housing proposals that the mayor had opposed. One longtime PACT leader traced the political decline of Mayor McEnery to this moment. In 1994, McEnery was heavily favored in a race with county supervisor Zoe Lofgren for U.S. congressional representative. Lofgren, a longtime PACT ally, won handily in an upset victory.[13]

In 1988, PACT's research and interviews with church members led it to focus on "the drug epidemic and the associated pain and violence touching the vast majority of South Bay families." From 1985 to 1994, the rate of violent felonies per 100,000 juveniles increased from 136 to 627—a 360 percent increase. PACT pressured McEnery for programs to curb drug sales. The day before his mass meeting with PACT in June 1989, in what is seen as a PACT victory, McEnery announced Project Crackdown, a $1 million effort to fight drugs in neighborhoods. At the meeting with over one thousand PACT members, McEnery agreed to make the drug issue a priority.

The next year, 1990, was an election year. At its mass action, PACT won commitments from the three mayoral candidates to deliver a comprehensive antidrug plan within six months of election and to consult with PACT. When former council member Susan Hammer was elected mayor, she honored PACT's demand for regular briefings. This began an eight-year relationship of both challenges and collaboration, resulting in many policy innovations proposed by PACT and implemented by the city. A cooperative city administration saw PACT as an ally to help advance its agenda of neighborhood-level reforms.

Nevertheless, PACT and Mayor Hammer fought over the use of Redevelopment Agency funds. In 1990–91, at the same time as crime, gangs, and drugs in neighborhoods increased, California experienced the worst recession since the Great Depression. State funds for cities were severely cut.[14] While the recession created pressure on redevelopment agencies statewide to shift funds from economic development to city operations and social services, San Jose Redevelopment Agency nevertheless sought to capture new monies for large building projects. With the mayor's support, the agency heavily subsidized downtown building projects through tax-increment financing.[15] It was estimated that its expanded borrowing capacity would capture over $1 billion in taxes that would otherwise fund city and county services.

In the early 1990s PACT launched a sweeping challenge to the Redevelopment Agency's appropriation of city resources. PACT leaders did not miss the irony of slashed social services juxtaposed with massive appropriations for palm trees and fine art downtown. Neighborhood services had no new programs or funding increases for five years. Meanwhile, the city was funding a hockey arena at a cost of $24.5 million more than the voter-approved amount, and the mayor had her eye on a major league baseball team and stadium. The 1990 Redevelopment Agency five-year plan totaled $789 million for downtown projects, including over $10 million of public subsidies to private developers.

In 1991 PACT demanded a comprehensive five-year plan for "youth and the drug epidemic" and asked the mayor to unveil it at the organization's June mass meeting. PACT proposed a funding mechanism called BEST that would divert 30 percent of all new revenues from the Redevelopment Agency's expanded taxing authority (less than 4 percent of Redevelopment monies) into youth and drug programs. Hammer fought the proposal for a year and a half, so PACT expanded its campaign to city council members, whom churches pressured in their council districts. BEST included a wide array of programs addressing delinquency, gangs, drug use, and crime, and PACT insisted on including progressive crime prevention and treatment programs as well as prosecution.[16] Predictably, the Redevelopment Agency fought this proposed use of its funds, claiming it was restricted by state law to building projects in designated areas.[17]

Initially the mayor and two council members supported minimal Redevelopment Agency funding for BEST ($1 million per year for five years) and a $1 million drug rehabilitation center for adolescents. However, at the last minute the powerful Redevelopment Agency director fought back, claiming the fund diversion was illegal. PACT leaders forcefully challenged this claim at their mass action. The mayor responded with a five-year, $6 million plan of programs funded by Redevelopment. Former PACT director David Mann explained:

> We were able with [the issue of] gang violence to make a very effective argument that the investment [Redevelopment] was making in the physical area of downtown needed to be protected by investing in the youth. You can tear the heart out of a neighborhood with youth violence as fast as you can build it up economically.[18]

PACT was rebuffed in its more sweeping demand to channel 30 percent of new Redevelopment revenues to youth and children's programming. PACT leaders acknowledge their failure to significantly alter Redevelopment Agency priorities. One said, "We were able to get a few crumbs from Hammer" because [city budget director and ally] Brownstein said, "Listen, I'll get you guys what you want, but don't try to go through Redevelopment, because our hands are tied."

Two days after the mass meeting, Mayor Hammer unveiled a $40 to $50 million plan to finance a major league baseball stadium and other developments. The mayor's strategic error was in proposing a utility tax to pay for the stadium. A coalition of stadium opponents framed the mayor's plan as taxing basic human needs—heat and electricity—for private gain. PACT distributed anti-stadium information to ten thousand voters in churches and neighborhoods. The mayor's initiative was defeated.

In 1992 PACT won a $1.8 million increase in program funding; but the following year, in an emotional meeting, budget director Bob Brownstein convinced PACT that in the current recession, the city was struggling just to maintain essential services like police and fire protection.[19] PACT failed to win a multiyear funding commitment and major reform in Redevelopment Agency priorities but won incremental program expansions.

In 1993, PACT identified another unmet need. First Congregational Church learned about homework centers, after-school academic programs that a sister PICO organization in San Diego had won. After school, when most juvenile crimes are committed, homework centers provide a safe alternative to gangs, free child care for working parents, and tutoring for low-performing students. They are not recreation programs but a response to parents' concerns about poor education. The church pressured two city council members to fund five pilot homework centers in their council districts. The centers were so successful and popular that PACT sought funding for one in each of the ten council districts.[20] Year by year the program was expanded. By 1995–96 the city supported 63 homework centers, for $645,382. By 1999, a permanent budget line item funded 163 centers, each with a paid director, and by 2003, all San Jose public schools had a homework center. Disappointed with the city's implementation of BEST, PACT fought not only for the program but for a specific program design, demanding paid directors, credentialed teachers, and adequate budgets. Although many students served are low-income, homework centers are not need-based and therefore attract broad support.[21] They have become a winning issue for the mayor and city council members.

As part of the fourteen-organization (now twenty) PICO California, PACT helped raise education issues in Sacramento. In 1995, PICO California had its first statewide action, an education summit in San Jose with 2,000 people, the California director of education, and the director of the U.S. Department of Education. The action was mostly a show of force but may have influenced the federal award of $25 million to California for school-to-career programs. In 1998, PICO California brought 2,500 members to a Sacramento town meeting with twenty state legislators. PICO pushed for the state's largest-ever bond act ($9.5 billion for school construction and repair, delayed by partisan conflict) and funding for after-school programs statewide. Both passed. After the action, Governor Pete Wilson included $50 million for after-school programs in his revised budget, in language adapted from the PICO proposal. PICO was part of a larger coalition but began to make a name for itself and gained its first experience mobilizing a grassroots citizens' movement at the state level.

Political Opportunity for PACT

The political context and institutions of San Jose in the 1980s and 1990s offered PACT favorable opportunities.

Gaining Political Access

Political access for grassroots challengers expanded in 1988 with the advent of San Jose city council elections by district rather than at-large. This created the opportunity for both PACT and San Jose ACORN to pursue local campaigns by targeting their district council members. PACT had member churches in six of ten city council districts, as compared to SJ ACORN's two. The potential to win a majority of council members' support opened the opportunity for PACT to pursue new citywide policies through the council as an alternative to the mayor's office. This, combined during the late 1980s with PACT's ability to mobilize mass meetings, forced Mayor McEnery to deliver Project Crackdown to fight drugs, gangs, and crime. This victory reinforced access to the mayor's office and, with this political capital, eventually to McEnery's protégé Mayor Susan Hammer. PACT steadily gained access to the officials it needed and developed credibility and influence with the Hammer administration. PACT used this access to press for even greater inclusion in city policy making.

To advance its issues, PACT mobilizes voters during election cycles. As in St. Louis, in San Jose the meaningful electoral competition takes place within the Democratic primary. PACT's grassroots constituency has influenced not only mayoral and city council elections but races for county supervisor and U.S. Congress. Officials to whom PACT has made claims found PACT valuable in mobilizing support for programs, and some became frequent allies.

Divisions among elites is one dimension of political opportunity, but there have been few divisions among economic elites for PACT to exploit. San Jose's pro-growth coalition has remained intact through two decades and four mayors. PACT attempted fundamental challenges to the pro-growth coalition, represented by the San Jose Redevelopment Agency. It set a precedent for diverting agency funds to neighborhood programs, but its significance lay more in its positive effect on neighborhoods and its value as a precedent than for the percentage of agency funds actually diverted. Its more fundamental challenges to the Redevelopment Agency—demands to channel new revenues to youth and children's programming, create a commission on new redevelopment priorities, and shift the majority of redevelopment spending into neighborhoods—PACT lost. Such ambitious challenges would have required a greater mobilization of voters and a viable, more sympathetic alternative to the last two decades of elected leadership. The potential cleavage between major Silicon Valley industries and developers might offer possibilities for PACT to exploit. The electronics industry seeks to recruit and retain its workforce and has led initiatives to improve quality of life so that the region can remain competitive.[22] With homework centers and school-to-career internships, PACT has capitalized on the corporate interest in improving public education. The industry's interest in affordable housing and mitigating traffic congestion, long commutes, and other byproducts of sprawl is at loggerheads with development interests.

Government Capacity

Unlike St. Louis, in San Jose an increasingly strong mayor and a ten-member city council had the authority and capacity to meet PACT's demands.

Divided authority—between mayor and council, among council member districts, between city and county—offered PACT more political openings than constraints. While St. Louis is restricted by charter from annexing adjoining land, San Jose annexed much of its surrounding land in the 1960s, so it controls much more area. Yet even in San Jose, fragmented governing authority sometimes poses difficulties. In its campaign for a residential drug treatment center dedicated to youth, in theory PACT could have used a commitment by the mayor to provide land and a building as leverage with the county supervisor to provide operating costs, and vice versa. But the separate authorities passed the buck to each other, each refusing to commit until the other did.

Since 1996, PICO California has increased its lobbying capacity with the State of California. The division of powers among Sacramento state legislators and local officials is well suited to PICO's federated structure. PICO's California organizations could target their local representatives in concert on statewide campaigns, yet exercise local autonomy.

PACT took advantage of opportunity—allies in the mayor's office, district city council elections—to initiate and institutionalize ongoing programs that benefit poor and working San Jose residents. It selected goals that were specific and realizable, backed by a large grassroots constituency. Along with MCU, it was not able to mount enough force to significantly challenge the pro-growth alliance of politicians and developers that supported development; however, it won significant concessions in the process of training a corps of effective and nontraditional activists in city politics.

Consolidating Its Gains, Expanding Its Challenges

New Small Schools

Since 2000, PACT has deepened its work on education. In 1999, an organizer formerly with PICO's Oakland Community Organizations (OCO) became PACT's new director. OCO has led campaigns for high-quality small schools and won twenty-five new schools in Oakland. PACT established a separate nonprofit organization in 2004, the ACE Public School Network, which has established three thriving small charter schools in the Alum Rock School District in Hispanic east San Jose.[23] PACT also gained legislators' support for alternative schools for at-risk youth.[24]

Health care is another critical issue for PACT constituents. In 1999, it worked with a coalition to preserve charity care in a hospital that converted to for-profit status. In 2000, PACT surveyed member congregations and learned that at some churches 45 percent of families had at least one member with no health insurance. More than 80 percent of uninsured families were headed by a full-time worker. PACT and its PICO California affiliates researched the issue and took three thousand members to Sacramento to lobby for using tobacco settlement funds for community health clinics. PACT also had an opportunity to address the issue closer to home.

The Children's Health Initiative

After Susan Hammer's term as mayor ended in 1998, her budget director Bob Brownstein became policy director of Working Partnerships USA (WPUSA), an innovative labor think tank in San Jose. Health care for the uninsured was a priority for both WPUSA and PACT. The strategy WPUSA and PACT crafted took advantage of new resources: state tobacco settlement funds. State Proposition 10, which levied a state tobacco tax to fund child health initiatives, generates about $700 million each year, $10 million for San Jose. As well, the state was increasing access to its Healthy Families plan, which reaches those ineligible for other programs but without private insurance. The WPUSA/PACT plan started with children, since universal coverage for all was not then feasible. With aid from the tobacco settlement, San Jose would have to commit relatively little—$2 to $3 million—to provide health care for all its children.

The Children's Health Initiative recruited social service and health provider allies, including Santa Clara County's public health agency. Later, these allies included PACT and WPUSA in designing the program. Other allies from academia, philanthropy, and health care gave the proposal the legitimacy it needed to win the *San Jose Mercury News*'s support. This was "a crucial breakthrough for the campaign."[25] However, Mayor Ron Gonzalez opposed the initiative. Because the tobacco money came with no strings, Gonzalez preferred to use it to keep his campaign promise to fund improved education. Santa Clara County's involvement in the proposal (the county provides health care) activated historic enmity between Gonzalez and county supervisors. Although his support could have won him national coverage as a trendsetter, Gonzalez opposed the health plan. He was strongly criticized by the *San Jose Mercury News* and alienated over one thousand PACT members at a June 3, 2000, action. According to an organizer, "He didn't even try to schmooze the audience. There was powerful testimony from parents. . . . Gonzalez was icy cold after forty minutes of lots of tension."[26]

The mayor pressured city council members and won their allegiance with pet projects for their districts, and PACT lost two council allies. The proposal lost by one vote. However, the Santa Clara County Board of

Supervisors endorsed and funded the plan. In 2001, Santa Clara County committed to insure 100 percent of its children. From 2002 to 2004 the county recruited 25 percent more children into the existing Medi-Cal and Healthy Families programs. It also created a new program, Healthy Kids, for children ineligible for these programs but below 300 percent of the poverty line (then $58,050 for a family of four). Healthy Kids enrolled another 15,000 children by 2004. The vast majority of Healthy Kids enrollees are undocumented immigrants well below 300 percent of the poverty level, who are ineligible for the state programs because of their immigration status.[27] The program brought $24.4 million in new state and federal dollars into the county, and twenty-seven other counties in California considered or implemented a similar program.

For PICO California, health care was also a primary issue. By 2001, PICO and its allies had won over $700 million in funds, including $400 million annually from the tobacco settlement, for clinics and health care (see Appendix C). San Jose PACT also deepened its involvement in education reform in underperforming Latino districts.

PACT's Impact and Potential

In the context of shrinking public resources and a national conservative ascendancy, PACT successfully forged a coalition of working-class, middle-class, and low-income members to win meaningful concessions. PACT used a piecemeal rather than a fundamental reform strategy and won incremental redistributive outcomes. In many cases, new programs became institutionalized. These are in no way adequate to withstand the fundamental national erosion of majoritarian social policies. However, given that for most of its history PACT included no more than fifteen churches, surely its achievements represent formidable leveraging of limited resources. PACT also benefited from the affluent philanthropic context of Silicon Valley and the relatively open political culture of a reform-style urban regime. It also benefited from the diffusion of policy ideas and political acumen that accumulated within the PICO Network. However, this was no guarantee of success. PACT had to combine resources with resourcefulness—the ability to learn from its failure to seriously challenge the Redevelopment Agency, to craft winning campaign issues, and to form constructive coalitions. Within the stark constraints of its time, PACT organizers and leaders exercised creativity not just in framing demands but in discerning problems and creating issues.

8

The Results of Organizing

We don't just want to focus on the issues, we want to empower these people to express their own dignity and sense of self-worth and to see themselves as equal to the politicians. But when push comes to shove, you organize around issues.

Priest of a PACT member church

This study has examined four community organizations in some depth, and compared the norms and practices of ACORN organizing to those of church-based community organizing. Ultimately, however, this study is concerned with results—the political, civic, and policy outcomes that organizing provides its participants, communities, and broader struggles.

Many causal factors influence social movement outcomes, so it is notoriously difficult to identify general patterns. Only a large representative study of organizations could support general causal claims. This chapter's aims, therefore, are more humble. I identify five outcomes that are significant for grassroots groups that seek to empower ordinary citizens, and I compare the four local organizations in these areas. To partially address the limitations of four local case studies, I also examine the broader work of the three national organizations. I include the most significant outcomes of the other locals in PICO, Gamaliel, and ACORN to get a better picture of the scale of other locals' work. Increasingly PICO and the Gamaliel Foundation as well as ACORN are undertaking national campaigns. I also compare data on these three national organizations.

The results of even four local case studies can be suggestive. If organizations in different cities are successful in one aspect of grassroots organizing *despite* dramatic differences in urban context, that would suggest that, at least in regard to this outcome, socioeconomic context is not destiny. Or if there are similar results in some areas between CBCO and ACORN locals, that suggests that the methods share important similarities or that in some areas other factors overwhelm the influence of organizational type. It is clear that national organizations exert powerful pressures for conformity through various mechanisms—centralized organizer training, ongoing consulting relationships between the nationals and their locals, national trainings for activists throughout the country, and in ACORN's case, its structure as one organization with centralized staff accountability and funding subsidies. This ensures consistency within each type with respect to organizational structure and broad mobilizing cultures. However, local and idiosyncratic features also influence results: availability of local resources, the skills and experience of local staff, local political regimes, and the ability of different racial groups to work together, to name an obvious few.

In this chapter I compare the four organizations with regard to five areas: (1) organizational strength; (2) engaging ordinary Americans, including underrepresented groups, in civic engagement and political action; (3) advancing issues important to poor Americans; (4) building coalitions across race and class lines; and (5) delivering policy outcomes.

Organizational Strength

I consider five components of organizational strength: (a) mobilization capacity, (b) leadership continuity, (c) organizational reputation, (d) regular access to authorities, and (e) ability to influence agendas.

Mobilization Capacity

All four local organizations seek to mobilize large numbers of people, the source of their strength—in organizing jargon, to achieve scale. All the organizers make enormous efforts to maximize attendance at their actions, whether they call or sign up members directly themselves (ACORN) or supervise activists in recruiting church members to events (the CBCOs).

The two church-based organizations mobilized significantly greater numbers to their events than the ACORN organizations.[1] This is not surprising, given religious congregations' access to institutions with social networks, their hierarchical chain of command that organizers and leaders use to mobilize members, and norms of accountability that pressure their leaders to produce attendance targets. During 1997–98, each ACORN chapter could mobilize from 15 to 50 people at local neighborhood events and from 30 to 100 at citywide ones. However, St. Louis ACORN had mobilized hundreds of north St. Louis residents in its campaign to keep a public hospital open—a reminder that mobilization capacity can wax and wane over time. The CBCOs could mobilize 100 to 300 at smaller, local events, and 750 to 1,000 at major events that year. There also, mobilization capacity waxed and waned—both PACT and MCU had mobilized as many as 2,000 previously and subsequently. Clearly, the different mobilization capacity of each organizational type is consistent with previous research on CBCOs.[2]

PACT and MCU had a similar mobilization capacity, even though MCU included fifty-seven churches and PACT had only seventeen. No matter how large the *potential* pool of activists, the actual pool was limited by the number of organizers. MCU's fifty-seven churches had only two organizers and no support staff. Strong leaders, church networks, and CBCO mobilizing culture allowed MCU to produce large mobilizations nevertheless. PACT had four organizers for seventeen churches; from one-third the organizational base, PACT could mobilize an equal or greater number. The simple structural factor of how many units (congregations) each organizer was responsible for (how well staffed was the organization) was fundamental.

However, raw structural availability says little about the dynamic mobilization process itself, which also varies. CBCO organizers' time is not spent in telephoning individual church members but in intense interaction with top leaders, analyzing their work, coaching them, seeking out potential new leaders, interacting with pastors—in short, the series of microprocesses the CBCOs call relationship building. PACT organizers aimed for at least fifteen one-to-one interviews per week. They also devoted much time to increasing activists' commitment and skills. More highly developed relationships create higher stakes for those who do not meet their commitments. Churches, especially large ones, are complex organizations with numerous committees and subassociations such as women's groups, ushers' guilds, youth groups, and sometimes subgroups based on language or ethnicity, such as Hispanic, Filipino, or Chinese groups. Activists use their web of social networks to set and meet demanding mobilization goals.

ACORN has developed tactics to help compensate for having to mobilize individual members and families directly rather than through a network structure. The organization takes advantage of its biennial national conventions to stage protests of about two thousand ACORN members from across the nation. Also, since ACORN has doubled the number of local offices since 2000 alone, it achieves larger local mobilizations by busing members from nearby cities to local actions.

Leadership Continuity

Grassroots organizations rely on volunteer leadership to build participation and power; if an organization relies on a constantly shifting pool of activists, it loses organizational skills, knowledge, and memory. Organizational memory is essential in long campaigns: St. Louis ACORN's campaign for a living wage ordinance took six years, and a PACT campaign for a drug treatment facility for youth has lasted over ten years. While leaders' power can ossify and keep an entrenched group in power, organizations in which leaders are chosen democratically have succeeded in avoiding this dilemma. In Figure 16 I measure leadership continuity by the number of years activists reported being active in their organization.[3] Among St. Louis ACORN leaders interviewed, none was active for less than two years and none was active for a period of seven to ten years; most had been long-time activists. This reflects the relatively small number of active leaders at that time (so that not all categories are represented) and the need to recruit lasting new leaders. All the organizations grapple with turnover and have leaders who have been active for years as well as newer recruits. All four organizations were founded in 1992 or earlier, but the proportion of leaders active for seven or more years varies from 50 percent of PACT leaders and 60 percent of St. Louis ACORN leaders to a quarter of MCU and San Jose ACORN

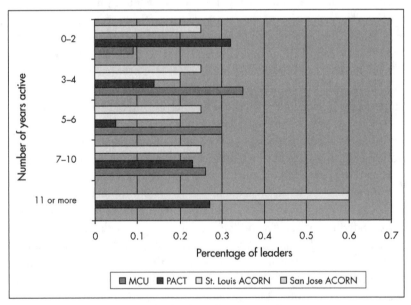

Figure 16. Number of years leaders have been active, by organization.

leaders. The fact that MCU for St. Louis and San Jose ACORN had no leaders active for eleven or more years is because both these groups were less than eleven years old at that time.

All the organizations have both members with long experience and some relative newcomers. St. Louis ACORN needed to recruit a new corps of active members, but had begun the job. San Jose ACORN leaders were impressive in the dense ties they had with their neighbors and their ability to recruit into the organization. At St. Louis ACORN leaders did not mobilize network ties to the same extent, due to weaker neighborhood ties, less effective mobilizing practices, or both. Residents of the San Jose ACORN neighborhoods are significantly better off than residents of north St. Louis. More research is needed to understand the relationship of poverty, ethnicity, local social networks, and neighborhood stability. Mobilizing practices likely play a role also, as the description of organizing practices in the case studies suggests.

Organizational Reputation

Authorities' perceptions of an organization's strength and effectiveness were influenced by many factors. Of the four groups, PACT had the widest public recognition.[4] San Jose ACORN was seen as effective in neighborhoods, though too small in 1998 to have a citywide impact. In 1998 MCU was not seen as powerful in the city as a whole, except in helping put urban sprawl on the region's agenda. St. Louis ACORN was well known, but informants were skeptical about its influence (before it won the living wage ordinance).

Regular Access to Authorities

A demonstrated usefulness to authorities (by helping achieve shared policy goals), ability to demonstrate power through mobilizing large numbers of voters, or significant victories helped groups win access to authorities.

The CBCOs had slightly better access because of their legitimacy and greater number of voters. However, when a new and less collaborative mayor, Ron Gonzalez, was elected in 1998, PACT had to struggle all over again for access to the city's top official.

While national ACORN has established relationships with national politicians, local ACORN chapters have less consistent access to their local politicians. St. Louis and San Jose ACORN had smaller mobilization capacity than the CBCOs, and their boisterous tactics sometimes angered officials, who then refused to meet. However, disruptive protest was often needed for new or weak chapters to win a meeting. Most of the time both ACORN chapters were able to meet with city officials and bureaucrats.

Ability to Influence Political and Policy Agendas

Even groups that cannot win individual campaigns can influence the public debate and, thereby, future campaigns. This was true for MCU's urban growth boundaries campaign and St. Louis ACORN's ballot initiatives for campaign finance reform and a state wage increase, which lay the groundwork for their living wage campaign. All four organizations launched proactive issue campaigns and defined new issues as significant. Appendix C lists the policy innovations the four groups introduced to their city and state agendas from 1990 to 2006.

Civic Engagement

Civic engagement has both breadth and depth. Organizing draws previously inactive citizens into action and deepens the engagement of others. It targets poor and working-class Americans, who are proportionately less active in civic and political life.

Mobilization capacity, discussed as a dimension of organizational strength, represents the breadth of civic engagement. The mobilizing capacity of MCU and PACT was consistent with Warren and Wood's survey of CBCOs, which estimated that in 2001 they mobilized between 1 and 3 million people, with 2,700 people on governing boards, and about 24,000 as active leaders.[5] ACORN mobilizes fewer people locally, but increasingly can compensate with multicity actions. Since the 2003–4 election cycle, all the groups engaged in unprecedented levels of voter registration and mobilization (see Appendix C, ACORN and MCU national accomplishments lists).

Leadership Training

The sheer number of people who attend meetings and protests or are mobilized to vote represents breadth of civic engagement but not depth. The number of activists and how thoroughly they were trained helps organizations run successful campaigns but is an outcome in its own right. Public leadership is skewed toward the affluent and well educated; even the leaders in these four organizations tend to be better educated than rank-and-file members.[6] Nevertheless, the groups train hundreds of poor, working-class, minority, and women leaders who have little political experience.

Almost all seventy-five ACORN and CBCO leaders interviewed, whether they were middle-class pastors, engineers, nurses, or teachers; working-class factory workers, secretaries, or truck drivers; or very low-income activists on public assistance, began with little confidence or experience in strategic political activism. Several experienced activists said things

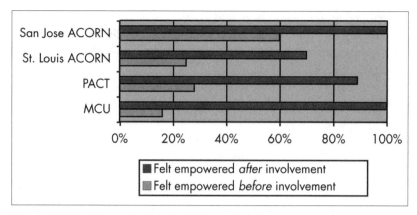

Figure 17. Participants' subjective feelings of empowerment.

like "I've never been afraid to speak my mind" or "I felt like I had lots of power . . . my [child-care] co-ops were my community . . . Now I belong to a larger community." But even most educated professionals felt that "there was no real way of making a change"; they felt "very uncapable" or that they could only exercise influence on a "more one-to-one or individual" level. Figure 17 shows that, in all four organizations, after participation the vast majority of activists interviewed felt far more political efficacy.

Civic Skills versus Strategic Knowledge

What political scientists who study participation have considered civic skills bears little resemblance to the complex strategic and leadership skills activists learned in these organizations. Survey data typically provide information on individual skills and categorize participation as aggregated individual acts, such as voting or public speaking. Such basic civic skills bear no relationship to the strategic calculations and familiarity with a political landscape that effective organizing requires. Even the educated middle class tend to have little experience beyond isolated or expressive acts such as voting, signing petitions, and attending protests. The more sophisticated and interactive political skills that some citizens have are not visible to most scholars of political participation. Yet these are precisely the most valuable skills that grassroots organizations like ACORN and the CBCOs impart.

Empowering leaders consists of both imparting *subjective* feelings of efficacy and teaching *objective* skills in moral and policy deliberation, research, and strategic planning. Chapter 1 illustrated that CBCOs emphasize training at all levels (in fact, PICO leaders are taught that the very mission of their organizations is to train leaders, not win issues). In ACORN, there is wider variation in organizers' expectations and leaders' responsibilities. In St. Louis and San Jose ACORN, strong leaders research issues and make strategic decisions, while weaker leaders' roles may be limited to mobilizing members for actions, running meetings, and speaking to the press. St. Louis ACORN's style was more off-the-cuff, while the San Jose members were carefully coached and rehearsed for actions.

All four organizations helped leaders feel more effective in the civic arena than they did before involvement. However, consistent with other research, interviews with CBCO activists suggested they learned more concrete skills.[7] This is unsurprising given the extraordinary emphasis CBCO places on leadership training, especially in PICO. Members were asked whether they had learned to "speak in public," "chair meetings," "conduct research on issues," "plan strategy," or "other" (the member named another skill such as conducting one-to-one interviews or translating during meetings). In MCU 69 percent and in PACT 100 percent of interviewees reported learning three or four of these skills. In St. Louis ACORN, the figures were 35 percent, and in San Jose ACORN, 25 percent.

Some of PACT's top leaders—primarily or all women—have become visible as effective advocates in other arenas. One former PACT president and another board member are teachers at the same Latino high school. In partnership with a state program, they founded an aviation academy within their high school that enrolled forty-five students in its first year. The impetus for the program was a PICO California Project Education Summit in 1995 that proposed educational reforms, including school-to-work programs.[8] Another Filipina PACT leader regularly advises her city council member and helped develop a comprehensive set of city programs to assist low-income immigrant parents at a middle school. Another top PACT leader successfully ran for San Jose city council in 2002, and a second ran in 2006 (but was not elected). A final example is Lupe, a formerly homeless, low-income Mexican single mother of seven with a sixth-grade education. This leader became active because, reportedly, she discovered the teachers at her children's school spent their days in the teacher's lounge rather than teaching. Lupe, who cannot yet speak English, played a critical role in several major PACT campaigns and is now a member of her area high school's governing council, which prepares the annual school plan and budget.

Advocating for Poor Citizens

For two decades, the income gap between rich and poor Americans has grown. In 1996 the federal government ended its commitment to support poor families through Aid to Families with Dependent Children (AFDC). In this context, we might ask whether organizations that pursue economic justice actually advocate for low-income, not just working- and middle-class Americans. ACORN and the CBCOs all seek to redistribute resources and power to poor and working-class people. The question is whether they advocate explicitly for poor people's issues *and* whether they win.

Although ACORN and CBCO constituencies overlap (many black members of ACORN belong to churches), ACORN reaches an unchurched low-income group. Like their white counterparts, many active members in black urban churches are now suburbanites who commute back to the urban neighborhoods of their youth. In a study of predominantly black churches in four cities, three-quarters or more of the members of roughly two-thirds of the churches lived more than one mile from their church.[9] ACORN's door-to-door and other recruitment methods enable it to reach both churchgoers and nonchurchgoers in poor neighborhoods.

ACORN consistently advocates for the poor and the working class. It is unconstrained by the need to satisfy middle-class constituents, so it can freely advocate for low-income issues such as welfare rights, higher wages, indigent medical care, and public housing tenants' issues. ACORN is an agenda setter for poor people's issues, consistently participates in coalitions representing their interests, and has won significant victories. Nationally, ACORN has achieved precedent-setting living wage agreements and low-cost loan programs. For example, predatory lending that targets the poor with excessive interest rates, fees, and penalties increased enormously during the 1990s.[10] In 2000, ACORN secured a three-year pilot program with the mortgage company Ameriquest. Using protest methods, ACORN pressured the company to commit $363 million in home loans for low-income families in ten cities with ACORN locals, including St. Louis.[11] ACORN successfully pushed a city ordinance outlawing lending abuses in Oakland, California, and allied with AARP, Consumers' Union, and others to pursue state legislation. Since then, ACORN has drafted model legislation and mounted campaigns in Philadelphia, New York, and Los Angeles, often in coalitions. By mounting successive local campaigns against the same national corporations, it has helped produce national momentum for reform and won significant improvements for poor people.

In contrast, the CBCOs are more economically diverse. Each local church has autonomy to select its issues, so if low-income people dominate a church, their issues will come to the fore.[12] For larger, citywide campaigns, CBCOs select issues that appeal to their broader and more diverse base. This means if their low-income church members share concerns with working- and middle-class members (typically issues not tied to family income, but to neighborhood conditions, crime, safety, services, and education), then MCU and PACT can successfully pursue them.

I found little evidence that low-income members in either MCU or PACT felt that their interests were unrepresented in citywide campaigns. Both groups selected major issues supported by members of all income levels. PACT selected youth services, education, and crime prevention in middle-class, working-class, and poor neighborhoods. MCU took on urban sprawl, which has major consequences for all St. Louis city and county dwellers, especially inner-city residents. CBCOs can take on issues that benefit solely low-income constituents if they can successfully be framed in terms of social justice or legitimate human needs, such as living wage laws or health care for all children (which the PICO California Project then expanded to include more adults). Cross-class coalitions are most unified when members of different classes have formed relationships of trust. PACT was old enough that its corps of top leaders had amassed significant experience and knowledge of diverse San Jose neighborhoods and their issues. Its middle-class leaders were strong advocates of issues such as preserving indigent hospital care and increasing low-income housing. The challenge of motivating less-involved middle-class members is mitigated in cities like San Jose, where Catholic churches with lower-income Hispanic members usually provide the largest mobilization capacity. Gamaliel projects that bring together inner-city and suburban churches arguably have the greater challenge, which they address with a metropolitan policy analysis that stresses shared interests.

During periods of movement demobilization, coalitions with the middle class through federations of churches can advance concerns of low-income Americans. Issues exclusive to poor people can also be addressed, but if they are culturally controversial, such as welfare and workfare issues, they are likely to get more attention from ACORN.

Building Coalitions across Race and Class

The ability to form cross-race coalitions is notable in itself, but more important, multiclass, multiracial coalitions may give low-income people and people of color greater leverage than they have on their own. Although it was an ongoing challenge, especially for MCU, the CBCOs built active coalitions across race and class. Including the middle class is not a stated goal of ACORN; however, ACORN bridges class divisions between the very poor, the working class, and some middle-class black and Hispanic professionals and small business owners.[13] ACORN is typically poor and working-class, while the CBCO members ranged from poor to middle-class. Racial and ethnic diversity often does not map neatly onto class diversity, so I consider the two to be separate dimensions.

CBCO Racial and Ethnic Diversity

Research indicates that CBCOs "bridge the racial divide," although their ability to do so is influenced by local racial-ethnic dynamics.[14] PACT, the most ethnically diverse of the four groups, has large white and Latino constituencies, some Filipinos, and very few black members (San Jose's black population is 4.3 percent). Four of its largest churches are Hispanic and Catholic. MCU, which is majority white, reflects the racial polarization of St. Louis. About seven to ten of CACI's churches are black, but gaining black pastors' trust remains one of MCU's biggest challenges. However, both black and white members felt strongly that MCU was successfully biracial relative to other St. Louis associations.

Although CBCO *locals* may have difficulty bridging local racial divides, the networks as a whole present a fully diverse picture. One Gamaliel Foundation organizer with experience in ACORN and many other groups described Gamaliel as

> very diverse, probably one-third black, one-third white, one-third Hispanic. This is the most diverse organization I've ever worked with. Because we have so many Latinos and immigrants in the organization we started seeing stuff happen to people. A guy in one of our congregations was taken out of his car after getting groceries and taken away in handcuffs and he died in prison in Missouri because he couldn't speak English. He kept telling them he was ill. You start to experience these problems in a diverse membership with a diverse staff.

CBCO Class Diversity

PACT and MCU and their combined churches were economically diverse. However, low-income members face barriers to leadership; they have as little time for voluntary work as the affluent, but less confidence and fewer civic skills.[15] Sometimes class maps relatively neatly onto religion, especially in high Latino areas: PACT's ten Protestant churches are mostly middle-class, while its six Catholic churches are much more poor and working-class.[16] The Catholic churches include 22,000 families, while the more middle-class Protestant churches claim only 2,065 families—less than 10 percent the number of Catholic members. MCU's Catholic churches also have more low-income parishioners than the Protestant churches.

Immigrants face barriers to leadership beyond class and race. The Silicon Valley cost of living requires that low wage earners work two or more jobs, and many immigrants are deterred from involvement by the language barrier. Maria, a Filipina who is a strong PACT leader, explained that immigrants are further inhibited from activism because "in our homelands when you spoke up you went to jail or got killed. We have to overcome that, coming from the third world countries. There's not the freedom in demanding your rights."[17] Maria saw herself as an indigenous community leader mentoring other immigrants, who begin by attending mass meetings and then become leaders on their church organizing teams and possibly in the city PACT leadership.

ACORN Class and Racial/Ethnic Diversity

Nationally, ACORN has a small white presence but is otherwise ethnically diverse (mostly black and Hispanic, judging from the 1998 national convention). As noted, both ACORN chapters are ethnically homogeneous; San Jose is about 90 percent Hispanic and 10 percent black, and St. Louis ACORN is almost entirely African American. In these local groups ACORN brings together poor and working-class members *within* one race. As noted above, ACORN does not aim to organize the middle class, although it does include relatively well-off blue-collar workers (or retired workers) as well as low-income members.

ACORN consistently advocates for low-income, especially poor minority, Americans. It does not aim to include many white or middle-class constituents. Because churches range across the entire ethnic and socioeconomic spectrum, the CBCO structure gives them a potential for racial and class diversity that they realize in varying degrees, highly influenced by local race relations and other factors.

Policy Outcomes

We know very little about the role of local or even national grassroots organizations in originating public policy proposals. Scholars have demonstrated how major federal policies have originated in large membership federations and mass movements.[18] However, in a political climate hostile to redistributive reforms, policy innovations at the grassroots may take on greater significance yet be all but invisible to observers. Many initiatives first gain visibility only after politicians officially endorse them (or co-opt them), or they produce national movements but the local associations that originate them remain obscure. More research on policy making from below would correct our understandings of policy making as well as what is possible for citizens' organizations in a hostile political climate. Appendix C includes data on specific policy outcomes for the four local and the three national organizations, whenever possible measured in dollars and/or number of people or level of jurisdiction affected, 1990 to 2006 (when available).

Local Organizations

MCU struggled in a difficult political context—a state legislature dominated by rural legislators and St. Louis and inner-ring suburban governments with limited resources and a disproportionate burden of poverty. With allies, MCU helped win new gains and, just as often, preserve redistributive programs threatened with elimination. MCU helped keep three schools open, helped establish the city's occupational high school, and kept a local hospital. It gained state legislative lobbying experience during the hospital campaign and through its work on urban growth boundaries and redevelopment and transportation projects.

When Gamaliel established a Kansas City, Missouri, affiliate, MCU became more adept at state-level politics and now plays a leading role in national transportation equity campaigns. MCU is a leading member of the national Transportation Equity Network (TEN), a project of the national Center for Community Change (see chapter 9). One of the Transportation Equity Network's achievements in 2005 was adding a Local Workforce Investment amendment, Section 1920, to the national transportation bill. This provision encourages states and localities to allocate 30 percent of construction work hours to people of color, women, and the economically disadvantaged. Although the amendment thus far has no teeth, it provides pressure that community groups can use to negotiate for these gains. Using Section 1920, MCU led a campaign that won an agreement with the Missouri Department of Transportation to allocate 30 percent of work hours on the rebuilding of Highway 64, or 150 union-scale jobs, to disadvantaged and low-income workers. MCU's increasing facility with state-level politics also enabled it to help preserve such programs as state tax credits for distressed communities and children's health insurance.

San Jose ACORN consistently produced neighborhood improvements and made headway in the east-side Alum Rock elementary school district, where ACORN members mobilized to unseat the ineffective, antireform school board. Four of five members were voted out of office. SJ ACORN pressured the district to supply new textbooks, won an addition to help ease overcrowding at one elementary school, and helped apply for a state grant for a parent governance program. As a young organization, its limited membership base restricted the scope of its activities, but it has grown significantly.

SJ ACORN now has an office of the ACORN Housing Corporation and is part of the thirteen-chapter California ACORN, active in state campaigns for education, housing, and a minimum wage increase.

St. Louis ACORN's most notable outcomes in the 1990s were produced by its ACORN Housing office. Its six-year campaign for a living wage agreement bore fruit in 2002. A new head organizer (director), an African American minister, started a sister chapter in East St. Louis and built alliances with other black clergy and churches in the city. Like MCU for St. Louis, SL ACORN responded to the imbalance of power between St. Louis City and the county by expanding organizing to include lower-income, African American suburbs. Not only are fewer resources needed to build power in smaller cities, but these give ACORN a base from which to pursue such metro-wide issues as transportation equity—investment in buses and light rail that benefit low-income people and people of color.

San Jose PACT was the most successful in gaining policy outcomes, having won conservatively more than $100 million in new city and county programs. A number of programs set precedents, becoming models for other city programs, and contributed significantly to PICO California state campaigns.

Evaluating the National Organizations

Among the three national organizations in this study, ACORN has led in the scope and scale of its national campaign outcomes. Both the PICO National Network and the Gamaliel Foundation are much newer to state and national organizing. Because of their decentralized structure, the aggregated impact of all their local affiliates is difficult to measure—which helps keep them relatively invisible. However, the impact of PICO's work in California is more visible, with its now twenty-member PICO California organization. The Gamaliel Foundation does not have a comparable presence in any one state, although it has some powerful city and regional affiliates. Appendix C presents detailed information on the policy outcomes of the four local and three national organizations in this study.

The Gamaliel Foundation

While Gamaliel excels at linking national policy analysts with grassroots leaders in training programs that link race, poverty, and national development policies, its policy outcomes nationally are modest thus far. Increasingly Gamaliel's campaigns for equity in development policy have focused on increasing national transportation funds to low-income and minority communities. Gamaliel took a major step in electoral organizing during the 2004 national election and is the lead organization in the national Transportation Equity Network, or TEN (see chapter 9). In 2005, TEN successfully lobbied Congress to include language in the SAFETEA-LU national transportation bill that encouraged local hiring on transportation projects, a de facto antipoverty program.[19] Community organizations in New York, Louisiana, Missouri, Illinois, and elsewhere have begun to use this provision to pursue campaigns for jobs and apprenticeships.

PICO National Network

PICO California contributed a mobilized mass base to state coalitions that won $13.4 billion in education and health funding (see Appendix C). Its Oakland affiliate is an important advocate of innovative small schools. California governor Arnold Schwarzenegger signed into law AB 1465, which allocates 10 percent of his $222.6 billion, ten-year infrastructure budget for thousands of new and small schools. A partial estimate of PICO's fifty affiliates' local redistributive gains as of 2006 (excluding San Jose PACT) is $2.23 billion in local community programs.

PICO began national organizing shortly after 2000. Because its culture is strongly rooted in local organizations, its initial step was for each PICO affiliate to research federal policy and power in its own locality. Like Gamaliel, prior to the November 2004 election, PICO coordinated public meetings with elected officials at the local, state, and national levels in major cities (thirty-seven of its fifty affiliates). PICO affiliate leaders came to Washington, D.C., for training, research, and lobbying meetings that began to build networks and capacity for future work. An organizer from PICO's Denver affiliate, Metropolitan Organizations for People, described the effect of this national exposure on local activists:

> In 2005 MOP took fifteen resident leaders (to join three hundred PICO leaders) to Washington, D.C., to become educated and informed about the link between national policy and local problems and pain. This was a deeply influential event for our organization. It captured the imagination of our members to dream and take action steps toward addressing federal policy issues and connecting them to local and state problems. Leaders who were only concerned about crime in their community some two years ago were now visiting congressional representatives and being trained by national policy institutes. They came back to Denver ready to lead MOP in efforts to fight federal cuts in Medicaid. They also came to understand the connection between shrinking health-care access for poor children and passage of [local measures] C and D in November's election.

Activists began to make links between issues, and according to the organizer, leaders held the largest meeting in recent history and "educated and involved people in complex issues that impact all of our children."[20]

ACORN

A conservative, independent (though ACORN-funded) study of ACORN redistributive outcomes from 1994 to 2004 estimated their value at $12 billion.[21] Even though its largest outcomes were realized as part of a broad coalition (like the other groups in this study), ACORN's policy outcomes are still impressive. A significant percentage comes from low-cost housing mortgages and legal settlements from its work on predatory lending. ACORN has the longest and most productive record of national organizing campaigns and has excelled at creative strategies, as detailed in chapter 3. As a national organization, ACORN commands attention from national political figures such as Ted Kennedy, Hillary Clinton, and John Edwards, all of whom were scheduled speakers at ACORN's 2006 national convention.

Locally, the two CBCOs were more successful than the two ACORN chapters in mobilizing large numbers, slightly more successful in gaining access to authorities, better at building coalitions across race and class at the local level, and better at leadership training. ACORN chapters were just as effective at influencing agendas and raising new political issues; excelled at advocating exclusively poor people's issues, such as income and wage issues; brought together poor and working-class people locally; and nationally, brought together diverse ethnic groups.

ACORN excels in winning concessions from nationally coordinated campaigns. The Gamaliel Foundation has led in metropolitan policy analysis and transportation equity advocacy, while PICO's national organizing has proceeded with the caution but thoroughness characteristic of that organization. Some critics argue that the CBCO (especially PICO) emphasis on deep local leadership development has allowed conservatives to cheerfully dismantle the federal welfare state without interference. (Of course, community organizing alone hardly had the power to prevent it.) They argue that if the community, labor, and other progressive sectors had united, AFDC might not have been dismantled. Others respond that the mobilization capacity required for major national campaigns is rooted in carefully nurtured local leadership. No single approach can successfully advocate for low- and moderate-income Americans, and since 2000, the community organizing sector has dramatically increased its capacity and commitment to higher-scale organizing. Chapter 9 considers the innovation and collaboration needed to realize the potential of this movement.

American Inequality and the Potential of Community Organizing

There is this sort of macho culture in organizing that makes it difficult anyway; you're not allowed to admit that any other model has anything worthwhile. Sometimes I've gotten the impression that organizations view each other as more the enemy than the enemy.

—Community organizer

Community organizing offers useful lessons for both scholars and practitioners of social movement activism. In a hostile political context, powerful forces prevent it from doing more. Even generous welfare states are under heavy pressure from global economic competition to curtail redistributive social programs and worker protections. More locally, contrasting urban contexts set different limits on the possible. Yet, I have argued, there is more scope for agency in social movements than scholars have acknowledged. Part of this is an artifact of the disproportionate concentration on national movements, whose goals are inevitably more ambitious and harder to realize. Another bias in the literature is a disproportionate focus on movements closer to Ideal Type A, particularly their expressive, symbolic aspects. This has obscured more strategic, pragmatic, and incremental dimensions of collective action. One PICO principle states, "The farther you are from a problem, the more you can philosophize." Because the organizing in this study addresses the immediate grievances of its constituency, it needs to win. Therefore, its strategies and tactics are important and revealing to those interested in strategic choices. These choices alone cannot roll back the dramatic increases in racial and economic inequality in the United States, but they can make the difference between success and failure in specific struggles, with billions of dollars at stake for working people. (Appendix C begins to quantify the policy outcomes of the four local groups in this study and, more consequentially, the three national organizations to which they belong.) Decisions by organizations and movement sectors on whether or how to collaborate toward larger goals have even greater consequences. This chapter examines implications of community organizing for other movements and for progressive reform efforts. Some barriers to success are internally imposed; others could be lifted if elite political allies so chose. I conclude with reflections on how this movement sector needs to confront a globalized political-economic terrain.

What We Can Learn from Community Organizing

Poor and Working-Class Americans Can Be Organized

Even in the best of times for social movements, scholarship suggests that poor and working-class Americans resist politicization and civic engagement.[1] Given these findings, one would conclude that politicizing poor and working-class Americans is a dubious prospect. However, these community organizations show how it can be done, despite a daunting and hostile political context. Church-based community organizing's cultural approach has united members of religious congregations across class and race lines. Its essential elements could be applied much more broadly, translated into a nontheistic language of values, rituals to connect daily work with larger meanings, using emotions explicitly in organizational processes, and attending to processes as well as results. ACORN uses a more task-oriented approach. Both styles have achieved impressive results.

Some argue that new vehicles for citizen influence, such as the public interest group and the Internet, help fill the advocacy gap left by the decline of traditional civic organizations. In *The New Liberalism,* Jeffrey Berry argues that public interest groups "engage their members in the political process in a meaningful way" and "are not the hallmark of 'thin democracy' but a reflection of people's abiding concern for the health of their society."[2] Debra Minkoff notes that national interest organizations can also act as nationally visible proponents of group claims and sources of "symbolic affiliation" that can play a powerful, life-affirming role for marginalized groups.[3]

Public interest groups perform a critical representative role, but they have limitations. First, they are strongly biased toward the affluent and too often do not speak for the poor or the working class. Second, they are not themselves democracies but are run by experts whose accountability to members is attenuated at best.[4] Thus they usually cannot provide the experience of democratic decision making, conflict and power, negotiating to achieve a shared purpose, and learning through action and struggle that democratically run organizations can provide.[5] Also, single-issue advocacy groups do not easily recruit citizens into new issue campaigns and expanded understandings, as older fraternal and civic organizations could do and as community organizing does today. No institutional mechanisms recruit environmentalists, for example, to advocate for educational equity or labor rights. Middle-class liberals have been able to separate such issues as environmentalism, nuclear weapons, peace, feminism, and gay rights from issues of class.[6]

The CBCO model of organizing provides a space for cross-class deliberation and learning. Coalitions between these groups, ACORN, and labor unions provide more opportunities for cross-class advocacy. But as Weir and Ganz argue, "Issue advocacy organizations must confront the fact that their opposition will always have the upper hand in a politics organized around money and technology."[7] Community organizing must draw on its traditional source of strength, organized members, to exert influence.

Organization Matters for Poor People's Movements

In 1979 Piven and Cloward's *Poor People's Movements* launched a debate about the comparative role of organization and mass disruption in poor people's campaigns. It has continued to prompt vigorous debate. Scholars have observed that the book makes a nuanced argument about factors necessary for movement emergence and success and that they foreshadowed McAdam's "cognitive liberation" and subsequent research on how emotions are linked to mobilization when they note participants' "indignation" and "joy" in meetings. An integral part of their argument is that movements can win concessions only during brief windows of opportunity. There seems to be a consensus among scholars that preexisting organization is more important for mass mobilization than Piven and Cloward admitted and also that their argument was more narrowly focused on bureaucratic, sectarian, party-like organization than organization and social networks broadly defined. If they oppose bureaucratically developed organizations, they do not deny the role of cadres.[8]

Other scholars take issue with their argument. This study shows the community organizing approach has produced significant gains on the local, state, and even national levels (such as their ongoing defense of the Community Reinvestment Act) during the decline of national political opportunity. ACORN is a poor people's organization, and CBCOs, while multiclass, pursue redistributive issues of jobs, housing, health care, and education designed to benefit poor and working-class people (often the young). As Joseph Kling writes, "It is simply not the case that only mass strikes and uncontrollable disruptions can attain significant gains for working people."[9] These gains would not have been possible without well-developed organizations.

Strategy Can Partially Counterbalance a Hostile Political Context

Mobilizing structures and cultures provide the material and conceptual resources for social movement leaders to exercise agency. Morris argues that institutions like SMOs are "agency-laden," replete with resources leaders can use to design strategy.[10] However, many scholars' structural bias and community organizers' ideological bias about bottom-up leadership by members have given the role of entrepreneurial decision making short shrift in explaining movement outcomes. It is a fixture of organizing ideology that organizers are coaches who train leaders (from among the membership) to own and lead the organization. ACORN has challenged this distinction somewhat by hiring large numbers of organizers from their constituents' neighborhoods and blurring the boundaries of who can speak for the neighborhood. Nevertheless, while staff with talent can advance from entry-level positions in all the organizations, the ideology of democratic control causes organizers to understate the importance of their own strategic expertise. This denies the important role of leadership in movements, another research topic whose neglect has begun to be rectified.[11]

Scholars in the political process tradition have argued that the configuration of political opportunities is the major force influencing movement leaders' strategic choices. Theory suggests that movement activism will emerge when there is general political instability, specifically, new access to the political system, divided elites, and new (often elite) allies.[12] Organizations and networks as well as successful issue framing are also key variables for scholars in this tradition; however, political opportunity appears to be "first among equals" as a predictor of new movement activity. The concept has come in for a barrage of criticism, for its ad hoc combination of variables and sometimes tautological application ("if mobilization occurred, there must have been political opportunity").[13] Research shows that movements have burst forth in contexts of no political openings and heavy repression. Scholars are increasingly acknowledging the room actors have to maneuver in choosing courses of action and the difference their choices make to outcomes.[14]

While the success of local organizations is influenced by different local political-economic contexts, the emergence of national campaigns and *over-*

all growth of community organizations from the midnineties to the present is better explained by the following:

1. Accelerating grievances and threats, especially under the George W. Bush administration.
2. Increased organizational capacity (members, staff, funds, and experience), as the national organizations gained experience and multiplied their number of affiliated organizations since 2000.
3. Strategic learning by organizational leaders. In this study we saw PACT choose incremental issues with multiple stakeholders and gradually universalize them (PACT's after-school centers), PICO California frame new issues locally and diffuse them throughout the state, ACORN diffuse many different tactics (such as living wage ordinances) through their locals across the nation, the Gamaliel Foundation creatively dovetail state with national organizing so that work to add redistributive provisions to the 2005 national transportation bill (SAFETEA-LU) enabled successful local campaigns, and ACORN develop nontraditional allies, new sources of funding, and multilevel, multitactic corporate campaigns.[15]

Through the prism of media, mass national mobilizations often seem to catch fire quickly and may just as quickly be extinguished. Their emergence may correlate with an opening in political opportunity. However, even without media attention and mass awareness, significant organizing for reform—enough to be called a movement—can expand and, in broad enough coalitions, win significant concessions.

Yet while strategy can make a difference even in a hostile context, that context sets limits on the possible. In 2000, PICO California and other health policy advocates won an agreement for $200 million in state matching funds that would have added 300,000 more parents of insured children to state health insurance programs. In 2001, then-governor Grey Davis agreed to use an *additional* $400 million per year of California tobacco settlement funds for health care programs. However, neither victory could be realized. When the Internet "dot com" industry collapsed early in the decade, the California state budget—heavily dependent on the stock market—was devastated. In another strategy, PICO had drafted legislation that would have altered state commercial property taxation, making more funds available for human services. However, such significant fiscal reform would have required a two-thirds vote in the California legislature, which the number of Republican legislators made unfeasible. PICO, ACORN, and their allies in California continue to weigh alternative strategies to reach their redistributive goals.

Since community organizing has raised its sights to the state and national levels, it confronts a global terrain foreign to Saul Alinsky.

Community Is Global: The Organizing Terrain Is Altered

Changes in American politics and the economy have created barriers to community organizing that activists in the sixties and seventies were only beginning to face. Threats to federal domestic programs resulting from new war and Homeland Security expenditures, a massive federal deficit, and major tax cuts for the affluent created grievances for poor and working Americans, already suffering from skyrocketing health care costs, housing costs, and shrunken budgets for human needs. Unions are threatened by a steady decline in membership, from a high of 37 percent in 1946, to 13.2 percent in 2002, to 12 percent in 2006.[16] Although since 1995 AFL-CIO leadership led a return to aggressive organizing, labor is struggling to regroup since the six-million-member Change to Win coalition of unions left the federation over what was seen as an inadequate commitment to organizing.[17]

At a time like this for urban organizing, Peter Dreier has asked, "Where is the power structure when you need it?"[18] St. Louis, like any city that has not annexed much of the surrounding land, cannot control suburban sprawl; the St. Louis region's municipal fragmentation, as well as a hostile development lobby and state legislature, meant that advocates of controlled development had an intractable political challenge. Increasingly local corporations have been sold to far-removed owners who have no locally-rooted commitment to the health of the urban community. The days when Alinsky could assume that the Daley machine or Eastman Kodak controlled local destinies are over.[19]

Students of contentious politics are probably more familiar with the shift in scale from national to transnational activism than they are with efforts to shift from local to state and national domestic activism. Because control of government resources has shifted upward, and capital has fled its local roots through corporate mergers and acquisitions, community organizing is attempting to shift scales.[20] However, grassroots resources—mass memberships—have more leverage in local action. Organizations are learning to operate in forms that are more isomorphic with their targets. One method is to select national targets that rely on local communities, such as a member of Congress seeking votes or a bank seeking to comply with the Community Reinvestment Act by issuing local mortgages. Another is to transcend the organizational chauvinism that plagued community organizing in the past and form the broad coalitions necessary for significant impact.

Organizations Have Transcended the Myopia of Localism

Chapter 2 shows that CBCOs effectively combine strengths from the two ideal types of American social movements described in the introduction, without falling victim to ideological purism familiar in some new social movements. But CBCO had its own brand of purism that is thankfully on the decline: an emphasis on localism and individual leadership development at the expense of significant policy impact. The local focus and bottom-up organizing tradition of CBCOs, especially of the PICO network, is a mixed blessing. What began as a pragmatic strategy to mobilize the hopeless and quiescent—choosing issues that are "immediate, specific, and winnable"— discouraged organizers from thinking beyond the local level. Valorizing immediate and local issues provided an inadequate basis for broader struggles. As such, local organizing was often criticized as conservative.

The Gamaliel Foundation is a leader at matching national policy experts with the problems of urban abandonment that their members experienced in the early 1990s. However, translating analysis into national campaigns is a separate challenge. In the 1990s, PICO's democratic and localist ideology seemed to overlook the fact that people cannot know what they need if they don't know the fundamental causes of their problems. In response to this argument, a senior PICO staff member argued, "They [the leaders] get there eventually . . . We get there, we bring the people along. It takes longer but it's better in the long run. [Regarding large victories:] If the people don't change, how long lasting is the victory? That's not really change for the long term." This view implies that long-term change takes place most fundamentally in hearts and minds rather than in institutional arrangements—from the inside out rather than the outside in.[21] But lasting change that is social, political, or economic can begin—and virtually always ends—with changed institutions.

Theda Skocpol described the dilemma confronting local community organizing in the 1990s:

> Purely local activists may not learn how problems and solutions are interconnected. And unless they speak for the most privileged neighborhoods, local activists are unlikely to enjoy sufficient leverage to make a real difference: to change the behavior of corporations, to persuade city, state, or local governments to act.[22]

During a national training in 2000, a PICO trainer said, "There is a danger: too much federated action with locals not doing anything leads to problems, because the self-interest of people is, or starts at the *local*."

However, two years earlier during a staff discussion of national campaigns, another senior PICO organizer said, "We've talked in PICO for a year about how our model limits us to neighborhood issues. We say we as organizers hold people back . . . We ask, "What's the problem in your *neighborhood*? And we limit them. We need to think about how to connect [larger issues] to the families on our block."

One PACT priest made the same point after returning to San Jose in 1998 after several years away. After the federal responsibility for welfare was jettisoned in 1996, he told PICO staff,

> All of a sudden I realize the heart has been ripped out of welfare and so-cial assistance in the three years that I was away . . . Now your commu-nity organizing is trying to get a little here in terms of food stamps and a little there, but none of you were doing anything at that time on the national level. PICO as a group never did a national lobby. And I said, now you're scrambling. And I said I was a leader of PACT, have great respect for what they do. My problem is it's naive politically. If all the money the Catholic Charities received doubled, and all the non-profits received double the amount they get now, it's a drop in the bucket com-pared to what we lose in terms of federal assistance. I said, were you sleeping during this time? Why weren't you doing something? Oh yeah, their theory is we're neighborhood—it has to come from the people and all that. I said, it *is* coming from the people, they're not getting food! It depends how you cut the question to them. Do you think we should use our political power on a national level in order to make sure children have health care no matter what their economic status, that children have food no matter what their economic status? No matter how you cut the question you get a positive response. You never asked the question.

In the ten years since the PICO organizers were struggling to combine local organizing with national goals, its culture has changed dramatically. One top organizer reported in 2007, "For ten years every PICO affiliate has been working on the state level." PICO has a truly national identity, and the fact that

> we'll be working together on federal policy is well established now. It was a struggle that took maybe five years; not a struggle for California affili-ates which had experience in working on state policy, but in other parts of the country that had it drilled into their head that it was all about local policy and nothing else. But we're there now: local policy is going to take

us to state and national level work. It's now well integrated into the PICO worldview.[23]

PICO has added enough new organizations to feel able to organize nationally. PICO California and the new National Voices campaign expose PICO leaders to the state and national policies at the root of local problems, and provide venues to engage in national campaigns. The Gamaliel Foundation has done likewise with voter registration and its work on federal immigration policy and the national transportation bill.

Organizations and Movements Need Each Other

If Piven and Cloward wrote an unjustified brief against organizations, the community organizing sector traditionally committed the opposite sin by fetishizing them. According to Stall and Stoecker, privileging the organization's endurance over its policy outcomes goes back at least to Saul Alinsky:

> In the Alinsky model, the organizer is not there just to win a few issues but to build an enduring formal organization that can continue to claim power and resources for the community—to represent the community in a competitive public sphere pluralist polity.[24]

This notion of the enduring interest organization that bargains for working people made it easy to dismiss loosely-run movements that rose up and faded away. However, this led organizing entrepreneurs to privilege building the organization even if it divided the larger movement. (ACORN always aimed to build a movement, but that did not stop it from privileging ACORN the organization.) Ann-Marie Szymanski shows in her study of the temperance movement that "movement *organizations* [e.g., the WCTU and the General Federations of Women's Clubs] thrive as groups by embracing a wide range of causes"; however, "social *movements* often flounder if their constituent groups fail to coalesce around shared goals when defining their political strategies." Szymanski argues that a "unifying purpose was a prerequisite for the development of a national—rather than a parochial—political strategy."[25]

Since 2000, ACORN, the Gamaliel Foundation, and the PICO National Network have articulated a national purpose for their own organizations—and also engaged in an unprecedented degree of cooperation.

Community Organizing Needs Vehicles for National Coordination

Scholars have demonstrated that mobilization by leaders and elites is a critical factor promoting widespread mass participation in politics, and that since the 1960s and 1970s movement cycle liberal leadership has declined.[26] In contrast, on the right, weekly meetings with competing factions held by conservative politico Grover Norquist helped coordinate the conservative resurgence. Dreier has argued that there is no comparable ongoing coordination of major progressive constituencies. The threat of a second Bush victory in the 2004 elections motivated a number of bodies to play a national coordinating role, including the George Soros–funded America Coming Together (ACT), and National Voice, which successfully coordinated about forty voter registration and mobilization efforts around the country. After the election, National Voice disbanded. George Soros ceased funding ACT in August 2005.[27]

There is no substitute for the kind of powerful national coordination visible in the 2004 presidential campaign. However, community organizing leaders have developed new vehicles for coordination among themselves.

The Center for Community Change

The Center for Community Change (CCC) formerly provided technical assistance to local community organizations. However, in recent years under the leadership of former ACORN organizer Deepak Bhargava, it has become in one organizer's words a "political machine"—that is, has begun to amalgamate organizations' local capacity in nationally coordinated campaigns on housing, immigration, transportation equity, and other issues. ACORN and the Gamaliel Foundation have been prominent participants in CCC-coordinated campaigns beginning with an effort to prevent cuts in the Temporary Aid to Needy Families programs.

In 2001, the CCC coordinated a national campaign to replicate the tactic of local housing trust funds at the national level. The campaign coordinated forty-four groups in twenty-nine states, including ACORN, Gamaliel, and numerous other grassroots groups.[28] Like the living wage strategy, and driven by the end of a national commitment to low-income housing, campaigns for local housing trust funds follow the "incremental groundswell" campaign model. Federal funds for low-income housing dropped from $71.2 billion in 1978 to $16.3 billion in 1997. In response, local housing trust funds have spread since the late 1980s. According to the CCC, today there are more than 350 housing trust funds in cities, counties, regions, and states, which have helped fund more than 200,000 units of affordable housing.[29]

ACORN, Gamaliel, the DART CBCO network and other groups are part of the organizing committee of the Center for Community Change's

Fair Immigration Reform Movement (FIRM). This effort has focused on supporting immigration reform and other legislative measures.

The Gamaliel Foundation is the lead organization among twelve in the Center's Transportation Equity Network (TEN). The goal of "transportation equity" is to ensure that low-income and minority communities receive a share of public resources for transportation infrastructure that benefits their residents, and that they do not bear a disproportionate burden of environmental impacts. MCU and the Gamaliel Foundation are leaders in campaigns for equitable transportation investment, mass transit rather than sprawl-enabling new highways, and transportation construction jobs for low-income, minority, and women workers.

The Organizers' Forum

Since 2000, ACORN and others have established the Organizers' Forum (http://www.organizersforum.org) in an effort to "explore common issues and learn from our mutual experiences."[30] The Board of Directors meets annually and the group sponsors strategic dialogues, cooperative organizer training sessions, and other joint projects. Most notably, all the major networks have participated, as well as other important allies such as the SEIU and AFL-CIO. Regular participants include John Calkins, director of DART, Mary Gonzales and Greg Galluzzo of the Gamaliel Foundation, and Scott Reed of PICO. Even the IAF—the original and traditionally most isolationist of the CBCO networks—sends representatives to both domestic and international gatherings of the Forum. In particular, collaborative relationships have developed between ACORN and each of PICO and the Gamaliel Foundation. The fact that their organizing models draw from different constituencies—individuals and families, versus congregations—enhances their ability to combine their strengths. The opportunity to build relationships of collaboration and trust enhances the possibility of broader and deeper collaboration in the future.

Hurricane Katrina: In Crisis Lies Opportunity

While the Gamaliel Foundation has thus far had no local affiliates in New Orleans, PICO and ACORN were entrenched in Louisiana organizing well before Hurricane Katrina struck in August 2005. During this emergency, PICO and ACORN, labor unions, churches, and numerous voluntary associations were almost forced to collaborate, not least to fill the vacuum of governmental inaction. Most basically, they sought to locate their members, ensure their safety, and provide emergency food and shelter. ACORN, deeply entrenched in Louisiana with a national office in New Orleans, engaged in a tremendous range of relief, reconstruction, voice-giving, and organizing activities (see Appendix C and http://www.acorn.org). Relationships were strengthened within PICO's statewide organization LIFT (Louisiana Interfaith Together) as Baton Rouge churches housed New Orleans members. Within the national PICO Network, thirty organizers from outside Louisiana flew in and conducted 3,000 interviews with displaced Louisiana members to identify their greatest needs. This research was used to develop a covenant for recovery priorities which the mayor signed. But more fundamentally, the disaster built relationships among organizers that have accelerated cooperation and the diffusion of organizing tactics. LIFT is now learning from PICO's San Diego affiliate about using community benefit agreements as a condition for new development. The director of LIFT, Rev. Jennifer Jones-Bridgett, reported the powerful memory of her thirty colleagues who helped "lift up [displaced residents'] voices. What happened could not have happened without the tremendous sacrifice from them and some leaders. They all slept in one house on the floor. Their sacrifice and love gave us what we needed to keep going."[31]

The catastrophe also strengthened relationships between the different organizations. ACORN's Wade Rathke, who lost his home in the hurricane, reported, "In a deep act of support [the Gamaliel Foundation's] organizing staff went into their personal pockets after Katrina and sent us more than $5000 to help us re-open our office in New Orleans." PICO's Jennifer Jones-Bridgett reported that an already positive relationship with Louisiana ACORN grew, and the two groups are exploring collaborative projects on housing, education, and voter turnout. She explained, "In new relationships it takes time to understand everybody's process. Before the storm I didn't know the intricate details of how ACORN was structured or operated, and at this point I do."

One sector with unique leverage to unify and coordinate organizing efforts is philanthropy.

Foundations Can Do More to Build National Organizing

Religious and philanthropic foundations have provided major funding for organizing, including the U.S. Catholic Bishops' Campaign for Human Development, the Ford Foundation, and many smaller funders. Community organizing staff devote much time to raising operating funds, and although they tout member dues (individual or institutional) as the essential route to self-sufficiency, their budgets reveal that dues generate only a percentage of revenue. All the national organizing networks and ACORN, as well as many or most of their local affiliates, seek foundation grants. They are pressured to compete with one another. They may stray from their core mission in order to "brand" themselves by developing distinct or faddish new programs. This of course encourages balkanization of the community organizing sector and discourages collaboration on large projects. Of course some funders only support local community development and social capital building efforts, but others seek policy change. Many of their priorities would support the view that foundations represent the co-opting goals of the elites who founded them—or they have that unintended consequence. Structurally, charitable foundations are 501(c)(3) nonprofit organizations, subject to the restrictions and social control functions of the tax code.

However, foundations do have some scope of action. They can, for example, fund base-building organizing based on which approaches and constituencies build power, instead of faddish diversions such as youth organizing that target a mobile population sector in transition rather than residents rooted in communities. They can create incentives for the national organizations to collaborate, such as seeking proposals for large joint campaigns.

Community organizations face fundamental choices, such as which allies to pursue in building coalitions. An obvious long-term coalition partner is labor. Each organization can remain isolated from its competitors in the community organizing sector, or it can reach out to other groups, as all the national organizations in this study have done. It can collaborate with unions, community institutions, single-issue advocacy organizations, or others. It can form temporary issue-based alliances, long-term partnerships, or both. Organizers can compete with existing organizations in particular cities while the vast majority of community members remain uninvolved, or they can cooperate in productive divisions of labor.

PACT has built local issue-based coalitions, and nationally PICO has cooperated with DART to prevent unproductive competition for organizing turf in Florida. MCU initiated positive collaborations with St. Louis environmentalists, inner-ring suburban officials, and local neighborhood associations. In San Jose, PACT and ACORN worked together on a campaign to protect renters from evictions, and both have a record of joining forces with labor. ACORN has recently led the way in forging local and national alliances, both with the Gamaliel Foundation and PICO, and far beyond them. However, community organizing can do much more.

The historic American national multi-level federations championed by some scholars responded to political opportunities and incentives that no longer exist. Instead, we must ask what new incentives and opportunities might allow entrepreneurs to build broad coalitions across race and class, drawing poor and working-class Americans into politics, training them for leadership, and winning significant gains. But we know what will *not* work: lack of participation and progressive politics as usual. More research and more action are both needed on the limits and possibilities of groups like ACORN, the PICO National Network, the Gamaliel Foundation, and their potential allies if we are to reverse the trends of privatism, political quiescence, and economic decline for millions of Americans.

Appendixes

Appendix A   Excerpts from "PICO Principles"

Appendix B   Methodological Appendix

Appendix C   Policy Outcomes for Selected National and Local Organizations since 1990

Appendix D   Agenda Setting: Selected Proposals Introduced by Four Community Organizations since 1990

Appendix A

Excerpts from "PICO Principles"

Power

Power is the ability to act.
Real power is often hidden.
Power is in the relationship.
Power respects power.
Power defines the rules.
Power is taken, not given.
Power: use it or lose it.
Who do you love?[1]

Leadership Development

The Iron Rule: Don't do for others what they can and should do for themselves.
You can't hold someone accountable for what they don't understand.
When in doubt, do a one-to-one [interview].
Take people where they are—not where you want them to be.
The first revolution is internal.
Challenge is relational.
A challenge outside of a relationship is an irritation.
You don't have a relationship until it's been tested by a challenge.
Change involves tension.
Empowerment is a journey.
If people can't say "no," what good is their "yes"?
Leaders have followers.
Organizers teach leaders; leaders organize.

Issue Development

Self-interest moves people; but self-interest changes.
Organizing is about people; people are about issues.
The farther you are from a problem, the more you can philosophize.
Push a problem and you get issues; push issues and you get values.

Strategy Development

Small is beautiful.[2]
Go in dumb, come out smart; go in smart, come out dumb.
He who defines the situation controls the outcome.
Stay within the experience of your people.
Surrender unto Caesar what is Caesar's—no more, no less.[3]

Action Development

No permanent friends, no permanent enemies.
The action is in the reaction.
Rewards go to those who do the work.[4]

Appendix B

Methodological Appendix

Protocol for Semistructured Interviews with Community Organization Members

1. What is your church/ward/subgroup? Are you an officer?
2. Can you remember when you first got involved with (name of organization)? When? Who told you about it? Why did you get involved? What were your thoughts and feelings about getting involved?
3. What is the first campaign you were involved with? Could you walk me through it?
4. What was the result of this campaign (if successful)? Is the achievement still in effect today? How is it being enforced?
5. Have you been involved in any campaigns or issues since then?

Respondent's Knowledge of the Organization and Level of Involvement

6. For any campaign they got involved with or one they know most about: Why was this chosen as an issue? Who chose it? In that campaign, who had the power to make the decision you wanted? Do you know why this strategy was chosen? Were there other choices?
7. What city, county, or other officials have you either targeted or worked with? Were there any corporate or other targets that are not government officials?

Member Empowerment and Internal Democratic Process

8. How are decisions made about issues and campaigns?
9. In your organization, have you done any research on issues? done any public speaking? chaired meetings? made strategy? had other responsibilities?

10. Does any one experience with (name of group) stand out in your mind? Why?

Organizational Alliances

11. Are there groups your organization has worked with on specific issues?
12. Do you consider (name of organization) to have any rival or competitor organizations?

Collective Identity and Ideology

13. If someone asked you, "What does (name of organization) stand for?" how would you best answer?

Organizational Stability

14. How many people are active in your ward/core team/local organizing committee/church?
15. How long have you been a leader? I want to ask about how much continuity or turnover there is in your organization. How long have other leaders/active members in your LOC/chapter been involved?

Class, Racial, and Gender Composition of Organization

16. Describe your core team/ward/organization's membership in terms of racial makeup. How about the number of women versus men involved? geographic areas represented? income level of members?
17. Can you think of an instance where race has been an issue or caused a conflict among members, leaders, staff? Are there other examples?
18. Has any other type of difference, such as income level or neighborhood, ever been an issue?

Respondent's Degree of Civic Engagement

19. When you got active in (name of organization), did you belong to any other organizations?
20. Did you have any other experience in community organizing? other volunteer community-based organizations or social service groups? labor? church? politics or political campaigns?
21. Are you currently active in other organizations?
22. What do you define as your community? How long have you lived in this community/been a member of this congregation? (If they say their church is their community) How long have you been a member of this church?
23. How do you feel about your community?
24. What are the main problems in your community?

Respondent's Subjective Feeling of Empowerment

25. Before you got involved with (name of organization), how did you feel about your ability to make a difference in the issues that affect you?

26. Since you have gotten involved with (name of organization), how do you feel about your ability to make a difference in the issues that affect you?

Process versus Task Emphasis in Organization

27. Do you see your job as a leader as setting goals and helping lead people to accomplish those goals? Or do you see your job as facilitating a discussion where everyone has input on the goals? Explain: why do you see your leadership that way?

Skills Respondent Exercised in Organization

28. What have you learned from (name of organization)?
29. Has (name of organization) taught you any new skills? Explain.
30. Have you been to formal trainings? What were they?
31. Can you think of a time you got an evaluation or were challenged by your organizer or another leader?

Values and Ideology of Respondent

32. Why do you continue to be active with (name of organization)?
33. What would you say are the values and beliefs that guide your life?
34. When we're active in a group, that may be because it somehow expresses our values and beliefs or it may be for other good reasons. Would you say your involvement in (name of organization) is connected to those particular values and beliefs you mentioned, or are there other reasons you are active? Explain.
35. What are the strengths of the organization? What are the weaknesses?
36. What are the strengths and weaknesses of the organizing staff?

Respondent's Social Networks

37. Who would you turn to for advice on strategy for a campaign?
38. How do you get the word out about a campaign you're starting? Who do you contact?
39. Are there any people in (name of organization) that you knew *before* you got involved? How did you know them?
40. Now that you are involved, have you gotten to know other members? I'm talking about significant working relationships. Do you have any contact with them outside the organization? How?

Respondent's View of Political System and Elected Officials

41. Since getting involved with (name of organization), has your view of the political system changed at all? of elected officials? of yourself and other leaders/members?

Demographic Information

42. Socioeconomic level: what is your occupation/are you working right now? educational level? age? race? gender?

Themes Identified in Interviews with Organization Members

Basis of Organizing

class (socioeconomic status)
neighborhood or community
racial/ethnic identity

Elements of Organization

research
expression
analysis of issues
planning
relationship building
recruiting

mobilizing people to events
actions
interactive processes
leadership
contention, combat
collaboration, negotiation

View of Politicians

no change
respondent knows more about them
respondent thinks they are more trustworthy
respondent thinks they are less trustworthy
mixed view of politicians, i.e., some are good allies, some not; or they can be good individuals, but system corrupts them

Goals of Organizing: How Activists See the Purpose of Organizing

political
problem solving
rational public policy reform
religious
moral: right/wrong, just/unjust, fair/unfair
valence language: mom and apple pie themes that are difficult to oppose, such as community, family, youth, children, "for the future"
service

Presence of Emotional Language

anger, fear, pain, etc.

A Note on Fieldwork and Interviews

I conducted numerous interviews with organizers and members in the course of participation-observation. I attended weekly ACORN staff meetings; staff meetings of CUCA, one of the MCU organizations; negotiation sessions between St. Louis ACORN Banking Committee and bank spokespersons; ACORN meetings with city officials; numerous board meetings of all the organizations; strategic planning and legislation drafting sessions; ACORN neighborhood chapter meetings; local ACORN, Gamaliel, and PICO leadership training events; the Gamaliel Foundation's 1997 national five-day training; the PICO Network's summer 2000 national five-day training; the 1997 Gamaliel Foundation's annual National Leadership Assembly in St. Louis; testimony at public hearings; Smart Growth Alliance monthly meetings; research committee meetings; organizational annual meetings; an MCU-CUCA annual prayer breakfast; an MCU-C4 meeting with a neighborhood association; and at least three foundation site visits (a Catholic Campaign for Human Development visit to St. Louis ACORN, an Interfaith Funders site visit to MCU, and a Needmor Fund visit to San Jose PACT).

Interviews

I would like to thank the organizers, city officials, funders, academics, journalists, and others listed below for generously sharing their time. Many agreed to multiple interviews. The list does not include the seventy-five semistructured interviews with members of the four local organizations.

> Steve Ables, Felix Alvarez, Jeanne Appleman, Ron Auer, Robert Blackburn, Chris Block, Bob Brownstein, Terry Christenson, Peggy Coleman, Lark d'Helen, Virginia Druhe, Peter Ellis, Kim Fellner, Janice Fine, Lew Finfer, Tim Fischesser, Richard Fleming, Dave Garretson, Joe Guerra, Susan Hammer, Charles Haun, Jim Helmer, John Hickey, Ellen Horstman, Terry Jones, Robert Kelly, Charles Kindleberger, Al Kirth, Mark Linder, Sarah Mehegan, Greg Mesack, Brian O'Neill, Toby Paone, Stan Rose, David Rusk, Robert Salisbury, Natasha Shawver, Jim Shrewsbury, Ron Smith, Lana Stein, Les Sterman, Wayne Tanda, Arthur Towers, Mark Tranel, Gloria Weber

ACORN

> Amy Cohen, Jon Eller, Nathan Henderson-James, Roosevelt Johnson, Jen Kern, Steve Kest, Brian Kettenring, Bertha Lewis, Matt Mayer,

Ken McCoy, Wade Rathke, Craig Robbins, Amy Schur, Amy Smoucha, Madeline Talbot, Kevin Whelan

Gamaliel Foundation

Laura Barrett, Greg Galluzzo, Pat Griffini, Gail Guelker, Kevin Jokisch, Denise McDuffie, Paul Scully, Cheryl Spivey-Perry, Ron Trimmer

PICO National Network

Jose Arenas, John Baumann, Kathy Chavez Napoli, Edith Friedman, Stephanie Gut, Matt Hammer, Lis Jorgens, Jim Keddy, David Mann, Bill Masterson, Diana Miller, Francois Pierre, Scott Reed, Maria Romero, Corey Timpson, Gordon Whitman

Industrial Areas Foundation

Ed Chambers, Arnie Graf, John Heinemeir

Catholic Campaign for Human Development

Bonita Anderson, Renee Brierton, Mary Beth Gallagher, Terry Iacino, Doug Lawson, Daniel Lizarraga, Sandy Mattingly-Ualen, Hector Rodriguez

Center for Community Change

Deepak Bhargava, Don Elmer

San Jose Mercury News

Scott Herhold, Tom Schmitz, Barbara Vroman

St. Louis Post-Dispatch

John Carleton, Bob Duffe, Repps Hudson

Appendix C

Policy Outcomes for Selected National and Local Organizations since 1990

The new policy or accomplishment is described in the left column, and the impact (if available, in dollars, number of people affected, or other measure) in the right column. St. Louis ACORN and San Jose ACORN policy outcomes are listed separately under "Selected St. Louis ACORN Accomplishments" and "Selected San Jose ACORN Accomplishments." Every effort has been made to confirm these claims with sources outside the organizations themselves. This includes verifying them using newspaper accounts or additional interviews with officials or opponents of the organizations.

Selected Recent ACORN Policy Outcomes

Living Wage Movement

Since 1996, ACORN initiated or led coalitions in twelve successful living wage campaigns and participated in four other successful campaigns.[1]	sixteen municipal living wage ordinances
ACORN maintains a Living Wage Resource Center with a full-time staff member who provides technical assistance to non-ACORN campaigns nationwide as well as to ACORN campaigns. The resource center Web site disseminates information on campaigns (140 successful campaigns), model ordinances, etc. ACORN sponsored three national living wage training conferences for ACORN and non-ACORN campaign organizers.	technical assistance to build a national movement, which moved from city to state-level campaigns
2004, New York:[2] The state minimum wage increased to $7.15 per hour, phased in over two years beginning with a raise to $6.00 on January 1, 2005.[3]	1.2 million minimum wage workers get wage increase

2004, Florida: The wage was raised to $6.15 per hour in May 2005, with annual increases indexed to inflation. Florida was the first southern state to increase its minimum wage above the federal level.	$1.7 billion in 2005 (average $2,000 annual increase for 850,000 workers)
2003, Illinois: The wage was raised to $5.50 in 2004, $6.50 in 2005.	first midwestern state to increase its minimum wage
1999, Massachusetts:[4] The minimum wage rose to $6.75 by 2002; the state earned income tax credit also was raised.	

Earned Income Tax Credit and Child Tax Credit Tax Refunds

2006: ACORN ran free tax preparation centers in seventy-five cities as part of the IRS's outreach program for low-income taxpayers eligible for these credits.	$36 million in tax refunds; 27,000 families received help filing tax returns
2005: ACORN ran free tax preparation centers in forty-five cities.	$19 million in tax refunds; 16,000 families received help filing tax returns
2004: ACORN ran its first pilot project for the IRS: free tax preparation centers in three cities.	average gain of $1,789 for eligible families; average savings per client of $250 on tax preparation fees and refund anticipation loans (RALs)[5]

Community Reinvestment

1986–2005: ACORN rehabilitated vacant and abandoned housing units.[6]	over 850 units rehabilitated
2004, Citigroup: ACORN negotiated a partnership to deliver new mortgage and bank account products for immigrants.	new loan products for immigrants by Citigroup
2000, Ameriquest: ACORN negotiated a three-year pilot loan program for low-income home buyers (a precedent-setting subprime lending program) in ten cities, administered by ACORN Housing Corporation.[7]	$360 million in loans for low-income home buyers
1986–2005: ACORN Housing Corporation provided loan counseling to low- and moderate-income first-time home buyers.	130,000 borrowers counseled
1989–91: ACORN was part of a coalition that won federal legislation that forced lenders to report not just loans made but also loans denied, categorized by race. This allowed community groups to demonstrate that minority communities were underserved, the basis of reform campaigns in many ACORN cities. Allies: Rep. Joe Kennedy, Ralph Nader, Center for Community Change.	Home Mortgage Disclosure Act

Predatory Lending Reform

2003: ACORN participated in a coalition that helped stop House Bill 833 (chief sponsor Rep. Bob Ney, R-Ohio).	helped prevent national legislation that would have preempted all state and local laws regulating predatory lending
2004, Citigroup: ACORN won a major campaign to reform subprime loan products.[8]	nation's largest bank reforms its loan products
2004, H&R Block: ACORN won a national agreement to eliminate an administration fee for RALs and to provide fuller disclosure.	nation's largest provider of RALS implements reforms
2004, Household Finance: ACORN won funding to administer a foreclosure avoidance program for at-risk borrowers.[9]	$72 million program for ACORN to help prevent foreclosures
2004, ancillary to ACORN campaign against Household Finance: Fifty state attorneys general settled a lawsuit that ACORN helped initiate by organizing formal complaints by Household Finance victims.	$484 million to compensate thousands of victims of Household predatory loans; $2 million annually in operating funds for ACORN
2001, Citigroup and Household Finance: ACORN successfully pressures the nation's largest bank and Household Finance to stop high-interest single-premium credit insurance to homeowners. These were the only two major lenders who offered the product.	two largest national lenders of predatory credit insurance cease selling the product
2005, Seattle: ACORN advocated that the city council pass anti-RAL legislation.[10]	Seattle law requiring disclosure and legal redress by RAL lenders
2004, Minnesota: ACORN collaborated with the state attorney general to win state legislation protecting homeowners at risk of foreclosure.	Minnesota law to prevent scams targeting families at risk of foreclosure
2004, Massachusetts: ACORN was part of a coalition that won protections against predatory lending practices.	legislation prohibiting loan prepayment penalties, requiring loan counseling, and limiting loan fees
2003, Connecticut: ACORN was part of a coalition that won state legislation.	legislation to reduce abuses of tax RALs
2003, New Jersey: ACORN helped win lending reforms.	new antipredatory lending legislation
2003, Arkansas: ACORN helped strengthen provisions of new antipredatory lending legislation.	stronger antipredatory lending legislation
2003, Arizona: ACORN led a campaign that prevented passage of an industry-backed bill.	bill defeated
2003, New Mexico: ACORN helped pass new protective legislation.	new antipredatory lending legislation

2001, California: A coalition including ACORN helped pass California Assembly Bill 489.	law limits interest to 8 percentage points above current yield on Treasury bonds. Loan fees cannot exceed 6 percent of the total loan.
2001, Oakland: ACORN led a successful campaign to ban features of predatory loans.	city of Oakland loan regulation

Voter Registration and Mobilization

2005–7: Bused New Orleans residents displaced by Hurricane Katrina from Little Rock, Dallas, and San Antonio to New Orleans to vote in municipal elections; helped survivors reach satellite voting centers to vote in the 2006 mayoral election.	Hundreds of votes cast by infrequent, low-income voters
2003–4: ACORN registered voters in low-income black and Latino neighborhoods for 2004 election in fourteen of seventeen presidential election battleground states.	1.1 million newly registered voters
1996, Illinois: ACORN sued the state of Illinois in 1996 for not complying with the National Voter Registration Act of 1993 (Motor Voter Law), one of five states that did not comply with the law, which directs states to offer voter registration to citizens in departments of motor vehicles, libraries, welfare offices, and other public offices.	
2003, New Orleans: ACORN mobilized voters in District 99.	turnout increased 17 percent in gubernatorial election
2003, Kansas City, Missouri: ACORN mobilized voters in Ward 3.	voting increased from 5 percent to 18 percent

Fielding Candidates in State and Local Elections

2005: ACORN member Wayne Hall ran for mayor of the Village of Hempstead, Long Island, New York, on the Democrat and Working Families Party line.	elected mayor of Long Island town
2003: ACORN member Letitia James ran for New York City Council.	victory by a third party candidate for New York City Council
1999: ACORN and labor allies backed two Democrats for Hempstead, Long Island, City Council, who were also running on the Working Families Party line.	elected two city council members; helped upset twenty-five-year GOP hold on Hempstead City Council

1999: Former Chicago ACORN president, endorsed by ACORN PAC, ran for alderman of Chicago's 15th Ward.	elected Chicago alderman
1998: ACORN, labor, and allies formed a third party, the Working Families Party, in New York and other states that allow third parties to endorse major party candidates (and thus win enough votes to retain their ballot line).	first community-labor party with official ballot status in New York state in more than fifty years

Education

2004: ACORN helped pressure the New York Department of Education to provide a new lead teacher program in South Bronx schools.[11]	$1.6 billion program
2001: Chicago ACORN won an agreement to hire almost double the number of new teachers hired in previous years.[12]	3,000 new teachers
2001: ACORN and the teachers' union pressured New York City not to privatize five public schools with the for-profit Edison Schools.	prevented privatization of five New York public schools
2000: Oakland ACORN won a three-year battle to reopen the abandoned Woodland Elementary School as an ACORN community school.	one charter school
1998, Chicago: ACORN High School, a dual-language charter school, opened in a Mexican American neighborhood.	one charter school
1997, New York: Two ACORN high schools open.	two charter schools
1997, New York: ACORN charged schools chancellor with racism when making assignments to gifted programs.	commitment to broaden access to gifted programs
1996, St. Paul: ACORN opened a trilingual elementary charter school using English, Spanish, and Hmong.	one charter school
1995, Seattle: ACORN pressured a low-income high school to create a library.	librarian hired; $20,000 for books

Welfare/Workfare Reform

2001, Los Angeles: ACORN-organized home child care providers sought reforms.	new grievance procedure
2000, New York: ACORN WEP (Work Experience Program, workfare) Workers Organizing Committee sought reforms for workfare workers.	new grievance procedure

1997, Philadelphia: ACORN sought transportation benefits for people moving from welfare to work within the city of Philadelphia.	free transit passes so work-fare participants can get to work
1997, Los Angeles: ACORN sought a grievance procedure for workfare workers, the first in the country.	new grievance procedure
1997, New York: The ACORN-organized Workers Organizing Committee won improved conditions for workfare workers. A judge ruled the Giuliani administration must provide WEP workers at sanitation and transportation departments with protective clothing, equipment, and other services. In an unofficial election, 99 percent of 17,000 city workfare workers voted for representation by ACORN.	improved conditions for 17,000 workfare workers

Housing

2002, New York: ACORN sought predatory lending reforms through the city council.	antipredatory lending ordinance
2002, Los Angeles: Housing LA Coalition, including ACORN, wins a housing trust fund.	$100 million
2002, California: The state senate passed ACORN-proposed SB 1403, a tenant-protection law giving renters sixty instead of thirty days to vacate when month-to-month rental agreements are terminated without cause.	all California renters get an additional month of rental protection
2001, St. Louis: A housing coalition including ACORN passed Proposition H, a tax to raise a trust fund for housing and health care for the poor. It taxes out-of-state purchases of more than $2,000.	$5 million each year since 2001
2000, Baltimore: ACORN helped pressure HUD to renegotiate FHA loans.	thousands of FHA loans renegotiated on more favorable terms for homeowners
1998, Dallas: ACORN convinced the city to increase funding to pay for home repairs for low-income elderly residents.	over five hundred senior citizens benefit

Utilities

2001, Chicago: A coalition including ACORN won concessions from Peoples Gas, including an additional $1 million for residents in arrears on high heating bills; the city of Chicago also increased aid by $2 million.	$3 million in aid for utilities payments

Hurricane Katrina Advocacy and Relief

Only specific policy outcomes are included. Enormous work accomplished in contacting displaced residents, providing immediate relief, and advocating at the local, state, and national levels is omitted.

2005 to present: Organized community-based forums to develop neighborhood rebuilding plans, with experts from Pratt Institute, New Jersey Institute of Technology, Cornell University, Louisiana State University, and Columbia University	First new specially designed, wind-resistant, elevated, pine homes, built for $125,000 each, with ACORN-arranged financing
2005: Formed the ACORN Katrina Survivors Association	Organization created to advocate for low-income hurricane survivors
2005: Launched Home Clean-out Demonstration Program	Mobilized volunteers to gut over 1, 850 homes in low-income neighborhood, enabling their preservation

Selected Recent PICO National Network Policy Outcomes

This section includes the outcomes of California state campaigns as well as selected outcomes of local affiliate groups. San Jose PACT outcomes are listed separately under "Selected San Jose PACT Accomplishments." Organizations listed by acronym only are local PICO affiliates best known by their acronym.

Health Care

2006: PICO and its allies placed Proposition 86, a cigarette tax initiative to fund children's health insurance, on the November ballot. The coalition, called Californians for Healthy Kids, included PICO California, PICO's Hollywood Interfaith Sponsoring Committee (HISC), the American Cancer Society, the American Lung Association, the American Heart Association, and other children's health advocates.	estimated $2.1 billion annually for health care plus $405 million for universal health insurance coverage to cover one million uninsured children in the state of California
2005, Roanake, Virginia: PICO's Faith Works and allies lobbied Congressman Bob Goodlatte (R-VA) to win federal designation of Southeast Roanoke as a medically underserved area (MUA), which paves the way for subsidized community health-care services.	$650,000 in federal funding for a community clinic
2004, South San Francisco Bay: Peninsula Interfaith Action (PIA) organized a coalition to save the health plan of San Mateo, a public health-care plan, from bankruptcy.	$4 to 5 million; more than 50,000 served

2003–4, Alameda County, California: COR mobilized support for ballot measure to fund Alameda County Medical Center, community clinics, and community-based programs. Measure A passed.	local health care funded
2002: PICO California organized thousands of letters and faxes pressuring U.S. Health and Human Services secretary Tommy Thompson to waive federal guidelines and allow the state to add the parents of children enrolled in the Healthy Families program. The HHS waived the federal guidelines.	parents added to children's health insurance
2001: PICO California and California Primary Care Association won grants for clinic infrastructure (Cedillo-Alarcon Clinic Investment Act of 2000) and annual funding increases for clinics for the uninsured through the Expanded Access to Primary Care Program.	$42 million for infrastructure; $10 million annual increase for clinics
2000: PICO California campaigned for state primary care health clinic infrastructure through the Cedillo-Alarcon Clinic Investment Act.	$50 million
2000: PICO California pressured the governor to drop the Medi-Cal quarterly reporting requirement, enabling half a million more people to obtain and keep health coverage.	500,000 people per year
2004: Contra Costa Interfaith Sponsoring Committee (CCISCO) mobilized voters to pass the parcel tax to keep a hospital in the community open.	$6 million per year; serves 330,000 people
2000, Alameda County, California: COR worked in coalition with PICO California affiliates on health-care projects, including a new clinic for the working poor in Hayward, California.	$100 million in total grants
2004, Alameda County, California: COR helped lead a coalition that won a new half-cent health-care sales tax increase to support the county public hospital, clinic system, and other health-care services.	$1.35 billion; $90 million annually for fifteen years for the public hospital, clinic system, and other health care services

Education

2006, San Jose: PACT won funding from philanthropist Reed Hastings for new small public schools in San Jose.	$1 million
2005, Anchorage: AFACT won a pilot program within the Anchorage School District to train staff in Native culture and communication styles.	$22,000, half of which will come from the school district itself

2005: PICO California won AB 1465 (sponsor, Wilma Chan, D-Oakland), which requires districts to disclose each school's budget and teachers' salaries. This information enables campaigns for equitable teachers' salaries in low-income school districts.	all public school systems in California
2005: Seven hundred parents from ten low-income schools mobilized to win an agreement to place a qualified teacher in every classroom and improve instruction and curriculum in their schools.	benefited ten such low-income schools
2005: Oakland Community Organizations (OCO) won thirty-six new, small, high-quality autonomous schools, twelve scheduled to open by the fall of 2006.	thirty-three autonomous schools with eight charter schools within Oakland; private investment of $8 million in school infrastructure with more startup grants from the state
2004, California: Governor Arnold Schwarzenegger signs PICO California–sponsored small schools legislation that funds incentives to build new small high schools and reconfigure large high schools into smaller communities. The legislation was based on PICO school reforms in Oakland, San Jose, and Sacramento.	$22 billion proposed for new, small high schools (10 percent of governor's $222.6 billion, ten-year infrastructure budget)
2004–6, Gainesville, Florida: Gainesville Action wins a model after-school youth program in cooperation with the Department of Education and school boards, which provided space.	$300,000 federal grant used in labor and human services; 360 students served per year
2004, Philadelphia: EPOP campaigned for restoration of Federal Title I support to the poorest city schools and won a ruling by the school district CEO, Paul Vallas.	more than $10 million dollars in federal grants
2003, Contra Costa County, California: CCISCO (Contra Costa Interfaith Sponsoring Committee) led a campaign to build the Central Richmond Middle School.	$37.5 million
1999, California: With Assemblywoman Nell Soto and the state secretary for education, PICO California developed legislation to fund parent-teacher home visits at statewide schools.	$30 million through 2003; home visits across 450 schools
1998, Alameda County, California: COR campaigned to redirect funds for after-school programs at most needy middle schools in Fremont, San Lorenzo, and Union City.	$500,000 of public funds redirected
1998, California: PICO California and a coalition helped win Proposition 1A for a school repair and construction measure.	$9.2 billion in grants

Since 2000, CCISCO of Contra Costa County successfully campaigned for a new Central Richmond middle school.	$37.5 million in funding
2005–6, Alameda County, California: COR won a commitment to convert Logan High School, one of the largest high schools in California, to small, more personalized learning communities.	massive high school converted to small learning communities
During the 1990s, the San Diego Organizing Project won after-school programs so schools are open 6:00 a.m. to 6:00 p.m.	130 programs
1998, California: PICO California convinced Governor Wilson and the legislature to allocate funds for a state After School Learning and Safe Neighborhood Program.	$50 million in grants; serves 140,000 low-income children daily

Immigration Rights

2005, Colorado: Northern Colorado CBCNC helped defeat a proposition to create a new immigration and customs enforcement unit within Weld County, where 35 percent of the population is Latino.	proposition defeated
2003–5, Alameda County, California: COR conducted Immigration Forums.	resources and free consultations with attorneys on immigrant rights

Affordable Housing

2006, Camden, New Jersey: CCOP (Camden Churches Organized for People) won a home improvement program after a survey showed that city residents believed the state's $175 million economic recovery plan (won by CCOP and black clergy association) had done more for hospitals, colleges, and the waterfront than for neighborhood residents.[13]	$7.5 million Camden Home Improvement Program; $20,000 each for three hundred low-income homeowners
2006, San Francisco: SFOP (San Francisco Organizing Project) won Board of Supervisors approval for increased low-income housing in coalition with Housing Action Coalition, Coleman Advocates for Youth and Children, and others.	$20 million in additional grants
2005, Denver: MOP (Metropolitan Organizations for People) proposed a law that required a percentage of low-income housing in middle-class areas.	inclusionary zoning law passed
2005, Kansas City, Missouri: CCCO proposed reformed housing policies.	$5 million

2005, South Bay Peninsula, California: PIA and League of Women Voters won new housing units for low-income families.	Fifty-three families served
2005, Los Angeles: The Hollywood Interfaith Sponsoring Committee (HISC) won a commitment to purchase land for supportive housing in Hollywood. Coordination was mainly by the HISC using the Corporation for Supportive Housing as a resource for information.	$5.8 million for purchase of land in October 2005; forty to sixty supportive housing units for community members
2004, Alameda County, California: COR proposed a program in Hayward to identify and resolve dangerous living conditions in rental housing.	rental inspection program implemented
2003, South Bay Peninsula: PIA and Community Working Group advocated purchasing land for a new Opportunity Center, a multiservice day facility with housing units.	$21 million dollars; ninety-five transition units
2003, Contra Costa County, California: Contra Costa Interfaith Sponsoring Committee (CCISCO) won an inclusionary zoning law that will require developers to create low- and very-low-income housing.	seventy-five new housing units; three hundred rental units projected through 2010; estimated $140 million total
2003, Alameda County, California: COR initiated a home loan counseling program for low-income families in Union City.	home ownership training and loan program initiated
2002, California: PICO California helped win Proposition 46, an affordable housing bond.	$2.1 billion in grants
2002, Alameda County, California: COR won affordable housing laws in four cities and new affordable housing to be implemented by the end of 2006.	affordable housing for one thousand families
2001, San Francisco: SFOP ran a YIMBY (Yes in My Back Yard) campaign to build low-income housing units, in collaboration with other housing advocates.	more than three hundred housing units built and one thousand more in planning and development stages
2002, South Bay Peninsula, California: PIA joined the Coalition for Affordable Housing Trust Fund from San Mateo County and Santa Clara County (the Housing Endowment and Trust). Both county supervisors agreed to support regional standards for local revenue sources and city land-use policies.	$3 million trust fund; $18 million commitment to affordable housing
2000, South Bay Peninsula, California: PIA prevented a HUD seniors' housing complex from being converted into a market-rate complex and reduced rate increases in low-income housing complexes.	preserved seventy-eight units of senior housing; reduced rate increases by 50 percent for eighty-eight units (three hundred renters)

Coachella Valley: Since 1999, Inland Congregations United for Change, California (ICUC) won new loans for tenant agricultural families. The Agricultural Worker Mobile Home Tenant Assistance Grant Program provides $30,000 in forgivable loans for renters to purchase new manufactured homes. The Mobile Home Park Assistance Loan Fund and Agricultural Housing Loan Fund provides two forgivable loans totaling $85,000 for property owners.	new homes for 250 families; seventeen rehabilitated mobile home parks, with spaces for 450 more tenant families and spaces for three hundred more in the process
2001, South Bay Peninsula, California: PIA helped gain passage of an impact fee of $6 to $12 per square foot.	up to $1 million dollars per year
2001, Alameda County, California: COR worked with the Alameda County Department of Public Health to bring low-income housing to the Decoto neighborhood.	new low-income housing
1998, South Bay Peninsula, California: PIA and other nonprofits won a housing ordinance.	ordinance providing below-market-rate housing
1998: PICO California campaigned for an increase in the state's low-income housing tax credit to help address a lack of affordable housing for families.	$20 million in grants
Philadelphia: Since 2000, EPOP has campaigned for a funding increase in the mayor's program for housing rehabilitation and for district council oversight.	$45 million in funding

Financial Justice and Predatory Lending Reform

2005, Kansas City, Missouri: CCCO pursued payday loan regulation.	first state legislation to cap interest rates on payday loans and regulate the industry
2005, Denver: MOP pursued a city earned income tax credit (EITC) policy (now repealed).	first city to win an EITC policy using city funds to match state and federal EITC
2005, northern Colorado: CBCNC sought an extension of bank credit to underserved sections of the community in Greeley, Colorado (mainly immigrants, regardless of legal status).	$1 million per year

Neighborhood Services, including Youth Programs

2006, Los Angeles: HISC, with a labor ally, Los Angeles Alliance for a New Economy (LAANE), won a commitment to fund a youth center from private developer JH Snyder & Associates.	$1 million proposed investment

2006, San Francisco: SFOP led a coalition that won additional funds for Avenues of Hope violence prevention programs including after-school and youth activities and crime prevention organizations. The coalition included Coleman Advocates for Children and Youth, Project CLAER, ACORN, and others.	$8.4 million dollars in additional grants
2003, Alameda County, California: COR developed a skateboard park and restroom at Cherryland Park, a neighborhood with few youth resources.	new park

Jobs

2005, San Diego: SDOP pursued new living wage and responsible contractor ordinances for subcontracted on-site permanent jobs.	ordinances passed

Community Preservation and Redevelopment

2006, Rochester, New York: Interfaith Action led lobbying for the city to apply for an additional $18 million of New York State aid.	$18 million
2006, Melbourne, Florida: The CCA won redevelopment of a low-income neighborhood with street beautification and a neighborhood watch.	$1.5 million in redevelopment; crime rate reduced by 40 percent
2005, San Diego: SDOP helped lead a coalition that won the largest redevelopment project in San Diego history, a community benefits agreement. It includes environmental green building (LEED) standards for over 1.5 million square feet of development and the first high-rise residential tower in the United States using LEED standards. It also includes a commitment for affordable housing for low-income families.	$1.5 million to seed affordable housing near downtown; 200,000 square feet of housing for families earning between 30 to 60 percent of area median income
2002 to the present: Los Angeles: HISC, with LAANE and the Yucca Residents Group, negotiated a community benefits agreement with the Community Redevelopment Agency for Hollywood and Vine. This included compliance with Los Angeles' Living Wage Ordinance, a 70 percent living wage goal for all on-site jobs associated with the development, a local hiring agreement, $50,000 for a job training program, $25,000 for the Health Care Careers Ladder Training Program, $15,000 for a health-care access outreach program, 20 percent of housing units reserved for low- and moderate-income families, and $500,000 for arts programs at Hollywood High School.	$350 million, including $95,000 for job training and health-care outreach and $500,000 for arts programs at Hollywood High School

Philadelphia: In the late 1990s, EPOP members negotiated a community reinvestment agreement resulting from a legal challenge of the First Union/CoreStates bank merger, including a commitment to keep ten branches.	$337 million community reinvestment agreement
2003, Roanoke, Virginia: Collaborating with the city, Faith Works won the South East By Design Project resulting in investment and redevelopment in Southeast Roanoke, new home construction, renovation of older homes, a police substation, a priority to enforce codes, street cleaning, traffic mitigation, business facade grants, and work to bring a sliding-scale-fee doctors' office into the community.	$3.7 million in federal block grants; total of $5 million including city funding
2005, Gainesville, Florida: Gainesville Action won funds in the Federal Transportation Equity Act to repair and redevelop roads in the Duval neighborhood of Gainesville, in cooperation with the Florida Department of Transportation.	$3 million; impacted lives of 1,200 people
2005, Anchorage, Alaska: AFAT mobilized support and campaigned for funding for a Weed and Seed grant for a five-year period.	$875,000 over the period 2005–9
2001–2, Camden, New Jersey: CCOP led a state campaign to win the Camden recovery initiative. CCOP organized 1,500 residents, clergy, business leaders, and public officials to win from then-governor McGreevey unprecedented state investment in Camden. CCOP partnered with two groups: Concerned Black Clergy of Camden City and the Greater Camden Partnership.	$200 million in new state investment
In the late 1990s, EPOP of Philadelphia played a key role in placing abandoned cars on the mayor's agenda and in creating the Office of Abandoned Vehicles.	city removed over 150,000 abandoned cars
1989–2002, Camden, New Jersey: CCOP initiated the Host Community Benefit Campaign for legislation that permits an annual host community benefit from the county sewage-treatment plant.	$3.2 million annual community benefit; $35 million to city residents and small businesses since 1994
1998, Camden, New Jersey: CCOP, with St. Joseph's Carpenter Society, won state funds to remedy housing blight.	$8 million in state funds; boarded up two thousand abandoned houses, demolished six hundred dangerous units, and rehabbed or built four hundred units

Public Safety and Crime Prevention

2006, Massachusetts: Massachusetts Communities Action Network won state programs to reduce gang violence.	$1.5 million witness protection program; $11 million for gang intervention and youth violence prevention

2004, Anchorage, Alaska: AFAT won overtime grants to increase policing in two high-crime neighborhoods.	$50,000 in federal grants
2004, Orlando: Orlando FOCUS won a juvenile assessment and monitoring program that increases the ratio of probation officers to juvenile offenders from 1 for 125 to 1 for 25.	$750,000 in annual state grants; reduced repeat youth offenders by 80 percent
2004, Oakland, California: Oakland Community Organizations (OCO) won Measure Y, a referendum for a parcel tax to support job counseling, placement services, policing, and job-centered crime prevention measures. OCO mobilized support from infrequent voters to win the ballot measure.	$15 million over ten years; sixty-three new positions for police officers created; mobilized ten thousand voters to win 70 percent of the vote

Hurricane Katrina Advocacy and Relief

Only specific policy outcomes are included. Enormous work accomplished in contacting displaced residents, providing immediate relief, and advocating at the local, state, and national levels is omitted.

2006: As a significant coalition member, PICO LIFT (Louisiana Interfaith Together) helped successfully lobby for federal housing funding.	$4.2 billion in supplemental funding, spring 2006
2006: With St. Peter Claver Catholic Church and Providence Housing, PICO secured commitment for new homes in New Orleans Treme neighborhood for tenants displaced from a public housing project.	1,500 new homes planned
2006: With the Vietnamese and New Orleans East community, PICO organized to close a landfill used for hazardous waste.	Closed Chef Mentuer landfill
2005 to present: Numerous local accomplishments.	Local services restored, such as postal delivery, city services, housing assistance

The Gamaliel Foundation Policy Outcomes

Includes outcomes of national campaigns as well as selected outcomes of local affiliate groups, noted in parentheses. MCU for St. Louis outcomes are listed separately under "Selected MCU St. Louis Accomplishments, 1992–2006."

Civic Engagement: Voter Registration and Mobilization

| 2003–4: Gamaliel affiliates conducted voter registration and Get Out The Vote (GOTV) campaigns in nineteen states and 1,600 congregations. | 47,000 newly registered voters; 400,000 voters mobilized to polls |

Immigration

2004: Mass showings in major city meetings helped win new Senate and congressional sponsors of the SOLVE Act (undocumented immigrants rights and protections).	fourteen new cosponsors of SOLVE Act
1998, Minneapolis: ISAIAH launched a campaign to improve services from the Immigration and Naturalization Service.	INS agrees to provide bilingual assistance and extended office hours for immigrant families seeking citizenship.

Jobs

2005: Gamaliel Foundation led national advocacy for federal SAFETEA-LU Transportation Bill to include a Local Workforce Development Amendment, which encourages community groups to negotiate with localities to hire low-income apprentices for living wage transportation construction jobs.	local workforce development amendment to transportation bill
Waterbury, Connecticut: Since 2000, United Action Connecticut has won a precedent-setting local hire ordinance.	$500,000 in state funds, 30 percent hiring on city reconstruction projects, 70 percent of new hires to low-income residents
Milwaukee: MICAH won a local hiring ordinance.	legislation that guarantees local hiring, prevailing wage, and affordable housing set-asides in new downtown developments
2005, Kansas City, Missouri: MORE2 campaigned for Project Prepare, a six-week union apprenticeship program.	prepares one hundred qualified candidates for entry into construction trade unions

Transportation Equity

2005: Gamaliel Foundation helped alter the Job Access and Reverse Commute Program (JARC) funding in a national transportation bill.	$700 million over the next six years
2005: Gamaliel Foundation pursued set-aside funds for transportation equity research demonstration programs.	$1 million per year
2004, Detroit: MOSES launched a federal Americans with Disabilities Act lawsuit against the Detroit Department of Transportation to improve handicapped accessibility on buses (40 percent of the wheelchair lifts didn't work); it involved two federal departments.	

2005, Detroit: MOSES sought funds for two high-speed rail corridors in the Detroit metro area.	
2003, Detroit: MOSES launched a ballot initiative to regionalize Detroit DOT bus service.	DARTA founded
Cincinnati: Since 2000, AMOS Cincinnati secured a commitment of $750,000 from the City of Cincinnati to assist in the $2 million Uptown Transportation Study to recommend innovative transportation policies.	$750,000 for Uptown Transportation Study

Community Preservation and Redevelopment

2002, Minneapolis: Minnesota ISAIAH won an agreement from St. Cloud and four other Minnesota cities for inclusionary zoning, including low- and moderate-income units in a new housing development.	agreement between five Minnesota cities mandating 15 percent affordable housing in all new development
2003, Minneapolis: Minnesota ISAIAH worked as part of a coalition since 2001 to win a housing trust fund.	Minneapolis Housing Trust Fund, $6 to $8 million annually
Minneapolis: Since 2000, Minnesota ISAIAH has helped lead a coalition that won funds to produce and preserve affordable housing. This includes a measure requiring that 15 percent of all new units developed be affordable. The group helped secure an increase in the Minnesota legislature's allocation for the production and preservation of affordable housing by $45 million over two years.	$45 million over two years; $68 million to redevelop urban polluted sites (brownfields) for redevelopment
Connecticut: Since 2000, United Action Connecticut and Interfaith Coalition for Equity and Justice have pursued the inclusion of affordable units in new development in East Lyme, Connecticut.	30 percent of units in a new development in East Lyme, Connecticut, zoned "affordable" (60–80 percent of median income)
Gary and East Chicago, Indiana: Since 2004, Interfaith Federation campaigned against medical waste processing plants in these cities.	waste processing plants rejected
Pittsburgh: Since 2000, PIIN won funds to tear down or board up abandoned houses in a five-block area being redeveloped by two member churches.	$150,000
2000, Shenango Valley, Pennsylvania: Shenango Valley Initiative won matching funds for an ongoing site cleanup.	$9 million
1991, Minnesota: Minnesota ISAIAH advocated for a community-controlled small business loan program.	$1 million in assets; twenty-one businesses started or expanded that had been rejected by traditional lenders

Education

2005, Minnesota: Minnesota ISAIAH sought additional funds for public education.	$800 million additional funding for public education
2006, Connecticut: UACT secured additional funds in the Connecticut state budget for low-income pre-kindergarten funding and placements.	$8.5 million; 700 more students in prekindergarten programs
2005, Connecticut: UACT secured an Education Cost Sharing Grant to fund public education.	$40 million

Regional Planning and Smart Growth

2004, Michigan: A Gamaliel affiliate pursued a new land use commission in Michigan.	established commission and won seats
1997 to the present, Detroit: MOSES worked to have Southeast Michigan declared a HIDTA (high-intensity drug-trafficking area).	$8 million since 1997 for broad, coordinated enforcement
2004, Detroit: MOSES campaigned for the Michigan governor to change the policy to "fix it first" (repair roads, sewers, schools) before building new infrastructure.	"fix it first" policy adopted
2002, Detroit: MOSES joined with twenty suburban mayors to prevent disinvestments in inner-ring suburbs.	Michigan Suburbs Alliance founded
Indiana: Since 2000, Interfaith Federation has secured a Northwest Indiana Regional Development Authority that will fund air, rail, and bus projects in the region.	$20 million

Prison Reform

Iowa: Since 2002, Quad-Cities Interfaith has won restoration of voting rights for felons with completed prison terms.	Iowa governor issued executive order

Selected St. Louis ACORN Accomplishments, Local and Citywide, 1992–2006

Information on local ACORN policy outcomes is incomplete because local staff organizers could not be reached in the course of compiling them.

1976 to the present: ACORN pressures local banks for lending agreements with low-income home buyers. In return, ACORN recruits and screens homebuyers and provides financial counseling and education.	500 home loans, estimated
2000: National ACORN agreement with Ameriquest Mortgage Co. yields $360 million in home loans for low-income families in ten cities with ACORN chapters.	undetermined percentage for St. Louis residents
1998: The Twenty-sixth Ward chapter campaigned for a first source agreement with the new Walgreen's.	ACORN is first source for job applicants for the store

1997: Using CRA provisions allowing community groups to challenge bank mergers, ACORN attacked Mercantile Bank's record of home loans in black neighborhoods in a hearing with federal bank examiners from the U.S. Treasury Department.	U.S. Treasury Department lowers rating of Mercantile Bank from "outstanding" to "satisfactory."
1994: One ACORN neighborhood group campaigned to prevent a medical waste incinerator from being built in an ACORN neighborhood.	incinerator rejected
1994: ACORN gathers 80,000 signatures and places a proposition for campaign finance reform on the state ballot. It passed by 74 percent. This success stimulated the Missouri legislature to pass Senate Bill 650, campaign finance reform legislation with higher funding limits. Most of Proposition A and SB 650 were thrown out in the 8th U.S. Circuit Court of Appeals; it was appealed to the U.S. Supreme Court in January 2000.	federal limits on campaign contributions upheld by U.S. Supreme Court (indirectly a result of Missouri ACORN Proposition A)

Selected San Jose ACORN Accomplishments, 1992–2006

Information on local ACORN policy outcomes is incomplete because local staff organizers could not be reached in the course of compiling them.

1993: ACORN sought traffic safety improvements for Cesar Chavez Elementary School—crossing guards, new crosswalks, and stop signs.	crossing guard, $15,000 per year; school grounds cleanup
1999: ACORN sought a working elementary school bathroom at Miller Elementary School.	$20,000 for new bathroom
1997: ACORN sought participation in police chief hiring.	ACORN participated in hiring process
1997: ACORN pressured the city to trim trees that blocked streetlights and promoted vandalism in the Tropicana neighborhood.	trees trimmed
1994: ACORN sought more effective street lighting.	new white streetlights installed
1996: ACORN sought a city ordinance banning new liquor licenses in the East Side area. The ordinance passed the city council, and in 1997 the ordinance was extended to twenty-four East Side census tracts.	ban on new liquor licenses in twenty-four census tracts
1995–96: ACORN won a new stoplight at a traffic intersection with many pedestrian injuries (McLaughlin Avenue and Appian Lane), and new lowered requirements for street intersection to qualify for stop sign.	$175,000 for new stoplight
1996: Police Athletic League organized local soccer league for boys and girls in Mayfair which had few other recreation opportunities.	$40,000

1996: ACORN sought improved traffic safety near Hillview Elementary School.	stop signs and speed limit signs installed near school with dangerous traffic
Two neighborhood cleanups per year in Tropicana neighborhood.	

Selected MCU for St. Louis Accomplishments, 1992–2006

Accomplishments of CUCA, CCCC, and CACI are included.

Jobs

2006: MCU won an agreement with the Missouri Department of Transportation to allocate 30 percent of all work hours on the Interstate 64 rebuilding project to minority, women, and low-income workers.	150 union-scale jobs for four to five years each

Health Care

2002: In a larger coalition, MCU won presumptive eligibility for Medicaid; children up to 225 percent of the federal poverty level could be enrolled into Medicaid.	over $1 million; 90,000 uninsured Missourians covered
2002: As part of a coalition, MCU won reauthorization of the Children's Health Insurance Program (CHIP/MC+) until July 2007.	CHIP reauthorized

Community Preservation and Redevelopment

2002: With a coalition, MCU helped to preserve the Tax Credits for Distressed Communities.	House Bill 1143 defeated
2002: MCU-ISAIAH won speeded-up road resurfacing, rescheduled from 2008 to 2005, in south St. Louis County.	road resurfacing rescheduled three years sooner
MCU: ISAIAH won reforms to housing code enforcement in the St. Louis County court system during the late 1990s.	Example: a data system to track repeat offenders
1998: C4 and coalition pressured St. Louis to demolish an abandoned Sears store and replace it with single-family homes.	Thirty single-family homes
Since 2000, C4, in coalition, helped ensure redevelopment of Gravois Plaza shopping center and saved the South Side National Bank from demolition.	redeveloped retail center; preserved bank
After 2004, MCU helped ensure reconstruction of Highway 367.	reconstruction of highway

Since 2000, CUCA helped win a commitment to re-develop the abandoned River Roads Shopping Mall.	development of middle-income housing and small businesses
2001–2: Helped win an agreement between the State of Missouri and the City of St. Louis to take over the ownership and maintenance of thirty-five miles of arterial roads in the city of St. Louis.	
In the mid-1990s, MCU established the St. Louis Reinvestment Corporation, a separate nonprofit organization that recruits and screens low-income home-buyers for its neighborhoods (mostly St. Louis and inner-ring suburban neighborhoods).	seven hundred low-cost home loans
1998: MCU won support from St. Louis City and County for the study of urban sprawl in the St. Louis region; results of the study were used to educate and recruit churches into an anti-sprawl campaign.	$20,000 contributed to $40,000 study
1997: In partnership with alumni, parents, and teachers, C4 and CACI helped keep Vashon High School open and helped pass a bond issue for a new building.	$30 million bond issue passed
CUCA pressured the state of Missouri to allow a local hospital to reopen in the mid-1990s.	community-serving hospital reopened
During the 1990s, St. Ann's Church of CUCA took on regional Shell Oil executives to clean up a toxic abandoned gas station.	Shell agreed to clean the toxic site
During the 1990s, CACI campaigned to keep an inner-city post office open.	post office preserved
CACI pressured NationsBank in the 1990s to provide all bank branches with security guards.	security guards in all bank branches
CACI helped broker an agreement between 1996 and 1998 to build an inner-city shopping center.	CACI leaders gain visibility as brokers; new development
CUCA helped unite five local governments in a joint development plan for the Lambert Airport buyout land.	18,000 living wage jobs
C4 with parents and local organizations during the mid-1990s helped keep three St. Louis neighborhood elementary schools open and secured renovations.	$12 million in renovations

Selected San Jose PACT Accomplishments, 1992–2006

Health Care

2000: Santa Clara County health initiative guaranteed health care to all children in the county. The number of children enrolled increased by 25 percent.	$24.4 million in state and federal funds; 13,500 more children enrolled

1999: PACT (in partnership with California Federation of Nurses, Consumers Union, and local city council members) delayed a nonprofit hospital's closing date and, as a condition of its change to for-profit status, Alexian Brothers were required to establish a charity care fund. This is the first time a citizens' group won this concession from Columbia Hospital Group, a national for-profit hospital corporation.	$14 million for fund to subsidize charity patients

Education

2004: Small schools opened in the Alum Rock school district.	three new schools
2000: PACT founded a separate nonprofit organization, ACES New Schools Center. Its goals are incubating new schools, instructional coaching and professional development, and a new schools grants program.	new nonprofit founded to develop more small schools
1993 to the present: San Jose's Homework Centers Program, designed and won by PACT, features academic supervision and tutoring until 6:00 p.m. in 100 percent of San Jose schools (over 180 schools).	$9,355,000 over eight years (1992–2000)
1996–97: PACT member Sacred Heart Church sought a rehabilitated educational research center in a monolingual Hispanic neighborhood and funds for programming at a resource center.	$150,000 and $80,000 respectively
PACT sought funding for Learn and Earn, a mid-1990s city program of internships for two hundred high school students.	$500,000
After 2000, extending PICO's success with after-school centers, it won state support for after-school programs. San Jose's program is San Jose Learns. The city also gained twenty-three low-income San Jose after-school enrichment/recreation/art programs. Every $1 of local funding gets $2 from the State of California. PACT leaders helped draft state legislation.	$1.8 million from the state and $3.6 million from the city
St. Maria Goretti Church won mandatory individual school safety plans for each school in the Hispanic Eastside Union School District, in the 1990s.	new school safety plans
During 1999–2000, Alum Rock United Methodist pressured its elementary school to reinstate the music program. It also won an ESL class for mothers at an elementary school.	music program reinstated and ESL class begun
First Congregational Church demanded a new bathroom in a local preschool.	new bathroom
1995: Cambrian Park and First Congregational Churches expanded their original pilot homework center into more middle schools.	expansion of homework centers

Affordable Housing and Tenants' Rights

Our Lady of Guadalupe Church organized twenty-nine sweat equity housing units to be built for low-income families.	$1.3 million in loans 29 housing units
St. Maria Goretti Church pressured the city attorney to sue the slumlords of Santee slum apartments during the mid-1990s.	city sued and jailed landlords

Community Development and Crime and Blight Prevention

1991: As part of a coalition that defeated an initiative to tax utility bills to fund a major league baseball stadium, PACT distributed fact sheets to over ten thousand voters.	stadium initiative defeated
St. Maria Goretti Church fought stock car racing in nearby fairgrounds in the 1990s.	stock car racing near neighborhood prevented
St. Patrick's Church, in a low-income downtown area, pressured the major local supermarket to clean up in the mid-1990s.	local supermarket cleanup
St. Patrick's Church sought increased lighting for crime prevention.	increased street lighting
1995: St. Patrick's Church pressured the city to implement Project Crackdown in the downtown area.	Project Crackdown implemented in low-income downtown area
1991 to the present: PACT won Project BEST, a package of forty neighborhood youth antigang, drug, and crime programs, including a new citywide antigang program coordinator ("czar") and a gang task force.	$21 million over eight years (1992–2000); set San Jose precedent for funding neighborhood social programs from the Redevelopment Agency
1993: Sacred Heart Church pursued an expanded Right Connection program, a summer gang prevention program with twelve staff members.	program expanded
1989 to the present: PACT pressured the mayor for Project Crackdown, a multifaceted neighborhood drug and crime prevention program.	$1,959,909 for 1998–2000
1989: St. Maria Goretti Church won the implementation of Project Crackdown in its neighborhood.[14]	Project Crackdown implemented in a low-income neighborhood
1992 to the present: St. Maria Goretti Church pursued a gang awareness program for grades 3, 5, and 7.	gang prevention program established for youth
First Congregational Church sought a local gang intervention program in the early 1990s.	won program

City agreed to revise the criteria for the BEST gang intervention in response to PACT.	city added crime prevention as well as intervention and suppression to program
1995: Cambrian Park and First Congregational Churches sought to retain two probation officer positions serving four local high schools.	officers retained; $100,000 per year
1995: Cambrian Park and First Congregational Churches sought a gang prevention specialist for grades 5, 7, and 9 in West San Jose.	$50,000 per year for a gang prevention specialist for youth
1995: Cambrian Park and First Congregational Churches allied to seek additional funding for Project BEST in their area.	funding won

Public Safety

Most Holy Trinity Church sought a new stoplight for an unsafe intersection in the mid-1990s.	$280,000
St. Maria Goretti Church sought a stoplight near the church at Southside Drive and Senter Road in the mid-1990s.	$150,000
1993: St. John Vianney Church sought a stoplight at Linda Vista and McKee.	approximately $150,000
1993–95: St. John Vianney Church initiated a combined state, county, and city traffic redesign, including a widened avenue and left-turn lane.	$1,500,000
A stoplight was installed at Kirk and Alum Rock Avenues in the mid-1990s.	$150,000
1995: St. Frances Cabrini Church sought local highway safety improvements.	$4,000
1997: The First Congregational Church PACT led a coalition of churches, schoolteachers, and parents to win a stoplight at an unsafe intersection at Sherman Oaks elementary school.	$280,000

Youth and Family Services

SAGE, a citywide after-school recreation program, was created during the 1990s after St. John Vianney PACT discovered that only forty-five students in their Council District 5 were served by such a program.	new citywide youth recreation program
1996–67: St. Maria Goretti Church sought a teen center at Fair School.	$200,000 plus operating costs

1998–99: St. Maria Goretti Church sought improvements to the Solari Youth Center.	improvements to youth center
PACT churches sought Fair Exchange in the mid-1990s, an all-inclusive, multiservice Healthy Start Program for families (largely low-income immigrants) at J. W. Fair Middle School, including homework centers, family counseling, and a teen center, all coordinated by one person.	$250,000 per year; $7,000,000 from Irvine Foundation for seven years
First Congregational Church, in partnership with Rose Glen Neighborhood Association, won a new community center at an elementary school in 1999–2000.	$500,000
1995–2000: St. John Vianney Church initiated a campaign for a new youth center.	$7,700,000 for Pala Youth Center
1991–99: St. John Vianney Church won a new neighborhood center at a local middle school.	$350,000
Cambrian Park United Methodist Church won a new youth center, added to an existing community center, in the late 1990s.	new youth center
Evergreen Valley United Methodist Church won a teen recreation specialist for a local community center in the late 1990s.	$240,000
First Congregational Church won three after-school recreation programs.	$8,000–10,000 each per year
1999–2000: Most Holy Trinity PACT, in coalition with other community groups, sought a new East Side community center.	new community center
Most Holy Trinity pressured the city to remodel a youth center during the 1990s.	$100,000
Our Lady of Guadalupe Church advocated for a portable room for the community center at Ryan Elementary School.	$300,000 for the portable room
Our Lady of Guadalupe won Police Athletic League soccer scholarships for forty low-income youths in 1998–99.	$2,000 in soccer scholarships
Sacred Heart Church won a new youth center in a monolingual Hispanic neighborhood in 1999.	$12,000,000 for a new youth center
In 1998–99, Sacred Heart Church won new jobs for youth.	two hundred jobs for youth
With the YMCA, the Westminster Presbyterian Church initiated a parent education class at a nearby school and expanded an after-school enrichment program in the late 1990s.	parent education class and expanded after-school enrichment program

Immigrant Rights

1994: PACT demanded that the Santa Clara County Board of Supervisors oppose state Proposition 187, which denied education and health care to children of undocumented immigrants.	resolution refusing to implement Proposition 187 passed by County Board of Supervisors; 52 percent of Santa Clara County voters voted against Proposition 187 (one of only eight counties out of fifty-eight that defeated it)

Agenda Setting: Selected Proposals Introduced by Four Community Organizations since 1990

St. Louis ACORN Proposals

ACORN Housing Corporation pioneered St. Louis's first program to match low-income homebuyers with bank lending programs. St. Louis now has eight to ten similar programs, which broker thousands more loans to low-income families.

The 1994 Missouri campaign contributions ballot initiative passed and then was struck down in court, but it triggered Missouri Senate Bill 650, which was upheld by the U.S. Supreme Court in January 2000.

1996 Missouri minimum wage ballot initiative failed; it proposed raising the minimum wage from $4.25 to $6.25 per hour.

Living wage agreement was passed in the Board of Aldermen in 2002.

St. Louis ACORN was a major advocate to preserve a public hospital and prevent the sale of a nonprofit hospital to a for-profit operator (efforts failed).

MCU Proposals

MCU helped lead an effort to establish the only city vocational high school in St. Louis.

The Smart Growth Alliance brought together churches, environmental groups, municipal governments, transportation planners, and environmentalists to combat urban sprawl.

Urban growth boundaries were proposed in the media and in state legislation.

MCU commissioned a major study of St. Louis urban sprawl.

MCU leads campaigns to redevelop shopping centers, banks, and schools.

MCU reformed housing code enforcement in the St. Louis County Court system, including a data system to track repeat offenders.

MCU used Missouri highway funds as incentives for hiring to obtain workforce diversity and to create jobs.

San Jose ACORN Proposals

San Jose ACORN won a city ordinance banning new liquor licenses in twenty-four census tracts.

San Jose ACORN advocated school district reforms, some successful, in a low-income Hispanic school district, including replacement of ineffective school board members.

San Jose ACORN used its Redevelopment Agency to pressure the city to hire San Jose residents first. It failed, but the mayor created a voluntary hiring program.

PACT Proposals

Santa Clara County Sobering Station is an alternative to incarceration for alcoholics and serves more than twelve local law enforcement agencies with an annual usage of 3,265 visits.

Project Crackdown is a multipronged antigang and anticrime program. It is a model for the federal neighborhood anticrime program Weed and Seed, which has been implemented nationwide.

Project BEST was inspired by a Los Angeles program. It set a precedent for diverting Redevelopment Agency funds to neighborhood social services.

PACT successfully proposed that the city coordinate all antigang programs under one governing board, the San Jose Gang Task Force, and one coordinator.

PACT proposed a joint city-county program, a drug treatment facility for youth, which is still in process.

PACT proposed after-school homework centers; implemented in 195 San Jose schools by 2000 and included all San Jose schools by 2003.

Learn and Earn is a city program providing two hundred high school work internships.

PACT partnered with Working Partnerships USA, a labor think tank, for the Santa Clara County Children's Health Initiative, the first national initiative to provide health insurance to all children below 300 percent of the poverty line in a county, using tobacco settlement funds. The number of insured children was increased by 13,500 (25 percent) and brought $24.4 million in new state and federal dollars into the county.

PACT initiated and helped design crisis response plans for school violence in all San Jose elementary, middle, and high schools by 2003.

PACT founded a separate nonprofit corporation for education reform in low-income, minority school districts, with three program areas: New Schools Incubator, Professional Development, and New Schools Grants Program. The first three new, small autonomous schools opened in 2004.

Notes

Introduction

1. The bill is the Safe Accountable Flexible and Efficient Transportation Equity Act—A Legacy for Users (SAFETEA-LU).

2. Evidence of diverse CBCO membership is consistent through multiple studies; see the survey by Warren and Wood, *Faith-based Community Organizing.* Another survey Hart conducted informed his *Cultural Dilemmas.* ACORN is largely black and Hispanic.

3. See Skocpol, *Protecting Soldiers and Mothers;* Skocpol, "Advocates without Members"; Skocpol and Fiorina, "How Americans Became Civic"; and Skocpol, Ganz, and Munson, "A Nation of Organizers."

4. See Morris, *Origins of the Civil Rights Movement.*

5. See Skocpol, *Protecting Soldiers and Mothers;* Skocpol, Ganz, and Munson, "A Nation of Organizers"; Skocpol and Fiorina, "How Americans Became Civic"; Gamm and Putnam, "Growth of Voluntary Associations." Skocpol, Ganz, and Munson identified forty-six federated organizations with memberships of at least 1 percent of the American population. According to one survey, congregation-based organizations represent an estimated 3 million Americans; however, they are not dues-paying individuals, but members of dues-paying congregations. Their financial support of their churches helps pay churches' dues to the federation. Each member congregation typically includes a committee of active leaders. Warren and Wood's survey *(Faith-based Community Organizing)* reported an estimated 100,000 citizens who attended at least one organizing event in an eighteen-month period. For ACORN, even the optimistic 200,000 members that ACORN claimed

as of 2006 is far smaller, but ACORN members pay significant dues: $160 per family per year. See Eckholm, "Antipoverty Group Plants Seeds of Change."

6. Mishel, Bernstein, and Allegretto, *State of Working America.*

7. Skocpol, *Protecting Soldiers and Mothers;* Skocpol and Fiorina, "How Americans Became Civic."

8. Piven and Cloward, *Poor People's Movements.*

9. What I call "congregation-based" or "church-based community organizing" is variously called "faith-based," "broad-based," and "institution-based" organizing. The first few labels obviously highlight its basis in religious congregations. "Congregation" and "faith" are both more inclusive terms than "church" because they include Jewish, Muslim, and other congregations. However, "faith-based" increasingly connotes the religiously-based *social services* championed by George W. Bush. I sometimes use "church-based" for brevity and because the vast majority of member congregations are Protestant and Catholic (Christian) churches. Some Unitarian-Universalist congregations are involved and, less often, synagogues. All the member congregations in the late 1990s in the two CBCOs in this book were Christian; since then, Unitarian-Universalist and Jewish congregations have joined them. The terms "broad-based" and "institution-based" indicate, respectively, that these are mass organizations and that their members are organizations, not individuals. Also, some of these include nonreligious organizations such as labor unions and community development corporations, and these terms are more accurate for them. Throughout I use "CBCO" for "church-based organizing."

10. The Industrial Areas Foundation (IAF) has been the subject of work by scholars, journalists, and practitioners. Book-length studies of the IAF include Orr, *Black Social Capital;* Osterman, *Gathering Power;* Rooney, *Organizing the South Bronx;* Shirley, *Community Organizing for Urban School Reform* and *Valley Interfaith and School Reform;* and Warren, *Dry Bones Rattling.* Organizers' accounts of the Industrial Areas Foundation include Chambers and Cowan, *Roots for Radicals,* and Gecan, *Going Public;* journalists' accounts include Freedman, *Upon This Rock,* and Rogers, *Cold Anger.* Many other works consider it along with other organizations: see Boyte, *The Backyard Revolution;* Day, *Prelude to Struggle;* Greider, *Who Will Tell the People;* Polletta, *Freedom Is an Endless Meeting;* Reitzes and Reitzes, *The Alinsky Legacy;* and many others; and Wilson cites it as an approach that could become *The Bridge over the Racial Divide.* The major CBCO networks are increasingly differentiated from the IAF and from one another. PICO and the Gamaliel Foundation are increasingly interested in forming alliances and mounting national campaigns. In *Doing Justice,* Jacobsen, a practitioner, reports on the work of clergy in the Gamaliel Foundation. Another guide to organizing is Pierce's *Activism That Makes Sense.* A few works compare CBCOs to other models: Wood compares PICO to the racially-identified Center for Third World Organizing in *Faith in*

Action. Hart compares CBCO to Amnesty International in *Cultural Dilemmas of Progressive Politics.* Smock compares several "ideal types" of community organizing in *Democracy in Action.* Her main focus is internal practices and community-level impacts rather than political influence. Earlier works on organizing include Fisher, *Let the People Decide,* and Lancourt, *Confront or Concede.*

11. For example, see the work of Theda Skocpol and Debra Minkoff. Skocpol's more recent work more closely examines organizational cultures and processes; see *Diminished Democracy.* Key examples of survey research are the work of Putnam, *Bowling Alone;* and Verba, Schlozman, and Brady, *Voice and Equality.*

12. Piven and Cloward, *Poor People's Movements.*

13. See McAdam, Tarrow, and Tilly, *Dynamics of Contention,* 92.

14. See, for example, Barker, Johnson, and Lavalette, *Leadership in Social Movements;* G. Davis et al., *Social Movements and Organization Theory;* Ganz, "Resources and Resourcefulness"; Polletta, *Freedom Is an Endless Meeting;* and Rose, *Coalitions across the Class Divide.*

15. Becker, *Congregations in Conflict,* 18.

16. Omitted are both the interactive processes of contention and the environment of opportunity or threats that motivate actors as well as condition their results.

17. See Benford and Snow, "Framing Processes and Social Movements: An Overview"; and Benford, "An Insider's Critique." For culturalist criticisms of the framing approach, also see Jasper, *Art of Moral Protest;* Goodwin and Jasper, *Rethinking Social Movements;* and Goodwin, Jasper, and Polletta, *Passionate Politics.*

18. Its affiliated organizations include ACORN Housing Corporation, which provides low-cost loans to low-income homebuyers; Arkansas Institute for Social Justice, the education and training arm; SEIU Local 880 and Local 100; and the ACORN Media Foundation, which runs radio stations in Little Rock and Dallas. ACORN was a key founder of the New Party and Working Families Party.

19. The fieldwork was conducted from September 1997 through March 1998 in St. Louis, and April through August 1998 in San Jose, California.

20. Berry, *The New Liberalism.*

21. Lichterman, *The Search for Political Community.*

22. These include Ed Chambers and Ernesto Cortes of the IAF, John Baumann of PICO, and Greg Galluzzo of the Gamaliel Foundation. Interviews by the author; also see Reitzes and Reitzes, *The Alinsky Legacy;* Chambers and Cowan, *Roots for Radicals;* and Gecan, *Going Public.*

23. Protestant Christianity, which overthrew priestly authority to establish the "priesthood of all believers," has always contained the seeds of both authoritarianism and radically egalitarian heresies. The multivocal Protestant Reformation included the Radical Reformation, led by radical protosocialists. Later, American

Protestantism included nonconformists like Anne Hutchinson, numerous utopian sects, and social reformers such as the Quakers. While the American church has devoted far more energy to charity than to social reform, it nevertheless inspired Progressive civic reformers and Social Gospel crusaders. More recently, the church undergirded movements for black civil rights, farmworkers' labor rights, peace, and human rights in Central America.

24. Putnam, *Bowling Alone*, 65; on church versus union membership, see Verba, Schlozman, and Brady, *Voice and Equality*.

25. Polletta has explored participatory democracy in American social movements, including CBCOs. See her *Freedom Is an Endless Meeting*.

26. Memo, Bruce Dorpalen, ACORN Housing Corporation, author's possession. In addition, Dorpalen calculates over $100 million in savings in interest rates and private mortgage insurance during the first year of mortgages alone.

27. Szymanski, *Pathways to Prohibition*. On suffrage, see Flexner and Fitzpatrick, *Century of Struggle;* and Wheeler, *One Woman, One Vote*.

28. I made this argument in "Setting the State's Agenda." For studies that integrate social movements and policy making, see Costain and McFarland, *Social Movements and American Political Institutions*.

29. Kingdon, *Agendas, Alternatives, and Public Policies,* 21, 71; Baumgartner and Jones, *Agendas and Instability in American Politics*. A few studies look at local policy making, but do not emphasize local or social movement organizations as policy innovators. See Berry, Portney, and Portney, *Rebirth of Urban Democracy;* and McCarthy, Smith, and Zald, "Accessing Public, Media, Electoral, and Governmental Agendas." But see Meyer, Jeness, and Ingram, *Routing the Opposition*.

30. The Progressives' program drew on earlier demands of the agrarian and populist movements, and the feminist, environmental, and consumerist movements not only generated pressure for new policies but in many cases proposed specific policies. See Costain, *Inviting Women's Rebellion;* McAdam, *Political Process;* and Sanders, *Roots of Reform*.

31. Tarrow, *Power in Movement,* 4.

32. On cycles, see ibid.

33. See Sampson et al., "Civil Society Reconsidered."

34. On moral reform in movements, see Giele, *Two Paths to Women's Equality;* Kersh and Morone, "How the Personal Becomes Political"; Morone, *Hellfire Nation;* Sorin, *Abolitionism;* Szymanski, *Pathways to Prohibition;* and Young, *Bearing Witness against Sin*.

35. On purist feminism in the ERA campaign, see Mansbridge, *Why We Lost the ERA;* on the antinuclear movement, see Downey, "Ideology and the Clamshell Identity"; on local environmental organizations, see Lichterman, *Search for Political Community*.

36. The Berrigan quote is found in Szymanski, *Pathways to Prohibition,* 1. On SNCC, see Polletta, "'It Was Like a Fever,'" 153, 152.

37. Ibid., 153.

38. Polletta, *Freedom Is an Endless Meeting.*

39. Arlene Stein argued twenty years ago in "Between Organization and Movement" that ACORN could benefit instrumentally if it built solidarity and collective identity through a richer, more expressive, value-laden internal culture.

40. European scholars nonplussed by new social movements that were organized along non-class-based goals and identities created an artificial new category that lumped identity-based movements (which often include redistributive economic goals) with causes for the public good such as peace, environmental, and antinuclear movements. Given American political culture, non-class-based movements were naturally less puzzling to American scholars.

41. Jasper, *Art of Moral Protest,* 10, 82. Jasper's division of social movements in the industrialized West into "citizenship" and "post-citizenship" movements is far preferable to earlier new social movement scholars' tacit division between class-based movements and "others." However, the ongoing significance of class in developed countries does not easily find a place in the "citizenship" and "post-citizenship" distinction. In another example, "protest" best captures the reactive, expressive element of activism; the use of "feminist protest" and "institutional protest" in Mary Katzenstein's important book on feminism in the church and military does not convey the planful, proactive, strategic, incremental—indeed, interest-group-like—efforts of feminists to alter military policies. See Katzenstein, *Faithful and Fearless.*

42. Lichterman's *The Search for Political Community* was an important exception for me.

43. Exceptions include Jasper, *Art of Moral Protest;* and Ganz, "Resources and Resourcefulness."

1. Different Mobilizing Cultures

1. Eliasoph, *Avoiding Politics,* 10, 17.

2. See Swidler, "Culture in Action: Symbols and Strategies," 273–86.

3. Oberschall, "Culture Change and Social Movements," 13.

4. I use the term "indoctrination" not pejoratively but descriptively, as these trainings are the most sustained opportunity for activists to learn what amounts to a doctrine of organizing.

5. Throughout this study "organizers" and "staff" refer to paid staff. "Staff" always refers to paid organizers and other employees. "Members" and "activists" refer to the membership—in ACORN, dues-paying members, and in PACT and MCU, participants from the member churches. All four organizations use the term

"leaders" to refer to the leading active members, not paid organizers, because in the ideology of community organizing those whom the group represents should be leading the group.

6. On emotion rules and emotion work, see Hochschild, *The Managed Heart.* On emotions in social movements, see the essays in Goodwin, Jasper, and Polletta, *Passionate Politics;* Taylor and Whittier, "Analytical Approaches to Social Movement Culture"; and Aminzade and McAdam, "Emotions and Contentious Politics."

7. For the fullest treatment of the Texas IAF, see Warren, *Dry Bones Rattling.*

8. Reitzes and Reitzes, *The Alinsky Legacy,* 149; Warren, *Dry Bones Rattling.*

9. In Oakland, California, in 1971, Jesuit priest John Baumann founded what became the PICO National Network of organizations, which adopted the CBCO model during the 1980s. Greg Galluzzo, a former Jesuit priest, reorganized the Gamaliel Foundation as church based. DART was founded in 1982 and is the smallest network.

10. Engel, "Influence of Saul Alinsky," 636–61.

11. The United Church of Christ allocated $1.1 million, the National Council of Churches $500,000, and the United Methodist Church $1.8 million, among others. The Catholic Church's first collection yielded $8.4 million, then the largest single collection in its history. Ibid.

12. A recent article by longtime organizer and sociologist Marshall Ganz is titled "Why David Sometimes Wins: Strategic Capacity in Social Movements."

13. Examples from national "weeklong training" are taken primarily from the PICO National Network training, with comparisons and contrasts from the Gamaliel Foundation training that often reveal interesting differences in the two organizations' ideologies. All the CBCOs borrow heavily from the original Industrial Areas Foundation training and its director Ed Chambers's philosophy of organizing. I attended the Gamaliel Foundation weeklong training in Chicago in March 1998 and the PICO training session at the Jesuit Retreat Center in Los Altos, California, from July 28 through August 3, 2000. PICO's training consisted of about seventeen one-to-three-hour modules led by PICO staff, including the PICO national director, assistant director, and several of the most experienced PICO organizers.

14. Of the ninety-three registered participants at PICO's July–August 2000 training session, seventy-one answered a brief survey. Of these, thirty-four were male and thirty-seven were female. Ages ranged from sixteen to sixty-nine, with about half the participants in their thirties and forties. The ethnic mix included 54 percent Anglo/white, 22 percent Hispanic, 20 percent African American, and a few others. The group was unusually well-educated by virtue of the twenty-nine clergy members who were present: thirty-four, or 49 percent, had a master's degree and only about a third lacked a college degree. The group was 51 percent Catholic, 45 percent Protestant (thirteen denominations), and a few non-Christians.

15. For the origin of this ideology, see *Roots for Radicals,* by longtime Industrial Areas Foundation director Ed Chambers. Chambers wrote that movements have "no large circle of well-developed leaders left to take up where they left off"; they seek instant redress of grievances; they are sporadic; they are geared more to attracting media than winning actual policy change; they are supported by "outside money from wealthy liberal supporters, rather than hard money raised from participants" that can be withdrawn whenever donors want (130–31). This presentation is a caricature, but reflects social movements' larger-than-life yet transitory quality. However, much of Chambers's characterization describes well-known drawbacks of 1960s social movements and the loose disorganization of a movement in its "moments of madness." I quote from Chambers because he was so influential in developing the CBCO mobilizing culture. The other CBCO networks drew heavily from Chambers and IAF training sessions. While CBCOs aim for financial self-sufficiency through member dues and fund-raising, this has proven impossible, although many raise significant funds internally. Instead of recommending self-sufficiency, the PICO trainer said, "You want a balanced portfolio. The more local you are the better."

16. Reitzes and Reitzes, *Alinsky Legacy.*

17. Hart, *Cultural Dilemmas.*

18. But see Wood, *Faith in Action,* 219–34, in which he describes a church in PICO's Oakland Community Organization that had a theology of saving individual souls and was therefore ineffective at community organizing. I did not observe this theology active in PACT or MCU churches. In fact, when PACT reviewed the city's administration of Project BEST in 1992, its many criticisms included the fact that one of the agencies funded for gang prevention and intervention had a "connection to evangelical Protestant ministry." "Summary of San Jose BEST," author's possession.

19. The 1977 Community Reinvestment Act was a major victory for community organizing and one of the few goals that community organizing groups all lobbied hard for and won.

20. The term is Hart's, from *Cultural Dilemmas.*

21. See Rodgers, *Contested Truths.*

22. This is also repeated in the series of three workshops given to new church organizing committees.

23. Hart, *Cultural Dilemmas.*

24. Ibid.

25. Exodus 2:23–25 reads: "After a long time the king of Egypt died. The Israelites groaned under their slavery, and cried out. Out of the slavery their cry for help rose up to God. God heard their groaning, and God remembered his covenant with Abraham, Isaac, and Jacob. God looked upon the Israelites, and God took notice of them."

26. Interview, March 1998, Chicago.

27. See Polletta's chapter on congregation-based community organizing in *Freedom Is an Endless Meeting.*

28. Ibid., 136.

29. See Hart, *Cultural Dilemmas.*

30. John Baumann, personal interview, Oakland, California, April 29, 1998.

31. The organization is United Action Connecticut. Information from http://www.gamaliel.org/UACT/faq.htm (accessed December 2005).

32. These associations are not natural or inherent, but socially constructed and conventional. They are, of course, nonetheless real and influence the level of familiarity and comfort for women and men in each of the organizations.

33. Alinsky, *Rules for Radicals,* 130.

34. This point has been made by scholars and activists alike. See Morris, "Reflections on Social Movement Theory." Alinsky wrote, "Never go outside the experience of your people" and "Wherever possible go outside the experience of your enemy" (*Rules for Radicals,* 127).

35. Lipton, "Giuliani Cites Criminal Past of Slain Man."

36. The pastors faced an unexpected development when Giuliani entered the meeting and they had to decide whether to walk out on the mayor. They caucused and compromised by sending one clergy member in. Ultimately they won the apology.

37. The term is from McAdam, Tarrow, and Tilly, *The Dynamics of Contention,* 6. The authors distinguish "contained" from "transgressive contention"; as I read them, either can occur within or without established institutions, and they are context specific, depending on cultural norms. So when the *form* of CBCO or ACORN interactions with authorities has become routine and accepted, it is contained. CBCO mass meetings are contained contention when they are accepted by authorities and routinized.

38. Balzer, "Finding Their Voice." Balzer interviewed AFSCME organizer Kris Rondeau. AFSCME is the American Federation of State, County, and Municipal Employees.

39. On gender and organizing, see Calpotura and Fellner, "The Square Pegs Find Their Groove"; and Stall and Stoecker, "Community Organizing or Organizing Community?"

40. When ACORN expanded beyond Arkansas, the name was changed to Association of Community Organizations for Reform Now. This brief history of ACORN is indebted to Delgado, *Organizing the Movement.*

41. Piven and Cloward, *Poor People's Movements.*

42. The Syracuse University School of Social Work had formed a training center in 1965 in which ideas from CORE and Alinsky-style tactics were com-

bined in the National Welfare Rights Organization. Trainers included Alinsky, Warren Haggstrom, and Fred Ross. The former chairman of Syracuse CORE, George Wiley, and other NWRO organizers went through the Syracuse training and learned about building organizations, CORE's direct action tactics, and Fred Ross's house meetings. Ibid.

43. In 1997 organizers started at $1,000 a month, with health benefits after three months, and $15,000 a year if they stayed a year. In 2005 the annual starting salary had risen to $23,285.

44. Fred P. Brooks, "Racial Diversity on ACORN's Organizing Staff, 1970–2003," in author's possession.

45. Charles R. Haun, memorandum to New Party, November 24, 1997, in author's possession.

46. http://www.ACORN.org/who_are_we.html.

47. Delgado, *Organizing the Movement*, 63–65.

48. Ibid., 163.

49. Eliasoph, *Avoiding Politics;* on episodic voluntarism having replaced long-term organizational commitments, see Wuthnow, *Loose Connections.*

50. Lichterman, *Search for Political Community*, 2.

51. For example, an elderly member (who happened to be the mother of the then-current St. Louis mayor) gave this opening prayer: "Heavenly Father, we come thankful to you . . . through many dangerous toils and snares . . . thank you, Jesus. Bless us and this organization in a special manner. Bless the hospitals, the sick and the wounded . . . in the name of the Father, Son, and Holy Ghost, every heart say amen." All present joined in with a murmured "amen" in a routine that was utterly familiar to them.

52. These and other unattributed quotes by members are from my interviews with grassroots leaders. All names of activists are pseudonyms in order to protect individuals' identities.

53. Delgado, *Organizing the Movement.*

54. "ACORN Members' Handbook, 1994–1995."

55. Data in Figure 5 are taken from interviews with seventy-five activists from all four organizations. They were semistructured interviews based on a protocol of forty-five questions, in Appendix B.

56. Interviews and e-mail correspondence with anonymous organizers, 1998–2000.

57. Chong, *Collective Action and the Civil Rights Movement.*

58. Delgado, *Organizing the Movement.*

59. These observations are based on St. Louis ACORN because I did not observe conflicts within San Jose ACORN.

60. Delgado, *Organizing the Movement*, 191.

61. Ibid., 193. I have been unable to get the current number of top-level female ACORN staff from ACORN sources.

62. Delgado, *Organizing the Movement*.

63. Personal communications.

64. A. Stein, "Between Organization and Movement."

2. Religion and Progressive Politics

1. Putnam, *Bowling Alone;* Wuthnow, *Loose Connections* and *I Come Away
Stronger;* Skocpol, *Diminished Democracy*.

2. On religious participation as a predictor of civic voluntarism, see Putnam,
Bowling Alone, 67; and Verba, Schlozman, and Brady, *Voice and Equality.* On the
stability of churches as voluntary associations, see Skocpol, "Advocates without
Members."

3. For example, see Rapping, *The Culture of Recovery;* Kaminer, *I'm Dysfunctional, You're Dysfunctional*.

4. Hart, *Cultural Dilemmas of Progressive Politics*.

5. For example, see Gitlin, *Twilight of Common Dreams.* A debate of this type
has simmered within the small world of community-organizing entrepreneurs. On
one side are those who argue for traditional community organizing that emphasizes shared class position (though not in that language) and avoids issues that
divide by race, gender, or sexuality. Mike Miller expresses the traditionalist view
in "Beyond the Politics of Place." On the other side are those who insist that class-
based community organizing must make room for race, gender, and sexuality issues. Representative statements of this view include Delgado, *Beyond the Politics of
Place;* and Fellner and Colpatura, *Square Pegs Find Their Groove*.

6. Dionne, *Why Americans Hate Politics,* 93.

7. For analyses and examples of working-class cultures and ideology, see Croteau, *Politics and the Class Divide;* Gamson, *Talking Politics;* Halle, *America's Working Man;* Lamont, *Dignity of Working Men;* Rose, *Coalitions across the Class Divide;*
Lichterman, *Search for Political Community;* Eliasoph, *Avoiding Politics.* On attitudes toward cultural elites and the middle class, see Dionne, *Why Americans Hate
Politics;* Croteau, *Politics and the Class Divide,* 78; Frank, *What's the Matter with
Kansas?* On American electoral coalitions, see, for example, Dionne, *Why Ameri-
cans Hate Politics;* Ginsberg and Shefter, *Politics by Other Means;* Katznelson, *City
Trenches;* Lipset and Marks, *It Didn't Happen Here*.

8. On the decline of leaders and organizations to mobilize working-class
Americans, see Rosenstone and Hansen, *Mobilization, Participation, and Democracy;*
and Ginsberg and Shefter, *Politics by Other Means.* The coalition of unions that broke
with the AFL-CIO in 2005 included the Teamsters, Laborers Union (LIUNA),
UNITE-HERE, Service Employees International Union (SEIU), United Food and

Commercial Workers (UFCW), United Brotherhood of Carpenters and Joiners, and United Farm Workers. The new federation pledged to devote 75 percent of its resources to organizing. Change to Win Coalition, "New Labor Federation Pledges to Carry Out Most Aggressive Organizing Campaign in 50 Years," press release, September 27, 2005, http://www.changetowin.org (accessed September 5, 2007).

9. On the working-class majority, see Teixeira and Rogers, *America's Forgotten Majority;* and Zweig, *Working-Class Majority.*

10. Levison, "Who Lost the Working Class?" 26, citing Halle, *America's Working Man.*

11. Lamont, *Dignity of Working Men;* and Willis, "Masculinity and Factory Labor." On the appeal of Bush versus Gore, see Levison, "Who Lost the Working Class?"

12. The "credential" for PACT and other PICO organizations means a short prepared statement that identifies the organization, its membership base of churches, number of families in those churches, and relation to the larger PICO network. This is meant to convey its legitimacy and power as a representative of local citizens. It is something like "PACT is a federation of seventeen local churches which together include 35,000 families . . . and as part of PICO is part of a network of forty organizations."

13. Suzanne Mettler argues that broad public-serving policies such as the GI Bill produce feedbacks in the form of civic engagement and positive attitudes toward government. See Mettler, *Soldiers to Citizens.* Today, GI Bill benefits have radically shrunk and their eligibility is governed by a bureaucratic maze of regulation, which reinforces the common working-class view that government does not support us, but takes from us in the form of taxes.

14. New social movement participants have high educational status, experienced economic security in their formative years, have relative economic security, and work in personal-service occupations. See Offe, "New Social Movements," 833; Croteau, *Politics and the Class Divide,* 31; Kriesi et al., *New Social Movements.*

15. Organizer Linda Stout gives the example of a middle-class activist who changed a flyer directed at a low-income community. The original read "Something has got to be wrong when the government spends so much money on the military and nothing on me." It was changed to "I don't understand why the government spends so much money on the military and nothing on me." Members of her organization were indignant, and said, "Of course we understand! Do you think we're stupid or something?" L. Stout, *Bridging the Class Divide,* 119.

16. Croteau, *Politics and the Class Divide;* Eliasoph, *Avoiding Politics;* Rose, *Coalitions across the Class Divide.*

17. Croteau, *Politics and the Class Divide,* 183.

18. Verba, Schlozman, and Brady, *Voice and Equality.*

19. Chambers, *Roots for Radicals,* 50.

20. Lichterman, *Search for Political Community;* Croteau, *Politics and the Class Divide.*

21. Material on working-class attitudes toward social movements is taken from Croteau, *Politics and the Class Divide;* Eliasoph, *Avoiding Politics;* and from fieldwork and training sessions.

22. Hart, *Cultural Dilemmas.*

23. The banking industry sought to weaken the Community Reinvestment Act. MCU was targeting Missouri senator Christopher Bond, who sat on the Finance Committee and had a swing vote.

24. The IAF is now building unusually broad federations; this CBCO, United Power for Action and Justice, includes three hundred organizations—not just congregations, but also labor unions, civic organizations, neighborhood groups, hospitals, and health centers.

25. How CBCOs address immigration will bode watching, since this issue is often a liberal-conservative fault line. Immigration has emerged as a priority for the major community organizing networks, and to my knowledge, campaigns have always focused on expanding immigrants' rights and protections.

26. Neal, "Talking Points: Race, Class Re-Enter Politics after Katrina."

27. See Wood's *Faith in Action,* a comparative study of CBCO and the race-based approach to community organizing practiced by the Center for Third World Organizing in Oakland, California.

28. See http://www.gamaliel.org/06.17.04AALCevent.htm (accessed October 4, 2004).

29. Polletta, *Freedom Is an Endless Meeting.* Including a wide range of contributors in deliberation is part of Marshall Ganz's notion of strategic capacity; see Ganz, "Resources and Resourcefulness."

30. Verba, Schlozman, and Brady *(Voice and Equality)* found that Americans of all income levels had a scarcity of time.

31. Warrren discusses this in *Dry Bones Rattling.*

32. On personalism, see Lichterman, *Search for Political Community,* 91. Also see Rose, *Coalitions across the Class Divide.*

33. Weir and Ganz, "Reconnecting People and Politics," 161.

34. When the mass base of the women's movement declined in both its first and second waves, some feminists withdrew and built alternative feminist or lesbian subcultures in lieu of claims making. Katzenstein *(Faithful and Fearless)* has shown how institutions that offer few avenues for internal reform, such as the Catholic Church, produce a feminist subculture that emphasizes radical discourse and cultural expression. See also Rupp and Taylor, *Survival in the Doldrums;* and Whittier, *Feminist Generations.*

35. Lichterman, *Search for Political Community*, 39.

36. "No leadership, no spokeswoman, no votes, action by consensus. It sounded so good. But what started out as a utopian vision has ended in a nightmare. . . . The no leadership/total equality line had damaging effects on the women's liberation movement. . . . Based on the dogma of exact equality among women, it denied the reality that some people are the first to dare and do, to provide clarity and insight, to teach others, to speak for themselves and for others who are not yet speaking for themselves directly." Hanisch, *Liberal Takeover of Women's Liberation*, 164–65. Jo Freeman's famous tract "The Tyranny of Structurelessness" challenged this refusal to designate leaders and build a decision-making structure. See also Baker, "The Problem of Authority in Radical Movement Groups"; and Purkis, "Leaderless Cultures."

37. Dionne, *Why Americans Hate Politics*. When the Kerner Commission concluded that unemployment, crime, drug addiction, and white racism were responsible for the riots, Nixon found a ready audience for his claim that the commission blamed "everybody for the riots except the perpetrators of the riots" (88).

38. For example, see Bennett, *Book of Virtues*.

39. Hart, *Cultural Dilemmas*.

40. On the 2004 election, see Carville and Greenberg, "Memo to Democracy Corps." Data on the 2000 vote is from Gore's pollster Stanley Greenberg, cited in Levison, "Who Lost the Working Class?" Recent studies shed light on how white working-class men see themselves and their status in society. Halle's 1984 study of blue-collar white male homeowners *(America's Working Man)* reinforces Katznelson's argument in *City Trenches* for working people's multiple identities.

41. Halle distinguished multiple sources of identity for working-class men: an occupational identity as workers, another identity as homeowners and therefore middle-class, and a national-populist identity as ordinary citizens against elites. In *What's the Matter with Kansas?* Frank argues that conservatives have successfully framed "elite" as a cultural, not an economic trait; thus liberals, and indeed the Democratic Party, become latte-drinking, academic, and professional cultural elites.

42. "Service in Louisiana Honors Soldiers" and "Bayou Interfaith Sponsoring Community Organization (BISCO) Held a Candlelight Peace Vigil," in *PICO Network News,* April 20, 2005, http://www.piconetwork.org (accessed September 5, 2007).

43. Lattin, "Multifaith Group Puts Own Spin on Values."

44. The historically mainline Protestant churches (Episcopal, Lutheran, Methodist, Baptist, Presbyterian) as well as Catholicism are frequently liberal.

45. According to some scholars, because their high demands generate high value for members. See Kelley, *Why Conservative Churches Are Growing;* and Finke and Stark, *The Churching of America*.

46. Anonymous, "PICO Issues," from PICO Web site, http://www.piconetwork .org/pico_issues.html (accessed June 21, 2006), emphases added.

47. Kraditor, *Means and Ends in American Abolitionism;* Sorin, *Abolitionism.*

48. Giele, *Two Paths to Women's Equality.*

49. Since the 1960s, Niebuhr has been so neglected that it is easy to forget his enormous influence not only on American religion, but on social scientists, scholars, and politicians. Niebuhr was not only a preacher, scholar, and public intellectual, but a political activist who helped found Americans for Democratic Action. On his death in 1971, Niebuhr's close friend Arthur Schlesinger Jr. wrote to Niebuhr's widow, "He had more intellectual influence on me than anyone I have ever known." Schlesinger, "Forgetting Reinhold Neibuhr."

50. Niebuhr cited in Imsong, "Reinhold Niebuhr and Christian Realism."

51. Hart, *Cultural Dilemmas.*

52. Observation of the Gamaliel Foundation weeklong training, March 1998, Chicago.

53. Gamaliel Foundation Web site, http://www.gamaliel.org/Leader/05.13 .04GTW.htm (accessed July 9, 2004).

54. Croteau, *Politics and the Class Divide,* 187–90.

55. On neighborhood decline, see Putnam, *Bowling Alone;* and Croteau, *Politics and the Class Divide,* chapter 10. On the privatization of public spaces, see Davis, *City of Quartz;* and Kohn, *Brave New Neighborhoods.*

56. On the proliferation of small groups, see Wuthnow, *I Come Away Stronger.* On the historic Protestant roots of American self-help, see Anker, *Self-Help and Popular Religion.*

57. For example, from among many possible ways to address the problem of drunk driving, the American solution is not increasing mass transit and reducing reliance on cars, but preventing individuals from drinking. See McCarthy, "The Interaction of Grass-roots Activists and State Actors." Trial lawyers provide a counterweight to this trend with such precedents as the successful framing of tobacco companies as responsible for promoting the individual behavior of smoking.

58. In fact, religious congregations are not clearly public *or* private, but incorporate aspects of both. They are legally private nonprofit corporations like any other private associations, but their domain includes the most private and personal aspects of life and addresses them publicly in worship and public advocacy.

59. Bales and Parsons, *Family, Socialization, and Interaction.* Scholars have traced how American Christianity was feminized in the nineteenth century as the church lost cultural dominance. See Douglas, *Feminization of American Culture;* and Welter, "Feminization of American Religion." Various religious movements reacted against this cultural shift, including stern, Calvinist neo-Orthodoxy and Reinhold Niebuhr's Protestant realism. Niebuhr confronted optimistic Christians

who sought to perfect society with the reality of intransigent power. In *Moral Man and Immoral Society,* Niebuhr reinforced the familiar domains of men and women in his distinction between home, women's arena of love and care, and the corrupt outside world, men's domain of struggle against power and injustice.

60. Eliasoph, *Avoiding Politics.* Activists made their way into the parade by the absurd argument that the local toxic incinerator wasn't "political" (conflictual) since "everyone in town agrees" about it except its owner.

61. Labor unions and other organizations have also harnessed this family discourse. The AFL-CIO's Internet mobilization vehicle is called the Working Families e-Activist Network, and a labor-community coalition third party in New York State is called the Working Families Party.

62. From PACT flyer and meeting agenda, undated, from late 1990s, in author's possession.

63. For example, see F. Ginsburg, *Contested Lives;* Harding, *Book of Jerry Falwell;* Maxwell, *Pro-Life Activists in America;* Ferree et al., *Shaping Abortion Discourse.*

64. Green, *American Religious Landscape and Politics.*

3. Experimenting with National Organizing Campaigns

1. Delgado, *Organizing the Movement,* 47.

2. Ibid.

3. The organization was BUILD, Baltimoreans United in Leadership Development. It launched the campaign in partnership with AFSCME, the American Federation of State, County, and Municipal Employees.

4. Only when a Democratic Congress was elected in 2006 was the minimum wage raised to $5.85 per hour, which went into effect on July 24, 2007. It will be increased to $6.55 on July 24, 2008, and finally to $7.25 on July 24, 2009.

5. Zabin and Martin, *Living Wage Campaigns.*

6. As of May 2005; more have passed since. See National ACORN Campaigns: Living Wage, on the ACORN Web site, http://www.acorn.org.

7. Hukill, "Chasing Amy."

8. ACORN, "Capital & Communities: A Report to the Annie E. Casey Foundation."

9. ACORN wanted the bank to "work with community groups to create loan counseling programs," alter rates for low- and moderate-income borrowers, establish lifeline bank accounts and government check cashing, expand branches in low-income neighborhoods, allow for local credit needs, and provide technical assistance for nonprofit housing development. Ibid.

10. The agreement provided $125,000 for ACORN Housing Corporation to help low-income and minority applicants in Dallas, Houston, and Washington,

D.C.; mortgages were fixed rate, down payments as low as $500, a 95 percent loan-to-value ratio, and interest rate 1 percent below market.

11. Maude Hurd, letter to federal banking regulators, October 17, 2001. At fanniemae.com/news/pressreleases/0710/html (accessed June 17, 2005).

12. Maude Hurd, Lisa Donner, with Camellia Phillips, "Community Organizing and Advocacy: Fighting Predatory Lending and Making a Difference," undated report, in author's possession.

13. *Retail Banker International*, "Household Losing the Public Relations Battle."

14. The coalition claimed that the house parties brought together parents, teachers, and community members to make plans "to take action and make sure that education is a priority" on "every level of government." Conyers, "4,000 House Parties Call for Quality Education," ACORN press release, September 24, 2004.

15. ACORN bylaws, author's collection.

16. Kest, "ACORN and Community-Labor Partnerships."

17. The wage was increased from $5.15 to $5.50 on January 1, 2004, and to $6.50 on January 1, 2005.

18. Interview, anonymous ACORN organizer.

19. Broder, "States Take Lead."

20. ACORN won a commitment to establish a poor people's commission, but in 1982 the Democratic National Committee essentially killed it. However, the campaign expanded ACORN and won it national visibility. From Delgado, *Organizing the Movement*.

21. Fusion used to be widespread in the United States, but the success of minor parties like the Populist People's Party, which used fusion, triggered bans on fusion by Republican-dominated state legislatures. Today fusion is legal in only ten states.

22. It was independent until 2003, when it approached both the Industrial Areas Foundation and ACORN to pursue affiliation. ACORN accepted the offer. Project Vote, "Our Mission," http://projectvote.org (accessed September 6, 2007).

23. "ACORN's 2004 Voter Participation Campaign," author's possession.

24. In 1986, former ACORN organizer Gary Delgado reported that 80 percent of ACORN's budget was internally generated, including membership dues, door-to-door canvassing in middle-class or affluent neighborhoods, and grassroots fund-raising events.

25. Chapter 5 on St. Louis ACORN provides more information on how an ACORN city organization mobilizes resources.

26. Ranghelli, "The Monetary Impact of ACORN Campaigns: A Ten-Year Retrospective," draft, February 16, 2005, author's possession. According to ACORN housing records, its offices "in 38 cities educated 175,057 potential buyers, counseled 115,660 clients, and assisted families in securing 48,566 mortgages"

whose estimated average value was $95,500: "Multiplying the average house price by the number of mortgages produces an aggregate of $4,638,053,000 in housing values." ACORN negotiates aggressively for the banks to cover some loan costs that would normally be passed on to borrowers (based on observation of negotiations between St. Louis ACORN/ACORN Housing Corporation and the Mercantile Bank, 1998).

27. In 2002 this included 4.9 million people, including 2.7 million children. A family of four with two children and one full-time worker earning $7 per hour would net $13,600 per year, several thousand dollars below the poverty line. This worker in 2004 qualified for an earned income tax credit of $4,300 and a child tax credit of $395. Llobrera and Zahradnik, "A Hand Up."

28. In 2003, the ACORN site in New Orleans ranked first among sixty-five sites, and in Miami first of thirty-nine sites, in number of tax returns prepared.

29. Smith, IRS chief of corporate partnerships, interview.

30. Gamson, *The Strategy of Social Protest.*

31. Evidence since 1997 includes extensive participant-observation, ACORN records and reports of campaigns, and news coverage.

32. For the relationship of tactics and movement collective identity, see Jasper, *Art of Moral Protest,* chapter 10; for conflicts between ends-means rationality and the expressive functions of tactics, see Pralle, "Venue Shopping."

33. "Principles of ACORN," principle 5: "If the issue is getting a stop sign, don't send a letter to the street commissioner when your members can go in person to his office." Going in person also helps train and develop new leaders and gives them the experience of success through action. This was confirmed in numerous interviews with organizers including executive director Steve Kest, August 4, 2004.

34. Observation; interviews with anonymous informants; Haun memorandum.

35. Delgado, *Organizing the Movement,* 165.

4. Organizing Is a Numbers Game

1. Names of organizers and members have been changed.

2. ACORN had four demands: that jobs pay $7.70/hour, or $8.70 if without health insurance; that jobs be targeted to city residents, with at least 25 percent for welfare recipients; that the hotel operator use ACORN as a first source for job candidates; and that the hotel operator be neutral in union-organizing efforts. ACORN wanted these provisions to be included in the lease agreement with the new convention center hotel.

3. Organizers guessed that City Hall security had recognized ACORN from a contentious recent campaign in 1997 to keep the city's only public hospital open (unsuccessful).

4. The mayor had been on the news for accompanying a group of young

urbanites on their tours of downtown night spots, an effort to focus attention on and revitalize downtown after business hours.

5. Campaigns in which ACORN played a part include New York City; Broward County, Florida; New Orleans; Boston; Chicago; Cook County, Illinois; Denver; Detroit; Hempstead, New York; Minneapolis; Oakland; San Jose; St. Louis; and St. Paul. These data are as of May 2005. They are listed on ACORN's Living Wage Resource Center Web site in a short "wins" list at http://www.livingwagecampaign .org/index.php?id=1959 and also in a longer list that describes the features of each ordinance.

6. A 1998 Tufts University study ranked Missouri's welfare reform among the ten most harmful programs for welfare recipients. See City of St. Louis, "St. Louis Five Year Plan." Rules for receiving federal funds prevent the city from providing job training to persons with drug problems or criminal records. According to the city, because of these restrictions the city's job training agency "has been able to spend only $740,000 of the $4.7 million that it received. The program has helped only 779 people, of which only 253 are in permanent fulltime employment."

7. For example, as early as 1985 Boatmen's Bancshares agreed to make $50 million in housing loans in low-income neighborhoods in St. Louis (*St. Louis Post Dispatch,* November 19, 1985). When ACORN challenged Magna Bank's merger with Landmark Bancshares, Magna Bank agreed in July 1991 to lend $15 million in poorer neighborhoods. Commerce Bank of St. Louis and Roosevelt Bank granted $7 million in home loans, with which they planned to make about 140 loans.

8. The Community Reinvestment Act, passed in 1977, allows community groups to challenge bank mergers and acquisitions if a bank has not adequately invested in its own community. ACORN uses these provisions to challenge bank mergers and win agreements to invest in ACORN communities, usually through loans to home buyers.

9. With its growth, the staff has increased. Out of fifty-eight organizers nationally in 1998, Missouri (St. Louis) ACORN's organizers were individually ranked eight, twelve, eighteen, twenty-five, and fifty-five in performance on June 17, 1998. During most of this study's observation period, only four organizers were on staff.

10. To derive this figure I took the mean of each north St. Louis census tract's median family income from 1989 census data.

11. A few whites were active, drawn in because ACORN was the only grassroots membership organization defending public health care. For much of 1997, St. Louis ACORN unsuccessfully fought the closing of the city's last public hospital. A key leader in this campaign was a young white activist who had worked as an advocate for Medicaid patients. After Regional Hospital was closed, St. Louis ACORN turned its attention to the impending purchase of the Catholic nonprofit St. Louis University Hospital by Tenet, the nation's largest for-profit chain of hospitals.

12. A quick look at budget data indicates that the average monthly income from dues (for the five months sampled) was $5,123. This computes to 1,024 $60 memberships in a year.

13. ACORN recruited the unemployed through flyers advertising a "Community Hiring Hall." One organizer ran the hiring hall by disseminating flyers ("Do you need a job?") and scheduling those who called the office for group "intake" sessions. Job seekers had to pay dues (often reduced for the unemployed) before they could receive job referrals. Besides recruiting, screening, and referring job candidates, the organizer sought agreements with companies to use ACORN referrals. In spring 1998 ACORN won a first source agreement from a new Walgreen's store. A first source for jobs means that ACORN would be informed of openings and have a window, such as forty-eight or seventy-two hours, in which it would be the only referral service for job candidates. The hiring hall also offered workshops on interviewing skills, employment skills, and the like.

14. The director estimated that St. Louis ACORN had a budget of $20,000 per month, or $240,000 per year. He estimated that member dues supplied about one-fourth of ACORN's income ($5,000 per month). He reported the following typical sources of income: canvassing, $6,000 to $8,000; dues, $5,000; tags (street collections), $500 to $1,000; and grants/other fund-raising, $11,500 to $14,000.

15. Haun memorandum.

16. These included realtors' ads that were listed in a book of realtors for ACORN housing clients to use, raffle tickets, telephone solicitation, fees banks paid to participate in bank fairs (where they could market home loans to prospective borrowers), and dinners and barbecues.

17. At one staff meeting, the director told his staff they needed to raise $1,800 in forty-eight hours. The subsequent flurry of brainstorming produced such ideas as selling more $500 tables to banks (those that worked with ACORN Housing) for the Christmas party, collecting money that was due from members' Christmas party ticket sales, etc.

18. Interview, anonymous informant; Haun memorandum.

19. The ACORN bylaws, article 9, section 1, state that the head of ACORN is "Chief Organizer." Although the chief organizer serves at the pleasure of the board of directors, he or she has the right to employ other staff. The national ACORN director appoints head organizers for states and regions, but (if a board exists in a state or region) the board of that region must ratify the chief organizer's recommendation. Other checks and balances exist: the chief organizer can suspend a state's head organizer, but so can a state or regional board. The chief organizer can transfer staff throughout ACORN.

20. Haun memorandum; interviews with staff. CACI (Churches Allied for

Community Improvement), the MCU suborganization in north St. Louis, has pursued abandoned buildings as a major issue.

21. The president of the St. Louis Labor Council (AFL-CIO) observed, "If we create a floor in wages that doesn't exist in the county, they'll have to put in toll roads to keep the businesses from leaving the city."

22. One local ACORN activist invited the director of the city agency responsible for abandoned buildings to a meeting (unknown to the bureaucrat, a tour of decrepit buildings to which media were invited). To the organizer's dismay, the activist revealed the address of the most dangerous vacant building ACORN had identified. The city promptly cleaned up the site, undercutting the organizer's plan to use the dramatic, weed-choked site as the action's focus.

23. During six months of 1997, I met at least six organizers who came and went, some in as little as a week. Two of the three organizers on staff during my observation also left later in the year. Others came and went in 1997–98.

24. The director was a white male college graduate in his thirties. One of the three organizers was a white male, thirty-four years old; the other two were black males, one in his late thirties, the other in his late forties or older.

25. This increased with seniority by about $1,000 per year. Organizers got health insurance after three months and paid vacation and holidays after six months.

26. Brooks, "Racial Diversity on ACORN's Organizing Staff, 1970–2003."

27. In the case of job referrals, ACORN could require membership (dues), while in the case of home loan seekers, it could merely request it. The Community Development Agency of St. Louis grants ACORN Housing Corporation and other organizations funds to cover borrowers' home loan closing costs. ACORN may not require that borrowers join ACORN as a condition of receiving loan referral services. However, ACORN could "request" that borrowers join ACORN, and many did. Organizers distributed flyers advertising ACORN Housing in low-income neighborhoods. The flyers were marked with the initials of the organizer who distributed them. When prospective clients of ACORN Housing called the ACORN number on the flyer, one organizer took the calls and asked if they met the minimum qualifications ($800 per month income and two or more consecutive years in a job). If they did, he scheduled a thirty-to-forty-minute intake session with the ACORN housing office. A small fee covered the cost of processing the credit check. Then he gave the pitch to join ACORN: "We request that everyone who participates in our programs becomes a part of our membership, because we are a nonprofit organization." If the caller could not afford the annual dues, the organizer asked for a half-year membership.

28. There was little discussion at staff meetings of fundamental or systemic reasons why organizers' productivity was low. With one organizer who had high

potential, it was addressed in private meetings I could not observe. The director had low expectations of another organizer, whom he ultimately fired.

29. When he discussed organizers' inability to reach dues or turnout goals with me, the director took responsibility for not adequately managing the organizing staff. He preferred direct organizing rather than staff management and believed his staff needed more supervision—particularly his presence with them in the office at night—in order to produce. The director regularly provided staff trainings on specific tasks, although these were irregularly scheduled so I was unable to observe them. One organizer reported that staff constantly debriefed actions, although I also did not observe this.

30. A. Stein, "Between Organization and Movement."

31. They felt the director tolerated poor performance and behavior from a white organizer that he never would have tolerated from a black organizer. The white organizer was ultimately fired. A sample of the angry comments: One black organizer described the annual all-staff retreat as follows: "It was just like a Klan rally! No joke! No organizers at the top are black! We're in the field, picking dues instead of cotton!" (This was a play on the term "field organizer.")

32. This organizer was an assistant pastor in a large AME (African Methodist Episcopal) Zion St. Louis church. His church income allowed him to work for ACORN's low salary, but the church competed for his time.

33. Interview, Robert Kelly; interviews with anonymous informants; ACORN Leadership School training booklet, 1998.

34. Gallagher, "Magna Agrees to Provide Low-Income Loans."

35. These organizations included black churches, the state social workers' association, health-care advocates, the NAACP, small neighborhood associations in north St. Louis, and some individual unions.

36. For example, ACORN chose to increase the wage from $4.25 to $6.25 even though polling data indicated that voters would only support a smaller increase. Interviews with Robert Kelly and an anonymous St. Louis activist.

37. Interviews with Arthur Towers and Robert Kelly. Towers suggested ACORN persisted in an underfunded campaign without union support even when it could have declared partial victory after the federal minimum wage was increased to $5.15 in June 1996.

38. Jen Kern, memo to ACORN staff, August 19, 2002, in author's possession.

39. Bryant, "St. Louis Judge Permanently Blocks Enforcement."

40. The judge found the provision that extended living wage coverage to tenants of developers too far-reaching. Ibid.

41. Kern, memo to ACORN staff.

42. "Mortgage Firm, Group to Provide Loans to Families," *San Jose Mercury News,* July 27, 2000, 2C.

5. A Seat at the Regional Table

1. Rusk, "St. Louis Congregations."

2. There are 550,000 Catholics in the St. Louis Archdiocese.

3. The mayor's representative did not commit at the meeting, but the mayor later provided the funds.

4. The eleven-county St. Louis region's population has remained steady at 2.5 million, but outlying St. Charles County grew 22 percent since 1990 while St. Louis County grew only 1.5 percent. The city of St. Louis's population declined from 850,000 in 1950 to 350,000 today and is declining faster than any other large U.S. city. Both 1998 and 1999 Sierra Club studies rank St. Louis second only to Atlanta as having the worst urban sprawl in the nation.

5. For example, the inner-ring suburb of Jennings collected $300,000 less in sales taxes and business fees in 1994–95 than in 1991–92. Johnson, "City Starts to Chart Course."

6. http://www.gamaliel.org/default.htm (accessed September 6, 2007).

7. The core team is the team of leaders within each church. Core team leaders identify issues, mobilize church members to attend actions, and have other functions. They are the basic building block of church-based organizing.

8. Measures to weaken the Community Reinvestment Act are regularly introduced in Congress. This proposal died in committee.

9. I use the term "deliberation" because it evokes Habermas's notion of an ideal speech situation in which all parties are equally heard. The goal of CBCOs, including MCU, is not primarily to create an alternative "knowledge community" with a "politics of reflection and reformulation" (see Katzenstein, *Faithful and Fearless,* 107); rather, it is to pursue goals that have been identified through one-to-one meetings and public debate in which excluded voices—those of ordinary citizens—are included.

10. In a chapter on tactics, Saul Alinsky advises, "Never go outside the experience of your people. Whenever possible go outside the experience of the enemy." *Rules for Radicals,* 127.

11. Here "confrontation" refers to nonviolent disruptive or transgressive behavior, such as breaking into closed meetings while picketing and chanting, or occupying an office and refusing to leave.

12. Glassberg, "St. Louis."

13. Ibid., 93–94.

14. Interview, John Carleton, *St. Louis Post-Dispatch.*

15. Civic Progress spearheaded major development projects and supported the highly successful light-rail system, Metrolink. It is staffed by the Fleischman-Hillard public relations firm, which also proposed St. Louis 2004. Funded by

Civic Progress member corporations at $2.3 million per year for eight years, this community development initiative evoked the glory days of 1904, when St. Louis hosted the World's Fair.

16. Rusk, cited in "Anti-poverty Strategy," *St. Louis Five Year Consolidated Plan Strategy,* http://stlouis.missouri.org/5yearstrategy/1999/app_d.html (1999).

17. Rusk was formerly mayor of Albuquerque, a member of the New Mexico legislature, and staffer of the Washington Urban League and U.S. Department of Labor. He has published works on urban policy including *Cities without Suburbs, Baltimore Unbound,* and *Inside Game, Outside Game.* Orfield is a Minnesota state legislator affiliated with the University of Minnesota, also a consultant in urban planning and policy, whose publications include *Metropolitics.* john a. powell is a scholar at Ohio State University who helps educate Gamaliel affiliates about race and poverty.

18. Rusk, "St. Louis Congregations."

19. Peirce and Johnson, "A Call to Action."

20. In 1973, the Oregon legislature mandated that urban growth boundaries be drawn around cities throughout the state. Portland has a directly elected regional government, which conducts land use and transportation planning for the 1.5-million-person metropolitan area. Development is prohibited outside the boundary. Prohibiting suburban sprawl and restricting development to within the boundary have both saved farmland and redeveloped the inner city. This means that Portland's black and inner-city neighborhoods are some of the very few in which property values have increased (Rusk, *Inside Game, Outside Game*). According to Rusk, when the Portland Metro recently redrew the boundary slightly to make a little more land available, "over the next 45 years, only about four square miles of current farmland will be urbanized—as much farmland as is subdivided in the state of Missouri every six weeks" (ibid., 251).

21. Ibid.

22. Rusk, "St. Louis Congregations."

23. MCU spokespersons and others, including St. Louis mayor Clarence Harmon, testified in favor of measures to halt sprawl. One committee member from St. Charles County invited the mayor out to his county "where he'd feel safe." This was perceived as a coded racial message, and sparked a reaction. *St. Louis Post-Dispatch* headlines reveal the flavor of the debate: "'Urban Sprawl' or 'Urban Choice'?"; "Officials Defend Sudden Growth of Towns in St. Charles County"; "Official Calls for Truce in Urban Sprawl Debate"; "St. Charles Mayor: Don't Blame Problems on Us: City, Counties Again Clash at Committee Hearings."

24. Sixty percent of St. Charles County residents work outside their county, helping create a demand for the highway extension.

25. "If they stop Page, we're going to come to a grinding halt out here,"

Alderman Jerry Hollingsworth, Second Ward, said. St. Charles County officials formed the Urban Choice Coalition. The rhetoric heated up as opponents of sprawl were called "social engineers." St. Charles County's Municipal League hired a public relations firm to "coordinate responses and rebut allegations," while its own members called sprawl opponents the "sprawl police" who were "preaching hate." A partial list of campaign donations supporting Page, in order of magnitude, includes builders and developers, $231,650; major corporations who are members of Civic Progress, $175,092; other St. Charles interests, $157,755; road builders, engineers, and unions, $136,600; miscellaneous others, $116,335; and real estate and finance interests, $10,950; a total of $828,382. Figures compiled by the St. Louis County Municipal League, December 20, 1998.

26. Interview, anonymous *Post-Dispatch* reporter, January 1999.

27. Rusk, *Inside Game, Outside Game,* 263.

28. Civic Progress, the organization of St. Louis's most powerful corporations, strongly supported a school tax measure but also supported the Page Avenue Extension. Interview, Tim P. Fischesser, director of the St. Louis County Municipal League, January 8, 1999.

29. This is partially because suburban readers are a growing market for newspaper subscriptions. The newspaper refused to print a list of the donors to the pro–Page Avenue extension campaign. However, the paper came out against the Page Avenue extension. Interview, anonymous reporter for the *St. Louis Post Dispatch,* 1999.

30. Nelson, *Making an Issue of Child Abuse,* 27. On valence issues, see Campbell et al., *Elections and the Political Order;* Stokes and DiIulio, "The Setting." Also see Carmines and Stimson, *Issue Evolution;* Cobb and Elder, *Participation in American Politics;* McCarthy, Smith, and Zald, "Accessing Public, Media, Electoral, and Governmental Agendas."

31. Interviews with organizing consultants, organizers, and foundation funders, from 1994 to 2000.

6. La Puebla Unida

1. All names of ACORN members and staff have been changed.

2. According to Sarah, the organizer, under the pressure of public performance ACORN leaders like Estella sometimes forget their ultimate goal.

3. Interview, Terry Christenson, San Jose State University. Former mayor Janet Gray Hayes and mayoral candidates Kathy Chavez Napoli and Pat Dando had a background of neighborhood activism. The city's director of Parks, Recreation, and Neighborhood Services was a former community organizer with the Industrial Areas Foundation, and his Lutheran church is a member of the church-based organization PACT (see chapter 7).

4. In this account, "chapter" refers to one of three neighborhood-level organizations. "Organization" refers to SJ ACORN as a whole. The Mayfair chapter covers the area bounded by Highway 101, Jackson Avenue, Alum Rock Avenue, and Highway 280. Hillview ACORN, just south of Mayfair, is bounded by King, Capitol Expressway, Story Road, and Ocala Avenue. Tropicana ACORN, west of Hillview, is bounded by Story Road and Cunningham Avenue, and King and 101.

5. Joint Venture: Silicon Valley Network, "Silicon Valley Index," 1999. Indexes from 2000 forward are available at http://www.jointventure.org/publications/publications. The 2007 data are from the 2007 "Silicon Valley Index."

6. The active members I observed during April–August 1998 were 90 to 95 percent Latino, with a few active black leaders and no Asians or whites. In the past, some whites had been quite active. Some responded negatively to ACORN's disruptive protest at the 1996 Republican national convention in San Diego. Leaders reported that Asians, specifically Vietnamese, were difficult to recruit because of the language barrier and their reluctance to get involved.

7. Interview, ACORN organizer, May 5, 1998.

8. The chapter's political campaigns were reduced during the observation period (April–August 1998) because the organizer was concentrating on recruiting staff. Although SJ ACORN's one organizer tried to replace herself throughout the six-month observation period, and national ACORN authorized a special $20,000 starting salary (compared to the normal $14,000), she was unsuccessful.

9. In 1990, the median price for a house in the six census tracts where ACORN is located, an area with a 20 percent poverty rate, was $175,700; in 2000, $252,375. From U.S. Census.

10. Andrade, "Los desmanes del Cinco de Mayo en San Jose son inaceptables."

11. The area is bounded by King, Jackson, Story, and Alum Rock Boulevard.

12. "Silicon Valley Index," 1999.

13. The campaign was won in November 1998. The city council voted to require companies holding city service contracts worth at least $20,000 to pay $10.10 an hour with health benefits, or $11.35 without. From http://www.livingwagecampaign.org.

14. Erkanat, "Stunned Redevelopment Agency."

15. http://factfinder.census.gov/servlet.

16. Interview, San Jose ACORN director, May 5, 1998.

17. Eliasoph, *Avoiding Politics.*

7. The Power Is in the Relationship

Note to epigraph: "Pins" are the demands that designated "pinners" make to the authorities at mass meetings. For example: "Will you commit to making Project BEST a permanent line item in the city budget?"

1. The names of all staff and members are pseudonyms.

2. Rombeck, "S.J.'s PACT Organization."

3. Interview, Fr. Bob Moran.

4. On PICO's leadership development and democratic process, see Hart, *Cultural Dilemmas.*

5. For example, in 1985 St. Patrick's members' median family income was $14,799, with 17 percent living below the poverty level. Yet in 1992–93, with an average mass attendance of 1,379, the church collected $205,889 from the Sunday offering alone. Data from St. Patrick's Church, San Jose, author's possession.

6. Letter, PACT to mayor, May 1, 1991, copy in author's possession.

7. Letter, May 1, 1991, from PACT chairperson Donna Furuta to Mayor Hammer; "PACT Churches Challenge Mayor and Council for Youth Budget—Hammer, Alvarado, Shirakawa Take First Step," press release, May 16, 1991, author's possession.

8. "Church Committee Wins One for San Jose's Youth," *Pacific, the Northern California/Nevada Conference Edition of United Church News,* September 9, 1993, 7.

9. See Alinsky, *Rules for Radicals,* 130.

10. "PACT 1990–1991 Drug Campaign Research Summary," June 4, 1991, author's possession. The Redevelopment Agency invests in areas that have been declared "blighted," recoups the increased taxes that result from increased property assessments for a specific time, such as thirty years, and uses them to pay off the bonds used to finance construction. Controversy arises because tax income is denied to other city and county needs during this period.

11. Los Angeles County Redevelopment passed through 8.2 percent, Riverside County Redevelopment passed through 13.6 percent, Orange County passed through 4.2 percent, but Santa Clara County passed through only 0.1 percent. Ibid.

12. The winner of the November election is typically the winner of the Democratic primary, held in June.

13. "How Lofgren Beat the Odds," *San Jose Mercury News,* June 9, 1994.

14. Schrag, *Paradise Lost.* In 1990, the mayor claimed that the city lost $6 million in state funding. By 1991, the city had a $20 million deficit.

15. PACT memo, "Legislative Issues concerning the Redevelopment Agency," undated, author's possession. Though the agency's ability to issue bonds and to tax was scheduled to expire in 2011, the Redevelopment Agency board (the city council) unanimously voted to extend its borrowing capacity past the year 2015. In 1991, the city threatened a $2.8 million cut in neighborhood services.

16. Prevention programs included continuation of Project Crackdown (targeting gangs and crime in specific neighborhoods and featuring code enforcement, neighborhood cleanups, stepped-up narcotics enforcement, etc.), drug and gang

prevention school curricula, special enforcement units, neighborhood watch programs, youth centers, extended recreation programs, expanded library hours, and neighborhood preservation. Treatment included a drug treatment facility for youth. Prosecution included stronger enforcement of the landlord law for drug abatement and drug-free school zones.

17. The law actually permitted wider use of the funds: for example, funds could be used for police and crime prevention if their purpose was to prevent crime, maintain safety, or protect the capital investment in Redevelopment districts. Redevelopment law had been revised in 1971 and now described its main purpose as "to expand employment opportunities for jobless, under-employed and low income persons" as well as to eliminate blighted areas. PACT argued that this permitted funding of neighborhood services and programs. The BEST plan directed Redevelopment monies to social programs by having the city "swap" budget line items with the Redevelopment Agency: Redevelopment could take on capital projects from the regular city budget that were located in official Redevelopment areas, while the city could redirect money allocated for these capital projects to neighborhood-serving programs. BEST is not a single program but a funding mechanism for a host of programs. In 1998 BEST funded thirty-one different social programs or agencies. Los Angeles implemented this strategy legally, and PACT proposed the same method.

18. David Mann, telephone interview, October 30, 1998.

19. PACT memo, undated, author's possession.

20. Peter Ellis, "Homework Center Program Evaluation," prepared for PACT, May 30, 1996; available from PACT. To contact Dr. Ellis, see Community Crime Prevention Associates, http://www.ccpahome.com/who.php (accessed September 6, 2007).

21. Each center had a teacher, a librarian, a community liaison, and volunteer tutors. Evaluations of the centers claimed that they significantly improved attendance and grades for about $1.50 per student per hour. Homework centers are extremely popular with parents, teachers, and students. Of the centers that participated in one evaluation, 72 percent of operating funds came from the city, 20 percent from the school district, and 8 percent from other sources such as corporations and parent-teacher organizations. Of participating students, 66 percent showed improvement in grades, 38 percent in attendance. Volunteers made up 46 percent of the staffing. The study did not measure what percentage of a school's students used each center but only studied those that did. An evaluation that included half of the centers found the following ethnic groups represented among participants: Latino, 38 percent; Asian, 29 percent; white, 27 percent, black, 6 percent. Ibid.

22. These include Workforce Silicon Valley, the Silicon Valley Manufacturing Group, the Technology Network, American Electronics Association, and Joint

Venture Silicon Valley Network, which monitors and seeks to improve local education, housing, traffic congestion, air quality, and the like.

23. In March 2006 Netflix founder Reed Hastings made a $1 million gift to the ACE Network for more small public schools in Santa Clara County. Hastings, an education activist, was president of the California State Board of Education from 2000 to 2004.

24. "My work with People Acting in Community Together has resulted in SB 1170" under which "charter schools serving at-risk youth would [get] $4,000 more per pupil." Sen. Elaine Alquist, *Gilroy Dispatch,* January 18, 2006, http://www .piconetwork.org/media-coverage/Alquist-Hopes-to-Curb-Drop-Out-Rate.pdf (accessed June 18, 2006).

25. Working Partnerships USA, Santa Clara County, "Children's Health Initiative Workbook," July 2003, p. 30, http://www.wpusa.org/publications/complete/ wpusa_chi.pdf (accessed June 22, 2006). This account is indebted to this excellent report of the campaign.

26. Interview, Rich Hammond, PACT director, July 25, 2000.

27. For Mathematica Policy Research Inc.'s multistudy evaluation of the Santa Clara Children's Health Initiative, see http://www.mathematica-mpr.com/health/ chi.asp (accessed April 8, 2004).

8. The Results of Organizing

1. Based on participant-observation; interviews with staff, leaders, and others; organizational records; and newspaper coverage of the organizations since 1992.

2. See Warren and Wood, *Faith-Based Community Organizing,* and the sources cited in chapter 1, note 11.

3. I obtained a list of the active current leaders from the organizers in each organization. During interviews with activists, I asked them for additional names in a "snowball" sampling procedure.

4. Susan Hammer, mayor from 1990 to 1998, found PACT to be "very valuable" in helping her realize her agenda for neighborhoods and youth. Interview, San Jose, August 1, 2000.

5. Warren and Wood, *Faith-Based Community Organizing.*

6. Verba, Schlozman, and Brady, *Voice and Equality.*

7. See, for example, Wood, *Faith in Action;* Warren, *Dry Bones Rattling;* and Hart, *Cultural Dilemmas.* There was significant variation between PACT and MCU. PACT is older than MCU, the other church-based organization, and its senior leaders had more experience.

8. Interview, Beth Gonzalez, September 21, 2000.

9. Smith, "Beyond the Boundaries."

10. Squires, *Organizing Access to Capital.* One study produced by the Self-Help

Credit Union, Durham, North Carolina, claimed the practice increased 1,000 percent since 1992.

11. "Mortgage Firm, Group to Provide Loans to Families," *San Jose Mercury News,* July 27, 2000, 2C.

12. Basing campaigns on what members will support, determined by scores of one-to-one interviews with members, helps ensure widespread representation. The effect of middle-class members' greater resources is somewhat buffered by the fact that funds come from institutions (church dues, foundations, corporations) rather than individuals.

13. ACORN was founded in 1970 to address the inability of an organization of welfare recipients (the National Welfare Rights Organization) to form alliances with workers and working-class Americans. ACORN defines its constituency as "low- to moderate-income people."

14. Warren and Wood's 2001 national survey of CBCOs found that of 2,700 governing board members, about 43 percent were white, 32 percent black, 21 percent Hispanic, and 2 percent Asian. About one-quarter were clergy and three-quarters were laypeople; the group was about equally divided between men and women. See Wood, *Faith in Action;* also see Warren, *Dry Bones Rattling;* and Wilson, *The Bridge over the Racial Divide.*

15. Verba, Schlozman, and Brady, *Voice and Equality.*

16. Only one of the Catholic churches is estimated to be majority middle-class (and that majority is only an estimated 65 percent). The rest estimated respectively 100 percent, 99 percent, 80 percent, 75 percent, and 60 percent poor or blue-collar membership. From undated internal PACT memorandum, "Profiles of PACT Member Churches," based on data provided by the churches, author's possession.

17. Telephone interview, September 21, 2000.

18. For example, see Skocpol, *Protecting Soldiers and Mothers;* Sanders, *Roots of Reform;* McAdam, *Political Process and the Development of Black Insurgency;* and Costain, *Inviting Women's Rebellion.*

19. Section 1920 reads, "It is the sense of Congress that Federal transportation projects should facilitate and encourage the collaboration between . . . Federal, State, and local governments, community colleges, apprentice programs, local high schools, and other community-based organizations that have an interest in improving the job skills of low-income individuals . . . and to help ensure local participation in the building of transportation projects." "TEN and Gamaliel Foundation Advance Local Hiring on Transportation Projects," press release, November 29, 2005, http://www.communitychange.org/issues/transportation/tenupdates/?page=112905#1 (accessed April 8, 2006).

20. MOP annual report for 2005, author's possession.

21. Ranghelli, "The Monetary Impact of ACORN Campaigns: A Ten-Year Retrospective," draft, February 16, 2005, author's possession.

9. American Inequality and the Potential of Community Organizing

1. Piven and Cloward, *Poor People's Movements;* Gaventa, *Power and Powerlessness;* and Verba, Schlozman, and Brady, *Voice and Equality.*

2. Berry, *New Liberalism,* 389.

3. Minkoff, "Producing Social Capital."

4. On a bias toward the affluent, see Strolovitch, *Affirmative Advocacy.* Skocpol has documented how this can slant policy proposals; experts' proposals for the GI Bill were far less inclusive than the membership-based American Legion's more comprehensive proposals. See Skocpol, "Advocates without Members."

5. Weir and Ganz, "Reconnecting People and Politics."

6. Fraternal and sororal organizations had multiple functions: socializing, recreation, service, and politics. Government segmentation of nonprofit organizations into separate categories has a chilling effect on recruiting individuals into politics. See McCarthy, Britt, and Wolfson, "The Institutional Channeling of Social Movements by the State."

7. Weir and Ganz, "Reconnecting People and Politics," 167.

8. On cadres, see Piven and Cloward, *Poor People's Movements,* 284.

9. Kling, "Poor People's Movements 25 Years Later."

10. Morris, "Reflections on Social Movement Theory."

11. Barker, Johnson, and Lavalette, *Leadership in Social Movements.*

12. McAdam, McCarthy, and Zald, *Comparative Perspectives on Social Movements;* Tarrow, "States and Opportunities." The role of state repression is more contingent, especially in Western democracies; newer modifications to the theory heighten the importance of threat. McAdam, introduction to *Political Process,* 2nd ed.

13. Gamson and Meyer, "Framing Political Opportunity." Also see essays in the first section of Goodwin and Jasper, *Rethinking Social Movements.*

14. See Kurzman, "Structural Opportunity and Perceived Opportunity"; Rasler, "Concessions, Repression"; Bronfenbrenner, *Organizing to Win;* and Levi, "Organizing Power."

15. This leaves aside the special opportunity for heightened electoral mobilization aimed at influencing the 2004 presidential election.

16. Bronfenbrenner et al., *Organizing to Win,* 2; Bureau of Labor Statistics, http://www.bls.gov/news.release/union2.nr0.htm, accessed December 24, 2003.

17. Change to Win includes the Service Employees International Union, UNITE HERE, United Food and Commercial Workers International Union, Teamsters, United Food and Commercial Workers International Union, United

Brotherhood of Carpenters and Joiners of America, Laborers' International Union of North America, and United Farm Workers of America.

18. Personal conversation, September 2005.

19. These campaigns are detailed in Alinsky's *Reveille for Radicals* and *Rules for Radicals*.

20. McAdam, Tarrow, and Tilly, *Dynamics of Contention*, 331; Tarrow, *New Transnational Activism*, 32, 120–140.

21. Swidler, "Cultural Power and Social Movements."

22. Skocpol, "Advocates without Members," 501.

23. Telephone interview, Jim Keddy, director of PICO California, May 9, 2007.

24. Stall and Stoecker, "Community Organizing or Organizing Community? Gender and the Crafts of Empowerment," 745.

25. Szymanski, *Pathways to Prohibition*, 10.

26. Rosenstone and Hanson, *Mobilization, Participation, and Democracy in America*.

27. For an account of the Norquist meetings, see Rick Pearlstein, *Before the Storm;* Peter Dreier, panel discussion at the annual meeting of the American Political Science Association, Washington, D.C., September 1, 2005; Edsall, "Soros-Backed Activist Group Disbands."

28. The study indicates a $5 billion national fund would generate 1.8 million jobs and nearly $50 billion in wages. "Housing Activists Release Study in DC, across the Country, Today," press release, September 6, 2001, http://www.commondreams.org/news2001/0906-03.htm (accessed February 19, 2003).

29. NLIHC (National Low-Income Housing Coalition), *Housing at a Snail's Pace: The Federal Housing Budget: 1978–1997*, August 1996, Washington, D.C.

30. Wade Rathke, letter to ACORN, May 15, 2007.

31. Telephone interview, September 25, 2007.

Appendix A

1. This asks activists with whom their loyalty lies. It is meant to remind them not to identify with the officials with whom they interact.

2. One PICO organizer interpreted this as a statement on picking winnable issues. Another noted that a small, tangible victory such as a stop sign can be both visible and symbolic. Telephone interviews, David Mann, November 26–27, 2001.

3. Explained one organizer, "This is about compromise in negotiations. Sometimes you can't try for the whole pie, because officials can't give up everything; but render unto Caesar what you must to get what you need." Another said this applied to the dangers of co-optation, and is a reminder to activists to "just do what you have to do, don't commit too much."

4. An organizer interpreted this to mean that those who have done the work on an issue, not just those most articulate or visible, such as the ministers, should be rewarded.

Appendix C

1. Cities in which ACORN led successful campaigns include Boston, Chicago, Cook County, Illinois, Denver, Minneapolis, New Orleans, New York City, Oakland, Sacramento, St. Louis, St. Paul, and San Francisco. In addition, ACORN participated in successful campaigns in San Jose, San Diego, Broward County, Florida, and Detroit.

2. The New York coalition was the $5.15 Is Not Enough Coalition, mobilized by New York's Working Families Party, of which ACORN is a founding member. In both the coalition and the party, ACORN and labor unions were primary driving forces.

3. Minimum wage for restaurant employees who receive tips was raised from $3.30 to $4.60 in two years.

4. The Massachusetts Needs a Raise Coalition (the Massachusetts AFL-CIO, Neighbor to Neighbor, the Tax Equity Alliance of Massachusetts, and the Coalition Against Poverty). Source: Greater Boston Legal Services Web site, http://www.gbls.org/employment/organizations.htm (accessed April 21, 2005).

5. RALs are short-term loans that provide people with their tax refunds earlier but at exorbitant interest rates that borrowers are often not informed of.

6. ACORN Housing Corporation was founded in 1986 and as of 2006 had offices in forty cities.

7. The program capped fees at 3 percent, included no prepayment penalties, held interest rates at half a percentage point below average, and featured no requirement for credit life insurance. ACORN provided financial education and loan counseling.

8. Citigroup agreed to reduce prepayment penalties and cap points and fees at 3 percent of the loan amount.

9. Provides interest-rate reductions, waivers of unpaid late charges, deferrals of accrued unpaid interest, and loan principal reductions to borrowers at risk of home foreclosures.

10. ACORN claims that tax preparers sold RALs to more than 17,000 low-income Seattle-area families in 2002.

11. This program is a project of the Community Collaborative to Improve District 9 Schools (CC9), made up of six community-based organizations, including ACORN. ACORN primarily contributes community organizing, while the others deliver services.

12. Chicago ACORN based its demands on its research on schools in four

low-income neighborhood schools. They characterized 28 to 40 percent of the teachers in the schools studied as underqualified.

13. Alan Guenther, "Housing Aid on Way for Camden," *Camden (N.J.) Courier-Post,* September 7, 2006.

14. Several major programs initiated by PACT are achievements at both the city and local levels. For example, in the case of Project Crackdown and the after-school homework centers, PACT pressured the city to implement them. However, the program structure provides the given service on the basis of competitive proposals from individual neighborhoods (for Project Crackdown) or schools (for homework centers). Simply because PACT as a whole has won a citywide program does not mean that it will be implemented in the neighborhood of an individual church. Therefore, that church's local organizing committee (LOC) must compete to get the service in that church's neighborhood or neighborhood school.

Bibliography

ACORN. "Capital & Communities: A Report to the Annie E. Casey Foundation on ACORN's Work to Revitalize Low and Moderate Income Communities." http://www.ACORN.org/index.php?id=686 (June 24, 2005).

Alinsky, S. D. "Community Analysis and Organization." *American Journal of Sociology* (1940–41): 797–808.

———. *Reveille for Radicals.* New York: Vintage, 1946.

———. *Rules for Radicals.* New York: Vintage, 1971.

Aminzade, Ronald, and Doug McAdam. "Emotions and Contentious Politics." In *Science and Voice in the Study of Contentious Politics,* ed. Ronald Aminzade et al., 14–50. Cambridge: Cambridge University Press, 2001.

Andrade, Mary J. "Los desmanes del cinco de Mayo en San Jose son inaceptables." *La Oferta Review,* April 15, 1998.

Angelos, Constantine. "Bare Shelves to Burst with Books—Sharples High School Gets Large Donation." *Seattle Times,* September 23, 1995, B8.

Anker, Roy M. *Self-Help and Popular Religion in Early American Culture.* Westport, Conn.: Greenwood Press, 1999.

Appleman, J. "Evaluation Study of Institution-Based Organizing." Discount Foundation, 1996. http://www.nfg.org/cotb/41discount.pdf (accessed April 8, 2004).

Atlas, John. "In Red State Florida, Victory for Working People." *Shelterforce Online* 139 (January/February), 2005. http://www.nhi.org/online/issues/139/organize.html (accessed August 10, 2005).

Auerhahn, Louise, Bob Brownstein, and Phaedra Ellis-Lamkins. "Squeezing the Middle Class: Santa Clara County Families Lose Ground." Economic Policy

Brief, Working Partnerships, August 30, 2005. http://www.wpusa.org/
publications/complete/wpusa_acs2004.pdf (accessed June 18, 2006).

Baker, Andrea J. "The Problem of Authority in Radical Movement Groups: A Case
Study of Lesbian-Feminist Organization." In *Leaders and Followers: Challenges
for the Future,* ed. Trudy Heller, Jon Van Til, and Louis A. Zurcher. Greenwich,
Conn.: JAI Press, 1986.

Bales, R. F., and Talcott Parsons. *Family, Socialization, and Interaction Process.*
New York: Free Press, 1955.

Balzer, Richard. "Finding Their Voice." *Boston Review* 18, no. 5 (September–
October 1993. http://www.bostonreview.net/BR18.5/findingvoice.html
(accessed April 8, 2004).

Barker, Colin, Alan Johnson, and Michael Lavalette, eds. *Leadership in Social
Movements.* Manchester: Manchester University Press, 2001.

Baumgartner, Frank, and Bryan Jones. *Agendas and Instability in American Politics.*
Chicago: University of Chicago Press, 1993.

Becker, P. E. *Congregations in Conflict: Cultural Models of Local Religious Life.*
Cambridge: Cambridge University Press, 1999.

Bell, Bill, Jr. "High Court Dismisses Living Wage Case." *St. Louis Post-Dispatch,*
September 6, 2002, B2.

Benford, Robert. "An Insider's Critique of the Social Movement Framing Perspective." *Sociological Inquiry* 67, no. 4 (1997): 409–30.

Benford, Robert, and David Snow. "Framing Processes and Social Movements:
An Overview and Assessment." *Annual Review of Sociology* 26 (2000): 611–39.

Bennett, William. *The Book of Virtues.* New York: Simon and Schuster, 1993.

Berry, Jeffrey M. *The New Liberalism: The Rising Power of Citizen Groups.* Washington, D.C.: Brookings Institution Press, 1999.

———. "The Rise of Citizen Groups." In *Civic Engagement in American Politics,*
ed. T. Skocpol and M. P. Fiorina, 367–94. Washington, D.C.: Brookings
Institution and Russell Sage Foundation, 1999.

Berry, Jeffrey, M. K. E. Portney, and Kent E. Portney. *The Rebirth of Urban Democracy.* Washington, D.C.: Brookings Institution Press, 1993.

Boyte, Harry C. *The Backyard Revolution.* Philadelphia: Temple University Press,
1980.

———. *Community Is Possible.* New York: Harper & Row, 1984.

Breidenbach, Jan. "The Coalition That Made a $100 Million Trust Fund Happen."
Shelterforce Online, no. 22 (April 2002). http://www.nhi.org/online/issues/
122/Briedenbach.html (accessed July 7, 2006).

Brint, S., and C. S. Levy. "Professions and Civic Engagement: Trends in Rhetoric
and Practice, 1875–1995." In *Civic Engagement in American Politics,* ed.

T. Skocpol and M. P. Fiorina, 163–210. Washington, D.C.: Brookings Institution and Russell Sage Foundation, 1999.

Broder, John M. "States Take Lead in Push to Raise Minimum Wage." *New York Times,* January 2, 2006, A1.

Bronfenbrenner, Kate, et al. *Organizing to Win: New Research on Union Strategies.* Ithaca, N.Y.: ILR Press, 1998.

Browning, Lynnley. "A $3b Welcome Mat: Marks's Group Lands Huge Mortgage Pact with Bank of America." *Boston Globe,* August 11, 1999, D1.

Bryant, Tim. "St. Louis Judge Permanently Blocks Enforcement of 'Living Wage' Ordinance; Voters Approved Measure by Wide Margin Last Year." *St. Louis Post-Dispatch,* July 19, 2001. Accessed in Lexis, "Mortgage Firm, Group to Provide Loans to Families," *San Jose Mercury News,* July 27, 2000, 2C.

Calhoun, C. "'New Social Movements' of the Early Nineteenth Century." *Social Science History* 17 (1993): 385–427.

California Department of Education, University of California at Irvine, with Healthy Start and After School Partnerships Office, 2002. "Evaluation of California's After School Learning and Safe Neighborhoods Partnerships Program, 1999–2001, Executive Summary." http://www.cde.ca.gov/ls/ba/as/documents/execsummary.pdf (accessed December 12, 2004).

Calpotura, F., and K. Fellner. "The Square Pegs Find Their Groove: Reshaping the Organizing Circle." COMM-ORG: The On-Line Conference on Community Organizing and Development, 2001. http://comm-org.utoledo.edu/papers96/square.html (accessed April 8, 2004).

Campbell, Angus, Philip E. Converse, Warren E. Miller, and Donald Stokes. *Elections and the Political Order.* New York: John Wiley & Sons Inc., 1966.

Carmines, Edward G., and James A. Stimson. *Issue Evolution: Race and the Transformation of American Politics.* Princeton, N.J.: Princeton University Press, 1989.

Carville, James, and Stanley Greenberg. "Memo to Democracy Corps RE: Solving the Paradox of 2004: Why America Wanted Change but Voted for Continuity," November 9, 2004. http://www.democracycorps.com/reports/analyses/solving_the_paradox.pdf (accessed April 8, 2004).

Center for Community Change—Transportation Equity. "Getting to Work: An Organizer's Guide to Transportation Equity." 1998. http://www.transportationequity.org/pdfs/Getting%20to%20Work.pdf (accessed April 8, 2004).

Chambers, Edward T., and Michael A. Cowan. *Roots for Radicals: Organizing for Power, Action, and Justice.* New York: Continuum, 2003.

Chong, D. *Collective Action and the Civil Rights Movement.* Chicago: University of Chicago Press, 1991.

Christensen, T. "San Jose Becomes the Capital of Silicon Valley." In *San Jose: A City for All Seasons,* ed. J. Henderson. Encinitas, Calif.: Heritage Press, 1997.

Christensen, T., and P. J. Trounstine. "Power in a Sunbelt City." In *Movers and Shakers.* New York: St. Martin's Press, 1982.

Christiano, Marilyn Rice. "The Community Reinvestment Act: A Case Study of the Role of Community Groups in the Formulation and Implementation of a Public Policy, Government and Politics." Ph.D. diss., University of Maryland, 1995.

City of Boston. "Boston and Denver ACORN Win Commitments from City Officials for First Source Hiring Programs." 1995. http://www.cityofboston.gov/bra/pdf/documents/LW-10-FY2005.pdf (accessed April 25, 1998).

City of St. Louis. "St. Louis Five Year Plan Consolidated Plan Draft." "Appendix E: Anti-Poverty Strategy." http://stlouis.missouri.org/5yearstrategy/pdf/APPENDIXA.pdf.

Clarke, John, et al., eds. *Working Class Culture.* London: Hutchinson, 1979.

Claus, Offe. "New Social Movements: Challenging the Boundaries of Institutional Politics." *Social Research* 54, no. 4 (1985): 817–68.

Clawson, D. *The Next Upsurge: Labor and the New Social Movements.* Ithaca, N.Y.: Cornell University Press, 2003.

Clemens, Elisabeth S. *The People's Lobby: Organizational Innovation and the Rise of Interest Group Politics in the United States, 1890–1925.* Chicago: University of Chicago Press, 1997.

Cobb, Roger W., and Charles D. Elder. *Participation in American Politics: The Dynamics of Agenda-Building.* Baltimore, Md.: Johns Hopkins University Press, 1972.

Cortes, E., Jr. "Reweaving the Social Fabric." *Families in Society* 78, no. 2 (1997): 196–200.

Costain, Anne N. *Inviting Women's Rebellion.* Baltimore, Md.: The Johns Hopkins University Press, 1992.

Costain, A. N., and A. S. McFarland, eds. *Social Movements and American Political Institutions.* Lanham, Md.: Rowman and Littlefield, 1998.

Croteau, David. *Politics and the Class Divide: Working People and the Middle Class Left.* Philadelphia: Temple University Press, 1995.

Davis, Gerald, Doug McAdam, W. Richard Scott, and Mayer N. Zald, eds. *Social Movements and Organization Theory.* Cambridge: Cambridge University Press, 2005.

Davis, Mike. *City of Quartz: Excavating the Future in Los Angeles.* New York: Vintage, 1992.

Davis, Robert, and Susy Schultz. "'Outsiders' Lend Vision, Hope to ACORN." *Chicago Sun-Times,* July 12, 1998, 7.

Day, Katie. *Prelude to Struggle: African American Clergy and Community Organizing for Economic Development in the 1990's.* Lanham, Md.: University Press of America, 2002.

Debare, Ilana. "Living-Wage Wildfire." *San Francisco Chronicle,* April 9, 1999, B1.

DeFao, Janine. "Oakland Moves to Prevent 'Predatory' Loan Practice; Home Refinancing Law Being Rewritten." *San Francisco Chronicle,* July 11, 2001, A1.

Delgado, G. *Beyond the Politics of Place.* Oakland, Calif.: Applied Research Center, 1994.

———. "The Last Stop Sign." *Shelterforce* 102 (November–December 1998). http://www.nhi.org/online/issues/102/stopsign.html (accessed April 8, 2004).

———. *Organizing the Movement: The Roots and Growth of ACORN.* Philadelphia: Temple University Press, 1986.

Dionne, E. J. *Why Americans Hate Politics.* New York: Simon & Schuster, 1991.

Donze, Frank, and Stephanie Grace. "ACORN Plants Its Support in Pennington." *New Orleans Times-Picayune,* February 22, 2002, 1.

Douglas, Ann. *The Feminization of American Culture.* New York: Farrar Straus Giroux, 1998.

Downey, G. L. "Ideology and the Clamshell Identity: Organizational Dilemmas in the Anti-Nuclear Power Movement." *Social Problems* 33, no. 5 (1986): 357–73.

Eckholm, Erik. "Antipoverty Group Plants Seeds of Change." *New York Times,* June 27, 2006.

Edsall, Thomas B. "Soros-Backed Activist Group Disbands as Interest Fades." *Washington Post,* August 3, 2005, A06. http://www.washingtonpost.com/wp-dyn/content/article/2005/08/02/AR2005080201849.html (September 23, 2005).

Edwards, Robert, and Michael W. Foley. "Social Capital and the Political Economy of Our Discontent." *American Behavioral Scientist* 40, no. 5 (1997): 669–78.

Eliasoph, Nina. *Avoiding Politics: How Americans Produce Apathy in Everyday Life.* Cambridge: Cambridge University Press, 1998.

Engel, L. J. "The Influence of Saul Alinsky on the Campaign for Human Development." *Theological Studies* 59, no. 4 (1998): 636–61.

Erkanat, Judy. "Stunned Redevelopment Agency called to task by ACORN," *El Observador,* March 15–21, 1995, 1–2.

Ferree, Myra Marx, William A. Gamson, Jurgen Gerhards, and Dieter Rucht. *Shaping Abortion Discourse: Democracy and the Public Sphere in Germany and the United States.* Cambridge: Cambridge University Press, 2002.

Finch, Susan. "Minimum Wage Increase in N.O. Upheld: Opponents to Appeal to LA Supreme Court." *New Orleans Times-Picayune,* March 26, 2002, 1.

Finder, Alan. "Marchers Call on Giuliani to Support Workfare Union." *New York Times,* December 11, 1997, B2, B24.

Fink, D. P. *The Radical Vision of Saul Alinsky.* Mahwah, N.J.: Paulist Press, 1984.

Finke, R., and R. Stark. *The Churching of America, 1776–1990: Winners and Losers in Our Religious Economy.* New Brunswick, N.J.: Rutgers University Press, 1992.

Fisher, Robert. *Let the People Decide: Neighborhood Organizing in America (Social Movements Past and Present).* New York: Twayne Publishers, 1997.

Fisher, Robert, and Joseph Kling. *Mobilizing the Community: Local Politics in the Era of the Global Community.* Newbury Park, Calif.: Sage, 1988.

Fleishman, Sandra. "Activists, Lender Join to Combat Abuses." *Washington Post,* July 27, 2000, E03.

Flexner, Eleanor, and Ellen Fitzpatrick. *Century of Struggle.* Cambridge, Mass.: Harvard University Press, Belknap Press, 1996.

Frank, Thomas. *What's the Matter with Kansas? How Conservatives Won the Heart of America.* New York: Metropolitan Books, 2004.

Freedman, Samuel G. *The Inheritance: How Three Families and the American Political Majority Moved from Roosevelt to Reagan and Beyond.* New York: Simon and Schuster, 1996.

———. *Upon This Rock: The Miracles of A Black Church.* New York: HarperCollins Press, 1993.

Freeman, J. "The Tyranny of Structurelessness." In *Radical Feminism,* ed. A. Koedt, E. Levine, and A. Rapone. New York: Quadrangle Books, 1973.

Fung, Amanda. "Baltimore: An Anti-Predatory Lending Model." *American Banker,* December 2000, 9.

Gallagher, Jim. "Magna Agrees to Provide Low-Income Loans." *St. Louis Post-Dispatch,* July 11, 1991.

———. "FIRSTAR Outranks Mercantile for Low-Income Loans; St. Louis Bank More Active at Home." *St. Louis Post Dispatch,* May 19, 1999, C1.

Gamm, Gerald, and Robert D. Putnam. "The Growth of Voluntary Associations in America, 1840–1940." *Journal of Interdisciplinary History* 29 (1999): 511–57.

Gamson, William. *The Strategy of Social Protest.* Homewood, Ill.: Dorsey Press, 1990 (1975).

———. *Talking Politics.* Cambridge, England: Cambridge University Press, 1992.

Gamson, William, and David S. Meyer. "Framing Political Opportunity." In *Comparative Perspectives on Social Movement,* ed. Doug McAdam, John D. McCarthy, and Mayer N. Zald. Cambridge: Cambridge University Press, 1996.

Ganz, Marshall. "Resources and Resourcefulness: Strategic Capacity in the Unionization of California Agriculture, 1959–1966." *American Journal of Sociology* 105, no. 4 (2000): 1003–62.

———. "Why David Sometimes Wins: Strategic Capacity in Social Movements." In *Rethinking Social Movements: Structure, Meaning and Emotion,* ed. James Jasper and Geoffrey Goodwin. Lanham, Md.: Rowman and Littlefield, 2003.

Gaventa, John P. *Power and Powerlessness: Quiescence and Rebellion in an Appalachian Valley.* Urbana: University of Illinois Press, 1980.

Gecan, Michael. *Going Public: An Inside Story of Disrupting Politics as Usual.* Boston: Beacon Press, 2002.

Giele, Janet Zollinger. *Two Paths to Women's Equality: Temperance, Suffrage, and the Origins of Modern Feminism.* New York: Twayne Publishers, 1995.

Ginsberg, Benjamin, and Martin Shefter. *Politics by Other Means: Politicians, Prosecutors, and the Press from Watergate to Whitewater.* 3rd ed. New York: W. W. Norton, 2002.

Ginsburg, Faye D. *Contested Lives: The Abortion Debate in an American Community.* Berkeley: University of California Press, 1989.

Gitlin, T. *The Twilight of Common Dreams: Why America Is Wracked by Culture Wars.* New York: Metropolitan Books, 1995.

Glassberg, Andrew D. "St. Louis: Racial Transition and Economic Development." In *Big City Politics in Transition,* ed. H. V. Savitch and John Clayton Thomas, Urban Affairs Annual Reviews, vol. 38. Newbury Park, Calif.: Sage Publications, 1991.

Goodman, Paul. *Of One Blood: Abolitionism and the Origins of Racial Equality.* Berkeley: University of California Press, 1998.

Goodwin, Jeff, and James M. Jasper. "Caught in a Winding, Snarling Vine: The Structural Bias of Political Process Theory." *Sociological Forum* 14, no. 1: 27–54, 1999.

———. *Rethinking Social Movements: Structure, Meaning, and Emotion.* Lanham, Md.: Rowman and Littlefield, 2004.

Goodwin, Jeff, James M. Jasper, and Francesca Polletta, eds. *Passionate Politics: Emotions and Social Movements.* Chicago: University of Chicago Press, 2001.

Green, John C. *The American Religious Landscape and Politics.* Pew Forum on Religion and Public Life, 2004.

Greenhouse, L. "Justices Uphold Ceiling of $1,000 on Political Gifts." *New York Times,* January 25, 2000, 1.

Greider, William. *Who Will Tell the People: The Betrayal of American Democracy.* New York: Simon and Schuster, 1992.

Griswold, Wendy. "A Methodological Framework for the Sociology of Culture." *Sociological Methodology* 17, 1987: 1–35.

Gusfield, Joseph R., and Jerzy Michalowicz. "Secular Symbolism: Studies of Ritual, Ceremony, and the Symbolic Order in Modern Life." *Annual Review of Sociology* 10, 1984: 417–35.

Hall, P. D. "Vital Signs: Organizational Population Trends and Civic Engagement in New Haven, Connecticut, 1850–1998." *Civic Engagement in American Politics,* ed. T. Skocpol and M. P. Fiorina, 211–48. Washington, D.C.: Brookings Institution and Russell Sage Foundation, 1999.

Halle, David. *America's Working Man: Work, Home, and Politics among Blue-Collar Property Owners.* Chicago: University of Chicago Press, 1984.

Hanisch, Carol. *The Liberal Takeover of Women's Liberation: Feminist Revolution, Redstockings of the Women's Liberation Movement.* New York: Random House, 1975.

Harmon, R. *New Season, New Tools.* Brooklyn, N.Y.: Brooklyn Ecumenical Cooperatives, 1985.

Harding, Susan F. *The Book of Jerry Falwell: Fundamentalist Language and Politics.* Princeton, N.J.: Princeton University Press, 2000.

Hart, Stephen. *Cultural Dilemmas of Progressive Politics: Styles of Engagement among Grassroots Activists.* Chicago: University of Chicago Press, 2001.

———. "The Cultural Dimension of Social Movements: A Theoretical Reassessment and Literature Review." *Sociology of Religion* 57, no. 1 (1996): 87–100.

Hevesi, Dennis. "New Curbs on Predatory Loans." *New York Times,* November 10, 2002, sec. 11, 1.

Hochschild, A. R. *The Managed Heart: Commercialization of Human Feeling.* Berkeley: University of California Press, 1983.

Holloway, Lynette. "Parents Explain Resounding Rejection of Privatization at 5 Schools." *New York Times,* April 13, 2001, B1.

Horwitt, S. D. *Let Them Call Me Rebel: Saul Alinsky, His Life and Legacy.* New York: Knopf, 1989.

Hukill, Traci. "Chasing Amy." *Metroactive,* October 15–21, 1998. http://www.metroactive.com/papers/metro/10.15.98/index.html (accessed April 8, 2004).

Hunt, S. A., and R. D. Benford. "Identity Talk in the Peace and Justice Movement." *Journal of Contemporary Ethnography* 22, no. 4 (1994): 488–517.

Hunt, S. A., R. D. Benford, et al. "Identity Fields: Framing Processes and the Social Construction of Movement Identities." In *New Social Movements: From Ideology to Identity,* ed. E. Laraña, H. Johnston, and J. R. Gusfield. Philadelphia: Temple University Press, 1994.

Hunter, J. D. *Culture Wars: The Struggle to Define America.* New York: Basic Books, 1991.

Iannaccone, L. R. "Why Strict Churches Are Strong." *American Journal of Sociology* 99 (1994): 1180–211.

Imsong, Imkong I. "Reinhold Niebuhr and Christian Realism." In *The Boston Collaborative Encyclopedia of Modern Western Theology,* 1999. http://people

.bu.edu/wwildman/WeirdWildWeb/courses/mwt/dictionary/mwt_themes
.htm (accessed September 7, 2007).

Jackson, Jesse, Sr., and Jesse Jackson Jr. "Stuck in Neutral on Motor Voter." *Chicago Sun-Times,* April 18, 1996, 28.

Jacobsen, Dennis. *Doing Justice: Congregations and Community Organizing.* Minneapolis: Fortress Press, 2001.

Jasper, James M. *The Art of Moral Protest: Culture, Biography, and Creativity in Social Movements.* Chicago: University of Chicago Press, 1999.

Johnson, M., "City Starts to Chart Course for Future Economic Growth." *North County Journal,* December 24, 1995, 3A.

Johnston, Hank, and Bert Klandermans. "The Cultural Analysis of Social Movements." In *Social Movements and Culture,* ed. H. Johnston and B. Klandermans. Minneapolis: University of Minnesota Press, 1995.

——, eds. *Social Movements and Culture.* Minneapolis: University of Minnesota Press, 1995.

Jordan, Robert. "Celebrating 'Living Wage.'" *Denver Post,* June 30, 1998, D4.

Joyce, Steven, Fr. "Voters Spoke Loudly on Living Wage Law [letter to the editor]." *St. Louis Post-Dispatch,* August 25, 2000, B6.

Judd, D. R., and T. Swanstrom. *City Politics: Private Power and Public Policy.* New York: Longman, 2002.

Kaminer, W. *I'm Dysfunctional, You're Dysfunctional.* Reading, Mass.: Addison-Wesley, 1992.

Katzenstein, Mary. *Faithful and Fearless: Moving Feminism into the Church and the Military.* Princeton, N.J.: Princeton University Press, 1999.

Katznelson, Ira. *City Trenches: Urban Politics and the Patterning of Class in the United States.* New York: Pantheon, 1981.

Keddy, James Edward. "Community Organizing as Christian Praxis." Unpublished paper, 1991.

Kelley, D. M. *Why Conservative Churches Are Growing: A Study in Sociology of Religion.* San Francisco: Harper, 1972.

Kersh, Rogan, and James Morone. "How the Personal Becomes Political: Prohibitions, Public Health, and Obesity." *Studies in American Political Development* 16 (2002): 162–75.

Kest, Steven. "ACORN and Community-Labor Partnerships." *WorkingUSA* 6, no. 4 (Spring 2003): 84–100.

——. "ACORN's Experience Working with Labor." In *Partnering for Change: Unions and Community Groups Build Coalitions for Economic Justice,* ed. David B. Reynolds. Armonk, N.Y.: M. E. Sharpe, 2004.

Kingdon, John W. *Agendas, Alternatives, and Public Policies.* Boston: Little, Brown, 1984.

Klandermans, B. "Mobilization and Participation: Social-Psychological Expansions of Resource Mobilization Theory." *American Sociological Review* 49 (1984): 583–600.

———. "Transient Identities? Membership Patterns in the Dutch Peace Movement." In *New Social Movements: From Ideology to Identity,* ed. Enrique Laraña, Hank Johnston, and Joseph R. Gusfield. Philadelphia: Temple University Press, 1994.

Kling, Joseph. "Poor People's Movements 25 Years Later: Historical Context, Contemporary Issues." *Perspectives on Politics* 1 (2003): 727–32.

Kniss, F. "Ideas and Symbols as Resources in Intrareligious Conflict: The Case of American Mennonites." *Sociology of Religion* 57 (1996): 7–23.

Kohn, Margaret. *Brave New Neighborhoods: The Privatization of the Public Sphere.* New York: Routledge, 2004.

Kraditor, Aileen S. *Means and Ends in American Abolitionism: Garrison and His Critics on Strategy and Tactics, 1834–1850.* New York: Pantheon Books, 1969.

Kriesi, Hanspeter, R. Koopmans, J. W. Dyvendak, M. Guigni. *New Social Movements in Western Europe.* Minneapolis: University of Minnesota Press, 1995.

Kurtz, Sharon. *Workplace Justice: Organizing Multi-Identity Movements.* Minneapolis: University of Minnesota Press, 2002.

Kurzman, Charles. "Structural Opportunity and Perceived Opportunity in Social Movement Theory: The Iranian Revolution of 1979." *American Sociological Review* 61 (February 1996): 153–70.

Lamont, Michele. *The Dignity of Working Men: Morality and the Boundaries of Race, Class, and Immigration.* New York: Russell Sage Foundation and Harvard University Press, 2000.

Lancourt, Joan. *Confront or Concede: The Alinsky Citizen Action Organizations.* New York: Twayne Publishers, 1997.

Lattin, Don. "Multifaith Group Puts Own Spin on Values." *San Francisco Chronicle,* November 19, 2004. http://sfgate.com/cgi-bin/article.cgi?file=/c/a/2004/11/19/MNGJN9U7JB1.DTL (accessed September 24, 2005).

Leege, D. C., and L. A. Kellstedt, eds. *Rediscovering the Religious Factor in American Politics.* Armonk, N.Y.: M. E. Sharpe, 1993.

Lerner, Stephen, et al. "Reviving Unions." *Boston Review,* April/May, 1996. http://bostonreview.net/dreader/series/revivingunions.html (accessed June 21, 2006).

Levi, Margaret. "Organizing Power: The Prospects for an American Labor Movement. Perspectives 1, no. 1 (March 2003).

Levison, Andrew. "Who Lost the Working Class?" *Nation* 272, no. 19 (2001): 25–32.

Lichterman, Paul. "Piecing Together Multicultural Community: Cultural Differences in Community Building among Grass-roots Environmentalists." *Social Problems* 42, no. 4 (1995): 513–34.

————. *The Search for Political Community: American Activists Reinventing Commitment*. Cambridge: Cambridge University Press, 1996.

Lipset, Seymour Martin, and Gary Marks. *It Didn't Happen Here: Why Socialism Failed in the United States*. New York: W. W. Norton, 2000.

Lipton, E. "Giuliani Cites Criminal Past of Slain Man." *New York Times*, March 20, 2000, B1.

Llobrera, Joseph, and Bob Zahradnik. "A Hand Up: How State Earned Income Tax Credits Help Working Families Escape Poverty in 2004 (Summary)." Center on Budget and Policy Priorities, 2004. http://www.cbpp.org/5-14-04sfp.pdf (accessed June 20, 2005).

Madrick, Jeff. "Economic Scene: Living Wages Are Practical and Don't Let Theory Get in the Way." *New York Times*, July 5, 2001, C2.

Mannies, Jo. "High Court Upholds Campaign Donation Limits; Justices Reject Assertion That Law Inhibits Free Speech," *St. Louis Post-Dispatch*, January 25, 2000, A1.

————. "Money in Politics: Hard Act to Break Up." *St. Louis Post-Dispatch*, April 28, 1996, 1B.

————. "Power of Compromise Forged Victory for St. Louis Use Tax." *St. Louis Post-Dispatch*, April 8, 2001, C2.

Mansbridge, Jane J. *Why We Lost the ERA*. Chicago: University of Chicago Press, 1986.

Maxwell, Carol J. C. *Pro-Life Activists in America: Meaning, Motivation, and Direct Action*. Cambridge: Cambridge University Press, 2002.

May, Meredith, and Janine DeFao. "Oakland Makes Big Step toward Smaller Schools: Woodland Reopens with Portables." *San Francisco Chronicle*, September 6, 2000, A15.

McAdam, Douglas. *Freedom Summer*. New York: Oxford University Press, 1999 (1982).

————. *Political Process and the Development of Black Insurgency, 1930–1970*. Chicago: University of Chicago Press, 1999 (1982).

McAdam, Douglas, John D. McCarthy, and Mayer N. Zald, eds. *Comparative Perspectives on Social Movements*. Cambridge, England: Cambridge University Press, 1996.

McAdam, Douglas, Sidney Tarrow, and C. Tilly. *The Dynamics of Contention*. Cambridge: Cambridge University Press, 2001.

McCarthy, John D. "The Interaction of Grass-roots Activists and State Actors in the Production of an Anti-Drunk Driving Media Attention Cycle. In *From Ideology to Identity in Contemporary Social Movements*, ed. J. R. Gusfield, H. Johnston, and E. Laraña. Philadelphia: Temple University Press, 1994.

McCarthy, John D., David W. Britt, and Mark Wolfson. "The Institutional

Channeling of Social Movements by the State in the United States." *Research in Social Movements, Conflict, and Change* 13 (1991): 45–76.

McCarthy, John D., and Jim Castelli. "Working for Justice: The Campaign for Human Development and Poor Empowerment Groups." Report prepared for the Aspen Institute Nonprofit Sector Research Fund, 1994.

McCarthy, John D., Jackie Smith, and Mayer N. Zald. "Accessing Public, Media, Electoral, and Governmental Agendas." In *Comparative Perspectives on Social Movements,* ed. Doug McAdam, John D. McCarthy, and Mayer N. Zald. Cambridge: Cambridge University Press, 1996.

Medina, Michael. "PACT Applauds Mayor's Drug/Gang Stand, But Demands More." *El Observador,* June 12, 1994, 1.

Melucci, Alberto. "A Strange Kind of Newness: What's "New" in New Social Movements? In *New Social Movements: From Ideology to Identity,* ed. E. Laraña, H. Johnston, and J. Gusfield. Philadelphia: Temple University Press, 1994.

Mettler, Suzanne. *Soldiers to Citizens: The G.I. Bill and the Making of the Greatest Generation.* New York: Oxford University Press, 2005.

Meyer, David S., Valerie Jenness, and Helen Ingram, eds. *Routing the Opposition: Social Movements, Public Policy, and Democracy.* Minneapolis: University of Minnesota Press, 2005.

Mihalopoulos, Dan. "Official Calls for Truce in Urban Sprawl Debate." *St. Louis Post-Dispatch,* October 30, 1997, 1A.

———. "Officials Defend Sudden Growth of Towns in St. Charles County; Tension Mounts at Hearing on Urban Sprawl Debate." *St. Louis Post-Dispatch,* October 30, 1997, 1A.

———. "St. Charles Mayor: Don't Blame Problems on Us: City, Counties Again Clash at Committee Hearings." *St. Louis Post-Dispatch,* October 31, 1997, 1B.

Milagros, Silvia. "NY Acorn/WEP Workers Organizing Committee." *Poverty and Race,* August 8, 1999, 7.

Miller, A. S. "Saul Alinsky: America's Radical Reactionary." *Radical America* 21, no. 1 (1987): 11–18.

Miller, Michael. "Beyond the Politics of Place: A Critical Review." 1996. Available at COMM-ORG Web site for community organizing, http://comm-org .utoledo.edu/papers96/miller.html (accessed September 4, 2007).

Minkoff, Debra C. "Producing Social Capital: National Social Movements and Civil Society." *American Behavioral Scientist* 40, no. 5 (1997): 606–19.

Mishel, Lawrence, Jared Bernstein, and Sylvia Allegretto. *State of Working America, 2004–2005.* Ithaca, N.Y.: Cornell University Press, 2005.

Mollenkopf, John H. *The Contested City.* Princeton, N.J.: Princeton University Press, 1983.

Morone, J. A. *Hellfire Nation: The Politics of Sin in American History.* New Haven, Conn.: Yale University Press, 2003.

Morris, Aldon. *The Origins of the Civil Rights Movement: Black Communities Organizing for Change.* New York: Free Press, 1984.

———. "Reflections on Social Movement Theory: Criticisms and Proposals." In *Rethinking Social Movements: Structure, Meaning, and Emotion,* ed. Geoffrey Goodwin and James Jasper. Lanham, Md.: Rowman and Littlefield, 2003.

Morris, Aldon, and C. M. Mueller, eds. *Frontiers in Social Movement Theory.* New Haven, Conn.: Yale University Press, 1992.

Nader, Ralph. "Banking Jackpot." *Washington Post,* November 5, 1999, A33.

National Fair Housing Advocate Online. "ACORN Teams with Prudential to Eliminate Insurance Redlining in Philadelphia." 1996. http://www.fairhousing .com/index.cfm?method=page.display&pagename=advocate_june96_page3 (accessed April 8, 2004).

Neal, Terry M. "Talking Points: Race, Class Re-Enter Politics after Katrina." *Washington Post,* September 22, 2005. http://www.washingtonpost.com/ wpdyn/content/article/2005/09/22/AR2005092200833.html?referrer=email (accessed September 23, 2005).

Nelson, Barbara. *Making an Issue of Child Abuse: Political Agenda Setting for Social Problems.* Chicago: University of Chicago Press, 1984.

Neuhaus, Richard. "The Uses of Confrontation (The Public Square: A Continuing Survey of Religious and Public Life) (Social Change and the Industrial Areas Foundation)." *First Things: A Monthly Journal of Religious and Public Life,* April 2002, 70.

Niebuhr, Reinhold. *Moral Man and Immoral Society: A Study in Ethics and Politics.* New York: C. Scribner's Sons, 1932.

———. "The Truth in Myths." In *Faith and Politics,* ed. Ronald H. Stone. New York: George Braziller, 1968.

Oberschall, A. *Social Conflict and Social Movements.* Englewood Cliffs, N.J.: Prentice Hall, 1973.

Offe, Claus. "New Social Movements: Challenging the Boundaries of Institutional Politics." *Social Research* 52, no. 4 (Winter 1985): 817–68.

Olmeda, Rafael. "Tenant Group Steps in, Led Fight to Turn Mott Haven VI Around." *New York Daily News,* December 8, 1997.

Orfield, Myron. *Metropolitics: A Regional Agenda for Community and Stability.* Cambridge, Mass., and Washington, D.C.: Brookings Institution Press and Lincoln Institute of Land Policy, 1997.

———. *St. Louis Metropolitics: A Regional Agenda for Community and Stability: A Report to the Metropolitan Congregations United for St. Louis.* Minneapolis: Metropolitan Area Research Corporation, 1999.

Orr, Marion. *Black Social Capital: The Politics of School Reform in Baltimore, 1986–1998.* Lawrence: University Press of Kansas, 1999.

Osterman, Paul. *Gathering Power: The Future of Progressive Politics in America.* Boston: Beacon Press, 2002.

Peirce, Neal, and Curtis Johnson. "A Call to Action: Region's Assets Provide a Strong Foundation." *St Louis Post-Dispatch,* March 9, 1997, 1B.

Perlstein, Rick. *Before the Storm: Barry Goldwater and the Unmaking of the American Consensus.* New York: Hill and Wang, 2001.

Peterson, Iver. "State Will Appoint Manager to Run Camden's Government." *New York Times,* May 25, 2001, B1.

Peterson, Paul E. *City Limits.* Chicago: University of Chicago Press, 1981.

Pichardo, Nelson A. "New Social Movements: A Critical Review." *Annual Review of Sociology* 23 (1997): 411–30.

Pierce, Emmet. "New Law Buys Renters More Time." *San Diego Union-Tribune,* December 15, 2002, I1.

Pierce, Gregory F. Augustine. *Activism That Makes Sense: Congregations and Community Organization.* Chicago: Acta Publications, 1984.

Piven, Frances Fox, and Richard A. Cloward. *Poor People's Movements: Why They Succeed, How They Fail.* New York: Vintage, 1979.

Polletta, Francesca. *Freedom Is an Endless Meeting: Democracy in American Social Movements.* Chicago: University of Chicago Press, 2002.

———. "'It Was Like a Fever . . .': Narrative and Identity in Social Protest." *Social Problems* 45, no. 2 (May 1998): 137–59.

Powell, Walter W., and Paul J. DiMaggio. *The New Institutionalism in Organizational Analysis.* Chicago: University of Chicago Press, 1994.

Pralle, Sarah B. "Venue Shopping, Political Strategy, and Policy Change: The Internationalization of Canadian Forest Advocacy." *Journal of Public Policy* 23 (2003): 233–60.

Purkis, Jonathan. "Leaderless Cultures: The Problem of Authority in a Radical Environmental Group." In *Leadership in Social Movements,* ed. Colin Barker, Alan Johnson, and Michael Lavalette. Manchester: Manchester University Press, 2001.

Putnam, Robert D. "Bowling Alone: America's Declining Social Capital." *Journal of Democracy* 6, no. 1 (1995): 65–78.

———. *Bowling Alone: The Collapse and Revival of American Community.* New York: Simon and Schuster, 2000.

———. "The Strange Disappearance of Civic America." *American Prospect* 7, no. 24 (December 1996): 34–48.

Rapping, E. *The Culture of Recovery.* Boston: Beacon Press, 1996.

Rasler, Karen. "Concessions, Repression, and Political Protest in the Iranian Revolution." *American Sociological Review* 61 (1996): 132–52.

Reitzes, Donald D., and David C. Reitzes. *The Alinsky Legacy: Alive and Kicking.* Greenwich, Conn.: JAI Press, 1987.

Retail Banker International. "Household Losing the Public Relations Battle," *Retail Banker International* 2 (May 13, 2002).

Rivera, Carla. "Day-Care Providers Say State Reimbursements Fail to Pay Living Wage; Labor: Workers Demand Investigation of California, L.A. County, Allege Violation of Minimum Wage Laws." *Los Angeles Times,* May 19, 2000, 3.

Robinson, J. *The Montgomery Bus Boycott and the Women Who Started It.* Knoxville: University of Tennessee Press, 1987.

Rodgers, D. T. *Contested Truths: Keywords in American Politics since Independence.* New York: Basic Books, 1987.

Rogers, Mary Beth. *Cold Anger: A Story of Faith and Power Politics.* Denton: University of North Texas Press, 1990.

Rombeck Janice, "S.J.'s PACT Organization a Promoter of Leadership: Everyday People Trained for Success." *San Jose Mercury News,* February 5, 2006.

Roof, W. C., and W. McKinney. *American Mainline Religion.* New Brunswick, N.J.: Rutgers University Press, 1987.

Rooney, Jim. *Organizing the South Bronx.* Albany: SUNY Press, 1995.

Roper Center. "A Vast Empirical Record Refutes the Idea of Civic Decline," issue of *Public Perspective* 7, no. 4 (1996).

Rose, F. *Coalitions across the Class Divide: Lessons from the Labor, Peace, and Environmental Movements.* Ithaca, N.Y.: Cornell University Press, 1999.

Rosenstone, Steven J., and John M. Hansen. *Mobilization, Participation, and Democracy in America.* New York: MacMillan, 1993.

Ruklick, Joe. "ACORN Demands School Board Fill Vacancies with Qualified Teachers." *Chicago Defender,* August 23, 2001, 3.

Rupp, Leila J., and Verta Taylor. *Survival in the Doldrums: The American Women's Rights Movement, 1945 to the 1960s.* Oxford: Oxford University Press, 1987.

Rusk, David. *Baltimore Unbound.* Baltimore, Md.: Johns Hopkins University Press, 1996.

———. *Cities without Suburbs.* Washington, D.C.: Woodrow Wilson Center Press, 1995.

———. *Inside Game, Outside Game.* Washington, D.C.: Brookings Institution Press, 1999.

———. "St. Louis Congregations Challenge Urban Sprawl." *Shelterforce,* January–February 1998.

Salisbury, Robert. "The Dynamics of Reform: Charter Politics in St. Louis." *Midwest Journal of Political Science* 5 (August, 1961): 260–75.

————. "St. Louis Politics: Relationships among Interests, Parties, and Governmental Structure." *Western Political Quarterly* 13 (June 1960): 498–507.

Salladay, Robert. "Protection for Consumers: Protection from 'Predatory' Lenders." *San Francisco Chronicle,* October 12, 2001, A19.

Sampson, Robert J., Doug McAdam, Heather MacIndoe, and Simón Weffer. "Civil Society Reconsidered: The Durable Nature and Community Structure of Collective Civic Action." *American Journal of Sociology* 111, no. 3 (November 2005): 673–714.

Sanders, Elizabeth. *Roots of Reform: Farmers, Workers, and the American State, 1877–1917.* Chicago: University of Chicago Press, 1999.

Scherer, Ron. "From Welfare to . . . Unions?" *Christian Science Monitor,* October 8, 1997, 1.

Schlesinger, Arthur, Jr. "Forgetting Reinhold Niebuhr." *New York Times Sunday Book Review,* September 18, 2005, http://www.nytimes.com (accessed September 5, 2007).

Schlozman, K. L., Sidney Verba, et al. "Civic Participation and the Equality Problem." In *Civic Engagement in American Politics,* ed. T. Skocpol and M. P. Fiorina, 427–60. Washington, D.C., and New York: Brookings Institution and Russell Sage Foundation, 1999.

Schrag, P. *Paradise Lost: California's Experience, America's Future.* New York: New Press, 1998.

Schudson, Michael. "What If Civic Life Didn't Die?" *American Prospect* 25 (1996): 17–20.

Shirley, Dennis. *Community Organizing for Urban School Reform.* Austin: University of Texas Press, 1997.

————. *Valley Interfaith and School Reform: Organizing for Power in South Texas.* Austin: University of Texas Press, 2002.

Sinisi, J. Sebastian. "Activists Demand Jobs in Projects 30 in ACORN Stage Rally." *Denver Post,* September 8, 1995, B1.

Skocpol, T. "Advocates without Members: The Recent Transformation of American Civic Life." In *Civic Engagement in American Politics,* ed. T. Skocpol and M. P. Fiorina, 461–510. Washington, D.C., and New York: Brookings Institution and Russell Sage Foundation, 1999.

————. *Diminished Democracy: From Membership to Management in American Civic Life.* Julian K Rothbaum Distinguished Lecture Series. Norman: University of Oklahoma Press, 2003.

————. *Protecting Soldiers and Mothers: The Political Origins of Social Policy in the United States.* Cambridge, Mass.: Harvard University Press, 1992.

Skocpol, T., and M. P. Fiorina. "How Americans Became Civic." In *Civic Engagement in American Democracy,* ed. T. Skocpol and M. P. Fiorina, 27–80.

Washington, D.C., and New York: Brookings Institution and Russell Sage Foundation, 1999.

Skocpol, T., Marshall Ganz, and Ziad Munson. "A Nation of Organizers: The Institutional Origins of Civic Voluntarism in the United States." *American Political Science Review* 94, no. 3 (September 2000): 527–46.

Slessarev, H. "Saul Alinsky Goes to Church." *Sojourners* 29, no. 2 (2000): 22.

Smith, Drew R. "Beyond the Boundaries: Faith-Based Organizations and Neighborhood Coalition Building." Prepared for the Annie E. Casey Foundation by The Faith Communities and Urban Families Project of The Leadership Center at Morehouse College, November 2003. http://www.aecf.org/publications/data/3_btbreport.pdf (accessed November 9, 2005).

Smock, Kristina. *Democracy in Action: Community Organizing and Urban Change.* New York: Columbia University Press, 2004.

Snow, D. A., and R. D. Benford. "Ideology, Frame Resonance, and Participant Mobilization." In *From Structure to Action: Social Movement Participation Across Cultures,* ed. B. Klandermans, H. Kriesi, and S. Tarrow, 197–218. Greenwich, Conn.: JAI Press, 1988.

Snow, D. A., E. B. Rochford Jr., et al. "Frame Alignment Processes, Micromobilization, and Movement Participation." *American Sociological Review* 51 (1986): 464–81.

———. "Brown Defends Funding, Leaps to Counter Harmon." *St. Louis Post-Dispatch,* October 27, 1997, 1.

Sonderegger, John. "'Urban Sprawl' or 'Urban Choice'?" *St. Louis Post-Dispatch,* October 26, 1997, 3D.

Sorin, Gerald. *Abolitionism: A New Perspective.* New York: Holt, Rinehart & Wilson, 1972.

Speer, Paul. "Empowerment in Pressure Group Community Organizations: Internal Processes and Associated Individual and Community Impacts." Ph.D. diss., University of Missouri–Kansas City, 1992.

———. "People Making Public Policy in California: The PICO California Project; Evaluation Report." Department of Human and Organizational Development, Peabody College, Vanderbilt University, May 2002. http://www.piconetwork.org/linkeddocuments/California-Project-Evaluation.pdf (accessed January 23, 2006).

Speer, Paul, and Joseph Hughey. "Community Organizing: An Ecological Route to Empowerment and Power. *American Journal of Community Psychology* 23, no. 5 (1995): 729–64.

Squires, Gregory, ed. *Organizing Access to Capital: Advocacy and the Democratization of Financial Institutions.* Philadelphia: Temple University Press, 2003.

Stall, Susan, and Randy Stoecker. "Community Organizing or Organizing

Community? Gender and the Crafts of Empowerment." *Gender & Society* 12, no. 6 (1998): 729–56.

Stein, Arlene. "Between Organization and Movement: ACORN and the Alinsky Model of Community Organizing." *Berkeley Journal of Sociology* 31 (1986): 93–115.

Stein, Lana. *Holding Bureaucrats Accountable: Politicians and Professionals in St. Louis.* Tuscaloosa: University of Alabama Press, 1991.

———. *St. Louis Politics: The Triumph of Tradition.* St. Louis: Missouri Historical Society Press, 2002.

Stokes, Donald E., and John J. DiIulio Jr. "The Setting: Valence Politics in Modern Elections." In *The Elections of 1992,* ed. Michael Nelson. Washington, D.C.: Congressional Quarterly, 1993.

Stout, David. "Bush Signs $286.4 Transportation Bill." *New York Times,* August 10, 2005. http://www.nytimes.com/2005/08/10/politics/10cnd-bush.html (accessed August 10, 2005).

Stout, Linda. *Bridging the Class Divide.* Boston: Beacon Press, 1996.

Strolovich, Dara. *Affirmative Advocacy: Marginalization, Representation, and Interest Group Politics.* Chicago: University of Chicago Press, 2007.

Sutin, Phil. "Area Leaders Call Time Out on Urban Sprawl; They Propose a Year of Study, Then Action." *St. Louis Post-Dispatch,* January 22, 1998, B1.

Swarts, Heidi. "Grassroots Community Organizations: Invisible Actors in American Urban Politics." Ph.D. diss., Cornell University, 2002.

———. "Political Opportunity, Venue Shopping, and Strategic Innovation: ACORN's National Organizing." In *Transforming the City: Community Organizing and the Challenge of Political Change,* ed. Marion Orr. Lawrence: University of Kansas Press, 2006.

———. "Setting the State's Agenda: Church-based Community Organizations in American Urban Politics." In *States, Parties, and Social Movements: Protest and the Dynamics of Institutional Change,* ed. Jack Goldstone. Cambridge: Cambridge University Press, 2002.

Sweet, Lynn. "U.S. Set to Sue Illinois Over 'Motor Voter' Law; Illinois Misses Jan. 1 Deadline For Compliance." *Chicago Sun-Times,* January 23, 1995, 7.

Swidler, A. "Cultural Power and Social Movements." In *Social Movements and Culture,* ed. H. Johnston and B. Klandermans. Minneapolis: University of Minnesota Press, 1995.

———. "Culture in Action: Symbols and Strategies." *American Sociological Review* 51 (1986): 273–86.

Szymanski, Anne-Marie. *Pathways to Prohibition: Radicals, Moderates, and Social Movement Outcomes.* Durham, N.C.: Duke University Press, 2003.

Tarrow, S. *The New Transnational Activism.* Cambridge: Cambridge University Press, 2005.

———. *Power in Movement: Social Movements, Collective Action, and Politics.* Cambridge: Cambridge University Press, 1994, 1998.

———. "States and Opportunities: The Political Structuring of Social Movements." In *Comparative Perspectives on Social Movements,* ed. Doug McAdam, John D. McCarthy, and Mayer N. Zald. Cambridge: Cambridge University Press, 1996.

Taylor, M. "Structure, Culture, and Action in the Explanation of Social Change." *Politics and Society* 17 (1989): 115–62.

Taylor, V., and N. Whittier. "Analytical Approaches to Social Movement Culture: The Culture of the Women's Movement." In *Social Movements and Culture,* ed. H. Johnston and B. Klandermans. Minneapolis: University of Minnesota Press, 1995.

Teixeira, Ruy A., and Joel Rogers. *America's Forgotten Majority: Why the White Working Class Still Matters.* New York: Basic Books, 2001.

Thomas, Ted, and Bessie Cannon. "The Little Guy Wins." Letter to the editor. *Chicago Sun-Times,* August 13, 1998.

Verba, Sidney, Kay L. Schlozman, and Henry E. Brady. *Voice and Equality: Civic Voluntarism in American Politics.* Cambridge, Mass.: Harvard University Press, 1995.

Verba, Sidney, Kay L. Schlozman, Henry E. Brady, and Norman H. Nie. "Race, Ethnicity, and Political Resources: Participation in the United States." *British Journal of Political Science* 23, no. 4 (1993): 453–97.

Waldman, Amy. "The 1998 Campaign: The Grass Roots; New Party Is Courting Liberal Constituencies." *New York Times,* November 1, 1998, 44.

Warner, Coleman. "ACORN: City Auction Unfair to Low-Income Buyers." New Orleans *Times-Picayune,* March 17, 1995, B3.

Warner, R. S. "Religion, Boundaries, and Bridges." *Sociology of Religion* 58, no. 3 (1997): 217–38.

Warren, Mark. *Dry Bones Rattling: Community Building to Revitalize American Democracy.* Princeton, N.J.: Princeton University Press, 2001.

Warren, M. R., and R. L. Wood. *Faith-based Community Organizing: The State of the Field.* Jericho, N.Y.: Interfaith Funders, 2001.

Weir, Margaret, and Marshall Ganz. "Reconnecting People and Politics." In *The New Majority,* ed. S. Greenberg and T. Skocpol. New Haven, Conn.: Yale University Press, 1997.

Welter, Barbara. "The Feminization of American Religion, 1800–1860." In *Dimity*

Convictions: The American Woman in the Nineteenth Century, ed. Barbara Welter. Athens: Ohio University Press, 1976.

Wheeler, Marjorie Spruill, ed. *One Woman, One Vote: Rediscovering the Woman Suffrage Movement.* Troutdale, Ore.: New Sage Press, 1995.

Whittier, N. *Feminist Generations: The Persistence of the Radical Women's Movement.* Philadelphia: Temple University Press, 1995.

Williams, Laura. "Called Up for Activist Duty Now She's N.Y. ACORN Prez." *New York Daily News,* May 17, 1997, 15.

Williamson, Tammy. "Citigroup to Kill Single Premium Credit Insurance; Bows to Pressure by Groups Claiming Loan was Predatory." *Chicago Sun-Times,* July 29, 2001, 53.

———. "Household Drops 'Maligned' Policy." *Chicago Sun-Times,* July 12, 2001, 56.

———. "ICC Shutoff Decision to Wait." *Chicago Sun-Times,* April 25, 2001, 62.

Willis, Paul. "Masculinity and Factory Labor." In *Culture and Society: Contemporary Debates,* ed. Jeffrey C. Alexander and Steven Seidman. Cambridge: Cambridge University Press, 1990.

Wilson, William Julius. *The Bridge over the Racial Divide: Rising Inequality and Coalition Politics.* Berkeley: University of California Press, 1999.

Wood, Richard L. *Faith in Action: Religion, Race, and Democratic Organizing in America.* Chicago: University of Chicago Press, 2002.

———. "Faith in Action: Religious Resources for Political Success in Three Congregations." *Sociology of Religion* 55, no. 4 (1994): 397–417.

———. "Religious Culture and Political Action." *Sociological Theory* 17, no. 3 (1999): 307–32.

———. "Social Capital and Political Culture: God Meets Politics in the Inner City." *American Behavioral Scientist,* 1997.

Wuthnow, Richard, ed. *I Come Away Stronger: How Small Groups Are Shaping American Religion.* Grand Rapids, Mich.: W. B. Eerdmans, 1994.

———. *Loose Connections: Joining Together in America's Fragmented Communities.* Cambridge, Mass.: Harvard University Press, 1998.

———. "Mobilizing Civic Engagement: The Changing Impact of Religious Involvement." In *Civic Engagement in American Politics,* ed. T. Skocpol and M. P. Fiorina, 331–66. Washington, D.C.: Brookings Institution Press, 1999.

———. *Sharing the Journey: Support Groups and America's New Quest for Community.* New York: Free Press, 1994.

Young, Michael P. *Bearing Witness against Sin: The Evangelical Birth of the American Social Movement.* Chicago: University of Chicago Press, 2006.

Zabin, Carol, and Isaac Martin. "Living Wage Campaigns in the Economic Policy Arena: Four Case Studies from California." Center for Labor Research and

Education, Institute of Industrial Relations, University of California–Berkeley, 1999. http://www.iir.berkeley.edu/livingwage/pdf (accessed January 30, 2005).

Zald, M. N. "Ideologically Structured Action: An Enlarged Agenda for Social Movement Research." *Mobilization* 5 (Winter 2000).

Zweig, Michael. *The Working Class Majority: America's Best Kept Secret.* Ithaca, N.Y.: ILR Press, 2001.

Index

Abolition, xxiii, xxvii–xxviii, 62, 234n34

Accountability: in CBCO mobilizing culture, 8, 17, 20–21, 44, 47, 52, 58–61, 147, 162, 193

ACORN (Association of Community Organizations for Reform Now): and Alinsky, 25–26, 43, 102; campaigns targeting banks and financial institutions, xxiv, 77, 203–4; compared with CBCOs, 29, 38, 40, 44, 71–72, 79, 80–81, 83–84, 89; disruption by, 37, 87, 92–94, 104–5, 139, 165, 255n6; and electoral politics, 82–84; emotion norms of, 42–43; and emotion work, 36–37, 44; empowerment in, 94, 98, 105; and experimental tactics in, 88–90; framing in, 32, 76, 89, 100; Hurricane Katrina and, 31, 187, 204, 207; labor and, 29, 72, 81–82; leaders in, 79–84, 88–89, 98–99, 101–2, 108; local-state-national campaign, 76–79; media and, 38, 75, 87–88, 233; and minimum wage campaigns, 74–76, 81–82, 201–2; mobilizing culture of, 25–43; as multifunction organization, 84–87; national organizing campaigns of, 72–80; as one central organization, 80–82; political strategy of, xvi, 71–90; and power, 71–72, 89, 93; power within, 80–81, 87; public and private distinction in, 32, 40–41, 103; as public interest group, 72; salaries in, 26, 239n43, 250n25; in San Jose, 138; and school campaigns, 79, 205; social class of members, 28, 33, 81, 169–70, 172, 176, 259n13; social class of staff, 26, 43; in St. Louis, 94–95, 103–4, 106–7, 227, 251n36, 262n2; training in, 26, 38–40, 82, 84, 99, 134–35. *See also* San Jose ACORN; St. Louis ACORN

Actions: in ACORN, 27–28, 37, 41; in CBCOs, 6, 8–11, 21–23

287

African Methodist Episcopal (AME) Church, 110

African Methodist Episcopal Zion (AME Zion) Church, 251n32

Agency: in social movement theory, xvii, xxvii, xxx, 177, 180; and working-class nonparticipation, 50

Agenda setting, xiv, xxv–xxvi, 234n29, 254n30; in ACORN, 88, 169, 176; as outcome of organizing, 166, 227–29

Agitation: in CBCO mobilizing culture, 14–16, 20, 44, 53, 55, 60, 67, 116

Alinsky, Saul: and ACORN, 25–26, 43, 102; and altered organizing terrain, 182; and CBCO cultural strategy, 51, 62–63; and history of community organizing, 3–5, 8, 232n10, 238–39n42; and MCU, 114, 252n10; and movements, 185; and PACT, 149; and polarizing the target, 21; and theme of self-interest, 13

AME. See African Methodist Episcopal

AME Zion. See African Methodist Episcopal Zion

Authority: in PACT, 146–47; in San Jose ACORN, 132–33; in St. Louis ACORN, 98–99

Baptist Church, 243n44; recruit black Baptist churches, 113

Baumann, John, 18, 200, 233n22, 236n9

Baumgartner and Jones, xxvi

Becker, Penny Edgell. See Edgell, Penny

Berrigan, Daniel, xxix, 235n36

Bloc recruitment, xv; of churches, xvii

Bond, Christopher (Missouri senator), 10, 38, 242n23

CACI, 112–14, 116, 219, 171; accomplishments of, 219–21

California Project. See PICO National Network

Catholic Campaign for Human Development (CCHD), 5, 199, 236n11

Catholic Charities, 149–50

Catholic Church, xxii, 4–5, 232n9; and abortion and homosexuality, 69; and MCU, 171, 252n1; mobilization capacity of, 170; mobilizing in, 16; and PACT, 144–46, 149–50, 171, 259n16; percent Catholics at PICO training, 236n14; and religious barriers, 47; social justice tradition, 9, 54; U.S. Catholic Bishops, 4, 188. See also Catholic Campaign for Human Development; Liberation theology

CBCO and CBCOs, xxv; and Center for Community Change, 186; compared with ACORN, 29, 38, 40, 44, 71, 72, 79, 80–81, 83–84, 89; cultural strategy of, xvi, xxi–xxii, xxxi, 45–70; and foundation funds, 26; and importance of organization, 179–80; and localism, 183; MCU, 110–26; mobilizing culture of, 1–25, 27–44, 114–16, 232–34, 236n13, 237n15, 259n12; PACT, 142–60; and policy innovations, xxii; and religion in American social movements, xxiii; and results of organizing, 162–63, 165–72, 176, 179; salaries in, 5; as tax-exempt, xxi

CCCC. See C4

CCHD. *See* Catholic Campaign for Human Development

Center for Community Change, 173, 186–87, 202

C4 (CCCC, Churches Committed to Community Concerns, component of MCU for St. Louis), 112–14, 116, accomplishments of, 219–21

Challenging: in CBCO mobilizing culture, 6, 10, 14–17, 20

Chambers, Ed, 3, 5, 13, 63, 233n22, 236n13, 237n15

Charter schools, xxvi, 85, 158, 205, 209, 258n24

Children's Health Initiative: in Santa Clara County, 159–60

Christian conservatives. *See* Christian Right

Christian Right, xxix, 9, 68–69

Churches Allied for Community Improvement. *See* CACI

Churches Committed to Community Concerns. *See* C4

Churches United for Community Action (CUCA, part of MCU United for St. Louis). *See* CUCA

Civic and fraternal associations: compared to community organizing, xv, 231n5; decline of, 47, 178–79, 231n5; in IAF ideology, 5

Civic engagement: and CBCO, 46–47, 64; and community organizing, xiv, xv–xvii, 231n5, 166; Gamaliel Foundation outcomes, 215; and GI Bill, 241n13; and liberal religion, 69; of poor Americans, 178; and religion, 240n2; voluntarism as, 30

Civic Progress, 118, 252n15, 254n28

Civic skills: in CBCOs, 53, 171; in community organizing, 167–68; in San Jose ACORN, 129; in St. Louis ACORN, 108

Class in United States: and ACORN, xx, 28, 33, 81, 141, 169, 172, 176, 259n13; and ACORN organizers, 26, 43; and CBCO cultural strategy, xvi, xvi, xxii, 4–5, 9, 46, 48–61, 64, 170–72; and civic engagement through organizing, 166–67, 169, 178–80, 190; cultures of middle- and working-class, xxx, 15, 23, 48–56, 64, 240–43; flight from St. Louis, 112, 114, 117–19, 126; and MCU, 113; middle-class flight from cities, 4, 20; and PACT, 145–46, 160, 259n12; and religion, xxii–xxiii; and San Jose, 129, 138, 141–42; and social movement theory and ideal types, xxvi–xxxi, 235n40, 240n5; in St. Louis ACORN, 94–96, 102

Clemens, Elisabeth, 1

Coalitions: and ACORN, xxiii, 89, 169–70; Alinsky and IAF, 51; CBCOs, 55, 57, 69; of community organizations, 179, 182, 189–90; and Gamaliel Foundation, xiv, 114; and MCU, 114, 120, 189; in PACT, 148, 151, 158, 160; pro-growth coalition in San Jose, 157; and race, 54; across race and class, CBCOs and ACORN compared, 169–72, 176; across race and class, within CBCOS, 47–62; in St. Louis ACORN, 107–9; in wage campaigns, 74–76, 81, 107

Collective identity, 2; in ACORN, 27–33, 41, 81, 235n39; in CBCOs,

6–11, 51–54, 67; in MCU, 116; in San Jose ACORN, 140; in St. Louis ACORN, 102–3, 105

Communities Organized for Public Service. *See* COPS

Community organizing: and ACORN mobilizing culture, 25–43; Alinsky and history of, 4–5; and CBCO mobilizing culture, 3–25; in contrast to middle-class movements, xxviii, xxx; invisibility of, xiv; "leaders" vs. "organizers" in, 3, 17; and public policy innovation, xxv–xxvi; and role in combating inequality, 177–90; and social movement theory, xxvi–xxvii; and training citizens in political strategy, 125

Community Reinvestment Act (CRA), 237n19; and ACORN, xxiv, 31, 77, 79, 95, 206, 248n8; and MCU, 10, 114, 242n23, 252n8

Conflict with authorities. *See* Confrontation with authorities

Conflict within organizations: in ACORN, 40–41; in CBCOs, 20–21

Confrontation with authorities: in ACORN, 41–42; in CBCOs, 21–23

Consensus decision making, xxvii, xxix, 243n36; in CBCOs, 11, 21, 56–57; in PACT, 145

COPS, 4–5

Cortes, Ernesto, 3, 5, 25, 63, 233n22

CRA. *See* Community Reinvestment Act

CUCA (part of MCU), 112–14, 119; accomplishments of, 220–21

Cultural strategy of CBCOs, xvi, 3–25, 45–70

Culture, organizational. *See* ACORN; CBCO and CBCOs; Cultural

strategy of CBCOs; MCU for St. Louis; PACT; San Jose ACORN; St. Louis ACORN

DART (Direct Action Research and Training), xxi, 4, 80, 186–87, 189, 236n9

Data used in study, xx, xxv, 2, appendixes B and C

Democratic deliberation, 242n9, 252n9; in CBCOs, xvi, 179; and leader empowerment, 167; in MCU, 114, 126

Democratic Party, 58, 82, 83, 243n41

Direct action, xxix; and ACORN, 30, 37, 41; and CBCOs, 69; in PACT, 149; in St. Louis ACORN, 91–93, 104–5

Direct Action Research and Training. *See* DART

Discipline: in ACORN, 27; in CBCO ideology and practice, 7–8, 16–17, 44, 56

Disruption, mass, xvii; by ACORN, 37, 87, 92–94, 104–5, 108, 139, 165, 255n6; by CBCOs compared to ACORN, 23, 116; in Piven and Cloward's *Poor People's Movements*, 179–80

Door knocking: in ACORN recruitment, 14, 26, 86–87, 169; in San Jose ACORN, 133; in St. Louis ACORN, 96–98, 100

Earned income tax credit, 247n27; ACORN campaigns on, 86–87, 202; PICO campaign on, 212

Ecumenical Sponsoring Committee (predecessor of PACT), 144, 149, 152

Edgell, Penny, xvii

EITC. *See* Earned income tax credit
Eliasoph, Nina, 1, 68, 245n60
Emotions: ACORN's emotion norms, 42–43; ACORN's emotion work, 36–37, 44; of CBCOs, 18–21, 24, 53, 66–69; emotion norms, 3; and gender, in CBCOs, 66–67; in MCU for St. Louis, 116, 123; in organizing poor and working-class Americans, 178–79; in PACT, 148; as part of organizational culture, 1–2; and religion, 46–47, 65
Empowerment, 5, 10, 14, 17, 18, 89; in ACORN, 94, 98, 105; and ACORN mobilizing culture, 27–43; in CBCO cultural strategy, 45–47, 53, 60, 61; and emotions in ACORN, 36–37; and gender, 23–25; as goal of CBCO mobilizing culture, 1–25; in MCU for St. Louis, 126; participants' subjective feelings of, 166–67; in San Jose ACORN, 140; of working-class women, 23
Episcopal Church, 6, 243n44. *See also* African Methodist Episcopal
ESC. *See* Ecumenical Sponsoring Committee

Family values, 65, 68
Federated civic, fraternal, and service organizations. *See* Civic and fraternal associations
Feminism, xxix, 13, 235n41, 242n34; and ACORN, 40, 136; and CBCOs, 23–24, 57
501(c)(3) nonprofit organizations. *See* Nonprofit organizations
Ford Foundation, 5, 188
Framing, in social movement theory, xxx, 180, 233n17; in ACORN, 32,

76, 89, 100; in CBCO, 11, 23, 51, 55; collective problems as individual in American culture, 64–65, 67, 244n57; family values as liberal, 68; of liberals by conservatives, 48, 59, 243n41; in MCU, 123; in PACT, 148; by PICO, 61, 64; in San Jose ACORN, 136
Fraternal organizations, xv, 179, 260n6

Galluzzo, Greg, 15, 24, 187, 233n22, 236n9
Gamaliel Foundation, 6; and CBCO cultural strategy, 55, 63–64, 67; and CBCO mobilizing culture, 8, 10, 15, 18, 20, 22, 24, 80, 111–12, 114; and coalition building, 188–89; and competition among organizing networks, 124; founding of, 236n9; and Hurricane Katrina, 188; and MCU, 110–26; and national organizing, 72, 175, 185–87; other studies of, 232n10; and policy analysis, 174, 176, 183, 253n17, 253n20; policy outcomes, 215–18; racial/ethnic diversity of, 171; and regional organizing, 4, 114, 170; and results of organizing, 161; and transportation equity, xiv, 173, 181, 187, 259n19
Ganz, Marshall, xviii
Gonzales, Mary, 24, 187
Gonzalez, Ron, 150, 159, 165

Hammer, Susan, 138–39, 150, 152–55, 157, 159, 199, 200, 258n4
Hart, Stephen, 8, 12, 59, 231n2, 233n10
Health care: and MCU, 126, 173; PACT campaign for Santa Clara

County, 15, 158–60; and PICO, 175, 181; and St. Louis ACORN, 104

Hispanics: in ACORN, xvi, 172, 174; in CBCOs, 259n14; in COPS, 4; in Gamaliel Foundation, 18, 171; in PACT, 145, 152, 158, 171; and PICO, 236n14; in San Jose ACORN, 28, 32–33, 127–41; and women organizers, 23

Housing issues and campaigns: ACORN Housing Corporation, 29, 31, 77–78, 84–87, 234n26, 245n10, 246–47n26, 250n27; housing trust funds, 186, 261n28; and MCU, 112, 114, 119–20; and PACT, 147, 150, 152–53; and San Jose ACORN, 135; and St. Louis ACORN, 95–96, 104, 248n7

Hurricane Katrina: and ACORN organizing, 31, 187, 204, 207; and PICO organizing, 187–88, 215; and race, 54

IAF. See Industrial Areas Foundation

Ideal types of American social movements, xxvii–xxviii, xxxi, 7–8, 13, 16; in CBCOs, 45–46, 56, 63, 89, 183; and managing conflict, 40; in social movement scholarship, 177

Ideology: in ACORN, 33–36; in CBCOs, 11–18, 45–70

Incremental groundswell: ACORN strategy, 74–76; in housing trust fund campaign, 186

Industrial Areas Foundation (IAF): and competition among organizations, 124; and history of organizing, xvi, 3–5, 232n10; and living wage campaigns, 74; and Project

Vote, 246n22; as source of CBCO ideology, 8, 45, 81, 51, 236n13, 237n15

Inequality in United States, xv; racial, and home loans, 88, 177–90

Interfaith Funders, 5, 199

Internal Revenue Service (IRS): and ACORN's earned income tax credit campaign, 86

Jasper, James, xxx, 235n41

Jesuits, xxii, 236n9

Jesus: referenced in ACORN, 239n51; referenced in CBCOs, 6, 12

Joint Venture Silicon Valley, 257–58n22

Kingdon, John, xxv, 25–26

Labor unions: and ACORN, 29, 72, 81–82; and altered terrain for organizing, 182; and CBCOs, 83; and Change to Win coalition, 240–41n8, 260–61n17; and coalitions, 179, 189; and gender in organizing, 25; and PACT, 151, 159–60; and PICO campaigns, 209, 212, 229; and San Jose ACORN, 138; and St. Louis ACORN, 104, 106–8, 204–5; and social movement theory, xxvi, xxviii; and working-class culture, 49–50; and Working Families Party, 245n61

Latinos. See Hispanics

Leaders: in ACORN, xxiv, 79–84, 88–89, 98–99, 101–2, 108; in CBCO cultural strategy, 52–70; and civic engagement, 166, 185–87; community organizing leaders, xv, xvii–xviii, xxvii; comparing leadership continuity among the organizations, 164–65; influence of class and immigration, 171–72; leadership development, 166–68, 170, 174–76, 185; in MCU, 115–16, 119–22, 125, 252n7; and mobilization capacity, 163; and mobilizing cultures, 1–44; vs. organizers, 236–37n5; in PACT, 142–49, 151, 154–55; in "PICO Principles," 193; in San Jose ACORN, 127–28, 132–37, 139–41; in social movement theory, 233n14; and strategic capacity, xviii–xix; 240n8; and strategy, 180–81. *See also* Training for community organizing leaders

Liberation theology, 5, 9, 54

LIFT. *See* Louisiana Interfaith Together

Living Wage Resource Center, ACORN's, xxvi, 76, 89, 201, 248n5

Local-state-national campaign: in ACORN, 76–79

Louisiana Interfaith Together, xxi, 4, 188

Lutheran Church, 243n44

MAC (Chicago), xxi

MCU for St. Louis, xiv, xx, xxi, xxv, 110–23, 125–26; and advocating for poor citizens, 170; agenda setting of, 166, 228; and CBCO cultural strategy, 45, 52, 54, 56, 57, 242n23; and CBCO mobilizing culture, 9–10, 18–20, 23–24, 174, 235n5; class diversity of, 171; in coalitions, 189; compared to PACT, 152, 158; and democratic deliberation, 252n9; as 501(c)(3) organization, 80, 110–26, 148; leadership of, 164, 168; and media,

115–16, 119, 121–23, 228; mobilization capacity of, 163, 166; policy outcomes of, 173, 220–21; political context of, 173; racial/ethnic diversity of, 170–71; reputation of, 165; results, 170–71, 173, 174, 189, 228; and transportation advocacy, 187

Media, 48, 57; and ACORN, 38, 75, 87–88; and CBCOs, 7, 11, 237n15; and mass mobilization, 181; and MCU for St. Louis, 115–16, 119, 121–23, 228; and PACT, 143, 151; and St. Louis ACORN, 99, 101, 103, 105, 250n22

Mediating institutions: churches as, 5

Members: of PACT, 145–48; of San Jose ACORN, 130–31, 133–34; in St. Louis ACORN, 100–102

Methodist. *See* African Methodist Episcopal; United Methodist Church

Metropolitan Congregations United for St. Louis. *See* MCU for St. Louis

Minimum wage, xiii–xiv, xx, 12; in ACORN campaigns, 74–76, 81–82, 94–95, 103–4, 106–7, 138, 174, 201–2, 227, 251nn36–37, 262n3; Florida campaign to increase, xiii–xiv, 82; public discourse about, 76; and public opinion polls, 74; 2007 federal increase in, 245n4

Mobilization: and ACORN, 94, 101, 133; in CBCOs, 14, 16–17, 58, 151; and leaders, 185–86; and Piven and Cloward, 179; and Project Vote, 84; of working-class Americans, 48

Mobilization capacity, xix, 44; comparing among the local organizations, 162–63, 165–66, 170, 176

Mobilizing culture: of ACORN,

25–43; of CBCOs, 1–25, 27–44, 114–16

Montgomery bus boycott, xiv–xv

MOSES (Detroit), xxi

National Council of Churches, 236n11

National Welfare Rights Organization. *See* NWRO

Needmor Foundation, 199

Neighborhood Funders Group, 5

Networks, social: in ACORN, 36, 38, 43, 101, 133, 140; in CBCO organizing, 7–8, 14, 16, 45, 53; compared, 163

New social movements, 17, 40, 235n40, 241n14

Niebuhr, Reinhold, 9, 54, 62, 244n49, 244–45n59

Nonprofit organizations: and ACORN, xx, 82; and CBCOs, 14, 80, 83, 148; 501(c)(3) organizations, 189

NWRO (National Welfare Rights Organization), 25, 105, 238–39n42, 259n13

Oakland Community Organization. *See* OCO

Oberschall, Anthony, 1

OCO (Oakland Community Organization), 158, 237n18

One-to-one meetings, 5, 14–16, 21, 25, 49, 53, 259n12; in PACT, 147, 163; and personalism, 57

Orfield, Myron, 119–20, 253n17

Organizational and political strategy: of ACORN, xvi, 25–27, 71–90; of MCU, 110–11, 114–26; of PACT, 142–44, 146–59; of San Jose ACORN, 127–29, 132–40; of St. Louis ACORN, 91–93, 98–109

Organizational structure: of ACORN, 80–81; of ACORN and CBCOs, xix; and ACORN organizational and political strategy, 82–85; of MCU, 110–11, 114–26; of PACT, 142–44, 146–59; of San Jose ACORN 127–29, 132–40; of St. Louis ACORN, 91–93, 98–109

Organizers: in MCU, 124; in PACT, 148; in San Jose ACORN, 134–35; in St. Louis ACORN, 99–100, 124

Outcomes, xix, 162–76, 177–90, 201–26; vs. organizational endurance, 184–85

PACT, xiii, xx, xxii, xxv–xxvi, xxxii, 124, 129, 142–60, 165, 168, 170–74, 184, 189; access to authorities, 165; and advocating for poor citizens, 170; agenda-setting proposals, 228–29; authority in, 146–47; and CBCO cultural strategy, 49–50, 52, 56–58; and CBCO mobilizing culture, 9, 11, 15, 16, 18–20, 24, 33, 34; class diversity of, 171–72; as 501(c)(3) organization, 80, 148; leadership of, 164, 168; and media, 143, 151; mobilization capacity of, 163, 166; policy outcomes, 174, 221–25; racial/ethnic diversity of, 171; reputation of, 165; and results of organizing, 161; and strategic learning, 181; working with San Jose ACORN on housing, 135

Page Avenue Freeway, 121–22, 254n28

Pain in emotion language. *See under* PICO National Network

Passion in emotion language. *See under* PICO National Network

Pentecostals, 6, 60

People Improving Communities through Organizing. *See* PICO National Network

PICO California. *See* PICO National Network

PICO National Network, xii–xvi, xx–xxi, xxv, xxxii; annual budget, 85; California Project/PICO California, xxi, 4, 22, 143–44, 156, 158–60, 168, 170, 174–75, 181, 185, 208–12; and CBCO cultural strategy, 60–61, 63, 66, 68, 72, 80, 83, 85; and CBCO mobilizing culture, 6–25; and data in study, 199–200; founding of, 236n9; and MCU, 124–25; national training, 236nn13–14; 241n12, 261–62; and PACT, 143–51, 154, 156–60; pain in emotion language, 8–9, 19–20, 67, 70, 153, 175; passion in emotion language, 13–14; "PICO Principles," 193–94, 261n2; and policy outcomes, 207–15, 222; and potential of community organizing, 181–85, 187–90; and results of organizing, 161, 167, 175–76; scholarship on, 232–33n10; typology of social action, 6–7

Piven, Frances: and Richard Cloward, xvii, 25, 179–80, 185

Policy. *See* Public policy

Political context: in St. Louis and San Jose, 173–74

Political opportunity, xviii; for MCU, 122–23; for PACT, 156–58

Portland, Oregon: and urban growth boundaries, 119, 253n20

Power: and access to authorities, 166; of ACORN, 176; within ACORN, 80–81, 87; and ACORN mobilizing culture, 27–43; anxiety about power in new social movements, 57; and CBCO cultural strategy, 45–48, 61, 70; and CBCO mobilizing culture, 1–25; CBCO theory of, 12–13; in democratic organizations, 179; expressed in "actions," 6, 21; of Gamaliel Foundation, 174; and gender in CBCOs, 23–25, 66; as goal of ACORN, 71–72, 89, 93; as goal of organizing, xv, xvi, xix, xxii, xxviii, xxxi; and leadership capacity in CBCOs and ACORN, 164–65; in MCU for St. Louis, 113–14, 116, 122, 125; in Niebuhr's thought, 245; through overturning norms, 21; of PICO, 175; in "PICO Principles," 193; in postindustrial cities, 182; and relationships, in CBCO, 14, 66; and religion, xvi, xxiii, 9–10, 12–13, 63, 66; and reputation, 165; in San Jose, 152, 155; in San Jose ACORN, 128, 141; in San Jose PACT, 143, 148, 150; in St. Louis, 117–18; in St. Louis ACORN, 98, 103, 107

Prayer walks, 10, 116

Predatory lending, xx, xxvi, 78–79, 87, 88, 169, 203–4, 206, 212

Presbyterian Church, 243n44

Protestant realism, 8–9, 54, 244. *See also* Niebuhr, Reinhold

Protestantism, 54, 232n9; and confessional narratives, 47; feminization of, 244n59; and Niebuhr, 8–9, 54; in PACT, 145–46, 147, 171; percent of Protestants at PICO training, 236n14; and Reformation, 233n23; and religious barriers, 47; and self-help, 65; strands of, 62

Public and private distinction: in
    ACORN, 32, 40–41, 103; in
    CBCOs, 10, 15–16, 59; linked by
    religion, 46–47, 64–66, 150
Public housing: tenant organizing, 85,
    169
Public interest groups, xx, xxiv, 46,
    178; ACORN as, 72
Public meetings ("actions"), 14, 17, 19,
    21–22, 110–11, 115, 175
Public policy: CBCO view of, 60,
    65; and community organizing,
    xxv–xxvi, xxviii; scholarship of,
    xvi, 172; in St. Louis, 119–23
Public schools: in ACORN campaigns,
    79, 205; in PACT campaigns,
    156–58
Public sphere: and Alinsky, 185; and
    emotions, 66; and family values, 68;
    and PACT, 142; and values, 63–64,
    65–70, 166
Public theology, 9

Quakers: and consensus decision mak-
    ing, xxix; and progressive reform,
    234n23

Race: in CBCOs, xxii, 47–48, 54–55;
    in MCU and in St. Louis, 118, 126;
    in San Jose ACORN, 32–33; in
    St. Louis ACORN, 31–32, 40
RAL. See Refund anticipation loan
Redevelopment: and MCU, 220; and
    PACT, 223, 228, 256nn10–11,
    256n15, 257n17; and San Jose
    ACORN, 228
Refund anticipation loan (RAL), 87,
    202
Religion, liberal, xvi; and building
    solidarity in CBCOs, 8–11; and

civic involvement, xxiii; and class
    diversity in CBCOs, 171; and
    gender, 24–25; in low-income
    neighborhoods, xxiii; and Niebuhr,
    244n49, 244n59; and progressive
    change, xxii–xxiii; and progres-
    sive politics in CBCOs, 46–70; in
    San Jose ACORN, 32; in St. Louis
    ACORN, 31
Religious Right. See Christian Right
Republicans: in PICO Network, 6,
    60–61, 83
Resource mobilization, xvii, 85
Resources, xviii, xix; of ACORN, 31,
    85–87, 246n24; of CBCOs, 36, 45,
    69; in MCU, 124, 126; of PACT,
    146, 259n12; PICO annual budget,
    85; of San Jose ACORN, 132, 141;
    of St. Louis ACORN, 96–97
Rusk, David, 119–20, 122, 199, 253n16
Rustbelt, xxiv

SAFETEA-LU transportation bill of
    2005, 1, 175, 181, 231n1
Salaries of organizers. See under
    ACORN; CBCO and CBCOs
San Jose, xiii, xix, xxiv, xxv, xxvii, 18,
    32, 34, 41, 81, 98, 101, 138; and
    PICO policy outcomes, 208–9. See
    also PACT; San Jose ACORN
San Jose ACORN, xxv, xxxii, 127–41,
    239; access to authorities, 165;
    and ACORN mobilizing culture,
    28, 30, 32, 33, 37, 39; agenda-
    setting proposals, 228; authority
    in, 132–33; class in, 138, 141–42;
    compared to St. Louis ACORN,
    96, 98, 101, 127–41; leadership,
    164–65, 168–73; and national
    ACORN strategy, 81; organization-

al reputation, 165; policy outcomes, 219–20; and San Jose PACT, 156

San Jose PACT. *See* PACT

San Jose Redevelopment Agency, 137–38, 152–55, 157, 160

Schools. *See* Charter schools; Public schools

Self-interest: in CBCOs, 13–14, 19, 62–64; and localism, 183–84, 194; and organizing ideology, xxviii

Service organizations. *See* Civic and fraternal associations

Silicon Valley, xxv, 138, 146, 152, 157, 160, 172, 257n22

Silicon Valley Manufacturing Group, 257n22

SMOs. *See* Social movement organizations

SNCC. *See* Student Nonviolent Coordinating Committee

Snowbelt, xxiv

Social class. *See* Class in United States

Social movement leaders. *See* Leaders

Social movement organizations, xiv, xvii, xxiii, 2, 234n2

Social movements, American, 9, 183, 185; Ideal Type A , xxvii–xxx; Ideal Type B, xxvii–xxx

Social movement theory, xxvi–xxviii, xxx; and class, xxvi; structural bias of, xxx

Sponsoring committee, 5; Ecumenical Sponsoring Committee, 144, 149, 152

Staff. *See* Organizers

St. Louis, xiv, xix, xxi, xxiv–xxv, xxvii, xxxi–xxxii, 22, 23, 26, 28–34; and poverty, 247n27, 248n6; power in, 117–18, 182, 253–54n25; and urban sprawl, 182, 246–47n26, 252n4,

253n23. *See also* MCU for St. Louis; St. Louis ACORN

St. Louis ACORN, xxv, xxxi, 91–109, 112, 227, 251n36, 262n2; and ACORN mobilizing culture, 26, 28–34, 36–43, 54, 60, 68, 71, 76–77, 87, 90; agenda-setting proposals, 227; authority in, 98–99; class in, 94–96, 102; compared to San Jose ACORN, 131–33, 135, 138–39; compared to San Jose PACT, 146, 152, 157–58; and influencing agendas, 166; leadership of, 164, 168; and media, 99, 101, 103, 105, 250; mobilization capacity of, 163; mobilizing members, 100–102; and national ACORN strategy, 87; policy outcomes, 173, 206, 218; racial composition of, 172; reputation of, 165; results of organizing, 163–66, 168, 172, 174

Strategic capacity, xviii–xix, xxvii, 242

Structure. *See* Organizational structure

Student Nonviolent Coordinating Committee, xxix

Sunbelt, xxiv–xxv, 127

Swidler, Ann, 1

Szymanski, Anne-Marie, xxix

Tactics, xviii; in ACORN, 88–90; in MCU, 114–17; in PACT, 148–52; in San Jose ACORN, 139–40; in St. Louis ACORN, 91–94

Taylor, Frank: of San Jose Redevelopment Agency, 138, 152

Temperance movement, xxvii, xxix, 62, 185

Templars, xxix

TEN. *See* Transportation Equity Network

Texas Interfaith Network, 4

Third parties. *See* Working Families Party

Training for community organizing leaders, xviii, xxii; by ACORN, 26, 38–40, 82, 84, 99, 134–35; by CBCOs, 2, 4, 6–25, 45–70, 111, 116, 144–58, 183, 236; of organizers, 162, 187; as an outcome of organizing, 166–68, 174–76, 190

Transportation bill of 2005. *See* SAFETEA-LU transportation bill of 2005

Transportation campaigns, 187, 259n19

Transportation Equity Network, 173, 175, 187

Unions. *See* Labor unions

Unitarian-Universalist denomination, ix, 5, 6, 97, 232n9

United Church of Christ, 236n11

United Methodist Church, 236n11

Urban growth boundaries, 119, 253n20

Weed and Seed, xxvi, 214, 228

Workforce Silicon Valley, 257n22

Working Families Party, 83, 204–5, 233n18, 245n61, 262n2

HEIDI J. SWARTS is assistant professor of political science at Rutgers University, Newark. She studies religion and social movements in American politics, with a focus on the policy and politics of community organizing in American cities.

(series page continued from ii)

Volume 16   Bert Klandermans and Suzanne Staggenborg, editors, *Methods of Social Movement Research*

Volume 15   Sharon Kurtz, *Workplace Justice: Organizing Multi-Identity Movements*

Volume 14   Sanjeev Khagram, James V. Riker, and Kathryn Sikkink, editors, *Restructuring World Politics: Transnational Social Movements, Networks, and Norms*

Volume 13   Sheldon Stryker, Timothy J. Owens, and Robert W. White, editors, *Self, Identity, and Social Movements*

Volume 12   Byron A. Miller, *Geography and Social Movements: Comparing Antinuclear Activism in the Boston Area*

Volume 11   Mona N. Younis, *Liberation and Democratization: The South African and Palestinian National Movements*

Volume 10   Marco Giugni, Doug McAdam, and Charles Tilly, editors, *How Social Movements Matter*

Volume 9   Cynthia Irvin, *Militant Nationalism: Between Movement and Party in Ireland and the Basque Country*

Volume 8   Raka Ray, *Fields of Protest: Women's Movements in India*

Volume 7   Michael P. Hanagan, Leslie Page Moch, and Wayne te Brake, editors, *Challenging Authority: The Historical Study of Contentious Politics*

Volume 6   Donatella della Porta and Herbert Reiter, editors, *Policing Protest: The Control of Mass Demonstrations in Western Democracies*

Volume 5   Hanspeter Kriesi, Ruud Koopmans, Jan Willem Duyvendak, and Marco G. Giugni, *New Social Movements in Western Europe: A Comparative Analysis*

Volume 4   Hank Johnston and Bert Klandermans, editors, *Social Movements and Culture*

Volume 3   J. Craig Jenkins and Bert Klandermans, editors, *The Politics of Social Protest: Comparative Perspectives on States and Social Movements*

Volume 2   John Foran, editor, *A Century of Revolution: Social Movements in Iran*

Volume 1   Andrew Szasz, *EcoPopulism: Toxic Waste and the Movement for Environmental Justice*